Phonological Knowledge

Phonological Knowledge

Conceptual and Empirical Issues

edited by

NOEL BURTON-ROBERTS,
PHILIP CARR, and
GERARD DOCHERTY

OXFORD
UNIVERSITY PRESS

OXFORD
UNIVERSITY PRESS

Great Clarendon Street, Oxford OX2 6DP
Oxford University Press is a department of the University of Oxford.
It furthers the University's objective of excellence in research, scholarship,
and education by publishing worldwide in

Oxford New York

Athens Auckland Bangkok Bogotá Buenos Aires Calcutta
Cape Town Chennai Dar es Salaam Delhi Florence Hong Kong Istanbul
Karachi Kuala Lumpur Madrid Melbourne Mexico City Mumbai
Nairobi Paris São Paulo Shanghai Singapore Taipei Tokyo Toronto Warsaw

and associated companies in Berlin Ibadan

Oxford is a registered trade mark of Oxford University Press
in the UK and certain other countries

Published in the United States
by Oxford University Press Inc., New York

British Library Cataloguing in Publication Data

Data available

Library of Congress Cataloging-in-Publication Data

Phonological knowledge: conceptual and empirical issues/edited by Noel Burton-Roberts, Philip
Carr, and Gerard Docherty.
p. cm.
Includes bibliographical references and index.
1. Grammar, Comparative and general—Phonology. 2. Phonetics. I. Burton-Roberts, Noel, 1948– II.
Carr, Philip, 1953– III. Docherty, Gerard J.

P217.P482 2000
414—dc21 00–49110

ISBN 0–19–824127–5

ISBN 0–19–924577–0 pbk

1 3 5 7 9 10 8 6 4 2

Typeset in Minion
by Mendip Communications Ltd, Frome, Somerset
Printed in Great Britain
on acid-free paper by
T.J. International,
Padstow, Cornwall

Contents

Abbreviations

ALP	Argument from Learning by Forgetting
ASL	American Sign Language
ATR	Advanced Tongue Root
CH	consonant harmony
CLS	Chicago Linguistic Society
CSPR	Conventional System of Physical Representation
CSPR$_{(L)}$	Conventional System for the Physical Representation of Language
CSLI	Center for Study of Language and Information
DM	Distributed Morphology
DP	Dependency Phonology
EPG	electropalatography
FA	Feature Algebra
FUL	Featurally Underspecified Lexicon [Model]
GP	Government Phonology
HDP	Head-Driven Phonology
HIL	Holland Institute of Generative Linguistics
HMM	Hidden Markov Model
IR	Intermediate Representation
LAD	language acquisition device
LAFF	Lexical Access from Features [Model]
LAFS	Lexical Access from Spectra [Model]
LF	Logical Form
LPM	Lexical Phonology/Morphology
MESM	Modified Extended Standard Modularization
ms	milliseconds
N	Numeration
OCP	Obligatory Contour Principle
OT	Optimality Theory
PF	Phonetic Form
SD	Structural Description
RcvP	Radical cv Phonology
RH	Representational Hypothesis
SO	Spell-Out
SPE	N. Chomsky and M. Halle, *The Sound Pattern of English* (New York: Harper & Row, 1968)
SR	surface representation
ToM	Theory of Mind
UG	Universal Grammar

UPSID   UCLA Phonological Segment Inventory Database
UR   underlying representation
VOT   Voice Onset Timing

Notes on Contributors

Sylvain Bromberger is Professor Emeritus at the Massachusetts Institute of Technology. A collection of his papers (on various topics) appeared under the title *On What We Know We Don't Know* (1992). He has written a number of papers on the foundations of phonology with Morris Halle. He was the dedicatee of *The View from Building 20* (1993), which includes his picture.

Mary Beckman is Professor of Linguistics at Ohio State University. A major proponent of Laboratory Phonology, she has developed experimental paradigms for the investigation of prosody and intonation and works on first/second-language phonological acquisition. Editor of the *Journal of Phonetics* (1990–4), she has published *Stress and Non-Stress Accent* (1986) and, with J. B. Pierrehumbert, *Japanese Tone Structure* (1988).

Noel Burton-Roberts is Professor of English Language and Linguistics, University of Newcastle upon Tyne. His interests include semantics, pragmatics, the architecture of the language faculty, the nature/status of phonology, and sign theory. He is the author of *The Limits to Debate: A Revised Theory of Semantic Presupposition* (1989) and *Analysing Sentences* (1997).

Philip Carr is Professor of Linguistics in the Department of English at the University Paul Valery (Montpellier III), France. His interests include phonology and the philosophy of linguistics. He is the author of *Linguistic Realities* (1990), *Phonology* (1993), and *English Phonetics and Phonology* (1999).

Gerard Docherty is Senior Lecturer, Department of Speech, University of Newcastle upon Tyne. His interests include phonetics, phonological variation, and disordered speech production. He is the author of *The Timing of Voicing in British English Obstruents* (1992) and co-editor of *Urban Voices: Phonological Variation and Change in the British Isles* (2000).

Jennifer Fitzpatrick is a research scholar in the Department of Linguistics, University of Konstanz. Her interests include intonation, prosody, typological phonology, the phonetics–phonology interface. Her recent published work concerns issues in phrasal phonology.

Paul Foulkes is Lecturer in Language Variation and Change, University of York. His interests include phonological acquisition and urban dialectology. With Gerard Docherty he is joint editor of *Urban Voices: Phonological Variation and Change in the British Isles* (2000).

Morris Halle is Institute Professor Emeritus at the Massachusetts Institute of Technology. His main interests lie in phonology and morphology. He is the (co-)author of numerous influential books and papers in these areas, including *The Sound Pattern of Russian* (1959), *The Sound Pattern of English* (with Noam Chomsky, 1968), and *An Essay on Stress* (with J.-R. Vergnaud, 1987).

John Harris is Professor of Linguistics at University College London. He writes on phonological theory, the phonology–phonetics interface, language disorder, and the history of English. His publications include *English Sound Structure* (1994) and *Phonological Variation and Change* (1985).

Harry van der Hulst, Director of the Holland Institute for Generative Linguistics until 1999, is Distinguished Visiting Fellow, Skidmore College, and Visiting Scholar, New York University. His interests are phonology, sign language, language acquisition and change, on which he is published widely. He is editor of *The Linguistic Review* and has (with C. Ewan) a textbook on non-linear phonology forthcoming.

Bob Ladd is Professor of Linguistics at Edinburgh University. His interests are intonation and prosody, on which he has published two books, *The Structure of Intonational Meaning: Evidence from English* (1980) and *Intonational Phonology* (1996). He is proponent of the development of Laboratory Phonology and was co-editor of *Language & Speech* (1994–2000).

Geoff Lindsey is Senior Research Fellow in the Department of Language and Communication Science at City University, London. His research interests include the phonetics–phonology interface, forensic phonetics, and intonation.

Scott Myers is Associate Professor in the Department of Linguistics, University of Texas at Austin. His research interests are in phonetics, phonology, and Bantu languages. Recent publications include 'OCP effects in Optimality Theory' (*Natural Language & Linguistic Theory*) and 'Surface Underspecification of Tone in Chichewa' (*Phonology*).

Janet Pierrehumbert is Professor of Linguistics at Northwestern University and a Fellow of the Simon Guggenheim Memorial Foundation. Her interests include intonation, prosody, allophony, and lexical representation, on which she has published widely. She co-authored, with M. Beckman, *Japanese Tone Structure* (1988).

Charles Reiss is Associate Professor in the Linguistics Program, Concordia University. His interests include phonology, morphology, language acquisition and change, learnability, philosophical foundations of linguistic theory, and cognitive science. He is co-author, with M. Hale, of several recent articles in *Linguistic Inquiry*.

Marilyn Vihman is Professor of Developmental Phonology at the University of Wales, Bangor, UK. Her interests include cross-linguistic study of language acquisition, acoustic analysis of prosody, developmental study of Welsh, and early phonology. She is the author of *Phonological Development: The Origins of Language in the Child* (1996).

Shelley Velleman is Assistant Professor of Communication Disorders, University of Massachusetts at Amherst. Her interests include normal/disordered phonological development, developmental verbal dispraxia, and the application of Optimality Theory to early phonologies. She is the author of *Making Phonology Functional: What Do I Do First* (1998).

Linda Wheeldon is a lecturer in the School of Psychology, Birmingham University. Her research in experimental psycholinguistics concerns prosody, lexical retrieval, the monitoring of inner speech, and the syntax of speech. She has recent papers in *Cognition* and the *Journal of Memory and Language*.

1

Introduction

Noel Burton-Roberts, Philip Carr, and
Gerard Docherty

1. PREAMBLE

This volume concerns the nature, status, and acquisition of phonological knowledge and, relatedly, the conceptual and empirical foundations of phonology, its place in and/or relation to the theory of language and of cognition.

Phonological enquiry is generally thought to be empirical in nature. But all enquiry depends for its empiricality on conceptual assumptions—about the nature of the data, the framework needed for their description and explanation, what counts as explanation within the domain, the scope of the enquiry, and the criteria by which its empirical success should be judged. These underlying assumptions are seldom examined explicitly. Where there is general agreement on such conceptual matters, it may not be necessary to examine them; it may even be felt to be beside the point.

But that is not the case in phonological theory. There seems to be almost no conceptual assumption in the foundations of phonological theory that is not controversial. Phonological frameworks are numerous, and they conflict in their underlying assumptions, even about what kind of entity phonological entities are. Disagreement can go so deep as even to affect what counts as a phonological fact. Different responses to the data may be persuasive in their own conceptual terms, but the terms may conflict.

Phonologists are not unaware of the conceptual questions raised by their discipline. But, rightly or wrongly, there is a view that holds that phonological theory holds pride of place at the empirical, 'observable' end of linguistic theory and that to focus on conceptual questions, rather than pursuing the eminently 'empirical' activity of 'doing phonology', could make no contribution to what phonology specifically and characteristically has to offer. We question this picture of things. We suggest that conceptual issues raise their heads more obviously in

The editors would like to thank John Davey, Sarah Dobson, and Hilary Walford at Oxford University Press for their help and care in preparing the volume for press.

phonology than elsewhere in linguistics and do so precisely in proportion to the extent that its supposed data appear (from a certain perspective) to be secure.

Anderson (1981: 495) asked 'should we or should we not limit the terms and constructs of linguistic theory to elements that can be given an extralinguistic foundation?' As put, the question has (and was intended to have) one possible (negative) answer. However, it is significant that Anderson was posing the question specifically in connection with *phonology* (responding to Donegan and Stampe 1979). But the question assumes we know what is 'linguistic' and what 'extralinguistic' independently of our conception of the nature and rationale of phonology and its place in or relation to linguistic theory. That assumption is itself controversial; it is precisely that assumption that was at issue—and is at issue in this volume. We seem to have a choice of conceptual strategy here, a choice between asking what (a certain conception of) language tells us about phonology and asking what (a certain conception of) phonology tells us about language. As the parentheses indicate, the choice is not straightforward and involves inspecting foundational assumptions.

It seems appropriate, then, to offer a forum in which contributors can stand back and reflect on the nature, origin, and rationale of phonological knowledge, the conceptual and empirical foundations of phonological theory. They were invited to do this either in general or from the perspective of some particular framework.[1] We believe the range of views expressed in the following chapters testifies to the conceptual ferment and tensions at the foundations of phonological theory. In what follows, we pick out some of the more salient issues, introducing the chapters in the light of them.

2. PHONOLOGY, KNOWLEDGE, AND LANGUAGE

As the title *Phonological Knowledge* indicates, we have assumed that phonological theory is about a form of knowledge. Even if this is uncontroversial, it remains to decide what that might mean and its implications. The assumption that phonological theory is about a form of knowledge is generally based on two other assumptions: (*a*) that phonological theory is part of linguistic theory, and, a specifically Chomskian assumption, (*b*) that linguistic theory in general is about a form of knowledge.

Although assumption (*a*) might be thought unexceptionable, we shall see it does not go without saying. As for assumption (*b*), 'knowledge' as understood in linguistic theory at least needs some explaining. In this context it has a particular (and even special) meaning. First, 'knowledge of language' is emphatically not, for Chomsky, 'knowledge-*how*'—that is, it specifically does not concern how to *do*

---

[1] All the chapters were written specially for the volume. However, that by Bromberger and Halle is a revision of an earlier paper that appeared in Sylvain Bromberger's book *On What We Know We Don't Know* (Chicago University Press, 1992), 209–28. That by Hale and Reiss is a revision and expansion of Hale and Reiss (2000). The chapters appear in alphabetical order of the first author's surname.

anything, abilities, or dispositions to behave (Chomsky 1986: 10, 36). This relates to Chomsky's rejection of the notion that generative grammar might be thought of as modelling any kind of behaviour. The conceptual foundations of generative grammar are not just anti-behaviourist, they are non-behavioural. Secondly, 'knowledge of language' notwithstanding, it is not in fact 'knowledge-*of*'—that is, it is not a relation between a 'knower' and some aspect of the external world that is 'known' of or about. Presumably, then, it is not 'knowledge-*that*', either. Rather than being *relational* in these senses, 'knowledge of language' is for Chomsky *constitutive*, in the sense that there is no distinction between what is known and the knowing of it. Language is thus said to have 'no objective existence apart from its mental representation' (Chomsky 1972: 169) and to be 'knowledge without grounds' (Chomsky 1980: 41; 1986: 12). In these terms, knowledge-of-language (= language) is a wholly internal, highly specialized (modular), informationally encapsulated, formal (rather than functional) state of mind/brain, essentially independent of sensory and motor apparatuses (Chomsky e.g. 1995a: 335), and linguistic enquiry is thus autonomous.

Assuming that phonological theory is an intrinsic part of linguistic theory, we should expect to understand 'phonological knowledge' as we understand 'linguistic knowledge'. However, given the generally assumed rationale of phonology specifically—and the very motive for thinking that the phonological is intrinsic to the linguistic—that conclusion is controversial. It is commonly—if not universally—assumed that language is externally manifested or realized in speech (or sign) or at least in the external physical phenomena produced by the behaviour we call 'speech' (or 'signing'). Otherwise, languages could not (as they clearly do) serve any communicative function and could not be (as they clearly are) acquired. The rationale of phonology is generally thought to lie precisely here. The phonological on these terms is that aspect of the linguistic that allows for its physical ('observable') realization in phenomena external to mind/brain (for example, sounds)—phenomena, furthermore, produced by a particular kind of behaviour (for example, speech) and needing to be processed in real time. On these terms, phonology is, at least in part, by its very nature *grounded* in phenomena external to mind/brain, their behavioural production and perception in communication, and crucially involves human sensory and motor apparatuses. This view is perhaps most clearly reflected in the influential line of research pursued over thirty years by John Ohala (see e.g. Ohala 1981, 1983, 1990, 1995).

For want of any better term, call this the 'traditional' view of phonology and its rationale. Something like this view seems assumed when Chomsky writes:

the information provided by L has to be accommodated to the human sensory and motor apparatus. Hence UG [Universal Grammar] must provide for a phonological component that converts the objects generated by the language L to a form that these 'external' systems can use: PF, we assume. If humans could communicate by telepathy, there would be no need for a phonological component ... (Chomsky 1995a: 221)

It is difficult to square the traditional view of phonology and its rationale with a wholly internal, non-behavioural, non-relational (constitutive), non-functional, understanding of 'linguistic knowledge' and hence (by its inclusion) 'phonological knowledge'. If phonological knowledge is not some kind of epistemic relation holding between an individual and those perceptual phenomena (that is, knowledge-of), or if it does not thereby confer the ability to speak and process speech (that is, knowledge-how), what is it and what is it for? If this presents a dilemma for Chomskian linguistic theory in general, it is one that originates in the conceptual and empirical foundations of phonological theory.

There are several possible responses to the dilemma, each with its consequences for how we conceive both of phonology and of language, involving a host of more specific and interrelated assumptions or arguments about modularity (both of mind and of language), the content of phonological elements and its relation to phonetic substance, the question of modality, the implications of sign languages for our conception of phonology, how phonological knowledge arises, the relation between 'language' and 'languages', the relevance or otherwise to linguistic theory of cross-linguistic and sociophonetic variation, the data and methods appropriate/ relevant to phonological enquiry. Several of these responses are represented in the chapters that follow. Here we sketch in broad outline four possible responses.

One response (A) would seek to insulate other parts of the language faculty from what would seem to be the (externalist, relational, behavioural, functional) consequences of the traditional view of phonology. Here phonology, albeit included within language, is simply 'different' from the rest of the language faculty, a view famously expounded by Bromberger and Halle (1989) and endorsed in places by Chomsky (1995a: 163, 212). In fact, within Chomsky's Minimalist Program, this 'difference' becomes ever more striking. This response involves at least a heavy qualification of Chomsky's concept of (knowledge-of-)language, calling for a distinction between 'core' and 'periphery'. On these terms, knowledge-of-language is wholly internal (non-relational, non-behavioural, and so on) but only 'at core'. Phonology (within Minimalism at least), while not actually excluded from the language faculty, is relegated to an 'extraneous' 'periphery'. It is not clear what answer to Anderson's question follows from this. In this connection, Chomsky's misgivings regarding core-periphery seem to the point: 'The core-periphery distinction should, in my view, be regarded as an expository device, reflecting a level of understanding that should be superseded as clarification of the nature of linguistic inquiry advances' (1995a: 163). The other possible responses constitute reactions to this (A) response.

Another response (B) would develop, on the basis of the assumed *centrality* of the phonological to the linguistic, a conception of the linguistic in the light of that traditional view of phonology and its rationale. Pushed to its logical conclusion, this would lead to an outright rejection of Chomsky's characterization of (knowledge-of-)language as divorced from communicative function and behaviour and the sensorimotor apparatus, insisting that the theory of language is the theory of communicative behaviour and its perceptual products. Here the functional character of phonology (and hence language) will be to the fore. It is consistent with this response to demand that linguistic theory—and phonological theory especially—properly reflect the psychological and physical processes involved in such behaviour (that is, have some measure of what some would call 'psychological reality') and be amenable to psycholinguistic and laboratory test and experiment; that it reflect the full range of factors entering into such behaviour—physiological, cognitive, perceptual, and sociological—and that it reflect the attendant fine-grained variation in that behaviour and its development (and historical change). This response would reject Anderson's characterization of such matters as 'extralinguistic' precisely on the grounds of the centrality to the linguistic of the traditional view of phonology.

Yet another response (C) would argue that, since phonology is indeed intrinsic to (knowledge-of-)language, phonology cannot be 'different'. If the Chomskian concept of language is to be sustained, our conception of the phonological *must* be accommodated to *it*, not conversely. This entails a rejection of the traditional view of phonology and of the idea that phonology is any more intimately related to overt behaviour, grounded in the perceptual products of that behaviour, or functional, than any other component of grammar. Pushed to its conclusion, response C would purge phonology of phonetic substance and modality, rejecting the assumption that language is 'accommodated' to external sensorimotor systems. Chomsky contemplates the possibility of such a (purely formal) phonology when he suggests that phonology is 'pure syntax, completely internalist' (1995b: 19). This response agrees with the conceptual priorities presupposed by Anderson's question, in deciding what phonology is in the light of a prior conception of what is linguistic and what extralinguistic. From the perspective of (A) and (B), response (C) raises a number of questions, not least why the language faculty should include a phonological component in the first place, and how internal language relates to external speech.

A fourth response (D) would seek to reconcile Chomsky's wholly internalist, constitutive concept of knowledge-of-language with a traditional view of the rationale of phonology by insisting that phonology on those terms is indeed so 'different' that it should be *excluded* from the language faculty so conceived. This response thus questions the presupposition of Anderson's question that the phonological falls within the scope of strictly *linguistic* enquiry. While agreeing with response (C) on the nature of the language faculty, response (D) would argue that it follows from (C) that phonology should be indistinguishable from syntax—and that this amounts to the exclusion of phonology as such. If, as the quote from Chomsky implies, the rationale of phonology lies in communication, response D makes a sharp separation between an essential element of the theory of communication (namely, phonological theory) and internalist linguistic theory. This, too, raises questions concerning the resulting architecture of the language faculty and the nature of the relation between it and (excluded) phonology, and that between language and communication (speech).

Not all the contributions focus directly on this general issue, or explicitly assume one of those positions, in quite the terms just presented. Nevertheless, the above highlights a major conceptual preoccupation of many of the contributions.

The chapter by Bromberger and Halle opens with a welcome and apposite discussion of phonology within the more general context of the philosophy of language. This paper is not primarily concerned to re-affirm their earlier contention that phonology is different from syntax and semantics—response (A). Rather, they assume that phonology is different and discuss the implications of this view for types and tokens in phonology. We return to this below.

The chapter by Pierrehumbert, Beckman, and Ladd is a wide-ranging outline of the conceptual foundations of phonology considered as a laboratory science, embedded within a discussion of what counts as science. Response (B) above quite accurately describes the stance Pierrehumbert *et al.* argue for. From the perspective of phonology—and Laboratory Phonology specifically—they question the modularity of Chomsky's concept of (knowledge-of-)language, arguing that linguistics (and phonology) is not autonomous and cannot be insulated from the methods (including statistical methods) and results of science as generally understood, and risks being unscientific when so insulated. The chapters by Docherty and Foulkes and by Fitzpatrick and Wheeldon also belong here. Although not couched in terms of the Laboratory Phonology programme, their arguments and conclusions are consistent with those of Pierrehumbert *et al.* Fitzpatrick and Wheeldon focus on recent rapprochements between phonological theory and experimental psycholinguistic research on spoken word comprehension, which they expect will afford relevant psycholinguistic work greater theoretical sophistication and lend phonological theory greater psychological reality. Docherty and Foulkes are particularly concerned with speech as a form of behaviour within social contexts and the significance of sociophonetic variation for the concept of phonological knowledge and the autonomy of phonology. We return to these issues below.

In sharp contrast, Hale and Reiss argue for a conception of phonology fully consistent both with Chomsky's constitutive (knowledge-of-)language and the assumption that phonology is linguistic. Their chapter is representative of response (C) above, perhaps the only chapter concerned to pursue (C) to its logical conclusion, seeking thereby to resolve a foundational tension they notice in Chomsky and Halle's *Sound Pattern of English* (*SPE*). Consistent with the informationally encapsulated, wholly formal character of the computation system assumed for human language, phonological computation operates without reference to phonetic substance—is, in Chomsky's recent terms, 'pure syntax'. Phonology, as linguistic, is grounded in (a module of) mind, not in phonetics. The computation treats features and the like as arbitrary symbols—and is best characterized in terms of a logical algebra. The symbols themselves are correlated, but not intrinsically, with phonetic substance by a *transduction* quite independent of the linguistic computation itself. Hale and Reiss mount a sustained criticism of the substance-based functionalism of proposed constraints in Optimality Theory, arguing that reference within the theory of grammar to acoustic salience, ease of articulation, phonetically based markedness tendencies, and the factors involved in sound change and acquisition simply duplicates extragrammatical principles and thus violates Occam's Razor. They characterize this as 'substance abuse'. On the assumption that sign languages have phonology, Hale and Reiss point out in passing that they constitute evidence that the transductive correlation between the symbols and substance must be arbitrary and incidental to the phonological computation.

Sign language is central to the chapter by van der Hulst, which also defends a version of response (C). It is argued that phonological theory must generalize over the modalities of spoken and signed languages and cannot therefore be modality specific. For van der Hulst, as for Hale and Reiss, phonology is not 'different', but subject to the same principles as operate in syntax. In that respect, he argues, phonology is not a module (not a distinguishable component of grammar). In some detail, van der Hulst shows how these ideas can be implemented in terms of a Radical CV conception of phonology, in which the substance implied by particular features is leached out of the system, leaving just the categories 'C' and 'V', which he suggests can, in turn, be replaced by 'head' and 'dependent'. On these terms, phonology is radically indeterminate (or 'polysemous') with respect to substance, both within and across modalities. Where Hale and Reiss appeal to transduction, van der Hulst invokes *instantiation*. (It is an interesting question whether these authors would regard those as the same relation—we suspect not.) Van der Hulst argues that, when the relevant principles and categories are instantiated in particular languages, modality and modularity *effects* arise. That is, the principles and categories are instantiated in particular languages in a modality-specific manner and in such a way as modularly to distinguish phonology from syntax.

Burton-Roberts argues for response (D), the radical exclusion of phonology from the language faculty. He agrees with Hale and Reiss that, if the Chomskian concept of (knowledge-of-)language is to include phonology, then phonology must be formal (substance free, and non-functional). However, he argues that the content and rationale of formal phonology are obscure. Burton-Roberts seeks to reconcile a wholly formal concept of language (L) with a view of phonology as substantive. Since phonology is external to L, functional/behavioural considerations can be acknowledged without, as Hale and Reiss would put it, violating Occam's Razor. Burton-Roberts argues that this resolves several tensions in Chomsky's Minimalist Program (tensions noted by Pierrehumbert *et al.*). This raises the question of where and what phonology is and how it *relates* to L. Burton-Roberts argues, not just that languages have phonology, but that they *are* phonological systems. The question of how phonology relates to L is thus the question of how particular languages relate to L. His answer is that spoken languages (phonologies) are systems of conventions for the external (phonetic) *representation* of internal expressions generated by L, the unique (phonology-free) language faculty. This Representational Hypothesis suggests that phonologies are conventionally representational, rather than realizational, of the syntactico-semantic properties of L. Sign languages, too, are Conventional Systems for the Physical Representation of L ($CSPR_{(L)}s$), but, since their representational medium is not *phon*etic, their conventions are not *phon*ological. With phonology excluded from L, there is no motive to insist that it must generalize across media/modalities.

The chapter by Carr adopts Burton-Roberts's Representational Hypothesis, and thus response (D). He contrasts the relation of *representation* assumed by Burton-Roberts and that of *transduction* assumed by Hale and Reiss, arguing that only the latter involves *conversion* and that, given the nature of transduction, the conversion is not arbitrary. Hence if, as Hale and Reiss assume, the transduction is between phonological symbols and phonetic substance, phonology is non-arbitrarily related to substance and thus inherently 'different'. He rejects the contention that phonology is subject to syntactic principles, arguing, for example, that it does not display recursion, and that 'head', 'complement', and so on, as understood in syntax, have only metaphorical or no counterparts in phonology. Parallelisms between them exist only at a level of generality at which almost anything would be like anything else and are explainable without specific reference to the linguistic. Carr also argues that, while linguistic theory is autonomous, phonological theory is not, but subject to a wide range of factors (including social factors). In this he agrees with Docherty and Foulkes. However, he disagrees (in the light of the Representational Hypothesis) that such factors are relevant to the nature of the language faculty. Relatedly, he argues that the Representational Hypothesis can and should reconcile a radically rationalist account of '(knowl-edge-of-)-language' with an essentially empiricist account of phonological acquisition.

In several respects Harris and Lindsey's chapter is consistent with those of Burton-Roberts and of Carr, in that they consider the possibility that the subject matter of phonology is epiphenomenal, by which they mean, not of any specific organ of body or mind and, in particular, perhaps not a modular component of grammar. They suggest the burden of proof lies with those who wish to defend a view of phonology as a modular component of grammar.

In a later section we return to questions that seem to arise here regarding the relation between the human language faculty (and UG theory) and particular languages.

3. QUESTIONS OF SUBSTANCE IN PHONOLOGY AND PHONETICS

Most of the contributions assume (sometimes in direct response to Hale and Reiss) that the phonological is more or less directly grounded in phonetic substance. But, even on that assumption, there is scope for disagreement as to what phonetic content consists in for the purposes of phonological theory, the exact nature of the relation between the phonological and the phonetic, and how we are to draw the boundary between them, both conceptually and developmentally.

The chapter by Bromberger and Halle takes speech to be primarily a form of intentional behaviour. In contrast to the proponents of Optimality Theory, which claims to have dispensed with rules and derivations, Bromberger and Halle defend the view that a speech event is the result of a phonological derivation, the levels of which are related by rules. Furthermore, the levels are all representable in terms of a single set of *phonetic* symbols. This might suggest a view of phonology as replete with phonetic substance. However, the symbols have different roles at different levels. In underlying representations they encode knowledge (of the phonological forms of morphemes), while in surface representations they encode phonetic intentions. These intentions, when executed, necessarily involve articulators. The derivation is said to effect 'a kind of transubstantiation ... through which mnemonic elements [are] converted into articulatory ones' (p. 30). Bromberger and Halle concede this requires further elaboration (for which see Bromberger and Halle 1997); however, they are here concerned with another matter. While allowing that phonetic intentions, when executed, result in the production of *tokens*, they reject the view that phonological theory therefore concerns *types*. We return to this below. Here it is enough to note that, at some point in the phonological derivation, the substance of phonological elements (features) is articulatory, as assumed in Chomsky and Halle (1968) and much of generative phonology since.

Harris and Lindsey's chapter, by contrast, is a sustained argument against the articulatory bias of much recent phonological theory, not least on the grounds that it is not articulations that carry the (signifying) *information* central to the rationale of phonology. It is the acoustic signifiers that matter, not the behaviour required to produce them (the latter may be quite varied). Furthermore, while conceding the close relation between acoustics and audition, Harris and Lindsey argue that these should not be conflated. They reject pure acoustics as a basis for phonology, since that would import into phonology factors that do not pertain to mental representation, which for them is the prime concern of specifically phonological theory. In taking phonological categories to be mental objects, they agree with Hale and Reiss (while leaving open the question whether they are specifically linguistic). Furthermore they concur with Hale and Reiss's appeal to Occam's Razor. Nevertheless they insist, against Hale and Reiss, that phonetic considerations cannot be expunged from phonology. They argue that the two are non-accidentally isomorphic. They defend the view, traceable back to Saussure, Sapir, and Jakobson, that phonological elements, as cognitive, are auditory images, illustrating their approach by means of a detailed compositional model of phonological vowel patterns in terms of the elements A, I, and U. Actual phonetic vowels are perceived as composed of these cognitive elements. While the elements are extracted from perceived properties of (and are used to parse) speech signals, they are ontologically distinct from them.

Myers, too, rejects reference to articulatory anatomy in phonological theory. His approach is acoustically based and he argues for a view of the phonology/ phonetics distinction that takes phonology to be discretely categorial in nature, free of gradient continuous effects, which are located within phonetics. It is gradience that distinguishes the phonetic from the phonological. Although the conceptual distinction is clear enough, Myers points up crucial difficulties in deciding whether a given pattern is phonetic or phonological—that is, whether it is best described in terms of gradient physical measurements or discrete categories. He points out, and illustrates, that this depends on the postulated categories. A gradient (and thus phonetic) distinction in one model with a few (broader) categories will emerge as categorial (and thus phonological) in another with more (and more fine-grained) categories. Transcriptions (which necessarily presuppose what the relevant categories are) cannot then provide a reliable basis for phonological research—a view shared by Pierrehumbert *et al.* and by Docherty and Foulkes. Myers argues that the physical measurements of Laboratory Phonology provide the only reliable basis and that categories are to be decided in the light of them.

Although Myers's categorial/gradient conception of the phonology/phonetics distinction is often assumed in earlier work in Laboratory Phonology, Pierrehumbert *et al.* here review that assumption. They argue that Laboratory Phonology requires both discrete and continuous mathematics and that it is an empirical issue which sort of formalism is most appropriate for a given phonological phenomenon. They suggest that phonological representations may appear rather more phonetic than hitherto thought. On the other hand, non-linearities in the domains of articulation, acoustics, and aerodynamics suggest that phonetics is partly categorial in nature. They claim, therefore, that knowledge of sound structure is spread along a continuum, with fine-grained knowledge of continuous variation lying at the phonetic end of the continuum and the more categorial distinctions lying at the phonological end. The Laboratory Phonology approach they outline avoids modelling the categorial/non-categorial distinction in modular terms and instead studies the factors that promote categoriality, such as cognitive processes that establish preferred regions in a continuous space and that maximize the sharpness and discreteness of those regions.

Docherty and Foulkes also point to increasing evidence that redundant phonetic detail may figure in the lexical representations of words and morphemes. In support of their general approach to sociophonetic variation, they question two assumptions that are widely adopted in generative phonology, and represented here in the chapters by Bromberger and Halle and by Myers. The first of these is that, as Myers puts it, 'for any given linguistic expression, there is one and only one phonological representation' (the Uniqueness Hypothesis). The second is that such representations are redundancy free. Docherty and Foulkes argue that these assumptions run into difficulties when confronted with the realities of speech perception and production. Both Pierrehumbert *et al.* and Docherty and Foulkes provide evidence for the claim that lexical representations are not maximally non-redundant. Docherty and Foulkes, in particular, review evidence that suggests that, for any given word, the speaker/hearer stores multiple memory traces, so that variability in the stimulus is directly encoded in lexical representations. Myers, while happy to allow for multiple traces, argues that they are not necessarily inconsistent with the Uniqueness Hypothesis.

Closely connected to the issue of the postulated gradience of the relationship between the phonetic and the phonological is the following developmental question. Is it possible to demarcate the point at which the child may be said to have begun to acquire a phonology, rather than engaging in 'purely phonetic' behaviour? Or is phonological development (viewed as phonetic-cum-phonological development) a completely gradual, continuous process? Vihman and Velleman take the view that phonetics provides the foundation for a child's phonology, which then assumes an organization and character of its own. They claim that discontinuity as well as continuity is evident in phonological development. One of the discontinuities in question is the emergence of word production templates in the child's mind (for example, a trochaic template for the stress contour of bisyllabic words). It is the emergence of word templates that marks the onset of the child's phonological system, according to Vihman and Velleman. These templates break free of phonetics and impose themselves upon words that do not fit the templates, leading to 'distortions' or 'adaptations' of adult pronunciations which were previously less distorted (for example, the uttering of a trochaic pattern for an adult target that is iambic). The development of the child's system can be tracked for each individual child in a distributional analysis in which the extent of parallel patterning across different word forms is established and tracked longitudinally, and this is what they do in their empirical study concerning the acquisition of segmental quantity (specifically, geminates in Finnish).

Fitzpatrick and Wheeldon, whose concern is with psycholinguistic models of speech perception, cast doubt on the idea that the phonological representations stored in the mental lexicon should be conceived of in the multiple-trace terms argued for by Docherty and Foulkes. Fitzpatrick and Wheeldon distinguish three hypotheses concerning lexical access and the nature of stored phonological representations in the mental lexicon. According to the first, the Intermediate Representation Hypothesis, the acoustic signal is analysed in terms of an 'intermediate' phonological unit, such as a stressed syllable, and this unit is then used to search the lexicon for appropriate matches. According to the second, the Underlying Representation Hypothesis (which Fitzpatrick and Wheeldon support), the information extracted from the acoustic signal is mapped directly onto underspecified underlying representations of the sort Docherty and Foulkes object to, with the access unit being the phonological feature. On the third view, the Surface Representation Hypothesis, the information extracted from the acoustic signal is mapped directly onto the surface representation of words, fully specified with all phonetic information, as in multiple-trace models. Fitzpatrick and Wheeldon find SR models implausible, on the grounds that they lead to over-proliferation in the lexicon. Against this, Docherty and Foulkes suggest that such proliferation is not necessarily over-costly. However, Fitzpatrick and Wheeldon cite psycholinguistic experiments on vowel nasalization in Hindi and English, the results of which, they claim, cannot be accounted for by the SR hypothesis, but are consistent with the UR hypothesis. In another experiment on voicing assimilation in Dutch, the results are likewise inconsistent with the SR, but consistent with the UR.

4. TYPES AND TOKENS IN LINGUISTICS AND PHONOLOGY

The distinction between types and tokens is often assumed to have special relevance for linguistics—and phonology particularly—since physical speech (or sign) phenomena are often regarded as tokens of linguistic types.

In an earlier paper (1989), Bromberger made three assumptions about types and tokens in linguistics: (*a*) that linguistic theory is about types not tokens; (*b*) that types are entirely abstract, platonic entities; (*c*) that the type/token distinction is *just* a distinction, implying no kind of *relation* (and furthermore that types do not enter into *causal* relations with tokens). In the light of those three assumptions, his paper posed the problem of how individuals can acquire knowledge of (abstract) linguistic types on the basis of (physical) tokens. This is a version of the problem of language acquisition, a version that sees it as an ontological problem.

The present chapter by Bromberger and Halle, while retaining assumptions (*b*) and (*c*), is concerned to retract assumption (*a*). Bromberger and Halle are agnostic on whether types as they understand them actually exist. However, even if types do exist, they argue that phonological theory is not about them. Rather, phonological theory (at least) is about physical utterance events and the mental conditions and capacities responsible for their occurrence. Their chapter thus disassociates itself from the abstract platonistic linguistics espoused by Katz (1990, 1996), which holds that the linguistic consists of purely abstract types and as such has an ontology wholly independent both of the human mind/brain and of the physical phenomena of speech.

Nevertheless, both Bromberger and Halle, and Katz, do make reference to 'tokens' and assume that the relevant tokens are physical utterance phenomena. For both, then, it is important that 'token' be understood non-relationally—that is, as not implying 'of a type'—assumption (*c*). For Katz, the relational understanding would suggest that linguistic types are in fact tokened/instantiated in (indeed are types *of*) physical utterance phenomena—difficult to square with his platonistic linguistics. For Bromberger and Halle, on the other hand, the relational understanding (coupled with the assumption that types are platonic) would readmit platonism into phonology, implying that utterance events were of interest to phonology qua tokens of platonic types. Bromberger and Halle are concerned to show that phonology is not a branch of metaphysics but is concerned with concrete particulars.

Assumptions (*b*) and (*c*) might well be controversial among those who subscribe to type/token thought as a way of conceiving of the relation between mind-internal linguistic entities and mind-external physical utterance phenomena. This view, common in one form or another, is closely related to that in which utterance phenomena are thought of as the 'realizations', instantiations, or externalizations of linguistic types, or as the physically constituted extensions of mentally constituted intensions. This view implies—against assumption (*b*)—that types can be thought of as located in mind, and—against assumption (*c*)—that type-token *is* a species of relation, that is, the terms 'type' and 'token' are inherently relational, each defined by reference to the other. Neither of these assumptions is actually inconsistent with the view of Peirce (1933, quoted by Bromberger and Halle), the originator of the relevant use of the terms 'type' and 'token', and in fact the relational understanding can be seen as implied by Peirce's discussion. Furthermore, if 'type' and 'token' are inherently relational and if types (at least) are mentally constituted, that would seem to make the problem of language acquisition less intractable—whether in terms of a nativist or an empiricist account of the origin of types.

It is worth asking—in the light of the last paragraph—whether Myers's reference to categories, van der Hulst's to C and V, and Harris and Lindsey's to auditory images, for example, could be interpreted as references to types. Myers's categories can be seen as types instantiated in (and therefore as types of) acoustic phenomena. Similarly for van der Hulst, who thinks of C and V as being instantiated in modality-specific physical phenomena. Harris and Lindsey insist on the ontological distinction between their cognitive (auditory) entities A/I/U and acoustic vocalic phenomena, but do not here discuss the precise nature of the relation between them. In earlier papers (Lindsey and Harris, 1990; Harris and Lindsey, 1993), they have written of 'realization' and of 'interpretation'. The chapter by Vihman and Velleman can be construed as concerned with the origin of types. By contrast, the relation of transduction assumed by Hale and Reiss would seem to be distinct from the type-token relation.

Several contributions make reference to 'phonetic implementation' of the phonological. This suggests a (behavioural) alternative to type-token as an account of the phonology–phonetics relation, if types are thought of as instantiated, rather than as 'implemented'. Consistent with 'implementation', Chomsky has written of the phonological as issuing 'instructions' to the sensorimotor apparatus. And Bromberger and Halle's 'phonetic intentions' sound like things to be implemented.

The Representational Hypothesis advocated by Burton-Roberts and Carr repudiates type-token as a model of the relation between objects generated by L and physical phenomena produced by speakers. A type-token view of this relation would imply that the linguistic is in fact instantiated/tokened in mind-external physical phenomena, which is not consistent with the 'radically internal' concept of the language faculty they defend. Their (and, they believe, Chomsky's) radical internalism implies that, if type/token is in fact needed in linguistics, then internal linguistic types will have internal linguistic tokens. Burton-Roberts offers an argument from compositionality in syntax for a distinction between I-linguistic types and tokens and E-physical types and tokens, a distinction he argues is anyway tacitly assumed in linguistic theory.

This rejection of a type-token model of the relation between the internal and the external is a central motive underlying their alternative—representational—account of the relation between what is internally *generated* (by a sub-personal language faculty, L) and what is externally *produced* (by speaking agents): the latter stand in a relation of representation to the former. A representation of *x* is *not* an instance/token of *x*, they insist. The Representational Hypothesis is consistent with 'phonetic implementation', in that physical utterance phenomena are regarded as produced by speakers implementing the (phonologically constituted) conventions of a language ($CSPR_{(L)}$). However, as representational, the conventions, and *a fortiori* their implementation, are external to the language faculty.

5. 'UNIVERSAL GRAMMAR', LANGUAGES, NATURE, AND SOCIETY

The reader of the foregoing sections might have felt some unease as to what exactly is meant by 'language' or 'phonology'. It is not always clear whether references to, and characterizations of, 'language' and 'phonology' are to be understood as a way of generalizing over languages and phonologies, or as referring to (and characterizing) something else. We have seen, for example, that, while Hulst argues that 'phonology' is neither modular nor modality specific, he allows that the phonologies of particular languages are both modular and modality specific. Hale and Reiss's concern is with *the* computation system of human language (*the* grammar), which, they maintain, is substance free. Thus phonology is substance free. But presumably the phonologies of particular languages are substantive. Is their appeal to transduction intended to relate (substance-free) 'phonology' to (substantive) particular phonologies/languages, or do languages include both substance-free phonologies and transductions?

What is at issue here is how we understand 'Universal Grammar (UG)', and its relation to 'languages'. Both Pierrehumbert *et al.* and Burton-Roberts note that UG can, on the one hand, be understood as providing an overarching description of what all human languages have in common (Burton-Roberts calls this the 'generic' or 'type' conception) and, on the other, as 'a real object of the natural world', a specific, and innate, state of mind/brain (Burton-Roberts calls this the 'realist/naturalistic' conception). By contrast with the realist/naturalistic, the generic conception is compatible with a view of UG as a derivative (even theoretical) concept, derived by generalizing and idealizing over actual languages.

This interpretation suggests that actual languages are, conceptually, the *instantiations* (or actual examples) of a generic concept 'Language' (UG). However, it has also been suggested that languages *instantiate* Language on the realist/naturalistic conception as well—but in a different sense: as an empirical process, in acquisition. Although only in passing, Chomsky (1995a: 6, 11) has recently questioned his earlier assumption that, in acquisition, UG is instantiated in languages. Pierrehumbert *et al.* and Burton-Roberts both question it here.

Pierrehumbert *et al.* claim that this view of the acquisition process is not supported by the available results on the acquisition of a phonology. They argue that the transition from the child's initially insufficient contrasts to robust, mature contrasts is a gradual one (although, as noted, Vihman and Velleman argue that there are both continuities and discontinuities in that transition). It is therefore best modelled, they suggest, using statistics over a continuous space, rather than being viewed as a process of logical instantiation. More generally, the discreteness of an emergent phonological system does not arise, they claim, from the logical instantiation of the discrete elements of an innate UG, but from the discrete limits of continuous processes. They do not either propose a distinct conception of UG or argue against the idea of UG *per se*. For them, as for Chomsky, the existence of UG is an empirical question, but for Pierrehumbert *et al.* the answer to that question awaits the results of further (experimental) research.

Burton-Roberts considers the implications for phonology of the contrast between the (generic) concept of UG as the theory of (all) languages, and the (realist/naturalistic) concept of UG as the theory of a natural object (L) independent of languages. On the generic conception, he argues, it is indeed conceptually necessary that UG include phonology—languages have phonology and (generic) UG is about languages. However, Burton-Roberts seeks to defend and develop the non-generic, realist/naturalistic conception. On this conception, he argues, it is neither necessary nor possible that L (and thus 'UG' theory of L) include phonology. It is not *necessary* because the properties of L are simply quite different from the acknowledged properties of languages, and UG theory is about L. The fact that languages have phonology need not then imply that L does. It is not *possible*, he argues, if only because the inclusion of phonology would introduce Saussurian arbitrariness/convention into L—not consistent with regarding L as natural. By the same token, the real natural object L cannot be thought of as being instantiated in the sociocultural, conventional constructs that languages are. For Burton-Roberts, the conventionality of languages not only distinguishes them from the natural object L but is the basis on which they relate to L: their (phonologically constituted) conventions are *for* the external representation of L.

The distinction between what is natural and what is sociocultural/conventional is important to Chomsky (and Burton-Roberts and Carr) in its own right and if linguistic theory is not to degenerate into 'the study of everything'. Pierrehumbert *et al.* reject this partition as a false dichotomy, insisting that human societies, the variety of sociolinguistic practices, and conventions are as much of the natural world as anything else. This general contention underlies their argument that linguistics is not autonomous. Carr argues that Pierrehumbert *et al.*'s use of 'natural' fails to distinguish the conventional from the non-conventional, a distinction he takes to be essential to phonology.

The relation between phonological knowledge and UG raises the question of the status of variation in phonology, a topic addressed by several contributors. Pierrehumbert *et al.* present an argument that variation *facilitates* the process of the acquisition of a language, rather than *impeding* it. Their general conclusion is that variability is the *cause* of abstraction: assuming that abstraction is cognitively costly, it would not exist unless there were variability that made abstraction necessary.

Docherty and Foulkes are also concerned with the significance for phonological theory of sociophonetic variation. They argue essentially that it is the 'generic' approach that is generally assumed in linguistics and phonological theory (that is, that they are about the actual languages and phonologies of individuals). Docherty and Foulkes suggest that, on that assumption, the fact that language-specific (and thus, learned) aspects of speech are present down to a very fine-grained level of analysis has major implications for phonological investigation. Phonological theory must therefore take account of patterns of variation among individuals and this means that social factors are as important as those normally considered by generative phonologists. It is impossible to exclude social and/or situational factors from a systematic account of the data. They therefore question the reliability of much of the data presented in generative analysis; it overgeneralizes and typically fails to give any indication of which speakers the data are supposed to be representative of, their characteristics (such as age, sex, class) or the communities that they belong to. This is not consistent with the fact that generative phonologists claim that their data reflect, in some sense, what speakers actually do. They argue that the lexical contrastive function of speech sounds is only one of many functions, and that, if studied to the exclusion of other functions as in mainstream generative phonology, it leads to a skewed picture of the function of speech sounds.

Within a broader discussion of scientific method, Carr notes that phonologists conceive of phonology as a scientific activity, and that several contributors rely on arguments from the nature of scientific method in support of their positions. But their interpretations of what that means vary, with some phonologists suggesting that certain types of phonological investigation are of doubtful scientific status, and that certain sorts of phonological analysis are not genuinely explanatory (for example, Pierrehumbert *et al.*). Carr adopts a conception of scientific method, based on falsificationism and scientific realism, and uses this to argue (*contra* Pierrehumbert *et al.*) that hypotheses in generative phonology are falsifiable and thus scientific. But Carr argues that the version of scientific realism adopted in generative phonology has varied between strong and weak realism. Under the former, phonological analyses are said to characterize mental representations and processes that are active during online processing and production. Under weak realism, any such claim is withdrawn, and the phonologist's analyses are said to constitute only an 'indirect characterization' of the speaker–hearer's phonological knowledge. Carr's worry is that weak realism comes very close to being instrumentalism, and that it is not easy to evaluate competing hypotheses on that interpretation. Carr suggests, with certain reservations, that a Laboratory Phonology that takes account of sociophonetic variation may indeed offer the best hope for a strongly realist interpretation of constructs in phonological theory.

This introduction has aimed to highlight a few of the more central issues, questions, and controversies that motivate the volume as a whole and the contributions that follow. It hardly does justice to the full range of topics they address nor to the quite intricate interrelations among them. Neither the volume nor this introduction settles any of the questions posed by phonological theory, but it is our hope that they will contribute to a clearer understanding of what the issues are and of how such conceptual issues in phonology lie at the heart of questions about the nature of linguistic knowledge.

REFERENCES

Anderson, S. R. (1981), 'Why Phonology Isn't Natural', *Linguistic Inquiry*, 12: 493–553.
Bromberger, S. (1989), 'Types and Tokens in Linguistics', in A. George (ed.), *Reflections on Chomsky* (Oxford: Blackwell), 58–89; repr. in S. Bromberger, *On What We Know We Don't Know* (Chicago: Chicago University Press, 1992), 170–208.
—— and Halle, M. (1989), 'Why Phonology is Different', *Linguistic Inquiry*, 20/1: 51–70.
—— —— (1997), 'The Contents of Phonological Signs: A Comparison between their Use in Derivational Theories and in Optionality Theories', in I. Roca (ed.), *Derivations and Constraints in Phonology* (Oxford: Oxford University Press), 93–122.
Chomsky, N. (1972), *Language and Mind* (New York: Harcourt, Brace Jovanovich).
—— (1980), *Rules and Representations* (Oxford: Blackwell).
—— (1986), *Knowledge of Language* (New York: Praeger).
—— (1995a), *The Minimalist Program* (Cambridge, Mass.: MIT Press).
—— (1995b), 'Language and Nature', *Mind*, 104: 1–61.
—— and Halle, M. (1968), *The Sound Pattern of English* (New York: Harper & Row).
Donegan, P. and Stampe, D. (1979), 'The Study of Natural Phonology', in D. Dinnsen (ed.), *Current Approaches to Phonological Theory* (Bloomington, Ind.: Indiana University Press).
Hale, M. and Reiss, R. (2000), 'Substance Abuse and Dysfunctionalism: Current Trends in Phonology', *Linguistic Inquiry*, 31: 157–69.
Harris, J. and Lindsey, G. (1993), 'There is No Level of Phonetic Representation', *UCL Working Papers in Linguistics*, 5: 355–74.
Katz, J. J. (1990), *The Metaphysics of Meaning* (Cambridge, Mass.: MIT Press).
—— (1996), 'The Unfinished Chomskian Revolution', *Mind and Language*, 11: 270–294.
Lindsey, G. and Harris, J. (1990), 'Phonetic Interpretation in Generative Grammar', in *UCL Working Papers in Linguistics*, 2: 355–69.

Ohala, J. J. (1981), 'Speech Timing as a Tool in Phonology', *Phonetica*, 38: 204–12.

—— (1983), 'The Origin of Sound Patterns in Vocal Tract Constraints', in P. F. MacNeilage (ed.), *The Production of Speech* (New York: Springer), 189–216

—— (1990), 'There is no Interface between Phonology and Phonetics: A Personal View', *Journal of Phonetics*, 18/2: 153–71.

—— (1995), 'The Perceptual Basis of Some Sound Patterns', in B. Connell and A. Arvaniti (eds.), *Papers in Laboratory Phonology IV* (Cambridge: Cambridge University Press), 87–92.

Peirce, C. (1933), *Collected Papers* (Cambridge, Mass.: Harvard University Press).

2

The Ontology of Phonology (Revised)

Sylvain Bromberger and Morris Halle

1. PHONOLOGY AND THE PHILOSOPHY OF LANGUAGE

Though many philosophers of language have views on empirical linguistics, few, if any, have given serious attention to phonology. Recent anthologies and books on the philosophy of language either do not mention phonology at all, or at best perfunctorily restate crude and outdated notions on the subject. This is somewhat surprising, since the facts that phonology studies are critical to the individuation of expressions and to their character as objects of speech perception or outputs of speech production. But for these facts, there would be no syntax or semantics of natural languages besides sign languages (also neglected by philosophers), and philosophers deliberating about such languages would have to be silent.

There are a number of explanations for this neglect. To begin with, recent philosophers of language generally belong to an intellectual tradition that admits no essential differences between natural languages and some of their contrived extensions. This was pointed out a long time ago by Strawson (1950), though he had other shortcomings in mind. Philosophic discussions thus generally abstract not only from differences between English, German, Japanese, and other natural languages, but also from differences between these real languages and notational systems used in mathematics, logic, physics, chemistry, biology, linguistics, etc. Such notational systems do have a syntax (albeit usually one that has very little in common with the syntax of natural languages), a semantics, and a pragmatics, but happen to have no phonology. Their minimal units are normally ideographs that encode wordlike units—rather than phonetic or even orthographic ones—open to many phonologically unrelated pronunciations (if pronounceable at all). Nothing in such notational systems corresponds to the phonologies of natural languages, and nothing about them can thus be captured in an overarching phonological

Chapter 2 is based on chapter 9 of *On What We Know We Don't Know*, by Sylvain Bromberger, copyright © 1992 by CSLI Publications, Stanford University, Stanford, CA 94305. The Publisher gratefully acknowledges the permission of CSLI Publications to include the revised version in this book.

We are grateful to Ned Block, Nancy Bromberger, George Boolos, Noam Chomsky, Leonard Clapp, Alec Marantz, Wayne O'Neil, Jean Michel Roy, and Linda Wetzel for comments on previous drafts of this chapter.

doctrine linked to the overarching semantic and syntactic doctrines studied by philosophers. So it is not surprising that, though Frege and his successors include signs in their Sign–Sense–Nominatum triad, they have nothing of interest to say about signs as things uttered and heard. Even philosophers who focus primarily on natural languages belong to that tradition and do not discriminate between aspects peculiar to real languages—that is, articulated languages whose inherently spoken tokens necessarily vanish as soon as produced, and aspects peculiar to conventional notational systems (including writing systems) with characteristically enduring tokens.

Furthermore, philosophers generally seem to believe that there cannot be anything of philosophic interest about phonology. This attitude flows naturally from the previous one. The ideographs used by scientists are adopted through open and explicitly published conventions that determine everything true of them qua signs. Since they are also semantically wordlike, or at least morpheme-like, their subsegments have no autonomous status and raise no philosophic problems. How could there be anything of philosophic interest about the shape of simple numerals, or about the horizontal segment in an inverted $\forall$ in a quantifier, or in the vertical line of the **F** for force? It is easy to pass from this outlook to the view that there cannot be anything of philosophic import about the spelling of words, and thence to the view that there cannot be anything of philosophic import about their pronunciation. And is not phonology 'just' about pronunciation?

Whatever the explanation for philosophers' neglect of phonology, we think that it has a cost. To begin with, we think that it is a mistake to lump all lexical systems together as forming some kind of natural family open to ready generalizations. It glosses over too many crucial differences, and attention to phonology can highlight important ones. Furthermore, we think that no theory about the relation between natural language signs and their referents (or their meaning, or their use) can be trustworthy that nonchalantly takes the nature of those signs for granted. Finally, we think an adequate understanding of the ontology of language—of the objects whose existence constitutes the reality of language—must include an adequate conception of the objects investigated by phonology. More specifically, an adequate conception of language must check our tendency, when we reflect about language, to slip thoughtlessly between talk about individual utterances and talk about types, as if such slips were always innocuous and easily fixed ways of avoiding pedantry. Spoken or subvocally produced tokens are transitory events that are finite in number, that occur in time and space, that can be perceived, that are shaped by their speaker's occurrent intentions, and that are subject to norms fixed in their speakers mental make-up. Types—if there are types—are abstract entities, neither in time nor in space, devoid of causal histories or causal consequences, hence beyond perception. Types—if there are types—outdistance tokens, in number (since there are infinitely many of them). Tokens and types—if there are types—are thus utterly different. Conflating them, or taking their connection as given, is bound to produce confusions and incoherence. But giving each its due, and understanding their connection, will not be possible unless we see how the type/token distinction fares in phonology.

2. THE ISSUES

Linguistics, like Gaul, is traditionally divided into three parts, syntax, semantics, and phonology, the latter being presumably concerned with the sound aspect of language.[1] The issues we plan to discuss in this chapter concern phonology directly and the other two branches indirectly. We take phonological theory to be about the world, about reality, and thus about certain items in the world—certain 'particulars', as metaphysicians[2] might put it—whose existence is attested to by the fact that people speak. What is the nature of these 'particulars'? In the first part of our chapter, we will address that question. Our answer will be that phonology is about concrete mental events and states that occur in real time, in real space, have causes, have effects, are finite in number, in other words are what metaphysicians would call CONCRETE PARTICULARS closely linked to, but distinct from, those described by traditional phoneticians concerned with articulatory or acoustic events. In the second part of our chapter we will consider a very different answer, according to which phonology is about types, a certain species of abstract, causally impotent, non-spatiotemporal entities, possibly infinite in number, and distinct from real live utterances.[3] Phonology, like the rest of linguistics, is normally expounded as if it were about types. But does this mean that the discipline is committed to there being such abstract entities as types? We will argue that it is not.

---

[1] This chapter is a somewhat modified version of a paper originally given in Uppsala, Sweden, at the Ninth International Congress of Logic, Methodology, and Philosophy (Bromberger and Halle 1994). All the references to actual utterances are to utterances produced by Sylvain Bromberger on that occasion. Readers should keep in mind that the chapter was intended for an audience of philosophers of language and philosophers of science—that is, an audience largely unfamiliar with phonology—and that one of our aims was to get such philosophers to appreciate the conceptual and ontological issues raised by phonology. The present version is still mostly untechnical and suited for an audience that knows little about phonology but is interested in the nature of language and its study. Since many phonologists, in practice if not in theory, write and talk as if the objects of their investigations were abstract entities—the sort of entities normally called types—the issues raised here will be pertinent to their interests as well. For a paper on how these issues arise in the debate between rule-based phonology and optimality theory, see Bromberger and Halle (1997).

[2] See Bromberger and Halle (1989) on why phonology is fundamentally different from syntax and semantics. We take morphology to be at the intersection between syntax and phonology.

[3] The type/token distinction, in the sense relevant to our discussion, is usually traced to a puzzling passage by C. S. Peirce (1933: iv., 423): '. . . there is but one word "the" in the English language; and it is impossible that this word should lie visibly on a page or be heard in any voice, for the reason that it is not a Single thing or Single event. It does not exist: it only determines things that do exist. Such a definitely significant Form, I propose to term a TYPE. A single event which happens once and whose identity is limited to that happening or a Single object or thing which is in some single place at any one instant of time, such event or thing being significant only as occurring just when and where it does, such as this or that word on a single line of a single page of a single copy of a book, I will venture to call

In the course of our discussion we will use some technical notation but we will keep it to a minimum and will explain it as we go. We will also talk from within a framework that some linguists may reject. That cannot be helped. Linguistics is in constant flux and full of controversies. Nothing of real interest in it is conclusively established once and for all and to everybody's satisfaction.

3. ON THE NATURE OF TOKENS

3.1. *The phonological representation of a token*

Let us begin by thinking about spoken tokens. And to fix ideas, let us focus on a very specific one, the one that I, the speaker,[4] will now produce:

(1) *The merchant sold shelves.*

That token is now history! Only time travel could enable us ever to hear it again. It could, of course, be duplicated, but it itself is gone forever. We will come back to the fact that it could be duplicated, but let us forget about that right now. Let us concentrate on the specific event that happened a few seconds ago. We will refer to it as event (1) since we are not able to display it again.

Actually many things happened when event (1) occurred. That is why it could be studied by more than one discipline and be analysed differently by each. So, for instance, noises happened, and event (1) therefore could be investigated under acoustics and given an acoustical analysis. Bodily movements happened, and event (1) could therefore be studied under motor behaviour and given an articulatory analysis. Brain and neurological events happened, and (1) could be looked at under neurology and given a neurological analysis. And so on.

However, we exhibited event (1) to illustrate a phonological event that is an event that can be examined in the light of phonological theory and given a phonological analysis.

What would such an analysis tell us about (1)?

Well, let us look at how phonologists would represent (1) in the notation of phonology.

They would represent it as follows (the dots between (2*a*), (2*b*), and (2*c*) represent 'lines' that we omit for present purposes):

TOKEN.' Thus tokens are actual utterances produced by specific persons, at specific times, at specific places. Types, if there are types, are not. It is important in this connection to distinguish tokens from OCCURRENCES of types. Thus the sentence type *Joe's cat hates Mary's cat* contains two occurrences of the type *cat* but contains no tokens, since types are not made up of tokens. For other discussions and attempts to clarify the distinction see Cartwright (1987), Quine (1987), Bromberger (1989), Hutton (1990), Katz (1990), Wetzel (1993), Burton-Roberts (1994, and this volume), Szabo (1999).

[4] We use the first-person singular to mention Sylvain Bromberger as producer of tokens displayed during the talk in Uppsala and use the first-person plural to mention ourselves, the two authors. We use script font to indicate displayed actual specific spoken tokens. Readers of the chapter should thus keep in mind that our use of script font is to point to episodes that they can no doubt imagine but that took place in Uppsala when this chapter was orally presented.

(2) (a) {[ðə], Art ... } + {[mərtʃənt], Noun ... } + {Q, Sing ... } + {[sɛl], Vb ... } +
{Q, Past ... } + {[ʃɛlf], Noun ... } + {Q, Plur ... }

. . . .

(b) {[ðə], Art ... } + {[mərtʃənt], Noun ... } + {Q, Sing ... } + {[sol], Vb ... } +
{Q, Past ... } + {[ʃɛlv], Noun ... } + {Q, Plur ... }

. . . .

(c) ðəmə-tʃntsoldʃɛlv z

In other words, they would represent it as a sequence of lines, a DERIVATION. Each line would purport to stand for some fact about (1), and the ordering would purport to stand for further facts about it.

What kind of facts?

We are going to go through the derivation step by step to answer that question. But before doing so, we want to describe the general character of that answer.

My production of event (1) was an action. Like other actions, it was therefore brought about by a distinctive kind of mental set—something we will call an INTENTION. But this term, as we use it, is not to be taken altogether literally. We use it to refer to a familiar kind of purposive mental stance. Think of someone aiming a rifle at a target. That person moved and positioned limbs, head, eyes, and so on in certain ways. But more went on. After all, the movements were not made accidentally, or by way of checking whether the barrel is in line with the butt. The person was set psychologically in a distinct way—that is, had distinct intentions. More specifically, a person who aims a rifle has certain effects in mind, plans moves in ways calculated to achieve those effects, and, crucially from our point of view, has the intellectual capacity to select those effects and to devise the gestures that achieve them. The uttering of (1), like the aiming of a rifle, also required a distinctive mindset, distinctive intentions on my part, intentions that I could not have formed without certain pre-existing intellectual capacities. Of course, I had many intentions when I produced it: I intended to give you an example, I intended to be understood, I intended to produce a sentence that you have probably never heard before. But only some of my intentions account for the fact that I PRONOUNCED (1), that (1) was an action of pronouncing something in a language I know, in my idiolect of English. Those intentions are the kinds of facts about (1) that we take (2) to represent.

3.2. *The last line of the derivation*

Let us now look at the last line of the derivation (2), that is (2c).

(2c) *could* be construed as a phonetic transcription of the utterance (1). Formally it is a string of letters from an alphabet in which each letter traditionally stands for a speech sound.[5] Speech sounds, as articulatory events, are not

---

[5] The fact that the utterance consists of sequences of discrete sounds is the insight on which all alphabetic writing systems are based. It may, therefore, appear to be self-evident. Yet, when we last asked our colleagues working on the automatic analysis of speech, we were told that no one has yet found a reliable mechanical procedure that can segment any arbitrary utterance into its constituent sounds.

unanalysable entities. They are rather complexes of (phonetic) FEATURES. Thus each letter in (2c) stands for a particular complex of features. In (3) we have given a partial list of the feature composition of some of the component sounds of English.

(3) p b m f v   t d n s z   k g
     – – – + +   – – – + +   – –   continuant
     – – + – –   – – + – –   – –   nasal
     – + + – +   – – + – +   – +   voiced
        labial   coronal   dorsal   major articulator

You will readily notice that the three sets of consonants in (3) differ from each other in that each involves action by a different major articulator; that is, [pbmfv] are produced with active involvement of the lips; [tdnsz], with that of the tongue blade or coronal articulators; and [kg], with that of the tongue body or dorsal articulator. It is the major articulator that stops the airflow from out of the mouth in [−continuant] sounds, but allows it in the sounds that are [+continuant].

In addition to the major articulators the production of consonants involves other articulators as well. In particular, the consonants m and n are produced with a lowering of the velum, which allows air to flow through the speaker's nasal cavities exciting thereby the resonances of these cavities. In all other consonants, the velum is raised, no air flows through the nasal passages, and their characteristic resonances are not excited. This information is reflected by the pluses and minuses in the second line of (3). The third line reflects the behaviour of the vocal cords. It is the vocal cords that implement the feature [voiced]. They vibrate in [+voiced] sounds such as [bmvdnzg] and they are stationary in the [−voiced] consonants [pftsk].

We said a moment ago that (2c) *could* be construed as a phonetic transcription—that is, as a record of articulator movements and positionings. However, that is not the way we construe it! We construe (2c) as standing for a series of intentions that generated those movements. Each letter in (2c) stands for such an intention, and each of these intentions called for an arrangement of articulators in the expectation of distinctive auditory effects. Each was also the intention to act so as to produce a specific English SPEECH sound, and thus required a capacity that I acquired when I acquired English.

Consider, for instance, the m in (2c). It represents an intention (at the time) that called for simultaneously closing my mouth at the lips, lowering my velum, adjusting the stiffness of my vocal folds, and thereby producing a sound *m*. That is what the expansion in feature notation reflects. However, it does not represent an intention that merely called for going through all that gymnastics to produce the sound *m*. I could have intended that much without intending to produce an English sound—for instance while intending to hum a tune, or to imitate a cow, or to express mild surprise. The m in (2c) represents an intention to act so as to produce a specific ENGLISH SPEECH SOUND. And I could not have formed that intention, that mindset, had I not acquired English.[6]

The other letters in (2c) stand for similar intentions to utter speech sounds in (1). Let us call them PHONETIC INTENTIONS.[7] What (2c) represents is, therefore, totally unlike what an oscillograph hooked to a microphone might have recorded, and this not only because some information recoverable from oscillograph records such as loudness, rate of speaking, fundamental frequency, and other characteristics of the speaker's voice cannot be inferred from (2c), but crucially because it stands for a different kind of event altogether. (2c) stands for the occurrence of phonetic intentions. Oscillographs hooked to microphones record the occurrence of noises.

But why not construe (2c) as standing for the actual movements that produced the noises rather than for mere intentions? The symbols, after all, were introduced in the discipline for that purpose! We have at least two reasons. The first is conceptual. (2c), as we shall see in a moment, represents the result of a mental computation. And we do not think that movements are necessary results of the kind of computation involved here. Results of such computations have content. (2c) happens to characterize a content that was executed, but need not have been executed.[8] It would not have been executed had we been reading or mulling subvocally. The second is empirical. When we execute a speech action we correct for all sorts of momentary impediments and conditions. (2c) says nothing about such corrections. It contains only linguistic information and takes into account only linguistic knowledge. As a description of the articulator actions, it might be false. So we use the traditional symbols, but we do not subscribe to their standard phonetic interpretation.[9]

3.3. *The first line of the derivation*

Let us now turn to (2a), the first line in the derivation. It represents another series of intentions responsible for event (1)—namely, the intentions to use certain words, for instance, the noun *merchant*, the verb *sell* marked for past tense, and so

---

[6] Compare with the availability of click sounds as phonemes to speakers of Bantu, but only as noises to speakers of English.

[7] For a related position see Liberman and Mattingly (1985, 1989), and Bromberger and Halle (1986), and Halle (1997).

[8] Elsewhere (Bromberger and Halle 1986a) we have called this kind of intentional content a SCORE, to mark the analogy with a musical score, something that can be executed through motions, but need not be executed, and often is not. Inner discourse probably stops at the formation of such scores.

[9] Our interpretation of event (1) commits us to the occurrence of the mental events we call intentions over and above acoustical events and articulatory events. We present some of our reasons in Bromberger and Halle (1989). Lenneberg (1967) pointed out a long time ago that the neural paths to the various articulators implicated in the production of a speech sound are of different lengths and that instructions to move them must therefore leave the brain at different times, thus providing possible evidence for the existence of brain events corresponding to such intentions.

on, in a certain order. This is reflected, for instance, in (2a) by the clustering of phonetic symbols into larger bracketed wordlike units.

Forming the intention to produce (1) clearly required that I know the words I used, and that I retrieve them from memory. So, before discussing in more detail how (2a) relates to (1), let us look at how some linguists represent knowledge of words.

None of us is born with the knowledge of the words of our native language. That children learn words as they develop is obvious and moreover massively documented, and we all know that the process goes on through life: most of us have only recently acquired such words as *intifada, glasnost, scud*. The proposition that an essential part of acquiring a language consists in storing in one's memory (something representable as) a list of words, something we will call the Vocabulary, is therefore one of the most securely founded in all linguistics.

Many words that any speaker of English knows are complex in the sense that they incorporate affixes of various kinds. We illustrate this in (4).

(4) (a)   shelv-es, child-ren, bough-t, sol-d
     (b)   pre-dis-pose, un-happy, in-secure
     (c)   un-poison-ous-ness, ex-pre-sid-ent, contra-in-dic-ate-d
     (d)   kibbutz-im, hassid-im

In linguistics the term STEM is used to designate the element to which an affix is added and the term MORPHEME is used as a cover term for both affixes and stems. Like stems, affixes too must be learned and committed to memory (see (4d)).

A speaker's knowledge of morphemes can thus be represented as a list of items containing information about each morpheme stored in memory.

What information?

Obviously information about its meaning, its functional structure, and the thematic roles it assigns. Also about its lexical category—that is, whether it is a noun, verb, preposition, adjective, conjunction. And certainly information pertaining to how the morpheme is pronounced—that is, phonological information. All this can be thought of as encoded in a COMPLEX SYMBOL, made up of elements that stand for meaning, lexical category, and so on. The markers pertaining to how the morpheme is pronounced are of particular interest to us here. We will refer to each of them as the IDENTIFYING INDEX. The Vocabulary as a whole can thus be represented as a long list of such complex symbols, each of which contains, among other things, an identifying index.[10]

We now turn to the information in identifying indices.

---

[10]   In talk about identifying indices we must take care to distinguish between what we presume to be 'in the mind' of the knower and representations in the notation of our theory. We use the term IDENTIFYING INDEX primarily to refer to representations in the notation of the theory, not what is 'in the mind'. We do, however, expect that research will eventually reveal elements of the mind/brain corresponding to these representations, and we may therefore sometimes avoid circumlocution by using the term and others like it to refer to these putative elements.

Most morphemes take on the same phonetic form regardless of syntactic and/or morphological contexts. Thus the verb *hint* shows up in the phonetic form representable as [hɪnt] whenever uttered. So that string of phonetic symbols is used as its identifying index.

Other morphemes assume different phonetic forms depending on syntactic and/or morphological contexts. For instance, the stems *sell* and *shelf* were pronounced differently in (1) than in the following utterance, which I now produce:

(5) *The merchant sells a shelf.*

The identifying index of such stems is also a string of phonetic symbols— namely, [sɛl] and [ʃɛlf] in the two cases at hand. We will come back to why those particular strings.

Not only do some morphemes, notably the English plural and past-tense affixes, assume different phonetic forms in different contexts, but these forms can also be utterly dissimilar, and sometimes they do not appear phonetically at all!

So note what happens to the plural affix in the following cases:

(6)   cat/s, child/ren, kibbutz/im, alumn/i, stigma/ta, geese, moose

and to the past-tense morpheme in the following:

(7)   bake/d, playe/d, dream/t, sol/d, sang, hit

Halle (1990) has dubbed morphemes such as the Plural and Past morphemes, which behave in this very irregular fashion, ABSTRACT MORPHEMES and he has used Q, a symbol that has no direct phonetic interpretation, as their identifying index.[11]

With all this in mind, let us look again at (2*a*).

(2*a*) is a sequence of complex symbols each made up of an identifying index and other grammatical markers, all copied from the Vocabulary.

What facts about event (1) does (2*a*) represent?

(2*a*), as we said before, represents the intention to use certain words, but we can now be more explicit. (2*a*) represents the fact that (1), besides being produced by my phonetic intentions in (2*c*) was also produced by my intention to use the words retrieved from my memory whose identifying indices (and lexical category) appear in (2*a*).

But what are the phonetic symbols doing in (2*a*)? Take the initial m in the identifying index of *merchant*. Does it represent an intention, already present at that stage so to say, to produce a token of the phoneme m—that is, to close my lips,

---

[11] Other elements in the lexicon may also lack specific phonological content—for instance, PRO, empty complementizers, case, expletives, etc.—yet not be represented by a complex symbol that includes any identifying index like Q. Whether or not some morpheme must be represented with an identifying index like Q or no identifying index at all is a contingent matter to be settled on empirical grounds. Halle's proposal is not that we adopt a convention for the sake of giving all complex symbols a common format. It embodies the claim that all unarticulated morphemes are not phonologically equal.

lower my velum, slacken my vocal folds, and so on? Offhand that may seem reasonable. But consider then the ε in the identifying index of *sell*. It cannot stand for an intention to produce a token of the phoneme ε, to undertake the relevant gestures. No such intention was executed in producing (1). Could I have changed my mind between the times I picked the words and pronounced them? That strikes us as a cute but vacuous idea, too literal minded about our use of INTENTION.[12] As we see it, the role of the phonetic symbols in (2a) and in (2c) is very different. In (2a) they play a computational role. Formulae such as (2a) have two functions. On the one hand, they model an event, represent aspects of that event. On the other hand they are used to compute other formulae IN THE FORMALISM OF OUR THEORY. Phonetic symbols appear in (2a) essentially to simplify computations within the theory. In (2c) they have that role, but they also represent phonetic intentions. These roles, though connected, are different.[13]

Note that in the Vocabulary phonetic symbols could not stand for intentions either. The Vocabulary is a representation not of intentions, but of knowledge. But its formulae too enter into computations.

3.4. *The second line of the derivation*

Let us now look at (2b).

(2b) stands between (2a) and (2c). It is like (2a), except that some of the phonetic symbols in the identifying indices have been changed. Unlike (2c) it is partitioned, contains lexical category labels and occurrences of Q.

What facts about event (1) does (2b) represent?[14]

It represents a stage between the formation of my intentions to use words in my memory—that is, the intentions represented by (2a)—and the formation of my phonetic intentions—that is, the intentions represented by (2c). Unlike (2a) and (2c), it does not represent intentions at all, though it does represent a mental set of sorts.

Remember events (1) and (5), the actual utterances? In the earlier one I pronounced the verb one way and in the later one I pronounced the same verb very

---

[12] See p. 23.

[13] For a different perspective, not committed to such an instrumentalist conception of phonological signs, see Bromberger and Halle (1997). In that paper—where we focus more closely on the semantics of phonological symbols—we assume that, WITHIN ANY THEORETICAL APPROACH TO PHONOLOGY, each phonological symbol must have the same semantic value wherever it occurs. We also explore there some consequences of that assumption in so far as it applies to symbols occurring in different lines of derivations and in different cells of OT tableaux.

[14] Some things we have said so far could be put in Austinian terminology (as in Austin 1975). (2a) modelled the formation of a PHATIC intention—that is, the intention to produce what Austin called a phatic act, 'the uttering of certain vocables or words ... belonging to, and as belonging to, a certain Vocabulary, conforming to and as conforming to a certain grammar'. (We leave out 'i.e. noises of certain types' as misleading.) (2c) modelled a PHONETIC intention—that is, the intention to produce what Austin called a phonetic act, 'the act of merely uttering certain noises'. (The 'merely' is unfortunate!) (2b) then models a stage in a mental process through which the phatic mental set (or intention) gets transformed into the phonetic mental set (or intention).

differently. The facts underlying the difference can be surmised from a vast body of evidence, though they also happen to coincide with common beliefs. When I acquired my idiolect of English, I not only acquired words and other morphemes, but I also acquired rules. In producing these utterances I applied appropriate rules, and this led to different pronunciations of the same verb.

(2*b*) stands for a stage in the application of these rules.

We can even tell what stage.

As noted before, the verb *sell* and the noun *shelf* appear in two distinct guises in different utterances. Specifically, the verb *sell* undergoes a vowel change when combined with the past tense (a morpheme in my memory), and the noun *shelf* undergoes a change of the final consonant, when combined with the plural (also a morpheme in my memory). In other words, in producing these utterances, I invoked something like the rules in (8)

(8) (*a*) Before [Q, Past] the stem vowel is [o] in the verbs *sell, tell, ...*
    (*b*) Before [Q, Pl] the stem-final consonant is [+voice] in the nouns *house, knife, life, wife, shelf, mouth, ...*

(2*b*) then represents a stage after the application of rules (8).

The rules in (8) are not the only rules I applied to produce (1). I also applied rules to pronounce the morphemes represented by Q in (2*a*). Halle (1990) has argued that the relevant rules are statable roughly as follows:

(9) Q → /n/   in env. X__ Plural if X is *child, ox, ...*
        /im/ in env. Y__ Plural if Y is *kibbutz, hasid, ...*
        /i/   in env. Z__ Plural if Z is *alumn-, radi-, ...*
        /ta/ in env. U__ Plural if U is *stigma, schema, ...*
        ø   in env. V__ Plural if V is *mouse, moose, ...*
        /z/   in env. __ Plural

(10) Q → ø   in env. X__ Past if X is *sing, write, ...*
         /t/   in env. Y__ Past if Y is *buy, dream, mean, ...*
         /d/   in env. __ Past

So (2*b*) also represents a stage before the application of those rules!

But what do the phonetic symbols in (2*b*) represent? For that matter, what do they represent in the statement of the rules? The answer here is as before. They play a role as symbols in the formal computations of the theory. We conjecture that they also stand for specific aspects of the production of (1), but what that comes to exactly is not something clearly understood at this time and that must wait for further understanding of the nature of linguistic capacities and their actualizations.[15]

This double role assigned to phonetic symbols, we should point out, has a shortcoming: it slights certain important phenomena. So, for instance, it does not

---

[15] But see n. 13.

show that between the formation of (2*a*)'s referent and (2*c*)'s referent a kind of transubstantiation occurred through which mnemonic elements were converted into articulatory ones.

4. ON THE NATURE OF TYPES

So far we have concentrated on a single and unique event, the utterance(1). We have done this because we hold that phonological theory, in so far as it purports to advance knowledge at all, is about such events and about the mental conditions and capacities responsible for their occurrence. Those are the sorts of things to which it is ontologically committed, or, as some followers of Quine would put it, those are the kinds of things over which it quantifies.

Our position may strike some as prima facie implausible, as simply conflicting with too many practices of phonologists.

Thus phonologists never mention or try to explain unique events like (1). Their papers and texts mention words, phrases, sentences, phonemes, that is, types, abstract entities outside time and space, devoid of causal histories and causal consequences. They do not mention utterances, events, or mental states. And, though phonologists do sometimes elicit tokens from themselves or from informants, they seem to do so only by way of getting facts about types. Thus their conclusions normally abstract from everything peculiar to such tokens, and, in so far as they seem to mention anything, they seem to mention types. In fact, no phonologists would probably interpret (2) as about (1), the utterance I produced umpteen minutes ago. How could they? How many have ever heard of that utterance! They would implicitly[16] take (2) as about a type possibly attested by something like (1) but attestable as well by other tokens—for instance, by the one that I now produce

(11) *The merchant sold shelves.*

And that last token, as Leibniz's indiscernability of identicals tells us, is not only numerically distinct from (1), since it occurred at a different time, but is also numerically distinct from its type, which does not occur in time at all.

Furthermore, phonologists, like all grammarians, strive for theories that neither undergenerate nor overgenerate, theories that predict some items and exclude others. But the relevant items cannot be tokens! If they were, any phonological theory, no matter how absurd, could always be trivially confirmed. Imagine, for instance, a theory that predicts that the following is in my language:

---

[16] We say 'implicitly' because, most phonologists explicitly avoid saying that they are theorizing about actual utterances by saying that they are investigating competence and not performance, as if that were sufficient to clarify the ontological nature of the entities they mention in practice.

(12) *The plmotpfu sell yesterday many shelf.*

I would have confirmed that theory simply by having produced the token (12)! What is more, every theory of any interest would be demonstrably false since it would predict an infinite number of tokens for each person, whereas the total number of tokens is bound to be finite. Life is short! Even the most loquacious of us, no matter how long they live, will shut up forever at some point!

That may all be true; none the less, we do not believe that there are types! And so phonology cannot be about types. We admit (on empirical grounds) internalized grammars, but those exist as mental attributes of concrete, specific human individuals. We admit (on empirical grounds) internalized vocabularies, but those too exist as mental attributes of concrete, specific human individuals; and we admit token events (again on empirical grounds) but those are spatiotemporally located concrete events like (1). But types, as a kind of individual, as a kind of entity, we think, belong, with useful fictions like virtual optical images and stellar constellations, in the null class.

We cannot prove that there are no types. The notion is surely not self-contradictory, or even incoherent. Bromberger (1989) has argued that it is a coherent and even useful one. We just do not see any reason to think that any entities correspond to that notion. And we do not believe that phonology provides any evidence for such entities, or must presuppose their existence.

On the other hand, we do believe that phonology provides overwhelming evidence that tokens cluster into scientifically significant similarity classes. That does not imply that there are types besides tokens (not even as sets, or mereological sums of tokens, though such sets and sums may well exist). But it is sufficient to justify most of the practices we have mentioned, to make sense of the demand that theories should neither overgenerate nor undergenerate, and perhaps to explain the source of the illusion that there are types.

We will now explain that position in more detail.

Instead of producing (1) when I did, I could have produced a very different token. In fact, to fix ideas, here I go:

(13) *Two elephants study in Uppsala.*

And we could now go on and produce a derivation analogous to (2) for this new token. It would be a different derivation from (2). The last line, the first line, the intervening lines, the rules invoked, the items said to represent morphemes retrieved from lexical memory, all would be different. However, the two derivations would have one crucial thing in common: they would incorporate answers to the *same* questions. Different answers, but the same questions.

In other words, event (1) was open to the following questions. What morphemes in memory were intended? What was the representation of these morphemes in memory? What articulatory gestures were intended? What rules were invoked in the course of the formation of these intentions? and so on. (2) provides the answers to these questions.[17] The last token (13) was open to the same questions. Its derivation, spelled out explicitly, would also provide answers to those questions, but the answers would be different. As we just said, different answers; the same questions. In fact, all spoken token events are open to these questions. Some warrant exactly the same answers. Token event (1) and the token event (11) do. Others do not warrant the same answers. Token events (1) and (13) do not. Token events that warrant the same answers are the ones we classify as BEING OF THE SAME TYPE. Those that do not, we classify as BEING OF DIFFERENT TYPES. Neither classification presupposes the existence of types. They presuppose only the possibility of certain similarities and differences among tokens.

That is all there is to talk of types, as far as we are concerned. But that is quite a lot, as we will now show.

Note, for instance, that each token warrants specific answers to these questions. We are unmitigated realists about this. We take the fact that each token warrants the specific answers it does to each of these questions to constitute truths about the world, not some artefact of our way of looking at things. It is a truth about the world that the answer to 'what was the first intended articulation underlying the production of (1)?' is 'vibration of the vocal cord (that is, [+voice]), constriction of the mouth cavity partially open (that is, [+continuant]), and so on', just as it is a truth about the world that the answer to 'How much does Sylvain Bromberger weigh?' is '175 lbs.'.

Note furthermore that we also take it as a truth about the world—and a very different sort of truth—but not an artefact of our way of looking at things, that (1) has the property of warranting such answers at all. We might put this somewhat more technically. It is a truth about the world that event (1) had the DETERMINABLE property of having intended morphemes. And it is a truth about the world that each spoken token also does. Other events, even events with acoustic properties, do not have that determinable property. Noises made by our coffee pot, or coughs for instance, do not have it. That fact is of the same order as the fact that swinging pendula have periods, while standing rocks do not; that positive numbers have square roots, while trees do not; that the manuscript from which we are reading has a certain gravitational mass, while the ideas we are expressing do not. Determinable properties, by the way, such as period, square root, weight, and so on, are a kind of property presupposed by what-questions such as 'What is the period of ... ?', 'What is the square root of ... ?', 'What is the weight of ... ?' Objects that do not have the property warrant no answer to the corresponding question. Those that do, and hence that have DETERMINATE instances of these determinable properties, warrant specific answers.

---

[17] Strictly speaking, to provide these answers it would have to be supplemented with references to the rules, as it was in the course of our discussion.

(1), (5), (13), and other tokens are, of course, open to many questions besides the ones answered in derivations such as (2). They warrant answers, for instance, to 'At what time was it uttered?', 'Where was it uttered?' If we were to use those questions to compare tokens as to sameness of type, we would end up with very different typological clusters. But we do not use those. We use questions that define the field of phonology. In other words, we use the questions that make phonology AS A THEORETICAL FIELD possible. That there are such questions, by the way, is also an empirical truth about the world!

An analogy that we have used elsewhere, taken from elementary chemistry, may be helpful here. Think for a moment about a sample of water, a real sample that you have 'experienced', as they say in California. That sample, like our tokens, is open to a number of questions—'Where was it situated when you experienced it?', 'Who owned it?', 'What did you do with it?'—that are of no scientific interest. But it is open to others that are of scientific interest, such as 'What is its boiling point?', 'What is its freezing point?', 'What is its molecular weight?' Other samples of stuff get the same answers to these last questions. They comprise all and only samples of water. Still other samples, though open to the same questions, get different answers. They comprise all and only the samples of other distinct substances—for instance, samples of gold all share one set of answers, samples of mercury share another set of answers, samples of sulphuric acid share yet another set, and so on. And still other samples of stuff do not hold answers at all to these questions. Pieces of sausage, for instance, or handfuls of mud, or buckets of shoelaces. These do not make up samples of a substance at all! The scientifically interesting questions collect bits of stuff into samples of SUBSTANCES. Not all bits of stuff. Some bits of stuff.

But what makes these questions scientifically interesting?

That should be obvious: the fact that their answers (when formulated in an appropriate notation) conform to lawlike, or at least computable, relationships. There are lawlike, or at least computable, relationships between boiling points, freezing points, and molecular weights. A theory can, therefore, be constructed on the back of these questions. And a certain attitude can be acquired. For instance, that these samples constitute a NATURAL domain, a domain that includes some (water, gold, mercury, and so on) but excludes others (sausage, mud, shoelaces); and that these samples have features that demand similar explanations. Of course, these attitudes are justified only if certain facts obtain—that is, only if certain lawlike relationships actually hold. For all we once knew, the world might have been otherwise.

A similar story, we believe, applies to utterances. Each utterance is open to a multiplicity of questions. The scientifically interesting ones are those whose answers across tokens stand in lawlike, computable relationships to each other. As we noted before, that there are such questions, if there are, is a fact about the world. An important and somewhat surprising fact. We believe there are such facts.[18] If we did not we would not spend time on linguistics. And we believe that the questions we characterized as defining the domain of phonology are among these questions. If we did not we would not pursue phonology as we do. All of that then is implicated in our talk about types. But none of it entails that there are types as well as tokens.

We want to stress one crucial further fact about questions of scientific interest. They are not all given, they are not part of ordinary common sense, they must be smoked out, discovered, and their discovery can be an achievement more revolutionary than the discovery of a new phenomenon. Newton, for instance, discovered many things about the world, but his most important discovery (outside optics) would not have been possible without the discovery that physical bodies have MASS. That was the discovery of a new kind of question (and determinable property), revolutionary because answers to it turned out to stand in marvellous computable relation to other questions (for instance, 'What force is required to accelerate such and such object one foot per second?'). Aristotle, a very good scientist, did not have the concept of mass, and therefore could not have asked what the mass of the moon was, could not even know that he did not know what the mass of the moon was, and, of course, could not have fathomed that the answer to that question was related in systematic ways to the answer to other questions about the moon. Celestial mechanics was beyond even his imagination!

The questions that make phonology possible also had to be discovered. And their discoverers are the heroes of our field: Panini, Rask, Bopp, Saussure, Jakobson, Chomsky. Without these theorists, doing phonology would still consist in pedantically collecting odd curiosities. But the work of discovering the right questions is far from finished!

As we mentioned at the very outset, utterances form a natural domain with other noises, the domain of acoustical theory. To deny this would be like holding that elephants, because they have a sex life, are not, like rocks, physical objects subject to the laws of mechanics! On the other hand, to deny that utterances constitute an autonomous domain, the domain of phonology, would be like holding that, because elephants are subject to the laws of mechanics, like rocks, they have no sex life! And to deny a priori that there are systematic relationships between these two domains would be like denying a priori that there are systematic relationships between the mass of elephants and the character of their sex life.

We can now tell what we make of the fact that (2), though about (1), contained no information about time, speaker, and so on, and could have served for (11) as well. (2) contains only answers to questions of interest from the point of view of theoretical phonology. It could serve for any token that holds the same answers to

---

[18]   The lawlike computable relationships are those that govern the production of utterances. Not of all utterances, but only of utterances produced by invoking rules and a lexicon. People can, of course, produce utterances without such invocation—when they produce gibberish, for instance. The crucial fact, not revealed by simple common sense, is that they can produce utterances that do invoke them.

those questions. Thus nothing about the abstract character of (2) entails that there be types besides tokens. Talk of types then is just a *façon de parler*.[19]

But that still leaves us with the requirement that phonological theory should not overgenerate or undergenerate. How do we construe the prohibition against overgeneration? Realistically: no phonological theory can be true of the world that generates derivations (combinations of answers to questions, like (2)) to which no token in our language (that is, produced as (1) was produced) can conform.[20] Phonological theories may not transcend the limitations on the production of tokens imposed by internalized rules and Vocabulary of the speakers. There is still no need to assume types.

What of the prohibition against undergeneration? We construe that also realistically: no phonological theory can be true of the world that cannot generate derivations to which tokens in our language (that is, produced as (1) was produced) could conform. Phonological theories may not exceed the limitations on the production of tokens imposed by internalized rules and Vocabulary of the speakers. There is again no need to assume types.

Our construal of these principles is stated with the aid of modalities (expressed by *could*) that vex many semanticists. But that is no reason to admit types. We find admission of types unenlightening as substitutes for these modalities, and at least as vexing.

Two final comments.

Some people may object to our way of looking at phonology on the grounds that it construes phonology as about performance and not about competence.[21] If they mean that we view phonology as about processes in real time responsible for the occurrence of tokens, they are right about our view. But we do not see this as an objection. If they mean that we view phonology as having to take into account contingencies of production over and above those traceable to knowledge of language, then they misconstrue our view. We do not.

Some will object that we have loaded phonology with unwarranted assumptions. Do speakers REALLY retrieve morphemes from their memory, invoke rules, go through all these labours when speaking? We think they do. In fact, we would like to know more about how they do it. We may be mistaken. Time will tell. But intuition will not. Clearly speakers are not aware of performing such actions. But then we perform many actions like zombies (to borrow a phrase from Ned Block). That is how we learn language, recognize faces, and solve most of our problems.

Some will object that our outlook leaves out entirely that tokens are not only

---

[19] We ourselves resort to this *façon de parler* even in this chapter, when, for instance, we speak of morphemes, phonemes, etc.

[20] Admittedly this answer requires elaboration. For instance, it seems to avoid commitment to phonological types at the price of commitment to types at the metalinguistic level—that is, at the level of the notation of the theory. We think that this appearance can be dispelled, but to do so would require a long discussion of theoretical formalisms. In any case, we are not claiming that there are no abstract entities at all. We are claiming that phonology is not about types.

[21] See e.g. Lindsey and Harris (1990).

uttered but are also recognized. That is indeed a big hole in our account so far. But it calls for another paper, not abstract types.[22]

Let us then return to the topic of our title, the ontology of phonology. What must the 'furniture of the world' include if phonological theory, as we conceive it, is to have a chance of becoming true of that world? It is a long list: agents with phonetic intentions, tokens, mind/brains with vocabularies and rules, articulators, and so on, in complicated interrelations. It does not have to include types. And if, perchance, the world does include types, phonology has nothing to say about them. But then, probably no branch of linguistics does.

REFERENCES

Austin, J. L. (1975), *How to Do Things with Words*, 2nd edn., ed. J. O. Urmson and M. Sbisa (Cambridge, Mass.: Harvard University Press).

Bromberger, S. (1989), 'Types and Tokens in Linguistics', in A. George (ed.), *Reflections on Chomsky* (Oxford: Basil Blackwell), 58–89. Also in Bromberger (1992).

—— (1992), *On What We Know We Don't Know* (Chicago: University of Chicago Press, CSLI Publications), 170–208.

—— and Halle, M. (1986), 'On the Relationship between Phonetics and Phonology', in J. S. Perkell and D. H. Klatt (eds.), *Invariance and Variability in Speech Process* (Hillsdale, NJ: Lawrence Erlbaum), 510–20

—— —— (1989), 'Why Phonology is Different', *Linguistic Inquiry*, 20/1: 51–70.

—— —— (1994), 'The Ontology of Phonology', in D. Prawitz, B. Skyrms, and D. Westerståhl (eds.), *Logic, Methodology and Philosophy IX* (Amsterdam: Elsevier), 725–743.

—— —— (1997), 'The Contents of Phonological Signs: A Comparison between their Use in Derivational Theories and in Optimality Theories', in I. Roca (ed.), *Derivations and Constraints in Phonology* (Oxford: Oxford University Press), 93–122.

Burton-Roberts, N. (1994), 'Ambiguity, Sentence and Utterance: a Representational Approach', *Transactions of the Philological Society*, 92: 179–212.

—— (this volume), 'Where and What is Phonology? A Representational Perspective'.

Cartwright, R. (1987), *Philosophical Essays* (Cambridge, Mass.: MIT Press), 33–53.

Chomsky, N. (1986), *Knowledge of Language* (New York: Praeger).

Halle, M. (1990), 'An Approach to Morphology', in J. Carter, R. Dechaine, W. Philip, and T. Sherer (eds.), in *Proceedings of North East Linguistic Society* (Armherst, Mass.: GSLA, Department of Linguistics, University of Massachusetts), 1: 150–84.

—— (1997), 'Some consequences of the representation of words in memory', *Lingua*, 100: 91–100.

Hutton, C. M. (1990), *Abstraction and Instance—the Type-Token Relations in Linguistic Theory* (Oxford: Pergamon Press).

Katz, J. J. (1990), *The Metaphysics of Meaning* (Cambridge, Mass.: MIT Press).

Lenneberg, E. H. (1967), *Biological Foundations of Language* (New York: Wiley).

Liberman, A. M. (1996), *Speech: A Special Code* (Cambridge, Mass.: MIT Press).

—— and Mattingly, I. G. (1985), 'The Motor Theory of Speech Revised', *Cognition* 21: 1–36.

---

[22] But on the relationship between production and recognition see Halle (1997) and Liberman (1996).

—— —— (1989), 'Specialization for Speech Perception', *Science* 243: 489–94.

Lindsey, G. and Harris, J. (1990), 'Phonetic Interpretation in Generative Grammar', *UCL Working Papers in Linguistics*, 2: 355–69.

Peirce, C. S. (1933), *Collected Papers of Charles Sanders Peirce*, iv, ed. C. Hartshorn and P. Weiss (Cambridge, Mass.: Harvard University Press).

Quine, W. V. (1987), *Quiddities* (Cambridge: Harvard University Press), 216–19.

Strawson, P. F. (1950), 'On Referring', *Mind* 235: 320–44.

Szabo, Z. (1999), 'Expressions and their Representations', *Philosophical Quarterly*, 49: 145–63.

Wetzel, L. (1993), 'What Are Occurrences of Expressions?', *Journal of Philosophical Logic*, 22: 215–20.

3

Where and What is Phonology?
A Representational Perspective

NOEL BURTON-ROBERTS

1. INTRODUCTION

There is a tension surrounding the *nature* of phonology, centring on phonological content and its relation to phonetic phenomena. The 'what' in my title concerns this. This chapter highlights the connection between that question and another concerning the *status* of phonology. The 'where' refers to this. Although this latter issue is seldom explicitly raised, the two issues are surely connected.

In asking 'where' phonology is, I am asking whether phonology should be thought of as included in the language faculty. As the linguistic is usually conceived, phonology *is* an essential component of the linguistic. So, in questioning the status of phonology, this chapter seeks to place the issue of the nature of phonology in the context of a general tension surrounding the nature of language.

I argue that phonology is not linguistic. This requires me to defend an understanding of 'linguistic' which, while not unprecedented, is not traditional. I contrast two concepts of 'Language' (and Universal Grammar (UG)) and show how the contrast relates to tensions in phonological theory. Equally, if phonology is not linguistic, we need an account of its *relation to* the linguistic. To this end I outline the Representational Hypothesis. This hypothesis offers a new conception of the relevance of phonology to linguistic theory. Simultaneously, it suggests a new conception of the distinction and relation between Language (thought of as the object of enquiry of UG theory) and particular languages.

2. TWO CONCEPTIONS OF LANGUAGE AND UNIVERSAL GRAMMAR

On one conception of Language and UG theory, the concept of 'a (particular) language' is taken for granted and is primary. English, Cantonese, and Swahili are

I am particularly grateful to Phil Carr, Soke Chng, Geoff Poole, and Charles Reiss for discussion. Preliminary versions were delivered at Trinity College Dublin, the Cambridge Linguistics Society, and the School of Oriental and African Studies, London. I am grateful to the participants at those seminars.

generally taken to be examples. UG is 'universal' in ranging over all such languages. UG is the theory of *languages*, capturing whatever is essential to their nature as languages, abstracting away from non-essentials. Particular languages furnish UG with *linguistic data*. They are thought of as instantiating Language, tokens of the type. That is why they are 'languages'.

Call this the GENERIC conception of UG/Language. It could also be called a 'type' or 'theoretical' conception. That is, it is not inconsistent with this conception to think of Language as a (merely) theoretical construct and to insist that the actuality, the reality, of the linguistic lies just in 'actual languages'. The distinction between Language (UG) and languages is, here, a matter of *theoretical level*. Chomsky's distinction between explanatory and descriptive adequacy can be construed this way (assuming the concept Language (UG) is explanatory of what theories of particular languages describe).[1]

The other conception can be called REALIST and NATURALISTIC. Here Language is, crucially, 'a *real object* of the *natural* world' (Chomsky 1995a: 11, emphasis added). It is an innately endowed state of mind/brain and thus, in Chomsky's terms, wholly 'internal'. As such, it has a reality quite independent of languages. UG is 'universal' because it ranges over, not all languages, but all individuals with the relevant endowment. 'I' stands as much for 'individual' as for 'internal' (Chomsky 1995a: 6; 1995b: 13). Here, 'theory of language' (UG) is exactly that: theory of the real, natural object Language; it is *not* the theory of languages ('E[xternal]-languages' for Chomsky). 'E-languages are mere artefacts. We can define "E-language" in one way or another or not at all, since the concept appears to play no role in the theory of language' (Chomsky 1986: 26). On this realist conception of Language, I will argue, the difference between Language and languages should be seen as a difference, not of theoretical level, but of *subject matter*. Here, Language is not an idealized construct or generic type. And particular languages offer not linguistic data but only indirect, defeasible evidence as to the objective—and distinct—character of Language.

The tension between these conceptions of Language arises from their being thought to be different conceptions of the same thing. In so far as each lays claim to the term 'Language', that might seem justified. However, in attempting to resolve the tension, we could start by granting that both of these conceptions do address some kind of reality. Having granted that, we can acknowledge that they focus on very different aspects of reality. Recognition of the difference as *a difference in subject matter* seems essential if the tension between them is to be resolved—and if, as I intend, the realist conception is to be defended. This is not to deny that those

---

[1] Chomsky is realist with respect to Language. However, the brand of realism implied by this explanatory-descriptive view of the relation between Language and languages amounts to what I would call 'instrumental (theory-derived) realism', illustrated by his comment (Chomsky 1995b: 1) that linguistics 'seeks to construct intelligible explanatory theories, taking as "real" what we are led to posit in this quest'. But there is also a distinct (and stronger) brand of realism evident in Chomsky's thinking, which I am about to contrast.

aspects of reality are clearly—even intimately—related. What is needed besides, then, is an account of the nature of the *relation* between them, one that will reflect the intimacy of their relation without compromising this claim about a distinction in subject matter. The Representational Hypothesis is designed to do just this. The next few sections motivate the hypothesis by pursuing this claim about an absolute distinction in subject matter and showing the central relevance of phonology to it.

3. PHONOLOGY AND THE DIFFERENCE

The generic conception of Language is committed to keeping faith with particular (E-)languages and/or individual speakers' (acquired) knowledge of them: anything conceivably essential to the character of such languages and such knowledge should be reflected in the generic conception of Language. Section 3.1 rests on a crucial but uncontroversial assumption, namely: it follows by *generic* reasoning that, since languages have phonology of essential necessity,[2] then (generic) Language/UG must include phonology. This, I shall argue in 3.2, distinguishes the generic conception from the naturalistic/realist conception.

3.1. Simply by including phonology, the generic conception of Language/UG keeps faith with a raft of features reasonably regarded as essential to the character of particular languages. This becomes clear as soon as we ask why phonology should be essential.

The fact that languages have phonology seems a necessary concomitant of their function in communication. Without phonology, allowing them to be 'realized' or 'externalized' in some perceptual medium, how could they serve that function? And how could any particular language be acquired? On the generic conception, the inclusion of phonology in UG is indicated on functional grounds.

Inclusion of phonology within (generic) UG/Language reflects the traditional assumption that languages are systems for pairing sound and meaning. It is thus intrinsic to their character that they are loci of Saussurean arbitrariness and convention. On the generic conception then, Language is conventional and thus not natural.

As conventional (Saussurean) sign systems, particular languages (and thus generic Language) have their being in the 'social collective' (the 'speech community'). They are thus external to the individual, not just because manifested in mind/brain-external physical (E-PHYSICAL) phenomena, but because they are sociocultural.

Individuals become members of the community by acquiring the local system of conventions. Thereby they become members of more than just a linguistic community. That is, it is difficult to identify the resulting knowledge as specifically and discretely linguistic. Davidson (1986: 446) suggests 'knowing a language' is

---

[2] More weakly: since languages with phonology have phonology of necessity . . . This allows that sign languages have something else. See below.

hardly distinct from 'knowing our way around in the world generally'. In the same vein, Chomsky (1992a: 102) remarks 'The study of language in [this, generic] sense verges on "the study of everything".' In short, it is not inconsistent with (and may even be the point of) the generic conception that Language is not well defined (or linguistics autonomous).

Given the complexity of factors entering into behaviour, that conclusion is anyway implied by the fact that the functionality and conventionality induced by the inclusion of phonology leads to a behavioural conception of Language. The function of languages is realized in behaviour. Relevant E-physical phenomena are produced by agents communicating (in part) by implementing the conventions of their language. On this conception, the conventions can be thought of as rules to be followed in behaviour. In characterizing the rules, we characterize an ability to speak. This behavioural, sociocultural orientation inevitably introduces a normative element into the generic conception.[3]

In including phonology, generic UG/Language incorporates what makes for the diversity of languages. Not only is diversity an inevitable concomitant of conventionality, it is generally assumed that diversity among languages is primarily a matter of 'realization', located in phonology (Chomsky 1995a: 7, 192), particularly if phonology includes morphology (Halle and Marantz 1993: 114; Chomsky 1995a: 231). If the generic conception is to keep faith with the diversity of languages, there must be severe limits to idealization if it is to avoid abstracting away from what is essential to their particular characters. Hence the typological character of generic theory. Parameters are a reflex of this.

I have assumed that languages are functional. They are even designed for use, if only in the circular sense that they are products of use. Given this and the diversity of the resulting designs, there can be no question of comparing the optimality of different languages. Each language just is how it is, the result of the accidental circumstances that brought it, particularly, into being. On these terms, there can be no coherent contrast between design and accident.

Nor can there be any conflict between the fact that languages are thus designed and the fact that they are messy (complex, irregular, redundant) and, from some conceivable perspective, less than 'perfect'. That is to be expected in what are designed for use only in the sense of being the accidental, changing products of use. And, if redundancy is an 'imperfection', it is an imperfection essential to languages; redundancy is essential to the efficiency of communication systems. This lack of 'perfection' is generally regarded as located in the (morpho-)phonology, precisely where the conventionality, diversity, and functionality of languages lie.

The phonological is thus intrinsic to the generic conception of Language. By its inclusion, that conception keeps faith with acknowledged features of *languages*:

---

[3] None of this implies (except by idealization) that languages are discrete and well defined. In fact, they are known not to be (Pateman 1987; Chomsky 1995b: 48–9). This is one sense in which (idealized) 'particular languages' are 'artefacts'. See also Docherty *et al.* (1997, and this volume).

their functionality, externality, non-natural conventionality, social basis in behaviour, normativity, diversity, redundancy and lack of definition, even their lack of perfection.

3.2. Chomsky's naturalistic realism contrasts with the generic conception in every respect. It is, as noted, a concept of Language as innate and natural. If 'knowledge of language' is 'knowledge' of real natural Language, it cannot be thought of as an empirically derived epistemic relation to the external world—let alone to any conventional, socio-cultural, locally normative aspect of it (Chomsky 1992*a*: 102). It is not a *belief* system. It is not acquired. 'Knowledge of language' is 'knowledge without grounds' (Chomsky 1980: 41; 1986: 12). There is, in fact, no distinction between Language and the 'knowing' of it: 'Language has no objective existence apart from its mental representation' (Chomsky 1972: 169). If 'knowledge' is the right term here, it is a quite special kind of knowledge, non-relational and subpersonal. All this is what I understand as implied by the language faculty being characterized as 'completely internal'—henceforth RADICALLY INTERNAL (by which I mean: neither internal*ized* nor externalizable).

Language on this conception—call it 'L'—*is* well defined. It is an autonomous, discrete, dedicated 'component of the mind/brain' (Chomsky 1995*a*: 2) with unique, specialized properties (ibid. 167), 'austere' (informationally encapsulated), not tied to sensory modality (Chomsky 1995*b*: 15–16), independent of behavioural abilities (e.g. Chomsky 1986: 10, 36). The internalist (subpersonal, non-agentive) concept of generation-by-a-grammar is absolutely distinct from production-by-a-speaker: 'A generative grammar is not a set of statements about externalized objects constructed in some manner' (Chomsky 1986: 24). Independently of that or not, L is (at core) 'rule free' (e.g. Chomsky 1995*a*: 29). It is formal not functional; 'it is not the case that language is readily usable or "designed for use"' (ibid. 18). It is even 'in many respects "dysfunctional"' (ibid. 162). In principle, it is unique, invariant (ibid. 7, 9, 131, 170–1, 359), not typological. The perspective from which *languages* are less than 'perfect' is precisely that of the theory of L, conceived of as 'something like a perfect system' (ibid. 1, 271), non-redundant, maximally economical, optimal, exceptionless, simple.

This is the conception pursued in the Minimalist Program. As the culmination of realist enquiry, minimalism contrasts self-consciously with the generic conception. Thought of as an idealization over *languages*, L could not but be thought of as a very extreme *over*-idealization. For that reason, I suggest, it cannot plausibly be thought of in terms of idealization over languages (and speakers' knowledge of them) but more fundamentally as having an entirely distinct subject matter.

Pursuing that idea, enquiry into the natural object L cannot concern *languages*—these, we have seen, involve non-natural convention. Nor could L be *instantiated* in particular languages. That would demand that a natural phenomenon be instantiated non-naturally.[4] Conceptually, this has a surprising, and thus interesting, consequence. On the generic conception, English, Swahili, and so on (as instances of Language) necessarily are 'languages'. But that is neither necessary nor possible on the realist conception. Since English, Swahili, and so on are not instances of Language on this conception, it follows strictly that they are not languages. The realist conception in fact tends to the conclusion that there *is* no language but L(anguage). (See Epstein *et al.* 1996: 3 ('there is, in effect, only one human language') and Chomsky 1995a: e.g. 7, 131, 170, 359.)

What of phonology on the non-generic, realist theory of Language (L)? Given all the above, there is no reason to suppose that even necessary features of languages are necessary features of L. It is at least conceivable, then, that L is phonology free—at least as 'phonology' is generally understood. In fact, given the contrast between the two conceptions and the centrality of phonology to the generic conception, I suggest it is *conceptually necessary* that the real natural object L be phonology free.

Naturalistic, internalist, and minimalist considerations in favour of excluding phonology are dealt with in later sections. Here I present a realist consideration. In generic terms, the linguistic is thought of as 'produced', 'realized', 'instantiated' in E-physical utterance phenomena. It is this assumption that underlies the motive for including the phonological within the linguistic. The overarching idea here is that utterance behaviour is productive of linguistic *tokens* (e.g. Bromberger 1989, Bromberger and Halle 1989, among many others). This depends on a CLASSICAL (Peircean) idea of type-token in which, while types are in some sense 'abstract', tokens are spatiotemporal E-physical (perceptual) phenomena—E-physical occurrences of linguistic types. But this classical view of type-token (with its insistence that linguistic tokens are perceptual) poses a problem when it comes to syntax. Consider 'I introduced him to your friend'. In asking this, I am asking the reader to consider, not an utterance, but a linguistic expression (LE). Translating into type-token as usually understood, the request concerns a linguistic *type*. Now that type (the LE) includes an instance/occurrence/token of a certain lexical item, the LE 'friend'. 'I introduced your friend to my friend' includes two tokens of that LE.

The problem is this. We want to allow that LEs *as such* (the types) can be syntactically composed of LEs, that LEs are instantiated (tokened) in the structure of LEs. Classical type-token cannot permit this. Since, classically, tokens are E-physical phenomena, we cannot say of any LE (any *type*) that it includes a *token*

---

[4] Chomsky does sometimes talk of L as being instantiated in particular languages, at least as known by individuals. However, he acknowledges a 'crucial inadequacy' with that idea (1995a: 6), adding 'what we call "English", "French", "Spanish" and so on ... reflect ... factors that cannot seriously be regarded as properties of the language faculty ... it is hard to imagine that the properties of the language faculty—a real object of the natural world—are instantiated in any observed system' (1995a: 11). This, I believe, has (negative) implications for the view of L as an *initial* state of mind/brain (i.e. one that has, or is instantiated in, distinct later states). See below.

of any LE: types, being abstract, are not constituted by physical phenomena and hence not by classical tokens. On these terms, only the (E-physical) *token* of an LE could be composed of tokens of LEs. But (classically) it is *utterance phenomena* that are linguistic tokens. Classical type-token thus obliges us to insist that an LE can occur/be instantiated only in the *utterance* (U) of an LE. Thereby the LE itself (the supposed type) is emptied of all structural and lexical properties, now only to be found in U (its supposed token). This results in a view of linguistic structure more externalist and anti-realist than intended or defensible even in the generic conception. (On the one hand, it is anti-realist with respect to the usual (non-phonetic) concept of syntax; on the other, it attributes to physical (e.g. phonetic) phenomena something they arguably do not have—namely, syntactic structure—otherwise syntax would reduce to phonetics.) In short, we buy the (classical) idea that the linguistic is tokened in perceptual phenomena by forfeiting a standard (or at least realist) concept of syntactic structure.

There is, I suggest, a simple solution. Apart from the classical insistence that linguistic tokens are E-physical (perceptual) phenomena, it seems entirely reasonable to allow that complex LEs (as types) are indeed composed of *tokens* of other LEs. So let us abandon that classical insistence and allow that there are two distinct concepts of 'occurrence' (or 'token') in play here. I propose there are different *sorts* of tokens and, correspondingly, different sorts of types. Certainly, types are 'abstract' in virtue of being types but, independently of that, we need to distinguish between E-physical types and Abstract (Formal) types. A type is an E-PHYSICAL TYPE if and only if it is a type having physical phenomena external to mind/brain as tokens (mercury, forked lightning, alphabet letters, phonetic phenomena). E-physical types, then, are the classical types usually assumed. By contrast, a type is an ABSTRACT (FORMAL) TYPE (independently of its abstractness qua type) if and only if its tokens are abstract, formal. Armed with this sortal distinction between types (in terms of the sort of their tokens), we are in a position to insist that *linguistic* types are Abstract types. In other words, tokens of *linguistic* types are *not* E-physical. As tokens of Abstract types, tokens of LEs are no less abstract or formal than the types (the LEs) within which they occur as constituents. On these (sorted) terms the usual, or realist, idea of syntactic composition poses no problem.[5]

This SORTED approach to type-token reflects a quite standard assumption in linguistics: that occurrence-within-the-formal-structure-of-an-LE is a sort of occurrence—namely, *linguistic occurrence* ('L-occurrence')—absolutely distinct from E-physical occurrence (a distinction corresponding to that between grammatical 'generation' and physical 'production', see below). Sorted type-token

---

[5] I believe 'sorted' type-token was anticipated by Bar-Hillel's (1970: 367) distinction 'between some abstract linguistic entity ... and its *equally abstract* occurrences' (emphasis added). Incidentally, I am using 'abstract' to mean 'not E-physical', allowing that in an ideally completed physics linguistic types and tokens will be I-physical (neurological).

effectively insists that the linguistic is tokened *linguistically*, not E-physically. If the linguistic is 'abstract' (= not E-physical) because mentally constituted (that is, in mind/brain), this amounts to saying that *linguistic tokens* are no less mentally constituted than their (linguistic) types.

But all this contradicts the (classical) idea that the linguistic is E-physically tokened in utterance. With sorted type-token, it is sortally incorrect to suppose that any E-physical phenomenon could be the token of a *linguistic* type. What we produce in utterance are tokens of E-physical, not linguistic, types. In short, any remotely realist concept of syntactic structure is simply not consistent with the linguistic being tokened (instantiated) in E-physical (for example, phonetic) phenomena. Nor, therefore, is any such concept of syntax consistent with the usually assumed motive for including phonology within the language faculty.[6]

Notice how this denial that the linguistic is instantiated (tokened) in external utterance (for example, phonetic) phenomena parallels the denial that L is instantiated (tokened) in 'languages'. But these denials—and the realist conception in general—raise urgent questions, which I now formulate.

4. REALIST QUESTIONS

Q1. *If phonology is not linguistic, what is its relation* to *the linguistic?*

On the generic conception, relevant external phenomena are 'relevant' because they are linguistic. The radical linguistic internalism of the realist conception surely denies this. But there is no call to deny that certain external phenomena (not others) are indeed 'relevant' to the linguistic. So:

Q2. *In what sense can an external phenomenon, without being linguistic, be 'relevant' to the linguistic?*

Relatedly, since the realist conception denies that what are produced by speakers are (instantiating) *tokens* of what is generated by L, and denies that what is generated is a *theoretical modelling* of production by speakers, we must ask:

Q3. *Given the realist* distinction *between linguistic generation and behavioural production, what is the* relation *between them?*

---

[6] Adjusting terminology might appear to dispel the problem: for example, by restricting 'occurrence' to occurrence-within-an-LE and stipulating that 'tokens' are not 'occurrences'. But the adjustment is surely artificial: tokens *are* occurrences (a token of lightning is an occurrence of lightning); furthermore it simply reaffirms the distinction between 'L-occurrence' and 'E-physical occurrence'. Legislating against the use of 'token' in respect of L-occurrence is beside the point, provided we do not confuse the tokening of linguistic types and E-physical types. (See Bach 1995; Bromberger and Halle, this volume, n. 3, though neither actually mentions any problem the adjustment might be thought to solve.) Incidentally, it seems to me that, when (as proposed here) we drop the insistence that linguistic types have E-physical tokens, type-token thinking loses much of its interest for linguistics.

The generic conception provides an account of the relation between Language and languages (in terms of instantiation). For that matter, it *constitutes* such an account. The realist conception conspicuously does not (for L and 'languages'). On the contrary, it suggests that there is just one language, L. The question then is:

Q4. *If so-called languages are not instances of L (and thus not 'languages'), what are they—and what is the nature of their relation to L?*

Most generally, in the light of the realist (double) rejection of type-token as a model of the I/E relation:

Q5. *Given a radical I/E distinction (such that only the I is linguistic), what is the nature of the I/E relation?*

These are the questions the Representational Hypothesis addresses. It offers a single answer to all five questions. In this it is intended as a defence of the realist conception. However, although (I insist) such questions do arise within the realist conception in principle, it has to be acknowledged they have in practice not been addressed or even contemplated. This needs explaining, if only to avoid the suspicion that the problems addressed by the hypothesis are artefacts of an oversimplified polarization of the two conceptions.

5. TENSIONS IN THE REALIST CONCEPTION

Thought of as a description of recent linguistic theory, the above polarization would indeed be an oversimplification. The fact is that Chomsky's naturalistic realism has retained fundamental features of the generic conception out of which it evolved and from which, as I understand it, it seeks to depart. Most saliently, it has retained the idea of a linguistic phonology. The questions of Section 4 are thereby pre-empted. But the inclusion of phonology in L gives rise to dilemmas and tensions, particularly in minimalism.

On the generic conception, the nature and (linguistic) rationale of phonology are as good as self-evident. A phonology is an *attitude* to certain external phenomena produced in a given community. By generic assumption, those phenomena are linguistic. Acquisition of such an attitude is necessary for practice of the given language. If the phenomena are acoustic and articulated in the vocal tract (that is, phonetic), then phonological elements, as constituents of an attitude to phonetic phenomena, must have phonetic content. On these (generic) terms, the phonological is both linguistic and SUBSTANTIVE.[7]

For the realist conception, by contrast, there is a dilemma. Briefly: if the real, natural object L is not phonology free, then phonology must be substance free. In other words, it must be wholly FORMAL. But, if phonology is formal, its content

---

[7] However, the phonological as such must then be just one setting of a 'modality parameter', since not all languages involve the phonetic.

and rationale are obscure and the motive for including it self-defeating. In what follows I show that, on the evidence of tensions in its treatment of phonology (both formal/substantive and included/excluded), the realist conception is sensitive to the dilemma.

On the one hand, substantive phonology, if linguistic, contradicts at least radical internalism, which denies that external phenomena are linguistic. If phonetic phenomena are not linguistic, there is no call for a *linguistically constituted* attitude to them—and certainly not if the relevant attitude is acquired, as seems necessary given the diverse particularity of relevant phenomena. On these terms, phonological elements, as linguistic, cannot have phonetic content. Consistent with this, although Chomsky allows that relevant elements 'can be called "phonetic"', he immediately warns 'but we should bear in mind that all of this is pure syntax, completely internalist' (1995*b*: 19).

A formal phonology is also implied by a problem, in realist terms, with substantive universals. If phonology is linguistic, we are committed to the discovery of *linguistic* universals in phonology. *Weak* universality consists in the idea of a universal bag of properties from which languages select. [Pharyngeal], for example, is universally available but not universally selected. *Strong* universality consists in the idea of a highly constrained set of (necessary) properties attested in *all* languages. The problem is that weak phonological universality, constrained as it is only by physiology between nose and larynx, is arguably (from a realist perspective) not discretely, strictly, linguistic. In the phonological domain, only strong universals can be relevant in the search for *strictly* linguistic universals. But then phonetic [pharyngeal] will not correspond to a phonological element properly called 'pharyngeal' in virtue of having that phonetic content. In at least this case, then, the phonetics–phonology relation will be arbitrary. And, if it is ever arbitrary, surely it is arbitrary by its nature, across the board.

Chomsky does not advance exactly this argument for formal phonology. However, he advances a similar argument from sign. If (as would be suggested by its inclusion in UG) phonology is necessary to the linguistic, then sign languages must be thought of as having phonology (van der Hulst 1993, this volume; Chomsky 1995*b*: 16; Hale and Reiss, this volume). But then, even phonetically strong universals will not be strongly universal—and the 'phonological' must equally be put into (necessarily arbitrary) correspondence with non-phonetic signs. On this basis Chomsky suggests that L (and phonology, since included) is 'not tied to specific sensory modalities' (1995*b*: 16). And, if not tied to any 'specific' sensory modality, it is not tied to sensory modality—period (consistent with the 'speculation that the essential character of C_{HL} is independent of the sensorimotor interface', Chomsky 1995*a*: 335). Hale and Reiss (this volume) give this and further arguments for a formal phonology, assuming phonology to be linguistic.

Against this, no *positive* account of formal phonological content is forthcoming. Nor is it clear what evidence could bear on the question. Chomsky's reference to 'pure syntax' is of help here only if intended to assimilate phonology to syntax, narrowly understood. But that would amount to excluding (a distinctive) *phonology* from L. On these terms, formal phonology is *sui generis*, 'tied' neither to (narrow) syntax nor to sensorimotor modality.

The inclusion of phonology, formal or substantive, is a departure from naturalism. But formal phonology entails a compound departure. That is, we are now looking at *two* loci of Saussurean arbitrariness: (*a*), the traditional locus, in the relation between phonology and Logical Form (LF) and, now, (*b*) in the relation between 'phonology' and modality. Hale and Reiss (this volume) notice this, proposing a 'Neo-Saussurean' extension of arbitrariness (for (*b*)), but don't address the conflict with naturalism. Chomsky acknowledges a problem (with (*a*)), but tacitly, mentioning Saussurean arbitrariness only among matters that 'I put ... aside' (1995*a*: 8) and 'henceforth ignore' (ibid. 169–70).

This compound arbitrariness further undermines the motive for including phonology. The arbitrary relation between non-phonological aspects of L (the syntactic derivation of LF) and the phonetic is generally held to be *indirect*, mediated by phonology. This is because the phonetic is thought of as *non-arbitrarily* (intrinsically, directly) related to the phonological specifically. But that assumes a substantive phonology. With a formal phonology, however, the phonetics–phonology relation is no less arbitrary than that between phonology and the syntax serving LF. In which case, why should the phonetic relate to phonology specifically? Why should it not relate to LF syntax directly? Phonological mediation, if formal, is an unmotivated complication of the arbitrary relation between the E-physical and (non-phonological aspects of) the linguistic. Conceptually, it is difficult to see what work a formal phonology—if genuinely formal—actually does.

The very idea of phonology, I suggest, is coherent only if substantive. Realist considerations apart, this conclusion is hardly controversial. Nor need it be inconsistent with the realist (formal) conception of L—provided, I have argued, phonology is excluded.

However, phonology *is* included in minimalism, and—notwithstanding any of the above (including the irrelevance to L of the communicative and functional character of E-languages)—on the basis of the very assumption that phonology is substantive:

The information provided by L has to be accommodated to the human sensory and motor apparatus. Hence UG must provide for a phonological component that converts the objects generated by the language L to a form that these 'external' systems can use: PF, we assume. If humans could communicate by telepathy, there would be no need for a phonological component ...   (Chomsky 1995*a*: 221)

Chomsky (ibid. 212, 163) in fact endorses Bromberger and Halle's conception of phonology, which deals in 'linguistic-phonetic behaviours', 'vocal tract gymnastics', and what 'enables a speaker to produce (a) sound sequence', and thereby 'implement', 'actualize', 'execute', 'token' the linguistic. Here the phonological reflects 'mechanical factors', including the fact that, 'like all physical systems ... articulators are subject to inertia', hence 'effects of the physics or physiology involved' are not merely physiological but 'are brought about through the application of language-specific rules that speakers acquire ... as part of their knowledge of their language' (Bromberger and Halle 1989: 54–8). In short, the nature/rationale of phonology is as assumed in the generic (non-discrete) conception.

In fact, minimalism, with its focus on reduction to the ineliminable, accords substantive phonology a new prominence in the architecture of grammar. While D-structure, S-structure, and much else are eliminated, the PF (Phonetic Form, π) interface with the articulatory-perceptual, and its relation to the LF (Logical Form, λ) interface with the conceptual-intentional, remain. Indeed, this 'double interface property' is, in principle, all that does remain (Chomsky 1995a: 169).

There is a certain irony in the fact that this double interface property—which, Chomsky (ibid. 2) observes, expresses 'the traditional description of language as sound with a meaning'—should figure so prominently, while the problem of Saussurean arbitrariness (sounds do not, as of *natural* fact, have meaning) has to be 'put aside' and 'ignored'.

Equally, the inclusion of phonology is attended by considerable overt misgiving on Chomsky's part. His endorsement of Bromberger and Halle (1989) is in fact a highlighting of their contention that phonology is 'different'. Considerations of conceptual economy might lead one to expect that, if phonology is to be included in L, it should display the same basic structural properties as the rest of L (Anderson and Ewan 1987: 283–4).[8] Within minimalism, however, the acknowledged difference of phonology becomes ever more marked as minimalist assumptions are implemented (e.g. Chomsky 1995a: 229, 230, 231, 324). Increasingly, phonology and the sensorimotor interface it serves are characterized as 'extraneous' to the essential nature of C_{HL} (ibid., e.g. 221, 229, 265, 271, 317). Furthermore, its inclusion calls for heavy qualification of the rule-free assumption: '(excluding phonology) there are no rules for particular languages' (ibid. 129, 131–2, 163). The uniqueness assumption too is undermined by the mapping to PF, which is assumed (with the lexicon—also phonologically constituted, in part) to be *the* locus of variation (ibid., e.g. 26, 169–70, 235, 271; 1998: 127)—and exceptionality (e.g. Chomsky 1998: 127). The perceived need to accommodate the sensorimotor interface induces 'departures from perfection', indeed 'a striking departure from minimalist assumptions' (Chomsky 1995a: 221–2; also 9, 265, 271, 316–17). For all essential purposes of the core derivation, that from the

---

[8] Efforts to make phonology look like (the rest of) L (see e.g. Kaye *et al.* 1985, 1990; Anderson and Ewan 1987; van der Hulst, this volume) are thus eminently well motivated, but only on the assumption that phonology is included in L. It is that assumption I am questioning. So I have no interest in making such efforts myself and can afford to be worried by the thought that, with enough ingenuity, anything can be made to look like anything else.

'Numeration' (N) to LF, phon(ological)-features are in fact irrelevant (ibid. 230), with chains needing to be formed only by the 'movement' of formal features (CH_{FF}), which lack phon-features. By contrast, movements of 'categories' (defined as having phon-features) form category chains, CH_{CAT}. Chomsky dolefully notes that 'CH_{CAT} should be entirely dispensable were it not for the need to accommodate to the sensorimotor apparatus' (ibid. 265).

Underpinning 'perfection' are two derivational conditions: INCLUSIVENESS (structures are constituted only by elements present in lexical items in the Numeration (ibid. 228)), and UNIFORMITY (operations can apply at any point (ibid. 229)). Phonology is seen as 'radically violating' both conditions (ibid. 236). As regards inclusiveness, the mapping to PF needs to introduce information not present in lexical items—for example, syllabic and intonational structure and 'a good part of the output phonetic matrix' (ibid. 381 n. 10). Uniformity is violated, because of the 'specific rule structure' of phonology and ordering of the morphological subcomponent within the phonology (ibid. 163 n. 2, 230–1).

This misgiving surrounding the inclusion of phonology is technically embodied in PROCRASTINATE, the economy principle whereby operations in N-LF should be delayed until after SPELL-OUT (SO), which strips out phon-features, feeding them to phonology. Pre-SO (overt) operations are less economical than post-SO (covert) precisely because they involve phon-features ('excess baggage' carried by 'categories').

But Procrastinate is problematic. Collins (1997: 116–17) identifies three problems. One is that, being global, it increases computational complexity (see also Chomsky 1998: 127; Poole 1998: 386). Another is that it introduces non-uniformity into the N-LF derivation itself. Thirdly, Procrastinate is unique among minimalist economy principles in being violable. For these reasons, Collins and Poole seek to eliminate Procrastinate in descriptive terms—but, in doing so, they ignore the *conceptual* misgiving Procrastinate reflects regarding (substantive) phonology. In the light of that misgiving, I suggest, the problems with Procrastinate can be seen to lie, not in Procrastinate, but in Spell-Out.

For example, in asking why Procrastinate should be violable (why less economical operations are tolerated at all), we are asking why there *are* overt, as opposed to covert, operations. This effectively questions the overt/covert contrast. And, since that amounts to the pre-SO/post-SO contrast, it touches on the existence of SO itself, without which Procrastinate would not be formulable.

The problem is aggravated by there being, as it were, metaviolations of Procrastinate. That is, there are violations that the theory cannot acknowledge as such without casting doubt on SO itself. The operations of Select and Merge, when they involve 'categories', should be subject to Procrastinate: they involve phon-features. Against this, violations by Select/Merge cannot be acknowledged because, were those operations delayable until after SO, there would be nothing to spell out. Assuming the necessity of SO, then, it must simply be stipulated that

Select and Merge are exempted ('cannot violate Procrastinate by definition' (Poole 1998: 386)).

For Collins, we have seen, it is Procrastinate that induces non-uniformity in the N-LF derivation. But that, I suggest, is a symptom of the non-uniformity induced by SO itself. While Pre-SO operations can deal in 'categories', post-SO operations cannot. Disregarding Procrastinate, then, it is still the case that 'categories' must, while non-categories need not, be selected/merged *before* SO (Chomsky 1995a: 232, 294).

It is SO itself, the perceived need to accommodate L to the sensorimotor that it reflects, that undermines minimalism, I suggest. What results is a kind of circularity: minimalism is achieved only 'essentially' and 'at core', where what counts as 'core' is precisely what remains after we have 'distinguished' as 'extraneous' or 'peripheral' that which detracts from minimalism (see e.g. ibid. 324). Misgiving here, too, is overtly reflected in Chomsky's (ibid. 163 n. 3) comment: 'The core-periphery distinction, in my view, should be regarded as an expository device, reflecting a level of understanding that should be superseded as clarification of the nature of linguistic inquiry advances.'

What would L be like were it minimalist without misgiving or qualification? I believe the above points to a single derivation, neither divided (N-PF, N-LF) nor subdivided (N-SO, SO-LF) but simply, and fully uniformly, N-LF—in which *all* operations are covert, involving only features serving (and, ideally, Fully Interpretable at) the LF interface. Since 'overt *versus* covert' would (with Procrastinate) be meaningless, 'covert' would yield to 'radically internal'. There would be no 'categories' in L, no phon-features or Saussurean arbitrariness in its (unique) lexicon, no Spell-Out. If L so conceived generates 'linguistic expressions'—and what else?—LEs could not be [π, λ] pairs.

In short, minimalist goals would be more fully realizable if phonology could be acknowledged as 'different' and 'extraneous' to the extent of being simply excluded. Chomsky does not pursue this course, but I believe he contemplates the possibility (e.g. ibid. 221; see also Hale and Reiss (this volume, section 7)). But it raises the questions of Section 4, which the reader might consider again here. Conceivably, the phonological has been included only for lack of answer to those questions about excluded phonology. Supplying an answer, I hope to show, will allow us to retain something resembling the assumed generic nature/rationale of phonology but in a manner more obviously consistent with a realist, naturalistic, radically internalist, radically minimalist concept of L.

6. THE REPRESENTATIONAL HYPOTHESIS

The Representational Hypothesis (RH), in summary, is the proposal that speakers produce external phenomena in aid of E-physically REPRESENTING linguistic expressions (LEs) generated by L, conceived of in the radically minimalist terms just outlined. In what follows I can only sketch enough of the general idea to show that it offers a way, not hitherto contemplated, of addressing the questions of Section 4 and resolving tensions within the realist conception and the tension between it and the generic conception.

6.1. To avoid misunderstanding, I shall be referring to M-REPRESENTATION, 'M' for Magritte. This is a reminder of Magritte's painting *La Trahison des images*, which includes some writing, 'Ceci n'est pas une pipe', itself a reminder that in looking at the painting we are not looking at a pipe, but at a representation of a pipe. In linguistics we are used to another sense of 'representation', '*not* to be understood relationally, as "representation *of*"' (Chomsky 1995*b*: 53, emphasis added). Call this C-REPRESENTATION, 'C' for 'Chomsky' or 'Constitutive'. A C-representation is constitutive of what it (!C-)represents. For example, in 'language has no objective existence apart from its mental representation' (quoted above), we clearly have C-representation: language as not distinct from, but constituted in, that 'representation'. 'Levels of representation' are generally understood, in linguistics, as C-representational. The rationale of my appeal to 'representation', by contrast, is that an M-representation (M-REP) is *not* constitutive of what it represents. M-rep emphatically is a relation, a relation between x and y where $x \neq y$. The distinction between representation (representans) and what-is-represented (representatum) is essential to the hypothesis.

The (Magrittian) point, in this context, is that what is M-representational of the linguistic is not thereby linguistic; on the contrary, it is thereby not linguistic. In terms of this conception of the I–E relation, the I/E distinction is to be thought of (and 'core-periphery' recast) as that between the *linguistic* and what is non-linguistically, E-physically *representational* of the linguistic (Q5). It is in this (M-rep) sense that external phenomena can, without being linguistic, be 'relevant' to the linguistic (Q2).

The relation of M-representation is distinct from any type-token relation. In producing an M-rep x of y, we produce x, not a *token* (instance, occurrence) of y.[9] M-rep(x,y) implies that y is instantiated independently of the fact of representation. Furthermore, an M-representation x of y is not an 'epiphenomenon' of y. Nor is any process of transduction involved in x's being produced with the intention of M-representing y. There is no sense in which an M-rep x of y is *caused* by y.

On these terms, speakers do not produce (or utter) LEs; they produce (/utter) only E-physical *M-representations* of LEs. With a realist distinction between generation and production, LEs (as generated) are not produced. With L constituted by a unique lexicon and derivation N-LF, it does not generate anything conceivably 'produceable' (utterable). What is produced-by-speakers thus stands

---

[9] I believe Peirce (1933: iv. 423) actually confuses his type-token (instantiation) relation with that of (M-)representation (the signing relation). An M-representational sign for x is not an instance of x.

in a relation of M-representation to what is generated-by-L (Q3). And what hearers parse are not LEs but M-representations. An LE, *qua* assumed representatum, is what is cognitively accessed as the result of a parse.

6.2. M-representation is an asymmetric relation, with representans unidirectionally oriented on its object, the representatum. Here again, possibly, my appeal to representation differs from Chomsky's. In so far as Chomsky thinks of the I–E relation in terms of M-rep, L itself ('accommodated to the human sensory and motor apparatus') is seen as providing linguistically constituted *internal* M-reps of *external* phenomena. This seems implied by his also offering 'intensional' and 'extensional' as glosses of 'I' and 'E'. Exactly the reverse holds in the RH. The hypothesis is that non-telepathic humans who seek to communicate (/express their thoughts) need to M-represent *externally* what is inescapably *internal*, L. If anything is 'accommodated' to anything else, it is the E-physical that is 'accommodated' to L, in the sense of being produced so as to be M-representational of L's ('strong') generative capacity.[10] This distinguishes M-REPRESENTATION from the more usual idea of REALIZATION. Underlying 'realization' is the idea that the linguistic is in part derivationally targeted on (and, as it were, results in) sensory output. By the RH, in contrast, sensory output is M-representationally targeted on the linguistic. I return to 'realization' below.

This logical orientation, *from* the E-physical *to* L, seems essential if L is to be thought of as radically internal and informationally encapsulated. That it is the *object* of external M-rep is not a fact about the nature of L. L is not, as object of external M-rep, oriented towards the external or 'externalizable', any more than *any* object is by its nature oriented towards what is M-representational of it. In such terms, there is no need or temptation to think of L (as representatum) issuing 'instructions' to sensorimotor systems.

The hypothesis is that, differences between painting and speech notwithstanding, those activities and their products stand in the same logical relation to their objects. It is then no more appropriate to think of there being external *linguistic performance* than it is to think that a representational painter, painting a wooden table, is performing (or producing a piece of) *carpentry*. Certainly the painter is deploying rules and abilities, but of M-representation, not of carpentry. Similarly where what is M-represented is linguistic. Speech, as a form of regular behaviour, does involve rule-following, abilities, even habits. But, with speech seen as M-representational of L, the rules/abilities/habits it involves are representational, not linguistic. With rule-guided behaviour and its relevance acknowledged but identified (on M-rep grounds) as non-linguistic, the temptation to treat linguistic principles as rules 'licensing' anything, let alone behaviour, is pre-empted. 'Competence-performance' as usually understood was unhelpful here, suggesting

---

[10] Anticipating Burton-Roberts (in preparation), I shall identify L and its ('strong') generative capacity. I will also assume there is no substantive distinction between LF and the derivation of LF.

competence-to-perform-(linguistically) and performance-of-(linguistic)-com-petence. In RH terms, competence-performance is orthogonal to L, applying wholly to M-representational knowledge and activity. In the light of Section 6.5 below, competence-performance can be allowed to apply in respect of 'languages' but is completely *in*applicable in respect of Language (L), which, I assume, is the object of enquiry for Chomsky.

6.3. By the RH, we are to understand 'Jones uttered $LE_{(y)}$' pretty much as we understand 'Monet painted Rouen cathedral', meaning he painted an M-rep of it. With painting, the locution is not evidence of conflation of representans and representatum, it being elliptical. By the RH, 'utter an LE' is no less elliptical. But here, I concede, the locution is a symptom of the opinion that LEs are literally uttered (produced), an opinion that (by the RH) results from representational conflation. The question then is: why should the ellipsis be so much less obvious here? Why the impulse to conflate when what is represented is linguistic, specifically?

There are several reasons, I suggest. With painting, the representational distinction (between representans and representatum) is perceptually manifest. Both M-rep and its representatum can be physically encountered. Each is independently accessible to consciousness. Functionally, it is manifest that we could enter/smoke representatum (cathedral/pipe) but not representans. Further, such (fine art) M-reps are of value and interest to us in their own right. Few of us put in the practice necessary for the development of such special representational abilities. For that reason the abilities and the fact of representation are *not* taken for granted. M-representation of the linguistic differs radically. Here, the E-physical phenomena are *only* of interest to us for their representational significance (singing and calligraphy apart). They have no other value or function. The M-rep distinction could not be perceptually manifest: the representatum L is not perceptual, but cognitive. Nor is it directly accessible to consciousness. All that is directly accessible to consciousness here are the external phenomena themselves and their significance, the latter deriving from the fact of M-rep. But we take that fact for granted, in part because we discount the abilities it calls for. Perceptually and consciously, then, speaker-hearers have only the external phenomena and their (M-rep) significance to go on. Given this, it seems inevitable that they will project onto the representans what they tacitly know of its representatum, and perception of relevant phenomena will feel like perception of the linguistic. By the RH (and radical internalism) it is not linguistic, though. The feeling and the projection are the predictable results of (M-)representational conflation.

6.4. M-representation is a non-natural relation. As noted, given M-rep(x,y), it is not a natural fact about y that it is the object of some M-rep. No more is it a natural fact about x that it is an M-rep. It is a matter of the intentions of x's producer that M-rep(x,y). As regards the perceiver of x, it is a matter of his interpretation of those intentions whether he responds to x as a representation and, if so, what he takes it to be a representation of.

Nor is it necessary for any physical M-rep to have any property in common with its representatum. This is crucial. M-rep can be iconic but, being non-natural, it does not have to be. It can be non-natural in the further sense of being *conventional*. An iconic M-rep (like Magritte's of a pipe) needs to share perceptual properties with (that is, resemble) its representatum. Conventional M-reps, by definition, do not. What is needed instead is a convention, in terms of which x is deemed to represent y. When x and y, such that M-rep(x,y), lie in the same perceptual domain, we can choose iconic or conventional, or a combination. Otherwise, it has to be conventional. In graphic M-rep of the phonetic and musical, for example, x and y lie in different perceptual domains. And with 'π', '$\forall$', '%', y is not even perceptual, but cognitive (conceptual). If the linguistic is cognitive (and radically internal), E-physical phenomena must be devoid of the (covert) properties in terms of which L wholly operates, and E-physical M-rep of the linguistic must be wholly conventional. (This is anyway implied by 'sorted' type-token.)

Both the M-representational relation itself and its conventionality are extra-linguistic. As one of the terms thereby *related*, L itself cannot be *constituted in* the relation. A major consequence of this is that L *can* now be thought of as wholly natural. On these terms, the thesis that L itself is a locus of Saussurean arbitrariness (generating $[\pi, \lambda]$ pairs), is the result of conflating one of the terms related with the relation itself.

E-physical phenomena used/recognized as M-reps will be cognitively signifi-cant. I distinguish between SIGNIFICANCE and, as understood in linguistics, MEANING. Sounds do not have meaning. However, the significance of relevant sounds is, as it were, supercharged by their being intended/recognized as representational of LEs, which do have meaning. If we can think of relevant sounds as (representational) 'signs', then this is where the Saussurean SIGN belongs, in the extralinguistic M-representational relation itself—not in the representatum, L.

6.5. The implications of the Representational Hypothesis for phonology and 'languages' and their relation to L (Q1 and Q4) seem clear, and clearly related. Take 'languages' first.

Nothing is, in itself, conventionally M-representational of anything. E-physical phenomena can only be intended/interpreted as conventionally M-represen-tational given a mutually manifest system of representational conventions—that is, a CONVENTIONAL SYSTEM OF PHYSICAL REPRESENTATION (CSPR).[11] By the RH, 'LANGUAGES' are CSPRs with respect to (that is, for the M-representation of) L.

---

[11] Mutual manifestness need not imply that interlocutors have the same CSPR. Their CSPRs need overlap only to the extent of allowing each to infer the CSPR of the other. (Cf. Davidson 1986.) The RH is highly consistent with Chomsky's (1992*a*) response to Davidson's contentions regarding 'a language' and their lack of bearing into naturalistic enquiry into L.

They are CSPR$_{(L)}$s. Their relation to L is thus M-representational, not instantiational. They instantiate, not real natural 'Language' (their representatum), but the generic type 'CSPR$_{(L)}$'. See Q4 above. In characterizing so-called languages as CSPR$_{(L)}$s, the RH offers an account of their common relevance (relation) to L coupled to an explanation of the sense in which they are *not* 'languages' (not instances of L). We might attribute their being *thought* of as 'languages' to the considerations of Section 6.3 above and to the related possibility that *conscious* access to L is made available (though indirectly) to an individual *i* only through CSPR$_{(L, i)}$ itself. I touch on access to L again, below.

Let us not be too exercised about terminology here, however. If so-called 'languages' aren't languages, no more is L itself 'a language' or even 'Language' as usually understood. If, despite this, we allow that 'L' is indeed for 'Language', we might as well call CSPR$_{(L)}$s 'languages'. If 'L' is for 'Language', it is only in terms of their representatum, Language, that the rationale of CSPR$_{(L)}$s can be understood. Whatever we call them, what matters is that, by the RH, they are conventional systems for the E-physical M-rep of natural Language, a view of the relation fully consistent with (and only with) a non-generic, radically internal concept of L. As a reminder of this, I will retain the scare quotes for 'languages' and continue reserving 'linguistic' for what pertains to L.

A CSPR$_{(L)}$ is what Chomsky calls an 'I-language'. Under the RH however, Chomsky's two glosses of 'I'—'individual' and 'internal'—drift apart. In fact, they are mutually exclusive. A CSPR$_{(L)}$ is 'I' only in the sense of being unique to an individual, *not* because it is radically internal. I assume that the CSPR$_{(L)}$ of an individual is developed largely on the basis of external influences more or less different from those of other individuals (see Carr, this volume). CSPR$_{(L)}$s, then, are individual *because* they are not radically internal. In complete contrast, L (the representatum) is radically internal but not individual (in the above sense). On the contrary, L is universally invariant—precisely because it is radically internal.

On these terms, diversity among 'languages' is M-representational diversity, not linguistic diversity. Such diversity has no implications calling for (typological, parametric) qualification of the invariance of L itself, the unique representatum. In fact, it follows from the RH that parametric variation (located as it is in 'languages') is—*by definition*—M-representational, not linguistic.[12] There is no call to suggest that the 'apparent richness and diversity' of CSPR$_{(L)}$ phenomena are 'illusory and epiphenomenal' (Chomsky 1995a: 8)—or that 'English is not Swahili, *at least not quite*' (Chomsky 1995b: 13, emphasis added). In so far as Swahili is identifiable, its identity consists precisely in its *difference*, as a CSPR$_{(L)}$, from other CSPR$_{(L)}$s. What English and Swahili, as CSPR$_{(L)}$s, have in common (their representatum, L) lies wholly outside of them.

From this perspective, there are two distinguishable domains of empirical

---

[12] Although this follows as a matter of conceptual necessity, the empirical details need working out. Section 6.7 below deals briefly, by way of illustration, with the 'Head Parameter'.

enquiry, LINGUISTIC (into the nature of L, the unique and natural representatum) and REPRESENTATIONAL (into 'languages', in all their diversity and conventionality). Data provided by M-representational phenomena in a given $CSPR_{(L,i)}$ are data for a theory of $CSPR_{(L,i)}$, not *data* for the theory of L (representational data, not linguistic data). However, $CSPR_{(L)}$s are not irrelevant to the theory of L—nor, of course, conversely. How L is conventionally (and thus differently) M-represented is a source of indirect *evidence* for the theory of L. The diversity is essential here, providing a (representationally comparative) triangulation of the object of enquiry, L. Since diversity is indicative of the conventional and thus of the M-representational, it functions as a touchstone as to what *is* M-representational, thereby contributing to the disentanglement of *what* is M-represented (L) from *how* it is M-represented.

As regards 'language acquisition', what is acquired is the ambient $CSPR_{(L)}$, or what the individual *believes* is the ambient $CSPR_{(L)}$ (cf. nn. 3, 11). I see no reason not to think of this as a form of learning (see Carr, this volume). We attain the $CSPR_{(L)}$s we have experience of, not those we do not. As M-representational, all this is orthogonal to the innateness hypothesis for L itself, which the RH supports in its strongest conceivable form.

Even so, the RH is not consistent with L being a 'language acquisition device' (LAD) as usually understood—or with the idea that L is an *initial* state, one that undergoes modification in the light of so-called primary linguistic data. It is true that without L there could be no $CSPR_{(L)}$s, but that does not make L an 'acquisition device' for $CSPR_{(L)}$s. It is not consistent with the directed asymmetry of the M-rep relation to suppose that the nature of L—as representatum—is such as to orient it towards, or anticipate, any system for its conventional M-representation. Relatedly, the idea of L as LAD is bound to the generic idea that L is instantiated in 'languages', impossible if 'languages' are in fact $CSPR_{(L)}$s and problematic on other grounds already noted (n. 4).

This is not to deny that L is implicated in the acquisition of $CSPR_{(L)}$s. It is implicated, not as a device for their acquisition, but as their unique/universal representatum. In accounting for the speed/ease of $CSPR_{(L)}$ acquisition, the assumption that infants have tacit access to L—a basic premiss here as elsewhere—is crucial. Endow them also with 'Theory of Mind' (ToM). These endowments will serve to make relevant external phenomena cognized as relevant (in roughly the sense of Sperber and Wilson 1986). Produced by fellow humans (by ToM assumption, intentionally, and with a Presumption of Relevance), those phenomena will be assumed to bear on what the child has tacit access to, namely L. That the rationale of this relevance to L *must* be (conventionally) M-representational in character follows from the internalist assumption that external phenomena are themselves devoid of linguistic properties.

If, in addition, a 'LAD' as such is necessary, L itself must be independent of it. Interestingly, this is consistent with Chomsky's (1992*b*: 213) speculation that organisms not thought to have 'languages' ($CSPR_{(L)}$s) might have L. On those terms, it would not be implausible to suppose that what is distinctive about humans is a general capacity for conventional M-representation. Although independent of L (phylogenetically at least), this would confer a capacity for E-physical M-representation of L. Assuming the kind of access to L that L-endowed organisms have is *direct* but *unconscious*, I speculate that the capacity externally to M-represent L confers a distinct kind of access to L—*conscious* but *indirect* (because mediated by convention). As a $CSPR_{(L)}$ is acquired, so is this latter (species-specific) kind of access. That the rationale of the relevance of relevant phenomena *can* be tacitly cognized as M-representational might be attributable to a capacity for conventional M-representation.

6.6. As regards PHONOLOGY, consider now $CSPR_{(L)}$s in which 'P' stands more specifically for 'phonetic'—that is, conventional systems for the PHONETIC M-representation of L—$CS\underline{P}R_{(L)}$s—a.k.a. 'spoken languages'.

A (substantive) phonology, we have assumed, is a particular kind of attitude to relevant phonetic phenomena. In RH terms, phonetic phenomena are 'relevant' in virtue of being produced and interpreted *as* M-representational of L. I suggest the attitude *consists* in so producing and interpreting them and is thus constituted in the $CSPR_{(L)}$ itself. If a $CSPR_{(L)}$ determines the physical form of M-reps, then the conventions that constitute a $CS\underline{P}R_{(L)}$ are phonological.

In short, $CS\underline{P}R_{(L)}$s *are*$_{(def)}$ phonological systems.[13] A *phonology* is a conventional system for the *phonetic* M-representation of the (phonology-free, unique) lexical and other semantico-syntactic properties of L. It is precisely a phonology that is acquired when a 'spoken language' is acquired.[14] It confers the ability to speak that 'language'. It is mentally (M-)represented and thus internal. That does not make it linguistic, though. There is more to the internal than the linguistic. And, unlike L, it is not *radically* internal.

On these terms, a 'phonological representation' $\pi_{(k)}$ is an internalized (acquired) M-representation of what, given a particular $CS\underline{P}R_{(L)}$ *i*, is required (*a*) to produce a phonetic M-rep *k*, of LE *j*, and (*b*) to apperceive (parse) a phonetic phenomenon (e.g. *k*) *as* the M-rep of an LE (e.g. *j*). We need have no misgiving here in thinking that, for an individual minded to produce *k*, $\pi_{(k)}$ functions as a set of articulatory instructions. M-representation is an activity (for the speaker, at least). A phonetic M-rep *k* is an event. It is *caused*, not by L or LE *j*, but by an agent who is minded to

---

[13] On these terms, a $CSPR_{(L)}$ will be *phonological* only if its M-reps are phonetic. 'Sign languages' then are non-phonological $CSPR_{(L)}$s. With phonology excluded from the language faculty, there is no motive (from the invariance of the language faculty) to insist that phonology must generalize across media/modalities. Burton-Roberts and Carr (1999) briefly discuss the relation between such $CSPR_{(L)}$s (spoken/signed languages) and (ideo/)graphic $CSPR_{(L)}$s (a.k.a. 'written languages').

[14] This is consistent with Chomsky's (1992*a*: 116) 'conclusion ... however surprising ... that nature has provided us with an innate stock of concepts and that the child's task is to discover their labels'. Of course, the child must also discover *whether* given features (including syntactic relations) of L are M-represented by the ambient $CSPR_{(L)}$ and, if so, *how*.

M-represent LE *j*, implementing the M-representational instructions encoded in $\pi_{(k)}$.

In calling $\pi_{(k)}$ a 'phonological (M-)representation', I am anticipating the possibility that, with $\pi_{(k)}$ thought of as a set of instructions to be implemented in the articulatory activity of producing *k* (with the intention of thereby M-representing *j*), there is no essential difference between phonological rules and phonological (C-)representations, the former being merely more general in their application than the latter. Equally, with the phonological firmly excluded from L, I see no need to identify any level of supposedly 'phonetic' 'representation' (for example, 'systematic phonetic') distinct from *k* itself. The motive for identifying such a level, I believe, stemmed from the dilemma inherent in making provision for external sensorimotor (and thus behavioural) systems *within* a radically internal and non-behavioural conception of L (see Harris and Lindsey 1995: Sect. 3.1). $\pi_{(k)}$ thus subsumes what are elsewhere thought of as 'underlying' and 'surface' (C-)representations.

As the implementation of the instructions encoded in $\pi_{(k)}$, *k* can be thought of as a REALIZATION of $\pi_{(k)}$. But *k* does not thereby 'realize' any (syntactico-semantic) property or feature of L itself. This is because what *k* is realizational of—the phonological ($\pi_{(k)}$)—is not itself *realizational* of those syntactico-semantic properties, but merely provides for (the possibility of) their wholly conventional *M-representation* by phonetic events such as *k*. *k* realizes, not LE *j*, but the (non-linguistic) *M-representation* (in *i*) of *j*.

The intrinsic properties of *k* itself are exclusively phonetic. It has no other properties—semantic, syntactic, or even M-representational. In attending to *k* as an M-representation (that is, as a sign), we are attending to the extrinsic, intended/assumed M-representational (phonologically defined) *function* of the phonetic event *k* in the mental life of its producer and interpreters. It is no trivial task to establish the (discrete) categories imposed upon the gradient nature of the medium in terms of which the conventions are expressed and the signs constructed (see Myers, this volume), which intrinsic features of such events are or can be exploited to serve the representational function (given physiological and auditory constraints and the trade-off between them), how directly they serve that function, and, if they do not or not directly, what other functions (if any) they do or could directly serve. These and allied questions recapitulate what I take to be the legitimate (E-physical, functional) concerns of phonological theory (see e.g. Ohala 1983, 1998; Keating 1988; Pierrehumbert *et al.*, this volume). These concerns can be reconciled with, and made relevant to enquiry into, a very 'different' (radically internal, wholly formal) concept of L by viewing phonologies as M-representational of, and thus excluded from, L.

As regards Spell-Out: REALIZATIONAL PHONOLOGY is tied to the idea that the linguistic is in part derivationally targeted on sensory output, Spell-Out being the derivational point in N-LF at which (overt) 'realization' in sensory output is inaugurated. By contrast, with sensory output targeted on the linguistic (L), by reference to a REPRESENTATIONAL PHONOLOGY (a $\underline{CSPR}_{(L)}$) wholly external to L, there *is* no operation of Spell-Out. There are no phon-features in L and hence nothing to spell out. This opens up the possibility of (indeed implies) a single, undivided, unique (invariant), fully uniform (wholly covert) derivation serving just the LF interface—maximally economical in that no violatable economy principle of Procrastinate is even formulable. External to L so conceived (and, as it were, beyond its ken) are a diversity of conventional systems for its M-representation, some of them *phon*ological.

Phonology on these terms genuinely is an INTERFACE—the locus of the functional *relation* between the object L, as representatum, and E-physical (phonetic) events representational of L. It concerns both but belongs to neither. It is phonology itself (excluded, substantive), then, that is the locus of Saussurean arbitrariness and convention. Since 'spoken languages'—as phonologically constituted $CSPR_{(L)}$s—provide for the conventional M-representation by phonetic events of the syntactico-semantic objects generated by L, they can perhaps be thought of as (indirectly) pairing sound and meaning. If so, the Representational Hypothesis reconciles this view of such 'languages' with a radically distinct (non-pairing, phonology-free) view of L (natural 'Language').

Hale and Reiss (this volume, p. 181) suggest 'that functionalism provides no insight into the nature of grammar'. If we take this to mean that functionalism does not or cannot show that the nature of grammar (L) is functional, the Representational Hypothesis is fully consistent with their suggestion. But we are still (in fact, especially) required to acknowledge and locate the functional and explain what relation it bears to the (by hypothesis) wholly formal nature of grammar (L). The RH is by definition *functionalist* in respect of grammar-external phonological systems, reconciling this with a wholly *formalist* concept of grammar (L) in terms of the relation of M-rep. On these terms, I have suggested, such functional (external, conventional, diverse) systems do provide insight (if only indirect) into the wholly formal (internal, natural, unique) nature of grammar—precisely in virtue of their (M-representational) function.

Fig. 3.1 (p. 62) is a schematic comparison of the Minimalism of Chomsky (1995*a*) and the Representational Hypothesis. Rectangles enclose L in each. Ovals denote kinds of relation.

6.7. The conceptual and empirical implications of the Representational Hypothesis and the questions its raises promise to be far-reaching and, as regards the derivation N-LF, radically minimalist in flavour.[15] Their investigation would take

[15] One expectation is that, relieved of the 'extraneous' need to serve the PF interface, N-LF will deal only in elements/relations interpretable at the LF interface and hence that nothing is (introduced into and) deleted from N-LF because uninterpretable at the (LF) interface. This I believe has a bearing on the distinction, or lack of it, between LF and its derivation (Chomsky 1995*a*: 223–5; Brody 1997; Epstein MS). With deletion permitted, properties not figuring in LF (as a C-representation) may figure in its derivation, thereby implying a real distinction between derivation and (C-)representation.

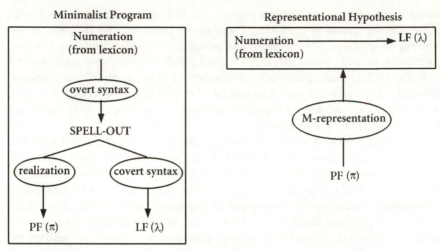

Fig. 3.1. The Minimalist Program and the Representational Hypothesis compared

us beyond the scope of both chapter and volume (see Burton-Roberts 1998, 1999, in preparation; Chng 1999; Carr, this volume), so I conclude with some remarks on the scope of phonology as conceived of here.

Phonology in the RH is necessarily much broader in scope than is traditional. In particular I have followed Chomsky in subsuming morphology under phonology. This is actually necessary in the RH because a phonology, as a $CSPR_{(L)}$, is conceived of as *determining the form of phonetic M-representations* of LEs—LEs of arbitrary complexity. Morphology is generally regarded as concerned just with 'words'. In the RH, WORDS (and the units from which they are constructed—a.k.a. 'morphemes') are M-representational entities.[16] The words of a 'language', then, are a *subset* of the phonetic M-representations (the signs) provided for by a phonology (a $CSPR_{(L)}$).

Since 'languages' are here identified as phonological systems, we can expect representational phonology to subsume not only the morphology of particular 'languages' but as much of (what elsewhere passes for) the 'syntax' of particular 'languages' as cannot—on the grounds of variation, on the one hand, and minimalist considerations of conceptual necessity, on the other—be thought of as pertaining to the syntax defined by L itself, the derivation N-LF.

Chomsky (1995a: 125) raises the question of the scope of phonology: 'there are open questions as to whether certain operations and properties we have assigned

---

[16] By the RH we need to distinguish the (unique) LEXICON of L and the VOCABULARIES of particular $CSPR_{(L)}$s. The latter consist of (wholly) phonological words. Since a vocabulary is not realizational (but M-representational) of conceptual elements in L's lexicon, there is no reason to expect the (M-rep) relation between (even morphologically simple, let alone complex) VOCABULARY ITEMS and LEXICAL ITEMS to be isomorphic (bi-unique).

to the LF component do not in fact belong to the PF component. Similar questions arise about the actual "division of labour" between the PF component and the overt syntax.' These are precisely the questions that can be expected to drive further research in an (M-)representational framework. Interpreted in the light of the Representational Hypothesis, they acquire a special significance. However, if L includes phonology, they *can* only concern 'division of labour' within (a theory of) L. As such, their significance is not as clear as it might be. Furthermore, the complexity of L is unaffected by divisions of labour within it, simplification being achieved in one part at the cost of increased complexity in another. In the RH, by contrast, it is *not* a question of division of labour. Whether a given feature is phonological or not is, more substantively, a matter of whether it is *linguistic* as such (L) or *M-representational* of L (and thus not L). This is a matter of what I have called 'representational disentanglement', a matter of identifying examples of, and resisting, the impulse to project onto L itself what we know of how L is M-represented and, equally, the impulse to project onto the M-representational phenomena of 'languages' what we know of their representatum. So put, I believe it exhibits more clearly the degree of conceptual and empirical significance that Chomsky (with his core/periphery distinction) in fact seeks to attach to it.

I conclude with a brief illustration of the widened scope of phonology in a representational framework. I assume with Chomsky that 'there is no clear evidence that order plays a role at LF or in the computation N to LF' (1995a: 334; also 289). What conceptual content might order have there? What function might it serve, apart from (in some obscure sense) anticipating the temporal order manifest in utterance phenomena? Accordingly, Chomsky (ibid.) assumes order is assigned in the phonological component of L, as part of a process that 'converts the objects generated by the language L to a form that ... "external" systems can use'. There is a difficulty here, however. It assumes order must be assigned to objects, those figuring in N-LF, because presumably they are not ordered. But they are not ordered because they are not linear (not temporal). Were they linear they would of necessity be in some order. We cannot impose order and thus linearity on what is by its nature non-linear.

It is essential to the Representational Hypothesis, by contrast, that nothing is, or needs to be, 'converted' into anything else. The properties related by conventional M-representation are disjoint—wholly and mutually independent. Linearity is a (temporal) property just of the physically articulated sounds. An important aspect of the conventionality of their M-representational relation to the linguistic lies precisely in their being *linear* (temporal) M-reps of *non-linear* structure generated by L. All CSP$R_{(L)}$s exploit temporal linearity for representational purposes, at least in their WORDS. Beyond words, they may or not may not exploit it (if not, we get so-called free word order). For example, a given CSPR$_{(L)}$ might demand that the physical M-rep of a head expression *H* be adjacent to and ordered before the physical M-rep of its complement expression *C* (as in English; or in reverse, as in Japanese) thereby exploiting physical order in aid of physically M-representing them *as* being in an *H-C* relation, and thus as the merged constituents of third expression, call it '*HP*'.

This is a wholly representational matter. It is not *H* and *C* themselves that are ordered, only physical M-reps of them. Nor does it follow that, in thus (effectively) M-representing *HP*, *the M-representation* of an LE-that-includes-*HP*-as-a-constituent has itself a (representational) constituent corresponding to *HP*. On the contrary, I assume that, beyond the word, physical M-representations do not themselves exhibit the hierarchical syntactic constituency they are M-representational of.[17] In such CSPR$_{(L)}$s, then, non-hierarchical linearity is physically M-representational of non-linear structural hierarchy. Other CSPR$_{(L)}$s—Latin, Czech, Waalpiri—do not exploit linear order in this way, leaving order free to be exploited for other (not strictly representational) purposes—theme-rheme, metricality, ease of parsing, or whatever.

Although traditionally regarded as syntactic, the Head Parameter in fact concerns CSPR$_{(L)}$-specific linear ordering (and thus the form) of phonetic M-representations. As such it must be phonological—*not* syntactic, nor yet 'epiphenomenal'—or 'realizational'—of the syntactic, but conventionally *M-representational* of the syntactic.[18]

REFERENCES

Anderson, J. and Ewen, C. (1987), *Principles of Dependency Phonology* (Cambridge: Cambridge University Press).

Bach, K. (1995), 'Type-Token Distinction', in *Cambridge Dictionary of Philosophy* (Cambridge: Cambridge University Press).

Bar-Hillel, Y. (1970), *Aspects of Language* (Jerusalem: Magnes).

Brody, M. (1997), *Lexico-Logical Form: A Radically Minimalist Approach* (Cambridge. Mass.: MIT Press).

Bromberger, S. (1989), 'Types and Tokens in Linguistics', in A. George (ed.), *Reflections on Chomsky* (Oxford: Blackwell), 58–89

—— and Halle, M. (1989), 'Why Phonology is Different', *Linguistic Inquiry*, 20/1: 51–70.

—— —— (this volume), 'The Ontology of Phonology (Revised)'.

Burton-Roberts, N. (1998), 'Language, Linear Precedence, and Parentheticals', in P. Collins (ed.), *The Clause in English: In Honour of Rodney Huddleston* (Amsterdam: John Benjamins), 33–52.

—— (1999), 'Ambiguity, Quotation, Grelling's Paradox: A Representational Approach', *Newcastle and Durham Working Papers in Linguistics*, 5: 75–98.

—— (in preparation), *Natural Language and Conventional Representation*.

[17] The evidence for this comes from so-called structural ambiguity and garden-pathing. It is also what motivates the more determinate M-representations used in linguistic theory, e.g. tree diagrams—but see Burton-Roberts (1998) on the representational conflation that tree diagrams embody.

[18] Kayne (1994), by contrast, proposes that linear (temporal) order falls out as an epiphenomenon of syntax (c-command). However, the syntax of L has to be modified and enriched to make this work.

—— and Carr, P. (1999), 'On Speech and Natural Language', *Language Sciences*, 21/4: 371–406.

Carr, P. (this volume), 'Scientific Realism, Sociophonetic Variation, and Innate Endowments in Phonology'.

Chng, S. (1999), *Language, Thought and Literal Meaning*, Ph.D. thesis (Newcastle University).

Chomsky, N. (1972), *Language and Mind* (New York: Harcourt Brace Jovanovich).

—— (1980), *Rules and Representations* (Oxford: Blackwell).

—— (1986), *Knowledge of Language* (New York: Praeger).

—— (1992a), 'Language and Interpretation', in J. Earman (ed.), *Inference, Explanation and Other Philosophical Frustrations* (Berkeley and Los Angeles: University of California Press), 99–128; repr. in Chomsky (2000), 19–45.

—— (1992b) 'Explaining Language Use', *Philosophical Topics*, 20: 205–31; repr. in Chomsky (2000), 46–74.

—— (1995a), *The Minimalist Program* (Cambridge, Mass.: MIT Press).

—— (1995b), 'Language and Nature', *Mind*, 104: 1–61; repr. in Chomsky (2000), 106–63.

—— (1998), ' Some Observations on Economy in Generative Grammar', in P. Barbosa *et al.* (eds.), *Is the Best Good Enough?* (Cambridge, Mass.: MIT Press), 115–27.

Collins, C. (1997), *Local Economy* (Cambridge, Mass.: MIT Press).

—— (2000), *New Horizons in the Study of Language and Mind* (Cambridge: Cambridge University Press).

Davidson, D. (1986), 'A Fine Derangement of Epitaphs', in E. Lepore (ed.), *Truth and Interpretation: Perspectives on the Philosophy of Donald Davidson* (Oxford: Blackwell).

Docherty, G. J., Foulkes, P., Milroy, J., Milroy, L., and Walshaw, D. (1997), 'Descriptive Adequacy in Phonology: A Variationist Perspective', *Journal of Linguistics*, 33/2: 275–310.

Epstein, S. (MS), 'Unprincipled Syntax and the Derivation of Syntactic Relations', Harvard University.

—— et al. (1996), 'Introduction', in W. Abraham, S. Epstein, H. Thrainsson, and C. Zwart (eds.), *Minimal Ideas* (Amsterdam: John Benjamins).

Hale, M. and Reiss, C. (this volume), 'Phonology as Cognition'.

Halle, M. and Marantz, A. (1993), 'Distributed Morphology and the Pieces of Inflection', in K. Hale, and S. J. Keyser (eds.), *The View from Building 20: Essays in Linguistics in Honor of Sylvain Bromberger* (Cambridge, Mass.: MIT Press), 111–76.

Harris, J. and Lindsey, G. (1995), 'The Elements of Phonological Representation', in J. Durand and F. Katamba (eds.), *Frontiers of Phonology* (Harlow: Longman), 34–79.

Hulst, H. van der (1993), 'Units in the Analysis of Signs', *Phonology*, 10: 209–41.

—— (this volume), 'Modularity and Modality in Phonology'.

Kaye, J., Lowenstamm, J., and Vergnaud, J.-R. (1985), 'The Internal Structure of Phonological Elements: A Theory of Charm and Government', *Phonology Yearbook*, 2: 305–28.

—— —— —— (1990), 'Constituent Structure and Government in Phonology', *Phonology*, 7: 193–231.

Kayne, R. (1994), *The Antisymmetry of Syntax* (Cambridge, Mass.: MIT Press).

Keating, P. A. (1988), 'Underspecification in Phonetics', *Phonology*, 5: 275–92.

Myers, S. (this volume), 'Boundary Disputes: The Distinction between Phonetic and Phonological Sound Patterns'.

Ohala, J. J. (1983), 'The Origin of Sound Patterns in Vocal Tract Constraints', in P. MacNeilage (ed.), *The Production of Speech* (New York: Springer), 189–216.

—— (1998), 'The Relation between Phonetics and Phonology', in W. Hardcastle and J. Laver (eds.), *The Handbook of Phonetic Sciences* (Oxford: Blackwell).

Pateman, T. (1987), 'What is a Language?', in T. Pateman, *Language in Mind and Language in Society* (Oxford: University Press), 43–80.

Peirce, C. (1933), *Collected Papers* (Cambridge, Mass.: Harvard University Press).

Pierrehumbert, J. B., Beckman, M., and Ladd, D. R. (this volume), 'Conceptual Foundations of Phonology as a Laboratory Science'.

Poole, G. (1998), 'Constraints on Local Economy', in P. Barbosa *et al.* (eds.), *Is the Best Good Enough?* (Cambridge, Mass.: MIT Press).

Sperber, D. and Wilson, D. (1986), *Relevance: Communication and Cognition* (Oxford: Blackwell).

4

Scientific Realism, Sociophonetic Variation, and Innate Endowments in Phonology

PHILIP CARR

1. INTRODUCTION

This chapter addresses two related questions that, I believe, lie at the heart of the conceptual and empirical foundations of phonological theory. First, in Sections 2 and 3, I address the question of whether, and to what extent, generative, variationist, and Laboratory Phonology approaches to phonological investigation may be said to be scientific in character. This issue is central to some of the objections to generative phonology raised by variationists and laboratory phonologists, who appear to question the putative scientific status of much generative practice. In order to examine this question, I first outline (in Section 2) the conception of scientific knowledge that I adopt here (Popper's), which embraces falsificationism and scientific realism. Having argued that hypotheses in generative phonology are typically falsifiable, and thus scientific in character, I then address (in Section 3) certain problems that have arisen in applying scientific realism in phonological theory. I show that these problems raise the second of the questions that I address here, that of the place of sociophonetic variation within a Rationalist approach to linguistic enquiry, and the related question of the role played by idealization in sociolinguistics and Chomskian Rationalist linguistics. In Section 3, I argue that the relation between E-language (the locus of sociophonetic variation) and Universal Grammar (UG) cannot be one of idealization. The question then remains of what the relation between sociophonetic variation and

Versions of this paper were given at the 5th Manchester Phonology Conference, May 1998; as one of a series of papers on Universals and Linguistic Diversity in May 1998, at the Centre for Research in Linguistics, Newcastle University; at the 2nd Current Trends in Phonology conference at the Abbaye de Royaumont, Paris, June 1998; and at a colloqium on phonological theory and variation in November 1999, at the Université de Toulouse-le-Mirail. My thanks to the participants for their responses, and to Noel Burton-Roberts, whose thinking on radical internalism and representation has reshaped my conception of the nature of phonological knowledge. This work was supported by a grant from the Arts and Humanities Research Board under its Research Leave Scheme.

UG might be. I seek to provide an answer to that question in the form of Burton-Roberts's Representational Hypothesis.

This question of the place of sociophonetic variation within a Rationalist approach to linguistic enquiry (which I address in Sections 4 and 5) has been put as follows: 'How could a nativist [henceforth, Rationalist[1]] theory of language development, such as Chomsky's, be integrated with some sociolinguistic theory of language practices?' (Pateman 1987: 81). The most prominent version of Rationalism in late-twentieth-century linguistics, that of Chomsky (1966, 1980, 1993, 1995*a*, *b*, and elsewhere), insists on the significance, for linguistic enquiry, of postulating a specifically linguistic, species-specific state of mind/brain, UG, which is said to be a natural fact: it is taken to constitute an aspect of the natural (specifically, biological) world. Under Chomskian Rationalism, UG is said *not* to be constituted in terms of behaviour, disposition(s) to behave, or *conventions* (norms) governing behaviour, all of which are said to fall outside the object of strictly linguistic enquiry.

However, others stress the *centrality* for linguistic enquiry of conventions (norms) of social behaviour (notably, speech and signing behaviour). These include variationists such as Milroy and Milroy (1985), Docherty *et al.* (1997), and Docherty and Foulkes (this volume), broadly Wittgensteinian philosophers of linguistics such as Itkonen (1978); and the laboratory phonologist John Ohala (1983 and elsewhere).

As Pateman (1987: 81) notes, these two sorts of approach to language study are generally taken as 'either rival accounts of the same domain or as having no relation to each other'. There is evidence that these two approaches are indeed taken as rival accounts of the domain of phonology. On the one hand, much phonological work that has Rationalist underpinnings (mostly, work within generative phonology) deliberately ignores sociophonetic variation, for reasons discussed below. On the other hand, work such as that of Docherty *et al.* (1997), which does not appear to adopt Rationalist assumptions, presents a variationist approach to phonology as an alternative, rival approach to such putatively 'theory-led' approaches to phonological phenomena. I seek to show that variationist approaches to phonology are compatible with Chomskian Rationalism (and how they are compatible). In order to do so, I argue (*a*) that allowing for innate endowments is compatible with the Empiricist tradition, (*b*) that the only coherent conception of UG is a radically internalist one (defined below), and (*c*) that an Empiricist account of the acquisition of a phonology (but with a Rationalist *raison d'être* (see below)) is viable, and can be squared with the idea of (radically internal) UG. I adopt Burton-Roberts's (1994 and this volume) Representational Hypothesis in order to show how this is possible.

This chapter may be taken to constitute an attempt at fleshing out a set of

---

[1] I use the term 'Rationalist', since the term 'Nativist' can be taken to imply no more than the postulating of innate perceptual capacities (see the definition of Nativism in Bullock and Stallybrass (1977), for instance). This conception of Nativism is, I claim below, fully consistent with Empiricism.

conceptual foundations for an approach to phonological realities that takes them to arise from the interaction of 'matter, mind and manners' (Ohala 1983). By the latter phrase, I take Ohala to mean facts concerning the articulatory apparatus and acoustic events (matter), general and specific perceptual and cognitive capacities (mind), and norms governing social behaviour (manners).[2] In setting out this set of conceptual foundations, I hope to show how, on the one hand, Laboratory Phonology and variationism, and, on the other, (certain aspects of) generative phonology and Rationalism might be brought into alignment with each other. The conception of phonological knowledge that is adopted here rests on the Rationalist assumption that it is reasonable to say that human beings are innately endowed with a specifically linguistic, species-specific, encapsulated state of mind/brain: UG. This is not the place to attempt to substantiate that assumption, but Sections 5 and 6 below contain discussion of the nature of UG and a defence of the claim that it is phonology free.

2. SCIENTIFIC KNOWLEDGE AND SCIENTIFIC REALISM

One cannot begin to assess whether a discipline is scientific in character (or not) unless one has a set of demarcation criteria that act as a means of distinguishing between scientific and non-scientific disciplines, and a relatively fleshed-out picture of the nature of scientific knowledge. It will not suffice simply to assume, without discussion, that it is self-evident as to what disciplines count as scientific disciplines, or that there is a self-evident distinction between the concerns of science and those of philosophy. The issues are contentious, and not just among philosophers of science; see, for example, the description of physics, by the laboratory neuroscientist Steven Rose (1993: 147), as 'this rather untypical science'. It is striking that the work of some linguists, such as John Ohala (1983 and elsewhere), while containing much that is of considerable importance and interest, contains many rather bold assertions as to the nature of science without any reference at all to the literature on the subject, or any allusion as to the possibly moot nature of the assertions being made. Similarly, several of the arguments proposed by Hale and Reiss (this volume) rely rather heavily on a conception of scientific method that appears to consist of little more than the application of Occam's Razor and the idea that scientific theories postulate a set of primitive elements and operations. This lack of serious reference to the literature, and thus the issues, on the nature of science seems to me to be regrettable, and I therefore

---

[2] No ontological distinction of a Cartesian sort between mind and matter is presupposed here, or in the work of Ohala. I assume that 'mind' is brain embedded within body, located in an environment and interacting with it in complex ways; the 'mind/matter' distinction adopted here is simply a terminologically convenient way of distinguishing between different aspects of human beings and their cognitive and social capacities and behaviour.

begin by laying out the core details of the conception of scientific knowledge that I will adopt here.

The work of Karl Popper (1959, 1963, 1982–3, and elsewhere[3]) constitutes what is arguably the most thoroughly worked-through attempt at providing a set of criteria for demarcating scientific from non-scientific hypotheses. I will be assuming, *contra* Feyerabend (1975 and elsewhere), and without argument (for reasons of lack of space), that there are such things as scientific, as opposed to non-scientific, hypotheses. I will accordingly base my discussion of the putative scientific status of phonological investigation on Popper's conception of science. I lack the space to examine Popper's main ideas in any depth here; Carr (1990) contains more detail. Some of the main components of Popper's philosophy of science are generally known, but some of the most salient aspects of his philosophy of science are often not properly appreciated. As a result, supposedly Popperian views are often criticized, views that Popper never held. Examples are criticisms of Popper's supposedly 'naïve (or instant) falsificationism', or of 'simplistic Popperianism' (Pateman 1987: 25), on which, see below. Other examples are putative alternatives to Popper's thought that crucially adopt positions actually held by Popper himself. An example here is Laudan's (1977: 66) claim to have developed the first-ever problem-based philosophy of science, since, according to him, 'no major contemporary philosophy of science allows for conceptual problems', a puzzling view, given that Popper stressed the centrality of what he called 'problem situations' in science (a complex mix of theoretical proposals, data, and problems raised by the interaction of the two, at a given point in time).[4] Another example is Bhaskar's (1975) 'alternative' to Popper's alleged 'positivism'. Bhaskar's philosophy of science centres on the putatively new and alternative idea that the physical world is an open system, an idea that, in fact, Popper himself insisted on. Given these unfortunate misinterpretations of Popper's thinking, it is worth sketching, however briefly, the main components of Popper's thinking on the nature of scientific method, even if, in doing so in such a summary manner, one risks being accused of the sort of misrepresentation just mentioned.

As is known, Popper stressed, in stark contrast to previous positivist thinking in the early twentieth century (thinking that is, alas, still with us: see below), the role of falsifiablity (rather than verifiability, which had played a major role in positivist thinking): a hypothesis is falsifiable, and thus scientific, if it logically excludes certain states of affairs. If those states of affairs can be shown to exist, then the hypothesis is falsified. That is, a hypothesis, to be scientific in nature, must admit of counter-evidence. The degree to which a hypothesis is falsifiable reflects the

---

[3] Note that the content of the three volumes, finally published in 1982 and 1983, of the *Postscript* to *The Logic of Scientific Discovery* (Popper 1959) was written in the 1950s, and not as a 'refinement' of earlier ideas in the wake of Kuhnian ideas, as is commonly supposed.

[4] Laudan's work is, I claim (*contra* Pierrhumbert *et al.*, this volume), a contribution to the theory of the social behaviour of scientific communities, rather than the nature of scientific knowledge *per se*. In this respect, it falls into the same category as the work of Kuhn.

degree of empirical content of the hypothesis. Hypotheses that do not admit of counter-evidence will appear true, no matter what states of affairs hold, and therefore lack scientific content. Popper famously claimed that this was the case for hypotheses in Freudian psychoanalysis and Marxist social theory, and it was this fact that led Marxist philosophers such as Bhaskar and Pateman to denounce Popper's conception of science as 'positivist', since it was crucial for them that social theory in general, and Marxist social theory in particular, be regarded as scientific (see below on the scientific status of sociolinguistics). Popper's falsificationism never included the view that science proceeds by means of 'instant' falsificationism, the view that scientists instantly abandon a hypothesis the moment counter-evidence comes to light. Nor did he claim that falsification is once-and-for-all. On the contrary, Popper (1959) stated quite clearly that 'no conclusive disproof of a theory can ever be produced'. This is an important point, since many philosophers, dating from Kuhn (1962) and including Bhaskar (1975), Laudan (1977), and Newton-Smith (1982), have continued to misrepresent Popper on this score, to the point where Kuhn's work is commonly taken to have represented a refinement on Popperian thinking. Rather, it is a refinement of ideas that Popper never held, a refinement of a caricature. Falsifiability is, Popper pointed out, a strictly logical property of scientific hypotheses; insisting on it does not amount to demanding that scientists state in advance the conditions under which they would be willing to abandon a hypothesis. Popper noted, very early on in his work, that his point was a point about *falsifiability in principle*, rather than the question of whether a hypothesis is in fact abandoned or modified.

Popper also argued that scientific knowledge arises from a methodology that is *both* top down ('theory driven') *and* bottom up ('data driven' (see my discussion below of Docherty *et al.* 1997)); put simply, data gained from observation is of no interest unless it is data that can count as evidence or counter-evidence with respect to some hypothesis or interlinked set of hypotheses, and such data are unlikely even to *be* gathered unless this is so. Put another way, there is no such thing as theory-free observation. Additionally, Popper stressed that all serious scientific theories rest upon a general picture of how the world (or a subpart of it) is; this general picture is what he called a metaphysical research programme; his main point about it is that it drives the formation of falsifiable hypotheses without itself necessarily being falsifiable. The point is an important one, and was taken up by Imre Lakatos (1970 and elsewhere), whose work on scientific research programmes can be seen as a development and elaboration of Popperian ideas, rather than an alternative to them. Popper famously pointed out that the general idea of natural selection is not itself falsifiable, but it is mistaken to conclude from this, as Rose (1997: 46–7) does, that Popper was thereby committed to claiming that the general idea of natural selection did not constitute a part of a scientific theory; rather, for Popper, it constituted the unfalsifiable part of a scientific theory (the metaphysical research programme) from which falsifiable hypotheses could be derived.

Another important aspect of Popper's view of the nature of scientific knowledge is his adoption of scientific realism. From the fact that observation is said by Popper to be theory dependent, it does not follow that one must retreat (as instrumentalists do) from the view that there are realities that exist outside our theoretical constructs. Popper stressed that, although we cannot achieve completely certain scientific knowledge, we can take our best hypotheses, those that remain unfalsified over time, to be our best approximations as to the way reality is. Popper also allowed that scientific realism necessarily entails idealization—that is, the factoring out of certain aspects of reality in order to arrive at a better comprehension of other aspects and the interaction between those different aspects.

The strategy of scientific realism seems well founded as far as the natural sciences are concerned, and seems to have yielded considerable results. Examples are not hard to find. When the physicist speaks of frictionless planes, he is not committed to saying that such things exist in the world of our everyday experience; quite the contrary: he is postulating such planes precisely *because* they do *not* occur in our everyday experience. The point in doing so is to isolate certain aspects of reality (in this case, energy conservation, force, mass, and acceleration, say) from each other and from others (for example, loss of energy and deceleration brought about by friction). In engaging in this sort of idealization, the physicist can then build up an account of the relationship and interaction between force, mass, acceleration, friction, and energy loss.

It would be entirely unreasonable to object to this methodological strategy (as various positivist[5] philosophers and scientists have done) on the grounds that it constitutes an unacceptable over-idealization, divorcing theoretical enquiry from everyday reality and sensory ('observational') data, engaging in unacceptable reification of notions such as 'force' and postulating non-existent, over-abstract notions such as 'total conservation of energy'. Quite the contrary: it is precisely via this strategy of scientific realism that the physicist engages with and explicates the nature of reality, and with considerable success. It is worth noting that, in speaking of such things as frictionless planes, the physicist is none the less speaking of planes. That is, idealization in physics does not involve idealizing from objects of one ontological category (for example, natural objects such as planes) to objects of a distinct category (for example, non-natural objects such as social conventions: see below on natural versus conventional), and must not, since any such idealization is untenable. The relevance of this observation for phonological theory should become clear below.

Positivist objections to this strategy have met with little success in the history of

---

[5] I use the term 'positivist' in its traditional sense—i.e. in the sense widely appealed to in much twentieth-century philosophy of science. 'Positivism', as used here, designates philosophies of science that refuse to assign real status to anything other than putatively directly observable entities. See Carr (1990) for considerably more detailed discussion of positivism. I do not use the term in the sense intended by Bhaskar (1975) or Laudan (1977).

science. Consider, for instance, Mach's (1893/1966) late-nineteenth/early twenti-eth-century instrumentalist[6] objections to the theoretical construct 'atom' in twentieth-century physics: no one now claims, as Mach did, that the notion 'atom', and indeed almost all constructs in physical science, is a mere reification, a departure from statements about sensory experiences, an over-idealization of (putatively) brute perceptual observation.

It is important to note that Popper also adopted fallibilism. The central Popperian notion of falsifiability as the hallmark of scientific hypotheses rests on our being able to accept certain statements ('observation' statements, which Popper referred to as 'basic statements', for obvious reasons), which allow us to say that a theory has, indeed, been falsified, as being true. Since we cannot be certain that they *are* true, we cannot be certain that what we have taken to be an instance of falsification is indeed such. Popper's fallibilism constitutes a recognition of this: Popper accepts that the entire edifice of scientific knowledge does not have absolutely certain foundations.

It is clear that, as is often the case in philosophy, only the more naïve versions of realism and instrumentalism are wholly at odds with each other; more sophisti-cated versions of the two doctrines are often very similar. For instance, Popperian fallibilist realism contains an element of pragmatism: Popper allowed that the granting of a realist interpretation of a construct is largely governed by the pragmatic factor of heuristic fertility (the success a construct allows us in the growth of scientific knowledge). This emphasis on heuristic fertility is found in most versions of instrumentalism.

None the less, it seems clear that, even with the most sophisticated versions of instrumentalism and realism, a fundamental difficulty remains for instrumental-ists: in stressing that competing theories are to be judged on their success (their heuristic fertility), but none the less withholding any ontological commitment as to the way the theory-external world actually *is*, the instrumentalist has no explanation as to *why* one theory should be more successful than another. The realist, on the other hand, can appeal to the notion of degree of correspondence to realities to explain why, for instance, our scientific accounts of, say, the sun and its relation to the earth (the solar system story) have resulted in our being able to travel to the moon, while earlier stories about the same objects, including many mythological stories, have not had that result. It is reasonable to say that both our current Western scientific story about the solar system and myths about the sun and moon are products of human imagination, but the former must surely be characterized in terms of greater correspondence to the real structure and function of objects in the physical world.

---

[6] To flesh out a little what I mean by 'instrumentalist', I mean any approach to theoretical constructs that views them as mere instruments for predicting and classifying observed data, a view that involves a refusal to grant that our theoretical constructs may be said to correspond to theory-external realities. See Carr (1990) for more details.

The question arises whether it is possible to adopt this kind of realism with respect to theoretical constructs in phonology, and whether any of the hypotheses proposed in that field could be said to be falsifiable (and thus scientific) in Popper's terms. I argue that this is possible, but that certain problems remain with respect to the application of scientific realism in phonological investigation; I discuss these problems in the following section.

3. AUTONOMOUS PHONOLOGY AND SCIENTIFIC REALISM

3.1. *Falsifiability and autonomous phonology*

I will take the term 'autonomous phonology' to refer to any approach to phonological investigation that assumes that the object of phonological enquiry can be studied in its own right, independently (or relatively independently) of the study of factors such as the social context in which speakers are located. Autonomous phonology, and autonomous linguistics in general, has a long history, stretching from the work of Panini (or earlier) to most of the work in present-day generative phonology. But the latter differs from much (but not, perhaps, all) earlier work in autonomous linguistics, since it is autonomist for a particular reason: it stems from a set of assumptions, proposed by Chomsky, about the nature of the object of linguistic enquiry and the way in which linguistic enquiry should be conducted.

The question arises whether it is reasonable to say that hypotheses in generative phonology are testable. It has been claimed by laboratory phonologists (see Pierrehumbert *et al.*, this volume) that frameworks elaborated within generative phonology (such as Lexical Phonology) are, in and of themselves, not subject to experimental testing, but that specific hypotheses proposed within those frameworks may be testable via the methods of laboratory phonology. Even if this is a valid point, it remains the case that such frameworks are testable, since the extent to which a framework is testable is a function of the extent to which its component hypotheses are testable. And this is usually the case in generative phonology.

For instance, in the case of the Lexical Phonology framework (and 'framework' here is equivalent to 'theory', in this case, a theory of phonology–morphology interactions), it seems to me that the following hypotheses are all testable: Structure Preservation, the Strict Cyclicity Condition, the Level Ordering theory of morphology–phonology interactions, and the claim that phonological generalizations may be divided into lexical and postlexical generalizations. Additionally, the claim that lexical and postlexical generalizations possess disjoint sets of properties is also testable. If this is true, then it follows that the Lexical Phonology framework is highly testable, even if the framework itself, as a whole, is not subject to experimental testing. I would claim, further, that most of these hypotheses are either clearly falsified by the available data, or are problematic. In particular, Structure Preservation and Strict Cyclicity (as applied to segmental generalizations) have been falsified (for relevant evidence, see e.g. Carr 1992, Harris 1989,

Hualde 1989, and McMahon 1990), and the Level Ordering hypothesis is deeply problematic, almost certainly false (see e.g. Szpyra 1989). The lexical/postlexical distinction apears to be robustly sustainable, but many of the proposed distinct properties of lexical and postlexical generalizations turn out to be false (see Carr 1991; Pandey 1997). This is not the place to substantiate these claims; the point I wish to stress here is that many of those claims can be shown to be false: they are falsifiable, and are thus properly scientific claims. I also claim that this is generally true of theories elaborated within generative phonology.

If it turns out that almost all of the hypotheses in all of the theories elaborated within generative phonology are false, then that raises interesting questions regarding the basic assumptions on which generative phonology rests. But it does not mean that theories within generative phonology are unscientific; in fact, it means exactly the reverse. If one adopts Popper's philosophy of science, the scientific status of hypotheses in generative phonology depends on their falsifiability *in principle*, not on the *mode* of falsification. Attempts at falsification (testing) of hypotheses may, but need not, involve laboratory techniques. The fact that theories in generative phonology are scientific in nature does not, of course, undermine Pierrehumbert *et al.*'s arguments about modes of testing, or the sorts of mathematics required to model phonological phenomena.

A central problem with generative phonology, with respect to its scientific status, is not the testability of its theories, but the question of the application of scientific realism to linguistic investigation by Chomsky, and thus by generative phonologists. One of the most important of the assumptions (for present purposes) underlying the autonomous linguistics proposed in Chomsky's earlier work (prior to the advent of the terms 'I-language' and 'E-language') concerned the notion of the ideal speaker-hearer in a totally homogeneous speech community, a notion that excludes from consideration the social context in which speakers exist and communicate, and thus excludes sociophonetic variation. It is the exclusion of those factors that sociolinguists have objected to (with, I suggest, considerable justification, as far as phonology is concerned). Similarly, in more recent work, Chomsky has asserted that sociopolitical notions such as 'English' are 'E-languages', which are said to 'play no role in the theory of language' (Chomsky 1991a: 9). Indeed, Chomsky claims that 'E-language, if it exists at all, is derivative, remote from mechanisms, and of no particular empirical significance, perhaps none at all' (1991a: 10). Again, sociophonetic variation is taken to fall outside the scope of linguistic enquiry, conceived of as the investigation of an object in the natural world (UG): the notion E-language 'involves complex and obscure sociopolitical, historical, cultural, and normative-teleological elements, which may be of some interest for the sociology of identification within and across various social and political communities and the study of authority structure, but which lie far beyond any useful enquiry into the nature of language or the study of meaning or the psychology of users of language' (Chomsky 1991b: 31).

Chomsky's aim in excluding the notion E-language from consideration is to isolate certain aspects of speaker-hearers' cognitive capacities (principally, UG) from others, such as constraints on short-term memory (Chomsky 1965), and the speaker-hearer's internalized sense of social identity. The aim is, ultimately, to examine the interaction between these different aspects of reality, on the entirely reasonable grounds that one cannot coherently speak of the interaction between two aspects of the world unless one has first distingushed them. This is the strategy of scientific realism. The alternative is to attempt to investigate any and every aspect of reality simultaneously, a strategy that seems ill-advised, to say the least. The adopting of the strategy of scientific realism is not, in itself, a problem, but certain problems arise from the way in which scientific realism has been adopted in generative phonology. I now seek to show what those problems are.

3.2. *Idealization, E-language, and Universal Grammar*

As is widely acknowledged, in engaging in idealization, one can idealize over (aspects of) specific speakers and arrive at the notions (say) 'New York English' and 'Tyneside English', and one can idealize over the two idealizations, and many others, to arrive at an idealized object '(contemporary) English'. One can then idealize over 'English' and 'Dutch' and other E-languages (assuming that one can reasonably say that such things exist); ultimately, one can idealize over all such E-languages and E-language groupings to arrive at an idealized notion 'E-language'. But that object cannot be UG, since E-languages are sociopolitical objects, not natural objects (see Section 5 for more discussion of the distinction between natural and non-natural objects), whereas UG is not: it is a natural object, identical in all members of the species, not subject to variation. As noted above, one cannot idealize over a set of objects that belong to one ontological category (in this case, sociopolitical objects) and thus arrive at an idealized object of a distinct category (in this case, UG, a natural object). The question therefore remains of what the relation might be between, on the one hand, E-languages (which are clearly the locus of sociophonetic variation) and, on the other hand, UG. I address this issue in Sections 4 and 5 below.

3.3. *Weak realism, strong realism, and derivationality*

There is another problem with the application of scientific realism within generative phonology. In order to explain what I take this problem to be, let us first note that Chomsky's understanding of a realist interpretation of theoretical constructs in linguistic enquiry varies between what I will call 'weak' and 'strong' realism. Consider the following quotation:

'Tentatively, accepting this explanation, we impute existence to certain mental representations and to the mental computations that apply in a specific way to these mental representations. In particular, we impute existence to a representation in which (12) [[S which for PRO to play sonatas on *t*]] appears as part of the structure underlying (5)

[What violins are sonatas easy to play on?] at a particular stage of derivation, and ultimately produces (5), identified now as ungrammatical because the computation violates the *wh*-island constraint when the rule of *wh*-movement applies to *sonatas* in (12). We attribute psychological reality to the postulated representations and mental computations. In short, we propose ... that our theory is true.'   (Chomsky 1980: 196–7)

Here, Chomsky appears to claim that the linguist's theoretical constructs are to be interpreted as claims about real, online processing of stored mental representations (since it is not clear that such talk of mental computations over mental representations could be about anything *other* than online processing in real time). This is what I will refer to as strong realism. On the other hand, there has been another tradition within generative practice in which talk of rules 'applying', 'having outputs', 'having (or failing to have) an effect', and 'applying one before the other', and talk of 'movement' in syntax are said to be 'purely metaphorical' talk, not intended to be interpreted literally (since one is not giving an account of any kind of mental process):

A generative grammar is not a model for a speaker or a hearer. It attempts to characterize in the most neutral terms the knowledge of the language that provides the basis for actual use of language by a speaker-hearer. No doubt, a reasonable model of language use will incorporate, as a basic component, the generative grammar that expresses the speaker-hearer's knowledge of the language; but this generative grammar does not, in itself, prescribe the character or functioning of a perceptual model or a model of speech production.   (Chomsky 1965: 9)

This position is one in which 'rules-as-processes' are interpreted in a weakly realist, 'purely metaphorical' manner. The least one can say about such metaphors, following Biggs (1987), is that they are unhelpful and misleading if one is not claiming to be describing actual mental processes. But there is a more deep-seated, conceptual, problem here, more grave than a mere unfortunate choice of metaphors: generative phonologists, following Chomsky, do indeed conceive of the object of phonological enquiry in terms of real-time processing of stored mental representations, while often at the same time, and again following Chomsky, denying that they do so. For instance, much of the 'abstractness' debate over *The Sound Pattern of English* (*SPE*) phonology was conducted almost entirely, by both critics and defenders of analyses involving absolute neutralization, on the assumption that the argument was about actual, real-time mental storage and processing. Critics of abstractness in *SPE* phonology, such as Lass (1984) and Hooper (1976), made this assumption; Lass questioned (with considerable justification) whether there was any justification for the claim that human beings prefer mental processing to mental storage. Dresher (1981), in a robust defence of abstractness in *SPE*, made exactly the same assumption, arguing that human beings are, after all, rather good at performing a series of mental operations one after the other. My point here is not to engage with the abstractness debate *per se*, but to emphasize that both sides were interpreting phonological rules and representations in dynamic terms, arguing about real-time mental processing and storage, despite the fact that strong disclaimers had been widely issued to the effect that rules and representations ought not to be interpreted in that way.

There were several reasons why a dynamic interpretation of rules was said to be mistaken, and they mostly clustered around the notion 'derivationality'. In syntax, the derivational theory of processing complexity had been shown to be falsified by the available psycholinguistic evidence. The response was not to abandon derivationality, but to withdraw to the 'indirect characterization of a cognitive state' position (weak realism), articulated by Chomsky as above. In *SPE* phonology, any strong realism was anyway impossible, since, in a rule-based derivational model, there would inevitably be representations intermediate in status between underlying and 'surface' representation, and it was vital that those intermediate representations not be accorded a realist interpretation, since, as in the derivational theory of syntactic processing complexity, it was not totally plausible that they, as it were, came into momentary being when a stored mental object was retrieved and processed.

This retreat from a realist interpretation of intermediate representations sits uneasily with a strongly realist interpretation of underlying representations as mental representations actually stored, retrieved, and mentally processed by specific individual speakers in real time, and an equally strong realist interpretation of surface representations as a species of mental representation actually 'produced' in real time as a result of the processing of underlying representations. If the former and the latter were to be given a strong realist interpretation, then so too must the intermediate representations. But they could not be. Thus the dilemma. Generative phonologists, therefore, had to retreat to weak realism, while at the same time speaking as if they were committed to a much stronger realism.

None of these problems has been resolved, or has been made irrelevant, since the heyday of the abstractness debate. Indeed, strong realism is currently explicitly adopted by Bromberger and Halle (1989, this volume), who take the phonologist's derivations to represent sequences of mental events that take place in real time, so that intermediate levels of representation are to be interpreted realistically as corresponding to real mental events. On this view, derivations are real events that eventuate in the production of utterance events. Again, there appeared to be, and there still appears to be, inconsistency within generative phonology as to how one should interpret the status of the phonologist's analysis, a discrepancy between what generative phonologists profess to be doing and what they are in fact doing.

With the advent of Optimality Theory (OT), the problem of the status of intermediate levels of representation is obviated to the extent that no such levels are appealed to. However, if any appeal to level ordering, cyclicity, or rules applying outside the system of constraints is made, then the underlying rationale of OT is abandoned, as has been pointed out by Halle and Idsardi (1997), and the problem of the status of intermediate levels of representation resurfaces. But weak realism remains the only version of realism available in OT, since it is presumably not the case that, in online retrieval and processing, every possible 'output' generated by Gen is actually assessed, in real time, for its optimality (this possibility being presumably even less plausible in terms of psychological reality than the derivations in *SPE*-type phonologies).

I have outlined two problems with respect to the adoption of scientific realism in phonology. First, the relation between E-languages and UG cannot be one of idealization. The question then remains of what that relation might be; I attempt an answer to that question in Sections 4 and 5 below. Secondly, generative phonology is inconsistent as between weakly and strongly realist interpretations of its theoretical constructs. I suggest that a resolution of this problem resides either in the adoption of a consistently weak realism, or in an attempted move towards a strong version of realism in phonology, in which any talk of phonological processes is intended as a direct characterization of actual, online processing in real time. It seems to me that certain developments in variationist and laboratory phonology, to which I turn shortly, offer some hope of a strongly realist interpretation of at least some theoretical constructs in phonological theory. However, as we will see, there are problems with the conceptual and empirical foundations of variationist approaches to phonological phenomena, and these then extend to Laboratory Phonology, which (rightly) puts variation at the heart of phonological enquiry.

3.4. *Variation and 'theory-led' versus 'data-led' approaches to phonology*

First, however, I outline a further problem regarding the putative scientific status of generative phonology, pointed out by variationists such as Docherty *et al.* (1997). It concerns the status of the material that generative phonologists typically present as representations of their data—namely, sets of IPA symbols enclosed in square ('phonetic') brackets, such as [fɪʔtɐ] ('fitter') *vs* [fɪɹɐ] ('fit her'), said by Carr (1991) to be pronunciations representative of the speech of Tyneside English speakers. One of the main claims made in that paper is that the glottalized realizations of /t/ are in complementary distribution with those (such as [ɹ]) that result from the application of the 'T-to-R rule'. But one is entitled to ask what the status of such data is. They are typically not presented, in generative work, as phonetic transcriptions of specific, spatiotemporally unique utterances. Instead, they are generally taken to be representative in some way of the speech of the members of certain speech communities (as they are in this case). Docherty *et al.* rightly object that, in much work in generative phonology, such data are not collected by means of sociolinguistically sensitive data collection techniques, and thus may fail adequately to represent the actual speech of the members of the communities in question. By contrast, their own approach does use such techniques, and, in the case of the two Tyneside English variants in question, reveals a quite distinct picture of their occurrence. Specifically, their research reveals the following:

(*a*) There are cases where Glottalization *does* apply foot initially (Carr's analysis claims that it never occurs in this position).

(*b*) There are cases where it applies *instead of* the 'T-to-R', rule—i.e. there is intra- and inter-speaker variation, with, e.g. [ʔt] ([ʔ]ʔ[7]) in *got a nice jacket* but [ɹ] in *got a little bow*.

(*c*) Word-list data do not exhibit the patterns suggested by Carr (1991), which are more appropriate, but still not accurate, for conversational data.

(*d*) There appears to be a 'lexical conditioning factor' for the occurrence of the [ɹ] realization (although, as Docherty *et al.* point out, this was already suggested by Carr (1991), and was one of the main points of that paper).

(*e*) Sentence stress is possibly also a factor governing the application of Glottalization and the 'T-to-R' rule, with 'T-to-'R' more likely to occur when the main phrasal prominence is not located on the syllable where the /t/ is the rhymal consonant. Thus 'T-to-R' is more likely in *get 'up* than in *'fit her.*[8]

(*f*) 'T-to-R' has a much more restricted social distribution than Glottalization.

(*g*) Glottalization is blocked in utterance-final ('and other pre-pausal')[9] positions.

(*h*) In Tyneside English, Glottalling and Glottalization, viewed from a sociolinguistic perspective, cannot easily be placed on a lenition scale, with Glottalling as the most lenited form. Thus Tyneside speakers might not be said to be implementing a process of 'lenition'. (Note that this observation does not undermine the general idea: Tyneside speakers may have borrowed a product of a lenition process.)

(*i*) It is necessary to distinguish between the [ɾ] and [ɹ] realizations, rather than categorize them together, as Carr (1991) does, since [ɹ] is favoured by working-class females, particularly those in the older group, but is rare in younger middle class speakers. The [ɾ] realization is more widely distributed socially.

Most of these points provide new and interesting data, and falsify the claim

---

[7] It is not clear from Docherty *et al.* (1997) whether the variants in question are [ʔ] or [ʔt]. They at times (pp. 291–4) distinguish glottal from glottalized variants, but at other points (pp. 291–4) do not. It is crucial to the claim being made that we know whether the data from Hartley (1992) cited by Docherty *et al.* show glottal or glottal*ized* variants: on the one hand, data from Hartley (1992) are said to show 'glottalized' variants (p. 291), while those same variants are described on the same page as 'glottal'. I make it quite clear in Carr (1991) that I am discussing glottal*ized* realizations, rather than glottal ones. If Hartley's data show glottal variants, they do *not* show, *pace* Docherty *et al.*, the application of glottalization, as discussed by me, although they are none the less problematic for my analysis.

[8] It is moot which syllable the /t/ occurs in here. If 'T-to-R' does indeed apply postlexically, then it is arguably in the second syllable, so the 'descriptive point' needs to be reformulated. This is a clear case of the relevance of 'theoretical' concerns for 'descriptive' claims.

[9] It is not clear that pre-pausal position can be anything other than utterance-final, if a spoken utterance is a stretch of uninterrupted speech. Some other definition of 'utterance' may be intended, but, if so, its definition is not offered by Docherty *et al.*

made by Carr (1991) that the glottalized realizations and 'R' realizations are in complementary distribution.

The main methodological point made by Docherty *et al.* is a fair, and important, one: adoption of sociolinguistic methodology in phonology is likely to allow a more strongly realist interpretation of phonological analyses qua analyses of aspects of E-languages (rather than UG: as we have seen, E-languages are the locus of variation; UG is invariant by definition).

But Docherty *et al.* (1997) also object that the kind of work they criticize is 'theory led', rather than 'data led', the implication being that 'theory-led' work is of more doubtful empirical (and thus scientific) status than 'data-led' work. The proposed distinction between 'theory-led' and 'data-led' work does not seem to be sustainable, precisely since, as noted above, all worthwhile scientific investigation must be simultaneously 'theory led' and 'data led'. Any attempt to apply Docherty *et al.*'s distinction seems to run into immediate difficulties. Consider the paper by Paradis and La Charité (1997), published in the same volume of the *Journal of Linguistics*. It is based on the Theory of Constraints and Repair Strategies. That would appear to indicate that it is 'theory led', in Docherty *et al.*'s terms. On the other hand, it is also based on a corpus of loanword pronunciations, which would seem to suggest that it is 'data led'. Examples of work such as this abound in the phonological literature, and little of it seems clearly (or insightfully) characterizable in terms of the proposed 'theory-led' versus 'data-led' dichotomy.

One might, of course, argue that the distinction concerns the *extent* of the role played by theory as opposed to data in a given piece of work, but there appears to be no way of assessing this, and it is unclear what would be gained if one could engage in such an assessment. The distinction therefore seems to have no obvious practical application or conceptual use, and anyway appears to be based on a conception of science that is unsustainable. Oddly, Docherty *et al.* themselves acknowledge that there is no such thing as theory-free observation, an acknowledgement that sits uncomfortably with their proposed distinction. Further, the issue for Docherty *et al.* is surely not whether phonological investigation should be 'theory led' or 'data led', but whether the theory in question should be autonomist or variationist; this, in turn, will determine what is to count as reliable and relevant data for the theory in question.

Whatever tension Docherty *et al.* are referring to (and there clearly is some sort of tension), it is not helpful or perhaps even accurate to describe it in terms of 'theory' versus 'data'. Rather, the question in phonological theory that Docherty *et al.* are (or should be) raising is whether the data that they (phonetically sensitive variationists) are considering are in fact the data upon which 'theory-led' phonological theories (regarded as theories of specifically linguistic objects) are based. The worry is that the things regarded as data by variationists do seem to be regarded as data not for a specifically linguistic theory, but for a theory in another domain. The tension boils down to the questions 'What is phonological theory a theory of?' and 'Is phonological theory part of a specifically linguistic theory?' I offer answers to these questions in Sections 4 and 5 below.

It seems to me that the variationist case against autonomous phonology would be strengthened were the proposed distinction between 'theory-led' and 'data-led' approaches abandoned. Additionally, the distinction between autonomous and variationist phonology is surely not characterizable as one between a methodology based on systematically collected data in the latter case and non-systematic data in the former case, as Docherty *et al.* suggest: *all* phonological data are necessarily systematically selected. What is at issue is the methodological and conceptual basis of the selection applied in the collection of data; that is where the strength of the variationist case lies.

When I argue that all phonological data is necessarily systematically selected, I have in mind the following sorts of features of phonological analysis. The data presented by Carr (1991) are systematically selected according to whether the relevant segment occurs morpheme-internally, across word-internal morpheme boundary, or across word boundary. They are also selected such that realizations of labial, coronal, and velar voiceless stops are systematically differentiated, and are presented on the basis of three distinct environments: V-V, VN-V, and VL-V. This kind of systematicity may be combined with quantitative systematicity. An example of this is the paper by Paradis and LaCharité (1997) referred to above. There, Fula pronunciations of French words are systematically presented on the basis of, for instance, word-initial consonant-plus-liquid vs. consonant-plus-glide branching onsets, while quantitative analysis is also given of numbers of adaptations and non-adaptations in Fula loanword pronunciations. Such systematicity is surely a sine qua non of phonological analysis.

Acceptance of the variationist objection to the sorts of data typically used in generative phonology, and thus of the importance of variationist studies, need not lead us to conclude that variationist phonology is not also open to worries about its scientific status. It is arguable that variationist linguists, just as much as generative linguists, seek scientific status. Evidence of the underlying concern felt among sociolinguists about the scientific status of their discipline comes from some of their uses of terminology. For instance, the expression 'second-order network contact', commonly appealed to by sociolinguists, and borrowed from social theory, corresponds exactly to the ordinary, everyday phrase 'friend of a friend': it contains no more conceptual content than the latter phrase. If we define 'jargon' as specialized terminology that does no more than recapitulate everyday terminology, then this use of terminology is properly described as mere jargon. Interestingly, this kind of usage stands in stark contrast to much of the terminology used in autonomous linguistics, such as, say, 'clausal complement to a transitive verb', which has no counterpart in everyday speech, precisely because social network membership is directly accessible to conscious awareness, and thus everyday discourse, whereas almost all of syntactic, semantic, phonological, and morphological structure is not.

The question arises why such terminology is used at all in social theory (and thus in sociolinguistics), since it serves no scientific purpose. The answer to that question seems clear: it serves the purpose of making the discipline appear objectively scientific in status, and thus divorced from ordinary everyday discourse about the world. But therein lies a paradox for the sociolinguist. On the one hand, there is a desire, on the part of social theorists and sociolinguists, to belong to a properly scientific discipline, whose discourse is, of necessity, distinct from the realm of everyday discourse. On the other hand, there is a desire to regard sociolinguistic enquiry as somehow more connected to everyday reality than autonomous linguistics. My point here is not just that this constitutes a major source of intellectual unease for the sociolinguist, and for the social theorist, but that, if sociolinguistics is to turn to any discipline for scientific respectability, social theory is about the last place to look. It is, however, a field that sociolinguists *must* turn to.

Variationist phonology exhibits this problem. It must appeal to notions such as social-class membership as a theoretical construct, but the scientific status of the notion 'social class' is even more open to question than the notions (such as 'syllable' or 'foot') appealed to in autonomous phonology. Consider the statement that speaker X is middle class. Is this an observation statement? Apparently not, since it is not difficult to conceive of the claim being debated by X's acquaintances. Is it a falsifiable hypothesis? If so, what data would count as counter-evidence to it? I do not argue that there are no such data, and my objection here is not to the necessary idealization involved in speaking of social-class membership (or indeed of 'Tyneside English' or 'Parisian French'); what I do suggest is that it is at least arguable that there is no very clear-cut sense of relevant counter-evidence, and that this is worrying, given a Popperian conception of science, especially since such statements appear to have to serve as observation statements in variationist work. Note too that there is no guarantee that the notion 'middle class' means the same thing when applied to sociophonetic variation in Tyneside English, as opposed to, say, Midi French (Armstrong and Unsworth 1998).

An additional worry stems from the fact that any discussion of social-class membership must entail appeal to the notion of personal identity: whether a given speaker is to be viewed as middle class will depend partly on how the speaker views himself or herself. But the notion 'personal identity' is a concept whose scientific status is, to say the least, open to question. The same remarks apply to categories such as age (Is a given 35-year-old individual middle aged or not? What kind of scientist could tell us? A sociolinguist?) and sex/gender (Is my gay, cross-dressing friend male or female? What *scientist* might one ask?), and, since these three categories are central to the sociolinguistic enterprise, it seems clear that some of the central concepts in that enterprise are problematic as far as their scientific status is concerned. The same remarks apply to the terms 'older' and 'younger', as used by variationists (such as Docherty *et al.*). If the scientific status of autonomous phonology may be called into question, the same is true, *a fortiori*, of sociolinguistics, and thus of variationist approaches to phonological phenomena. Paradoxically, then, autonomous phonology is, in one sense, the best contender for a phonology as a properly scientific discipline. But, as we have seen, a fully autonomous phonology is unsustainable, since the data to be accounted for cannot be divorced from social context and are inherently variable.

Variationist work also appears to lack any interest in a coherently worked-out set of assumptions about the nature of human cognition or the place of language within it. This is surely unsatisfactory in a discipline that stresses the importance of studying real speakers in real societies, since such speakers *must* be possessed of mind-internal representations that constitute their sociophonological knowledge. The risk run by a sociolinguistics that is divorced from mentalism was well put by Fodor in another context: 'If, then, the notion of internal representation is not coherent, the only thing left for a linguistic theory to be true of is the linguist's observations ... Take the notion of internal representation away from linguistic metatheory and you get positivism by subtraction' (Fodor 1981*b*: 202). The same point is surely true of any sociolinguistic theory. And a positivist approach to scientific enquiry has been justly discredited for over half a century.

Some of the problems with variationism appear to be inherited by lab phonologists, who convincingly point out (see Pierrehumbert *et al.*, this volume) that mind-internal phonological abstractions are made necessary by the existence of variations in the input to which the child is exposed, and that variability facilitates, rather than impedes, the process of phonological acquisition. My point here is that the sorts of variation discussed by Pierrehumbert *et al.* must include socially determined variants, and that the problem of the scientific status of social theory must therefore be faced by laboratory phonologists. It is not at all clear that hypotheses in social theory can be tested by the experimental methods rightly advocated by laboratory phonologists; at any rate, a case needs to be made that they can. The question is not whether the data collected by sociolinguistically sensitive methods are subject to laboratory testing (they are, of course), but whether predicates such as 'is middle class' can be thus tested. To the extent that they cannot, variationist phonology is not Laboratory Phonology.

To sum up thus far, I have suggested that variationist and Laboratory Phonology approaches to phonology have much to offer in expanding our understanding of the phonetic (articulatory, acoustic) properties of speakers' speech behaviour and its products. The question is what bearing this has on phonology. And that in turn depends on what we take phonological theory to be a theory of. If phonological theory is a part of specifically linguistic theory as conceived of by Chomsky, then perhaps such approaches have little to offer linguistic theory, thus conceived. Conversely, if Laboratory Phonology and variationism have much to offer phonological theory (which, I suggest, they do: they are our best hope of strong realism in phonology), but not linguistic theory, then the question again is 'What is phonological theory a theory of?'. An equally urgent question is: how does phonological theory relate to linguistic theory (thus conceived)? I attempt to answer those questions in Sections 4 and 5.

Both Laboratory Phonology and variationist approaches appear to lack an overarching conception of the nature of human language that includes a theory of syntactic and semantic knowledge. No one has yet shown, to the best of my knowledge, how laboratory phonology might become laboratory linguistics, containing experimentally testable hypotheses about the full range of syntactic and semantic phenomena. Additionally, as we have seen, variationist linguistics appears to lack any coherent set of assumptions about cognitive states, despite the fact that these must be implicated in any account of the phonological knowledge possessed by speaker-hearers. Generative phonology, on the other hand, does appear to be embedded within a set of assumptions that constitute a serious attempt (however flawed or inconsistent) at an overarching conception of the nature of human language and human cognitive structure, and generative linguistics does seriously set out to offer a set of theories of the nature of the relation between phonological, syntactic, and semantic knowledge. But generative phonology often fails to take sufficient account (or any account at all) of the sorts of data that are central to work in variationist and Laboratory Phonology. What the discipline of phonology requires, I suggest, is an approach that combines the advantages of the two perspectives, while overcoming their respective short-comings, an approach that places variation and laboratory work at the heart of phonological enquiry, but at the same time rests on a properly articulated overall conception of the nature of human language, human cognition, and the structure of human languages.

In what follows, I try to sketch the conceptual foundations of such an approach. I begin with a discussion of the Empiricist tradition in philosophy and psychology, and its relevance for work on the acquisition (and thus the status and nature) of phonological knowledge. What I will be proposing is a sketch of a philosophy of phonology that combines an Empiricist approach to phonological knowledge with the Rationalist notion of UG.

4. EMPIRICISM AND THE ACQUISITION OF PHONOLOGY

4.1. *Rationalism, Empiricism, and innate endowments*

Although they are sometimes equated, I will distinguish here between Nativism in general and Rationalism in particular. Recall that Nativism can be defined entirely in terms of innately endowed perceptual capacities. Rationalism is a specific version of Nativism, which involves postulating an encapsulated, specifically linguistic, species-specific innate endowment (UG), distinct in kind from innately endowed perceptual capacities and general cognitive capacities. I am thus allowing for a Non-Rationalist Nativism, which may form a part of an Empiricist approach to the acquisition of phonology.

Empiricists need not (indeed *cannot*) deny that humans possess innately endowed mental capacities, such as perceptual capacities, the capacity for mimicry, the capacity to categorize, and the capacity to form inductive generalizations on the basis of abstraction. For instance, Locke's 'blank sheet' 'is meant to indicate that the understanding (and hence the mind) is originally empty of objects of thought, such as ideas; but it has whatever apparatus is necessary to acquire them, and then to derive knowledge by comparing and contrasting them with each other' (Harris 1977: 27). It seems clear that Hume too (1748/1962: 53) was presupposing certain innately endowed capacities, such as the capacity to form inductive generalizations, and to connect two events in terms of the cause–effect relation (see Russell 1961 for this kind of reading of Hume).

Nor need Empiricists claim that the organism has a purely passive, Lamarckian role in acquiring knowledge; Piaget, and the work of present-day neo-Piagetians (e.g. Elman *et al*. 1998), both allow for complex interactions between organism and environment in the acquisition of knowledge. So too does the work of experimental biologist Steven Rose (1993, 1997). Earlier work in the Empiricist tradition, in the seventeenth and eighteenth centuries (Locke and Hume) and more recently (in the late twentieth century) shows that early twentieth-century Empiricism, such as the work of Skinner (1957), is the exception in the Empiricist tradition in attributing a largely passive role to the organism in the acquisition of knowledge, and in adopting an anti-mentalist outlook.

Empiricism need not be anti-mentalist, and has, generally speaking, not been such. Indeed, one can hardly conceive of Locke and Hume as anti-mentalists: their concern was, after all, with the nature of human knowledge, and thus mind. But this is not to say that there is no distinction to be made between Rationalist and Empiricist approaches to the mind in general, and 'language' in particular. Work in the Empiricist tradition typically emphasizes the role of inductive generalization as a means of arriving at human knowledge. It also emphazises sensory input as the basis for knowledge (Locke, Hume). The Empiricist dictum (cited by Fodor 1981*b*) that 'nothing is in the mind which was not first in the senses' has both a phylogenetic and an ontogenetic interpretation. If one allows that some of what is in our minds at (or before) birth was in our biological ancestors' senses, one gets (phylogenetic) innate endowment. The Empiricist need not be committed to the ontogenetic interpretation—that is, to the claim that everything that is in the mind of the individual member of a species gets to be there solely through the sensory input that the individual experiences (*cf*. in this respect, more sophisticated versions of Empiricism with respect to phonology, such as Locke 1993). Additionally, Empiricism can accommodate innate endowments that are general, and not domain specific; again, see the work of Piaget (Piatelli-Palmarini 1980; Boden 1994) and the connectionist neo-Piagetians (Elman *et al*. 1998).

It is normal practice to distinguish between at least two sorts of specificity with respect to innately-endowed capacities (*cf*. Plotkin 1997; Elman *et al*. 1998): species specificity and domain specificity. While Rationalists postulate UG as an innately endowed cognitive capacity that is both species specific and specifically linguistic,

Empiricists typically claim that the phenomena that UG is said to explain can be explained by appeal to innate capacities that are general, in one or both senses. Examples are the capacity (*a*) for inductive generalization (involving abstraction/idealization), (*b*) for internalization from the environment, (*c*) for categorization, and (*d*) for mimicry.

It is important to note that, if UG is conceived of as innately endowed disposition to behave, that is arguably an Empiricist conception of UG. It is also, I suggest, a *vacuous* conception of UG, in which 'G' is so general as to be void of content. It is true that one can speak reasonably of, for instance, 'the grammar of the genes', 'the grammar of vision', or 'the grammar of architectural objects'. But the term 'grammar' here merely means 'structure' (it is an awareness of this fact that induces the use of scare quotes whenever linguists speak of, for instance, the 'grammar of vision': see Hale and Reiss, this volume). If the 'G' in 'UG' is to have any real content, it must mean something much more specific than this. It must be used to refer to an encapsulated, specifically linguistic endowment, distinct in kind from perceptual, general cognitive, and behavioural capacities. If the word 'grammar' in 'UG' is taken to subsume such capacities, then that amounts to an abandonment of Rationalism with respect to linguistic knowledge. There is only one sustainable conception of UG, one that takes it to be *radically internal*, in the sense that it is an innate endowment that does not consist of perceptual capacities, behavioural dispositions, general cognitive capacities, or capacities that are not species specific. It follows that UG cannot coherently be conceived of in terms of (innately endowed) disposition to behave, and that UG is not, *pace* Pinker (1994), an instinct (or a set of instincts), parallel to the innately endowed web-spinning capacity of (certain species of) spiders. It is an awareness of this requirement for radical internalism that leads Chomsky, one suspects, to say that the innermost part of 'I-language' is an encapsulated module of mind, distinct from both behaviour and perceptual systems.[10]

Note that weak internalism (in contrast to what I am calling radical internalism) allows for internal states that are arrived at by means of internal*ization* from sensory input from the environment. Memories are an example, and an important one, since, in possessing a lexicon, one presumably is in possession of a species of memory (this is to simplify radically; I appreciate that there are important distinctions to be made between distinct kinds of 'memory'; cf. Rose (1993); I will use the term 'images' below). The important point here is that weak internalism is compatible with Empiricism, and, if one's mentally stored phonological representations get there *via* a process of internalization, that is compatible with Empiricism.

---

[10] I lack the space to discuss in any detail Chomsky's notion 'I-language'. See Carr (1997), Burton-Roberts and Carr (1999), and Burton-Roberts (this volume) for more detail.

4.2. *Innate endowments, Universal Grammars, and the acquisition of a phonology*

Bearing in mind these general remarks about the Empiricist and Rationalist traditions, I now want to suggest that an Empiricist approach to the acquisition of phonology looks highly plausible. I will assume, without argument (owing to lack of space), and *contra* van der Hulst (this volume), that sign languages *do not* have a phonology (or have something other than a phonology). I will also assume that phonetics and phonology are closely intertwined—that is, that phonology is substance based, *pace* Hale and Reiss (this volume). I make this assumption since I take it that the onus is on proponents of a substance-free phonology to show what such a phonology would look like. I argue below that Hale and Reiss have not succeeded in doing so. Given these assumptions, it seems clear that some innate capacities have a facilitating function, but are not crucial to the acquisition of a phonology. These include the human/primate face-recognition capacity (Goren *et al.* 1975), for which there are parallels for this in other species—for example, chickens, ducks, and monkeys.

But other innate capacities that are either not species specific or not specifically linguistic seem *necessary* for the acquisition of a phonology, such as disposition to vocalize, which is not unique to humans, and the vast human capacity for recognition (as opposed to recall) of internalized images, including acoustic images, central to the study of phonological knowledge. These are not specifically linguistic: compare Rose's (1993) discussion of Standing's research on recognition of visual images, which almost certainly extends to mapping of acoustic input to acoustic (subsuming phonological) images. The point here is that most visual images are not linguistic in any sense, so that the vast capacity for rapid recognition is not specifically linguistic. Interestingly, this research included recognition of images of written words, which almost certainly interact with adult phonology. Additionally, the capacity for recognition of acoustic phenomena produced by conspecifics seems necessary for the acquisition of a phonology, and is not species specific. It is present in, for instance, various species of insects, frogs, and songbirds. Even phonetic category recognition, such as the capacity to recognize a given acoustic event as a token of the type 'unaspirated (versus aspirated) stop', is not species specific, since both humans and chinchillas possess it (Kuhl and Miller 1975; Marler and Peters 1981). The capacity for mimicry (Meltzoff and Moore 1977; Meltzoff 1986) also seems crucial if the human child is to acquire a phonology, but it is clearly not a capacity that is restricted to *homo sapiens*. Nor is it restricted, in humans, to mimicry of speech sounds. The acquisition of a phonology could not proceed without the capacity for normalization (for example, the filtering-out of variation in the characteristic pitch of the voices of individuals), but that too is not a species-specific capacity (frogs and crickets normalize calls from conspecifics). While the notion 'critical period' has been appealed to in the Rationalist linguistic literature, critical periods are not unique to *homo sapiens*, and are anyway perceptual/behavioural capacities (compare vision in kittens and native speaker pronunciation capacity in humans).

So the existence of a critical period in phonological acquisition need not imply that it is directed by a specifically *linguistic* module of mind (UG).

It seems clear that the sorts of innate endowment that are necessary for the acquisition of a phonology fail to meet the requirement that they be specific in both senses. They could not, therefore, constitute part of UG, construed in any coherent manner. An account of the acquisition of a phonology can allow for a major role for innate endowments independent of UG, disposition to behave, repetition and habit (speech habits). None of this undermines the case for UG. The claim that phonological acquisition involves general (not specifically linguistic) innate endowments undermines the case for UG only if it is insisted that phonology is an essential component of UG. But, if phonology can be allowed to fall outside UG, the claim—far from undermining the case for UG—actually results in a more robust (that is, more plausibly innate, radically internal, encapsulated) conception of UG. I suggest here, following Burton-Roberts and Carr (1999), that phonological knowledge does indeed fall outside UG, and that an account is required of the relation of phonology to UG that does not undermine the case for UG (see Section 5 below, and Burton-Roberts, this volume).

One of Chomsky's problems in this connection is, I suggest, that he likens UG to 'an organ', and sets up an analogy between blueprint innate endowments and UG, such that UG 'develops', under triggering from environmental input, into language-specific knowledge. An example of such an analogy, suggested by Chomsky (1965), concerns depth perception in lambs, the principle point being that, while visual input is vital to such development, it has a *facilitating* (triggering) function, rather than *determining* the nature of depth perception. While the distinction between facilitation and determination is a valid and important one, all of these analogies are, it seems to me, damaging to Chomsky's case. They invite the kinds of attack made by Dennett (1995: 388), since (*a*) they often concern perceptual systems, whereas linguistic knowledge is said by Chomsky not to be a kind of perceptual input/output system, and (*b*) organs are functional by definition, whereas Chomsky insists that the initial state is not functionally oriented. What is required is an account of UG as an innate endowment according to which it is not like behavioural or perceptual endowments, of the sort that develop under triggering, and which excludes phonology. On that (more robust) conception, UG is an innate endowment that does not undergo development. Rather, what develops is our epistemic access to UG (for a little more detail on this issue, see Burton-Roberts and Carr 1999).

4.3. *Putative syntax–phonology parallelisms*

Against this, it might be argued that, even if all of these non-UG endowments are brought to bear on the acquisition of a phonology, there is *also, in addition, a set of specifically phonological* constraints, and/or principles and/or parameters that *does* fulfil the criteria for inclusion in a coherently conceived of UG. Possible candidates might be certain OT constraints or Government Phonology principles and parameters, or other parallelisms between syntactic and phonological structure. However, if any of these make crucial reference to universals of physiology and/or acoustic events and/or human sensory perception, or events and objects in general, they are not good candidates for inclusion in UG (since this is the wrong sort of universality: it is not specifically linguistic, and might not be species specific). I now seek to show that they do make reference to such non-linguistic universals.

I begin with one such postulated parallelism between phonological and syntactic structure: Pierrehumbert's (1990) claim that phrase and syllable structure are parallel, in that both can be represented by means of 'rewrite rules' of the form: S→ NP + VP and, it is claimed, Syllable → Onset + Rhyme. Van der Hulst (this volume) similarly claims that both syntactic phrases and phonological objects possess the property of compositionality. But the parallelism amounts to nothing more than the parallelism between any two (or more) objects or events that have internal structure (that is, almost all objects and events). Consider: Spectacles → lenses + frame, or Kir Royal → champagne + crème de cassis. The notation '→' here means only 'consists of'. True, this is a parallelism, but one that is of no particular scientific interest, since complex objects and events have subparts by definition. It is unsurprising, therefore, that the hand signs used in sign language can be viewed as consisting of component parts. The term 'compositionality' is apparently not intended by van der Hulst to convey anything more significant than 'has component parts'. For instance, if the semantic notion of compositionality were to be intended, the parallelism would fall apart, since phonological objects do not have a semantics. What *is* of scientific interest here is what *distinguishes* syntactic phrases and syllables. One such difference is striking, and of some interest: syntactic phrases possess the property of *recursion* (S within S within S, *ad infinitum*; NP within NP within NP *ad infinitum*, and so on), as van der Hulst (this volume) concedes, whereas syllables do not: there is no such thing as a syllable within a syllable, an onset within an onset, or a rhyme within a rhyme.

It has also been suggested that phonological knowledge is organized in terms of the relation of government (the head-dependent relation). The relation of government is a good candidate for inclusion in UG since there is no obvious sense in which mind-external objects could be said to contract that (apparently purely syntactic) relation, and nor is it a behavioural or a perceptual relation: when one says that two syntactic objects contract a relation of government, it seems reasonable to say that this is a strictly linguistic relation that is 'austere' in the sense intended by Chomsky (1993). However, it seems to me that attempts to show that the purely syntactic relation of government holds in phonology have not been successful. Two main interpretations of the government relation occur in the phonological literature.

One interpretation takes two phonological objects (elements of segmental structure, for instance, or syllabic nuclei) to be perceptually more salient than another (for example, coda consonants), the former being referred to as the head or governor, and the latter as the dependent. This tradition can be seen in work on Dependency Phonology (Anderson and Ewen 1987), Government Phonology (Kaye *et al.* 1985, 1990) and in Radical CV Phonology[11] (van der Hulst 1994, this volume). But there are two reasons why this interpretation of headhood precludes its inclusion in UG.

First, it is often offered as an interpretation that concerns sensory perception. For instance, the acoustic effect of palatality may be said to be more salient than the effect of lowness in a high-mid vowel, and vice versa in a low-mid vowel, and the 'head' nucleus of a foot may be said to be perceptually more salient than the other nuclei in the foot. It is thus inappropriate for inclusion in UG because it is a perceptual relation. And the parallelism fails since the notion 'head' in syntax is quite different from this: it does not make any reference to salience, let alone *perceptual* salience.

Secondly, the relation 'perceptually more salient than' is general–cognitive: it is the figure–ground relation. That relation cannot be said to constitute part of UG, since UG, by definition, excludes general cognitive capacities. One could, of course, argue that perceptual prominence and 'semantic prominence' could be subsumed under a more general category of cognitive salience. But, in doing so, one is, again, emptying the notion UG of any content if it is to be said to subsume anything as general as this.

Another tradition, also seen in work on Government Phonology, seeks to define the government relation formally, in terms of, for instance, universally defined, strictly syntactic, relations between skeletal slots. But all of the phenomena (for example, lenition phenomena) that this approach seeks to explicate anyway have other-non-government explanations, in terms of, for instance, perceptual salience and ease of articulation. More tellingly, the putative government relations postulated are strikingly unlike government relations in syntax, in that the former can be given independent semantic and distributional justification, whereas the latter lack any such independent justification. Complements of verbs, for instance, considered as syntactic objects that are governed by their verbs, are said to be obligatorily present, and are said to stand in a stateable semantic relation to the verbs that are said to govern them. Contrast this relation of government in syntax with the government relation postulated in Government Phonology, where it is said that the skeletal slot occurring to the right of a nucleus (what is elsewhere referred to as the coda slot) is governed by the nuclear slot. The independent semantic and distributional evidence that justifies this kind of claim in syntax is simply absent in the case of the nucleus–coda relation. There is no semantic relation between the two slots, and there is no sense in which the 'governed' element is obligatorily present (a nucleus cannot be said to demand the presence of a coda in any sense). It is, therefore, hardly surprising that the 'governed' slot in question has variously been described as an adjunct and as a complement in the

---

[11] Referred to in later developments as Head-Driven Phonology (see van der Hulst, this volume).

Government Phonology literature. The reason for the variation in terminology is not hard to find: the adjunct/complement distinction, widely attested in syntactic organization, is simply absent in phonological organization, as indeed is the syntactic relation of head/dependent, and the specifier/head relation.[12] Note too that there can be no question of subcategorizing 'heads', such as the 'heads' of metrical feet, according to the 'types of complement' that they take. This is unsurprising if it is acknowledged that the head–complement relation is inapplicable to phonological objects.

It is easy to be misled into thinking that, because one can, in some cases, draw tree diagrams in attempts at representing the structure of syntactic phrases and that of feet and syllables (and even intra-segmental structure), one is therefore depicting parallel (or identical) relations between the elements of structure in question. This, it seems to me, is the motive that drives the observation that syntactic and phonological objects both possess arboreal structure. One can draw tree diagrams to represent the relations between, say, members of a family or the parts of a business organization, but it does not follow from this that the objects in question contract relationships parallel to those contracted by syntactic objects. The same point applies to putative parallelisms between phrase and syllable structure. I conclude that the relation of government is simply inappropriate for understanding the nature and structure of phonological knowledge. This is unsurprising if the government relation is provided by UG and if phonology falls outside of UG.

4.4. *Phonological generalizations as inductive generalizations*

A further argument for an approach to phonological knowledge that excludes it from UG concerns the role played by inductive generalizations over internalized phonological representations. When one asks, for instance, whether children learn word-stress assignment lexically or by rule (Fikkert 1995), one is posing a false dichotomy: the child can memorize stress patterns of particular words and then generalize over what is internalized (inasmuch as there are generalizations to be had). There is no reason why this should not be true for *all* phonological generalizations, including the set of phonological contrasts in a language (Hayes 1999), even if the set of possible contrasts is limited by certain innately endowed capacities. In addition to the roles played by repetition and mimicry, induction also appears to play a major role in the acquisition of phonology, and all of these capacities are consistent with an Empiricist approach to phonological acquisition.

---

[12] It might be argued (Marc Plénat, p.c.) that talk of government in phonology is 'purely metaphorical'. But that is clearly not what is intended either by Pierrehumbert, by Government Phonologists, or in van der Hulst's Head-Driven Phonology: the parallelisms they propose are intended as empirical claims. This is unsurprising: it is hard to see the point in adopting the notion of 'government' relations between phonological objects as a purely metaphorical mode of description when non-metaphorical modes of description are already at hand (e.g. descriptions appealing to the idea of assimilation).

It is hard to resist the conclusion that the phonetic/phonological data which the child is exposed to are *not* impoverished or degenerate in any sense—that is, there is no 'poverty of the (phonological) stimulus', or underdetermination of phonological knowledge. Phonological knowledge is *not* 'knowledge without grounds', as Chomsky has described linguistic knowledge. If anything, the sensory data are *more than complete*: there are, if anything, more data available to the neonate than is strictly required for phonological acquisition. The possession of capacities such as the normalization capacity aids immensely in important filtering out of irrelevant acoustic input. Clearly, specific properties of the ambient language play a role in phonological acquisition (Vihman 1996; Vihman and Velleman, this volume), but it does not follow from that fact that the child is possessed of a phonology-specific innate capacity. However, even if one *could* demonstrate that some of the relevant innate 'phonological' capacities were species specific and phonology specific, that would not count as evidence for UG unless the capacity were non-perceptual and non-behavioural. Note too that the capacities to form inductive and deductive generalizations must be innately endowed, but neither is likely to be either species specific or specifically linguistic.

If these arguments for an Empiricist account of the acquisition of a phonology are well founded, and if Rationalist arguments for a specifically linguistic innate endowment (UG) are well founded, they raise the question of the nature of the relation between phonology and UG. The foregoing discussion implies that the strictly formal relation 'generate' (as opposed to the non-formal relation 'produce') holds directly between UG and an infinite set of linguistic objects, and that there must be a gulf between these objects and a phonology (this is an extension of a claim made by Harris and Lindsay 1995). In that case, the relation between the two *cannot* be one of instantiation (or realization, or manifestation), since realizations of a type must be of the same ontological category as the type itself (see Burton-Roberts and Carr 1999, and Burton-Roberts this volume, for more detailed argumentation). What might the relation be, then? Burton-Roberts (1994; this volume; Burton-Roberts and Carr 1999) suggests it is a relation of *conventional representation*. I turn to this now.

5. ACCOMMODATING UNIVERSAL GRAMMAR AND SOCIOPHONETIC VARIATION

5.1. *Natural versus conventional facts*

In what follows, I will assume that the set of natural facts is a subset of the set of physical facts: not all physical facts are natural facts (tables, and artefacts in general, are physical, but not natural, objects). I also assume that there is a valid distinction to be made between facts of nature and *conventional* facts. In doing so, I will distinguish between two senses of 'natural'. There is a broad sense in which any fact about human beings must be a natural fact. Any species of ant constitutes a part of the natural world, and thus any facts about ants, such as facts about their internal states and social behaviour, are natural facts. By the same token, *homo sapiens* is part of the natural world, and any facts about human beings (such as facts about their internal states and social behaviour) are also natural facts. I will call this species of fact a *broadly* natural fact. However, there is also a valid distinction to be drawn, with respect to (perhaps only to) human beings, between *broadly* natural and *narrowly* natural facts. A human being who abides by the conventions of (some version of) vegetarianism is not thereby a member of a herbivore species: the fact of being a vegetarian is a natural fact in the broad sense (it is a fact about the behaviour of a member of a species in the natural world), but not in the narrow sense. Any narrowly natural fact is also a broadly natural fact, but not vice versa.

This leads us to a distinction between conventional facts and narrowly natural facts. For instance, while it is a natural fact about the present author that his hair is black, it is a conventional fact that his hair has a side parting. By 'conventional fact' here, I mean the following. First, while the presence of a hair parting is a physical fact, it is not a natural fact: hair partings are not part of our genetic endowment, and do not emerge in ontogenetic development in the way that, say, binocular vision does. Secondly, it is a physical fact that comes into being by adherence to some socially constituted convention. The convention, in the society in which this author lives, is something like: men should either not wear a parting, or should wear a single parting in the middle or on either side of the front of the head; multiple partings or partings solely on the back of the head are not conventional for men. The ontology of any social convention governing hair partings appears distinct from the ontology of the partings *per se*. I will, therefore, take conventional facts to be facts that arise from the adherence to conventions of social behaviour. This latter fact about a hair parting is an example of a natural fact in the broad sense, but not in the narrow sense.

It also appears necessary to identify natural facts as a subset of the set of physical facts: as we have seen, not all physical facts are natural facts. Conventional facts are, therefore, part of the natural world in the broad sense, but they are not natural facts in the narrow sense. Henceforth, unless otherwise indicated, I shall be using the word 'natural' in the narrow sense, and contrasting it with 'conventional'. It is an interesting question how conventionality can arise in the course of evolution, but I shall have nothing to say here about that question.

It is as well to emphasize at this point that the distinctions just made do not constitute any sort of metaphysically objectionable dualism, of the sort objected to by Pierrehumbert *et al.* (this volume). Rather, they arise as a matter of conceptual necessity. It is a conceptual error to equate, say, the phenomenon of vegetarianism in humans with herbivore status in other species, just as it is a conceptual error to equate the initial conditions for a solar system with generalizations over the equilibrium states that may evolve from those conditions (Pierrehumbert *et al.*, this volume). Indeed, it seems to me that Pierrehumbert *et al.*'s distinction between the sense in which phonological categories are natural and the sense in which

which they are language specific is an example of the kind of distinction I propose here.

5.2. *The Representational Hypothesis*

I now proceed to a necessarily brief sketch of Burton-Roberts's Representational Hypothesis and its implications for the natural/conventional distinction, and thus for the relation between UG and sociophonetic variation. Burton-Roberts's view is that relevant acoustic events (the acoustic products of speech events), and indeed the visual events that occur during signing, are produced as *implementations of conventions of representation* of the (radically internal) objects generated by UG. Here, 'representation' is to be understood in its ordinary sense as a transitive verb (or two-place predicate), rather than in the specialized Chomskian sense, under which linguistic objects as mental representations are *constituted* as mental representations (not *of* anything, least of all mind-external objects[13]). Burton-Roberts refers to the latter as C-representations (C for Chomsky or constitutive) and the former as M-representations (M for Magritte, after his painting *La Trahison des images*, in which the point is arguably made that a visual representation of a pipe does not constitute an instance of a pipe, does not constitute a token of the type 'pipe').

   One of the main points here is that this conception of the relation between the relevant mind-external acoustic events and the radically internal objects and relations defined by UG is consistent with the gulf between the two that Harris and Lindsey (1995), and indeed Chomsky, insist on. By contrast, the instantiation/ implementation/realization conception is not, since it is a type/token conception, and tokens of types must necessarily belong to the same ontological category as their types. Chomsky himself seemed to have recognized this when he noted that it was hard to see how UG, a natural object, could be instantiated in a cultural object (an E-language):

> what we call 'English', 'French', 'Spanish', and so on, even under idealizations to idiolects in homogeneous speech communities, reflect the Norman Conquest, proximity to Germanic areas, a Basque substratum, and other factors that cannot seriously be regarded as properties of the language faculty. Pursuing the obvious reasoning, it is hard to imagine that the properties of the language faculty—a real object of the natural world—are instantiated in any observed system.'   (Chomsky 1995b: 11)

   Talk of this gulf is not Cartesian dualist talk. For Burton-Roberts, as for Chomsky, mind is physical, and the principal distinctions being made are those between (*a*) radically mind-internal realities (UG and the objects and relations it defines), (*b*) weakly mind-internal realities (for example, acoustic and visual images stored in the mind via a process of internalization from the environment),

---

[13] Chomsky is, in fact, inconsistent in his conception of 'representation'; see Burton-Roberts and Carr (1999: 393) for discussion and exemplification.

and (*c*) mind-external events. Allowing for such distinctions is no more Cartesian dualist than allowing for a distinction between the parts of a bicycle and the functions of those parts. The parts have specifiable spatiotemporal coordinates, while the functions do not (the two are thus distinct from each other), but the functions are none the less part of the physical world.

Reserving the term 'linguistic' for UG and the objects and relations it defines, Burton-Roberts makes the point that neither the relevant mind-external events, nor the relation of representation, are themselves linguistic. (It is important to bear in mind here that it is unimportant what terminological distinction one adopts in order to distinguish between these two sorts of thing; if 'linguistic' versus 'non-linguistic' is objectionable, then some other set of terms will suffice; see Burton-Roberts, this volume, Section 6.5.) Radically-internal linguistic objects, on this view, are, as it were, innocent of the fact of being represented, and are not, therefore, conceived of as instructions to perceptual or articulatory systems, as Chomsky (1995*b*) suggests (see Carr 1998 for further discussion of this point). The main point here is that linguistic objects cannot be radically internal at the same time as being instructions to perceptual and/or sensorimotor systems: if they are like such instructions, they must be weakly internal.

5.3. *Sociophonetic variation and Universal Grammar*

This brings us to the natural/conventional distinction and to the role of norms (conventions) of social behaviour, and thus the relation between sociophonetic variation and UG as a natural object. For Burton-Roberts, a specific, mentally stored, internalized phonological representation is constituted as a convention (a norm), or set of conventions, specifically a convention governing representational behaviour. But that claim does not exclude the claim that there are internal (inductive) generalizations over those conventions that may interact in complex ways, this interaction being the stock in trade of the autonomous phonologist. This allows us to accommodate (*a*) the complex systems of conventions that govern sociophonetic variation with (*b*) UG as an object in the natural world, and with the object of most generative phonological enquiry. Such conventions are norms of social behaviour, and can have simultaneous, multiple, social, and linguistic (representational) functions, as Docherty *et al.* (1997) have pointed out. For instance, variation in the pronunciation of the coronal stop in a word such as *better* among speakers of Tyneside English as, among other things, a glottalized stop or a coronal approximant may involve *both* representational activity *and* the signalling of group membership simultaneously.

This approach reconciles the diversity of individual languages with the uniqueness of UG. Since individual languages (and thus their phonologies[14]) are

---

[14] In fact, individual languages, as conceived of here, as conventional systems of representation, are phonologies, and the notion 'phonology' is thus extended to include any facts about sequentiality, as opposed to syntactic relation. I lack the space to elaborate this point here; see Burton-Roberts (this volume) for a little more detail.

viewed here as conventional systems of representation, those systems, being conventional, will be subject to diversity and variation. UG, on the other hand, is invariant. The sorts of factor that the variationist is concerned with (age, sex, social class membership, solidarity, formality of discourse, and so on) are to be found within such systems of conventions, determining, to some extent, those systems.

Notice that it does not follow from the representational hypothesis *in itself* that linguistic objects, understood in the radically internalist sense, lack a phonology. But if such objects do have a radically internalist phonology, then it must be 'phonology without substance', as proposed by Hale and Reiss (this volume; see also van der Hulst, this volume). However, it seems to me that Hale and Reiss do not succeed in formulating a conception of phonological objects that is genuinely substance free, for the following reasons.

First, for Hale and Reiss, the relation between (*a*) strictly linguistic, 'purely formal' phonological objects and (*b*) phonetic substance is one of transduction. A transducer is an input/output device that takes signals as input and yields signals as output. Examples are the mouthpiece on a telephone (which has sound waves as input and yields electrical signals as output), an eye (which has light waves as input and chemico-electrical signals as output), and a neuron (which has chemico-electrical impulses as both input and output). It is in the nature of transduction that the input and output signals of transducers are inter-transformable: just as acoustic input can be transduced into electrical signals, so can those electrical signals be transduced back into acoustic signals (as is the case with the earpiece in a telephone). This means that the input and the output of a transducer are intimately connected, and that they stand in a non-arbitrary relation to each other: the properties of the output depend crucially on properties of the input. It therefore appears that, in adopting the transduction conception of the relation between phonetic substance and 'purely formal' phonology, Hale and Reiss undermine their view that the two are not intimately connected.

Secondly, while it is reasonable to insist, as Hale and Reiss do, that the human visual perception system constructs objects (percepts) that are not *directly* induced by the visual stimulus it is exposed to (such as the triangle constructed by the visual system in the example they give), it is equally reasonable to insist that the percept is *indirectly* induced, that the properties of the percept in question depend crucially on properties of the visual input, as is always the case with transduction. That is, the percepts in question may be said to have intrinsic visual content (they are a species of visual image). Again, it is problematic to assume that the relationship between acoustic (speech) input and phonological representations, considered as strictly grammatical objects, is one of transduction. If it is, then that leads naturally to the idea that phonological representations have intrinsic acoustic content, that they are a species of acoustic image (and thus not purely formal in the intended sense).

Thirdly, according to Hale and Reiss, the universe of discourse of linguistic theory does not include seeing, and does not, therefore, include processing of visual images. This is because, on Hale and Reiss's assumptions, the strictly linguistic excludes the human visual perception system. By the same token, Hale and Reiss must surely argue that the strictly linguistic must not include processing of acoustic images, because it excludes the human auditory perception system. Again, it is therefore problematic to assume that the relationship between acoustic input and phonological objects is one of transduction, since that would imply that the phonological *does* include the processing of acoustic images. And, if the relationship is not one of transduction, then the question remains what the relationship might be.

Fourthly, intrinsic articulatory content also seems to find a place in Hale and Reiss's conception of the putatively strictly formal properties of phonology-within-UG. For instance, they claim that UG places conditions on rule application that refer to Place features. It is rather difficult to see what content 'Place' can have, other than articulatory content. True, the conditions in question are stated in terms of variables such as 'F' for feature, which makes them appear purely algebraic in nature, but if the features in question are defined in articulatory terms, then they are substantive, and the conditions in question are conditions on objects that have intrinsic phonetic content. Again, the desired aim of leaching all substance out of phonology appears not to have been achieved.

The choices here are: (*a*) maintain the position that phonological objects are substance free, and seek a conception of the relation between substance and phonology that is consistent with that claim, or (*b*) abandon the claim that phonological objects are substance free and maintain the transduction (or some other) conception of the relationship between phonetic substance and phonological representations. It seems to me that the former option has yet to be successfully sustained.

Given this, and the kinds of evidence cited above, which strongly suggest that the acquisition of phonological knowledge is intimately tied up with a variety of perceptual, general-cognitive, motor-control, and social factors, it seems unlikely that linguistic objects, understood in the radically internalist sense, have a phonology. Rather, phonological systems *constitute* conventional systems of representation. It seems to us (see Burton-Roberts and Carr 1999) that, if phonological systems are regarded this way, this resolves the dilemma, attested throughout the history of twentieth-century phonology, whereby phonologists often wish to regard phonological systems as 'purely formal' ('substance free', to use Hale and Reiss's term, 'A-modal' in van der Hulst's), and thus parallel to objects that contract purely syntactic relations, while at the same time allowing (explicitly or implictly) that they have intrinsic phonetic content (as, I suggest, is the case with, for instance, 'Place' in the work both of Hale and Reiss and van der Hulst).

5.4. *Phonology, Universal Grammar, and learning by forgetting*

In arguing for a phonology-free UG, I have claimed that, for an innate capacity to be subsumed within UG, it must fulfil two criteria: it must be uniquely human, and it must not be a perceptual, behavioural, physiological, or general-cognitive capacity. The following argument (Jacques Durand, p.c.; Phil Harrison, p.c.) might be raised against the position adopted here. While both human beings and chinchillas possess the capacity to discriminate aspirated versus unaspirated stops, human beings alone undergo 'learning by forgetting', whereby the innate capacity (for instance) to discriminate aspirated from unaspirated stops becomes 'submerged' for the child acquiring (most varieties of) English, under the generalization that aspiration is non-contrastive in English stops. In acquiring English, the human child 'forgets' the distinction, and has to be given training in phonetics classes in order to recover the capacity consciously to notice the distinction (the capacity to perceive the distinction at some level is, clearly, not lost).

The argument (let us call it the Argument from Learning by Forgetting (ALF)) is that this phenomenon provides an example of a capacity that is specific in both of the required senses: it is unique to human beings, and is a specifically phonological capacity. Thus, the argument goes, there are indeed innate phonological capacities of the sort that fulfil the two proposed criteria, and that can, therefore, be said to be present in UG. The ALF constitues a claim that UG includes phonology. Additionally, the capacity in question is, according to the ALF, said to be not only species specific and specifically phonological, but also perceptual in nature. It follows from the ALF that UG must be at least partly perceptual in nature, a claim that is problematic, as we have seen.

Several observations are in order here. When we say that a human child, or a chinchilla, can discriminate aspirated from unaspirated stops, we mean that, on exposure to sets of acoustically distinct, but none the less similar, spatiotemporally unique, acoustic events, some will be categorized as belonging to the class 'aspirated', while others will be categorized as belonging to the 'unaspirated' class (within limits defined by innate, non-species-specific psychoacoustic categories). That is, both the human child and the chinchilla will, at birth, take certain acoustic events to 'count as instances of the same thing'—that is, to belong to the same category.

The capacity for categorization is, quite clearly, a *general* cognitive capacity: it extends over the full range of perceptual (and perhaps other) domains (visual, olfactory, tactile, acoustic, taste based). To be sure, a distinct *mode* of categorization is attested for consonant, as opposed to vowel, perception, but it is categorization none the less. Furthermore, since categorization subsumes both vowel and colour perception, and is thus a *general perceptual* capacity, it is not restricted to the perception of human speech sounds (although, even if it were, that would not warrant its inclusion in UG, since it is a perceptual capacity). It is also not species specific: other species can (and presumably *must be able to*) categorize in this way. That capacity cannot be subsumed within UG, since it fails to fulfil either criterion.

A given acoustic event will count as a token of the type, say, unaspirated coronal stop, and various acoustically distinct, but none the less similar, acoustic events will also count as tokens of that type. It seems reasonable to assume that both aspirated and unaspirated event-types already count as instances of more general categories (for example, stops), prior to the emergence of a phonological system. We may refer to those more general categories as 'supertypes'. The relation between a type (supertype) and its subtypes is distinct from that between types and their tokens (I owe this observation to Noel Burton-Roberts). Subtypes are not instances/tokens of (super)types. Since stops are instances/tokens of the type Stop, they are instances/tokens of all the types that Stop is subtype of (e.g. Consonant, etc.). But no type (super- or sub-) is a token.

There is no upper limit on the extent to which a given type may be subsumable under a more general type, since everything resembles everything else, at a sufficiently broad level of generality (all consonants are instances of speech sounds; all speech sounds are instances of acoustic events; all acoustic events are instances of events). What is required is the capacity to recognize differences and similarities and to generalize over those in order to arrive at categories. This is the capacity for inductive generalization, a capacity that could not be present in UG.

The question of why chinchillas do not undergo learning by forgetting amounts to the question of why they do not attain phonological systems. The answer to that question is that they possess neither UG (for the representation of which phonological categories are formed and utilized) nor the capacity for representation (which is not, itself, a linguistic capacity: human beings can represent objects other than the linguistic objects made available by UG). Phonological systems emerge as a result of the acquisition of a conventional system for the physical representation of those linguistic objects. That is, phonological contrastivity has a representational function.

To be sure, in adopting the Representational Hypothesis and radical internalism, Burton-Roberts and I are accepting that UG plays a crucial role in the explanation of why only humans undergo learning by forgetting and acquire a phonology. But what radically distinguishes our position from that advocated by proponents of the ALF is our conception of the nature of UG and the role it plays in this process. The ALF is unsustainable for the following reason. In order to account for the fact that human beings, but not other species (even those that share some of our innate psychoacoustic capacities) attain phonological categories, one needs to postulate (*a*) UG in humans but not in chinchillas, (*b*) the innate capacity for representation, again present in humans but not chinchillas (or any other species, apparently), and (*c*) the capacity to form categories, which is not specific to humans, and is anyway a general cognitive capacity (which therefore falls outside UG). None of this requires the postulating of an innate, species-specific, capacity oriented exclusively towards the formation of phonological categories.

Note that the functionality of phonological contrastivity is explainable only with respect to UG: the function in question is *representational* function. Thus the acquisition of a phonology has a Rationalist rationale, but all of the capacities that are harnassed in the process of the acquisition of a phonology (that is, a representational system) are consistent with Empiricism.

6. SUMMARY

I have attempted to sketch here the essentials of a philosophy of phonology based on Popperian falsificationist realism, radical internalism, the Representational Hypothesis, and an approach to phonological acquisition whose rationale is rooted in Rationalism, but where the capacities harnassed during acquisition are fully consistent with Empiricism. I have shown how this approach to phonological knowledge allows an accommodation between both variationist and labphon approaches to phonology, on the one hand, and the Rationalist notion of UG as a radically internal part of the natural world, on the other. The conceptual work done by the Representational Hypothesis in allowing for an accommodation between Empiricism and Rationalism, and between Rationalism and variationism, seems both genuinely novel and immensely useful in clarifying the conceptual foundations of phonological investigation.

REFERENCES

Anderson, J. M. and Ewen, C. (1987), *Principles of Dependency Phonology* (Cambridge: Cambridge University Press).

Armstrong, N. and Unsworth, S. (1998), 'Sociolinguistic Variation in Southern French Schwa', *Linguistics*, 37/1: 127–56.

Beckman, M., Ladd, R., and Pierrehumbert, J. (1996), 'Laboratory Phonology', in J. Durand and B. Laks (eds.), *Current Trends in Phonology: Models and Methods* (2 vols.; Salford: European Studies Research Institute).

Bhaskar, R. (1975), *A Realist Theory of Science* (Brighton: Harvester Press).

Biggs, C. (1987), 'Chomsky and Artificial Intelligence', in S. Modgil and C. Modgil (eds.), *Noam Chomsky: Consensus and Controversy* (Lewes: Falmer Press).

Boden, M. (1994), *Piaget* (2nd edn., London: Fontana).

Bromberger, S. and Halle, M. (1989), 'Why Phonology is Different', *Linguistic Inquiry*, 20/1: 51–70.

—— —— (this volume), 'The Ontology of Phonology (Revised)'.

Bullock, A. and Stallybrass, O. (1977), (eds.), *The Fontana Dictionary of Modern Thought* (London: Fontana/Collins).

Burton-Roberts, N. (1994), 'Ambiguity, Sentence and Utterance: A Representational Approach', *Transactions of the Philological Society*, 92/2: 179–212.

—— (this volume), 'Where and What is Phonology? A Representational Perspective'.

—— and Carr, P. (1999), 'On Speech and Natural Language', *Language Sciences*, 21/4: 371–406.

Carr, P. (1990), *Linguistic Realities* (Cambridge: Cambridge University Press).

—— (1991), 'Lexical Properties of Postlexical Rules: Postlexical Derived Environment and the Elsewhere Condition', *Lingua*, 85: 255–68.

—— (1992), 'Strict Cyclicity, Structure Preservation and the Scottish Vowel Length Rule', *Journal of Linguistics*, 28/1: 91–114.

—— (1998), review of Chomsky, (1993), *Journal of Linguistics*, 33/1: 215–18.

Carr, P. (forthcoming), *Phonology, Nature and Convention* (Oxford: Oxford University Press).

Chomsky, N. (1965), *Aspects of the Theory of Syntax* (Cambridge, Mass.: MIT Press).

—— (1966), *Cartesian Linguistics* (New York: Harper & Row).

—— (1980), *Rules and Representations* (New York: Columbia University Press).

—— (1991*a*), 'Linguistics and Adjacent Fields: A Personal View', in A. Kasher (ed.), *The Chomskyan Turn* (Oxford: Blackwell), 3–25.

—— (1991*b*), 'Linguistics and Cognitive Science: Problems and Mysteries', in A. Kasher (ed.), *The Chomskyan Turn* (Oxford: Blackwell), 26–55.

—— (1993), *Language and Thought* (Rhode Island: Moyer Bell).

—— (1995*a*), 'Language and Nature', *Mind*, 104: 1–61.

—— (1995*b*), *The Minimalist Program* (Cambridge, Mass.: MIT Press).

Dennett, D. C. (1995), *Darwin's Dangerous Idea* (Harmondsworth: Penguin).

Descartes, R. (1637/1970), *Discourse on Method*, in E. Anscombe and P. T. Geach (eds.), *Descartes: Philosophical Writings*, (2nd edn., Wokingham: Van Nostrand, 1970), 5–57.

Docherty, G. and Foulkes, P. (this volume), 'Speaker, Speech, and Knowledge of Sounds'.

—— —— Milroy, J., Milroy, L., and Walshaw, D. (1997), 'Descriptive Adequacy in Phonology: A Variationist Perspective', *Journal of Linguistics*, 33/2: 275–310.

Dresher, B. E. (1981), 'Abstractness and Explanation in Phonology', in N. Hornstein and D. Lightfoot (eds.), *Explanation in Linguistics* (London: Longman), 76–115.

Elman, J. L., Bates, E. A., Johnson, M. H., Karmiloff-Smith, A., Parisi, D., and Plunkett, K. (1998), *Rethinking Innateness: A Connectionist Perspective on Development* (Cambridge, Mass.: MIT Press/Bradford Books).

Feyerabend, P. (1975), *Against Method* (London: Verso).

Fikkert, P. (1995), 'Acquisition of Phonology', *Glott International*, 1: 3–7.

Fodor, J. A. (1981*a*), 'Methodological Solipsism as a Research Strategy in Cognitive Psychology', in J. A. Fodor, *Representations* (Brighton: Harvester), 225–53.

—— (1981*b*), 'The Present Status of the Innateness Controversy', in J. A. Fodor, *Representations* (Brighton: Harvester) 257–316.

—— (1989), 'Why Should the Mind be Modular?', in A. George (ed.), *Reflections on Chomsky* (Oxford: Blackwell), 1–22.

Fudge, E. (1999), 'Words and Feet', *Journal of Linguistics*, 35/2: 273–96.

Goren, C. C., Sarty, M., and Wu, P. Y. K. (1975), 'Visual Following and Pattern Discrimination of Face-Like Stimuli by Newborn Infants', *Pediatrics*, 56: 544–49.

Hale, M. and Reiss, C. (this volume), 'Phonology as Cognition'.

Halle, M. and Idsardi, W. (1997), '*r*, Hypercorrection and the Elsewhere Condition', in I. Roca (ed.), *Derivations and Constraints in Phonology* (Oxford: Oxford University), 331–48.

Harris, J. (1977), 'Leibniz and Locke on Innate Ideas', in I. C. Tipton (ed.), *Locke on Human Understanding* (Oxford: Oxford University Press), 25–40.

Harris, John (1989), 'Towards a Lexical Analysis of Sound Change in Progress', *Journal of Linguistics*, 25: 35–56.

—— and Lindsey, G. (1995), 'The Elements of Phonological Representation', in J. Durand and F. Katamba (eds.), *Frontiers of Phonology: Atoms, Strucutres, Derivations* (Harlow: Longman), 34–79.

—— —— (this volume), 'Vowel Patterns in Mind and Sound'.

Hartley, S. (1992), 'A Study of the Effects of Sex and Age on Glottalisation Patterns in the Speech of Tyneside Schoolchildren', unpublished undergraduate dissertation, (University of Newcastle upon Tyne).

Hayes, B. (1999), 'Phonetically-Driven Phonology: The Role of Optimality Theory and Inductive Grounding', in M. Darnell, E. Moravcsik, M. Noonan, F. Newmeyer, and K. Wheatley (eds.), *Functionalism and Formalism in Linguistics*, i. *General Papers* (Amsterdam: John Benjamins), 243–85.

Hooper, J. (1976), *An Introduction to Natural Generative Phonology* (New York: Academic Press).

Hualde, I. (1989), 'The Strict Cycle Condition and Non-Cyclic Rules', *Linguistic Inquiry*, 20: 675–80.

Hulst, H. van der (1994), 'Radical CV Phonology: The Locational Gesture', *UCL Working Papers in Linguistics*, 6: 439–77.

—— (this volume), 'Modularity and Modality in Phonology', 164.

Hume, D. (1748/1962), *An Inquiry Concerning Human Understanding*, in A. Flew (ed.), *David Hume on Human Nature and the Understanding* (London: Collier Macmillan).

Itkonen, E. (1978), *Grammatical Theory and Metascience* (Amsterdam: John Benjamins).

Kaye, J., Lowenstamm, J., and Vergnand, J.-R. (1985), 'The Internal Structure of Phonological Elements: A Theory of Charm and Government', *Phonology*, 2: 305–28.

—— —— —— (1990), 'Constituent Structure and Government in Phonology', *Phonology*, 7: 193–231.

Kuhl, P. and Miller, J. (1975), 'Speech Perception by the Chinchilla: Voiced–Voiceless Distinction in Alveolar Plosive Consonants', *Science*, 190: 69–72.

Kuhn, T. (1962), *The Structure of Scientific Revolutions* (Chicago: University of Chicago Press).

Lakatos, I. (1970), 'Falsification and the Methodology of Scientific Research Programmes', in I. Lakatos and A. Musgrave (eds.), *Criticism and the Growth of Knowledge* (Cambridge: Cambridge University Press) 91–196.

Lass, R. (1984), *Phonology* (Cambridge: Cambridge University Press).

Laudan, L. (1977), *Progress and its Problems* (Berkeley and Los Angeles: University of California Press).

Locke, J. L. (1993), *The Child's Path to Spoken Language* (Cambridge, Mass.: Harvard University Press).

McMahon, A. (1990), 'Vowel Shift, Free Rides and Strict Cyclicity', *Lingua*, 80: 197–225.

Mach, E. (1893/1966), *The Science of Mechanics* (Peru, Ill.: Open Court).

Marler, P. and Peters, S. (1981), 'Birdsong and Speech', in P. D. Eimas and J. L. Miller (eds.), *Perspectives on the Study of Speech* (Hillsdale, NJ: Lawrence Erlbaum), 75–112.

Meltzoff, A. N. (1986), 'Imitation, Intermodal Representation, and the Origins of Mind', in B. Lindblom and R. Zetterstrom (eds.), *Precursors of Early Speech* (New York: Stockton Press.)

—— and Moore, M. K. (1977), 'Imitation of Facial and Manual Gestures by Human Neonates', *Science*, 198: 75–8.

Milroy, J. and Milroy, L. (1985), 'Linguistic Change, Social Network and Speaker Innovation', *Journal of Linguistics*, 21/2: 339–84.

Myers, S. (1997), 'Expressing Phonetic Naturalness in Phonology', in I. Roca (ed.), *Derivations and Constraints in Phonology* (Oxford: Oxford University Press), 125–52.

Ohala, J. J. (1983), 'The Origins of Sound Patterns in Vocal Tract Constraints', in P. F. MacNeilage (ed.), *The Production of Speech* (New York: Springer), 189–216.

Newton-Smith, W. (1978), 'The Underdetermination of Theories by Data', *Aristotelian Society*, 52 (supplement): 71–91.

—— (1982), *The Rationality of Science* (London: Routledge & Kegan Paul).

Pandey, P. K. (1997), 'Optionality, Lexicality and Sound Change', *Journal of Linguistics*, 33/1: 91–130.

Paradis, C. and LaCharité, D. (1997), 'Preservation and Minimality in Loanword Adaptation', *Journal of Linguistics*, 33/2: 379–430.

Pateman, T. (1987), *Language in Mind and Language in Society* (Oxford: Oxford University Press).

Piatelli-Palmarini, M. (1980), (ed.), *Language and Learning: The Debate between Jean Piaget and Noam Chomsky* (London: Routledge & Kegan Paul).

Pierrehumbert, J. B. (1990), 'Phonological and Phonetic Representation', *Journal of Phonetics*, 19: 375–94

—— Beckman, M. and Ladd, D. R. (this volume), 'Conceptual Foundations of Phonology as Laboratory Science'.

Pinker, S. (1994), *The Language Instinct* (London: Penguin).

Plotkin, H. (1997), *Evolution in Mind* (London: Allen Lane).

Popper, K. R. (1959), *The Logic of Scientific Discovery* (London: Hutchinson).

—— (1963), *Conjectures and Refutations* (London: Routledge and Kegan Paul).

—— (1982–3), *Postscript to the Logic of Scientific Discovery*, London: Hutchinson (3 vols: vols i, ii: 1982; vol. iii: 1983; Totowa, NJ: Rowan & Littlefield).

Rose, S. (1993), *The Making of Memory* (London: Bantam).

—— (1997), *Lifelines: Biology, Freedom, Determinism* (Harmondsworth: Penguin).

Russell, B. (1961), *History of Western Philosophy* (2nd edn., London: Allen & Unwin; repr. London: Routledge, 1991).

Skinner, B. F. (1957), *Verbal behavior* (New York: Appleton Century Crofts).

Szpyra, J. (1989), *The Phonology-Morphology Interface* (London: Routledge).

Vihman, M. M. (1996), *Phonological Development: The Origins of Language in the Child* (Oxford: Blackwell).

—— and Velleman, S. (this volume), 'Phonetics and the Origins of Phonology.'

5

Speaker, Speech, and Knowledge of Sounds

GERARD DOCHERTY AND PAUL FOULKES

1. INTRODUCTION

Our aim in this chapter is to offer a reflection on the theme of 'where and what is phonology' from the perspective of investigators whose prime interest is to develop an understanding of variability in speech production. Recent work by the authors (e.g. Docherty *et al.* 1997; Docherty and Foulkes 1999; Foulkes *et al.* 1999; Milroy *et al.* 1999) has investigated aspects of 'sociophonetic' variation in a number of varieties of British English. In carrying out this work, we specifically set out to look at what value could be added to our understanding of sociolinguistic variation by bringing to bear a more refined (auditory and instrumental) phonetic analysis than is typically employed in the analysis of consonantal variation, and by considering the findings in the light of accounts of phonological alternations in English appearing in the recent phonological literature. As a result of taking this approach, we have been led to reflect on the interface between these three areas—phonetics, phonology, and sociolinguistics—particularly in respect of whether, jointly, they provide a coherent account of the systematic properties of speech production. The nature of this interface lies at the heart of the issues that are tackled by this volume.

In dealing with this theme we differ from many of the contributions to this volume by presenting a perspective on phonology that is largely formed by work *outside* mainstream phonology. Our goal is to shed light on phonology by exploring how it connects with what we know about speech from other perspectives (phonetics and sociolinguistics). While this leads us to be rather critical of a number of aspects of phonological theory, we have no particular axe to grind with phonology *per se*, and we make no particular attempt to discriminate between the merits of different theoretical positions within phonology. The point

We would like to thank the following for their valuable comments, which have helped us in the preparation of this chapter: Noel Burton-Roberts, Phil Carr, Ghada Khattab, John Local, April McMahon, Jim Scobbie, Jane Stuart-Smith, and Dominic Watt. Preparation of this chapter has been supported by a grant from the UK ESRC (R000237417).

we seek to drive home, however, is that observations of the systematic properties of speech production do seem to have a number of implications for our understanding of what phonology is actually a theory of (or what it cannot be a theory of). We are not in a position to provide any firm solutions to the challenges that we raise; indeed, we are to some extent taking on a devil's advocate role in highlighting them. However, we believe that raising the profile of these issues does help clarify the sorts of questions that can and should be addressed by those interested in gaining an understanding of speech production/perception/acquisition and by those interested in understanding phonology, and the extent of any overlap between these domains of enquiry.

The chapter begins with an overview of what we perceive to be the central goals of most phonologists. We then compare these with our own research goal of identifying precisely what language-/accent-/speaker-specific properties of speech production must be learned. We discuss the extent to which these two goals are compatible, identifying in the process what appears to be a conceptual impasse in this area. While phonology seeks to be a theory of speakers' knowledge of native language sound patterns, there is considerable and mounting evidence that what speakers learn about the sound patterns of their native language extends beyond the domain of phonology as it is usually conceived. The key issue is how phonology might respond to this situation and what these responses entail about the nature of phonological theory; we discuss some of the responses that have been proposed, concluding with a call for greater clarity in respect of the objectives of phonological theorizing.

Throughout this chapter we make use of the terms 'phonology'/'phonologists' as if they were homogeneous categories. Of course, this is far from the truth (as we make clear below, and as is amply illustrated by the contributions to this volume). Nevertheless we do feel that most, if not all, of the points we make below do apply rather generally to the majority of investigators who consider themselves to be doing 'phonology' (see further our discussion in Section 2), and for this reason we have decided to make use of this general terminology.

2. THE SCOPE OF PHONOLOGY

In dealing with the 'conceptual foundations of phonology' it is important to state what we understand phonology to be in the first place. This question is fundamental to the aims of this volume, and it is a matter that we return to in greater detail towards the end of this chapter, but for now let us consider the following definition of the domain of phonology provided by Kenstowicz (1994) in his advanced textbook *Phonology in Generative Grammar*:

Phonology is the component of our linguistic knowledge that is concerned with the physical realization of language. Possession of this knowledge permits us to realize words and the sentences they compose as speech (or as gestures in the language of the deaf) and to recover them from the acoustic signal (or visual sign display) ... knowledge of the pronunciation of lexical items must be stored in memory. (p. 2)

Kenstowicz then gives his view of the key questions which are addressed by phonology:

For any given language, what are the phonological representations and rules that have developed from U[niversal]G[rammar] in individual speakers as a result of exposure to the language of their environment? How do these rules apply to compute the phonetic representation? At a more theoretical level, what is a possible rule and representation? What elements are representations composed of? What principles cover their combination? Precisely how does UG develop into G_{Korean} G_{French}, and so on, in response to the language of the environment? (p. 10)

Not every phonologist would sign up to exactly this definition of the scope of phonology. Nevertheless, we do not think it would be controversial to claim that the bulk of work that would be generally considered to fall within the field of phonology does fall broadly within the bounds of Kenstowicz's overview description.

 We interpret the first part of Kenstowicz's definition as a claim that at least one of the tasks fulfilled by phonology is to provide a theory of lexical representations that are used as the basis for the pronunciation of words by speakers (they presumably also have a reciprocal role in speech perception). The second part of the quotation firmly locates the study of phonology in the framework of UG. Many phonologists have been far less explicit than Kenstowicz about this underlying goal of their work, but it is a feature that is pervasive, and continues to be so in the more recent work within the framework of Optimality Theory that has developed in the period since the publication of Kenstowicz's book. (There are a few exceptions to this general picture, but the basic point remains true that the bulk of work following *The Sound Pattern of English* (*SPE*) (Chomsky and Halle 1968) sees itself as seeking to shed light on the phonological component of (Universal) Grammar.) One consequence of this is a focus on identifying the most economical analysis of a particular set of observations, enabling maximum generalization within a language and across as many languages as possible.

 It is also important to note that phonology has a prime focus on lexical contrast (as the key function of a phonological system) and how this is achieved in different languages; that is, phonology is conceived of principally as being *the* means of allowing for a large and expandable lexicon with finite sound-generating resources. From our point of view, it is noteworthy that this lexical contrastive function of speech is predominant in most work on phonological theory largely to the exclusion of any other functions fulfilled by the sound patterns produced by speakers, and we return to this point later.[1]

---

[1] A notable exception to this general statement is work on intonational phonology, where a certain amount of work has focused on the systematic correlations between patterns of f0 movement and particular pragmatic functions (Ladd 1996).

This interest in cross-language generalization and the focus on lexically contrastive aspects of sound patterning result in a tendency for hypothesized lexical representations typically to contain only that which is 'not predictable' from other factors, as explained in the following quote from Anderson (1985: 10):

It is often taken as self-evident in phonological studies that underlying ('phonemic' or 'phonological') representations should contain only *distinctive* or non-redundant material. That is, arriving at the phonological representation of a form, one of the steps involved is the elimination of all predictable properties, and the reduction of the form to the minimum of specification from which all of its other properties can be derived by general rule. For many, indeed, such a step establishes the fundamental difference between the 'phonological' and the 'phonetic' representation of a given form.

The characteristics of phonology just described reflect strongly the influence of Chomsky and Halle (*SPE*) and the Minimalist Program (Chomsky 1995). Similarly, the focus on lexical contrast shows an influence of structuralist principles that can be traced back at least as far as the Prague School—e.g. Trubetzkoy (1969: 10): 'It is the task of phonology to study which differences in sound are related to differences in meaning in a given language, in which way the discriminative elements ... are related to each other, and the rules according to which they may be combined into words and sentences.' As with the overall goals of phonology, it is rare that these general principles are explicitly discussed, and even more unusual for them to be questioned.

From our perspective, there appears to be a distinct tension in the dual focus of phonological theory on the 'language general' and the 'language specific'. On the one hand, a concern for the pronunciation of words by speakers requires investigation of language-specific aspects of speech production and other aspects of speech performance; however, working within a UG framework involves a completely opposing orientation, one that seeks to cut through the differences between speakers and to identify the deep (and presumably innate) phonological knowledge shared by all speakers. Indeed, some proponents of UG would want this deep knowledge to transcend modalities—for example, to apply equally to speech and sign language (cf e.g. the quote from Kenstowicz given above, and van der Hulst, this volume). Later in this chapter we return to the question of whether a concern for 'the physical realization of language' is compatible with an agenda that seeks to identify the characteristics of UG. First, however, we would like to focus on the domain of phonology expressed in the first part of the quotation from Kenstowicz—namely, that phonology is to do with speakers' knowledge of sounds. In doing so, we begin by outlining the general issue that we are addressing in our own work and provide examples of the sorts of speech-production phenomena that we are seeking to understand. We then discuss the extent to which phonology can contribute to this understanding.

3. VARIABILITY IN SPEECH PERFORMANCE

The starting point for our work is the fundamental observation that speech produced naturally and situated in a communicative context is abundantly variable. Pisoni (1997: 16, based on Klatt 1986) points to the following different types of variability found in the speech signal: ambient conditions (e.g. background noise and reverberation), within-speaker variability (e.g. rate, voice quality, precision), cross-speaker variability (e.g. accent, rate, voice quality), segment realization variability (e.g. coarticulation, prosodic modulation), word-environment variability in continuous speech (e.g. connected speech processes, phrasal effects on duration). Note that this variability does not reside exclusively in the acoustic signal that is the external physical stimulus generated by uttering a word or phrase, but is also present in the articulatory and neuromuscular activity that gives rise to the acoustic signal. Not only do different speakers use different articulatory strategies in producing the same lexical item (e.g. Lindau 1975; Pandeli 1993), but even individual speakers do likewise across token-to-token repetitions (Abbs 1986).

We should supplement Pisoni's list with the insights regarding adaptive variability that have arisen from Lindblom's 'H&H theory' (1990). Lindblom points out that speakers appear to be continually tuning their performance online up and down a continuous scale that has hyper (overarticulated) speech at one end and hypo (underarticulated) speech at the other, and that the key driving force in this process is the speaker's perception of how much information actually needs to be in the speech signal for communication to be successful in any particular instance (that is, speaker performance is enormously situation sensitive).[2]

One consequence of this variability in speech performance is the perennial 'non-invariance problem'—that is, the problem that, in natural speech production, invariant phonetic correlates (at whatever level of analysis) that apply across multiple tokens of the 'same' lexical item have proven to be extremely elusive (Labov 1986; Lindblom 1986). In some cases, the variability that is observed could be classified as fluctuation around a mean (for example, the distribution of Voice Onset Timing (VOT) in aspirated stops), but in other cases the effect of variability is to render two tokens of the 'same' word quite dissimilar. It seems then that we are dealing not simply with a 'noisy' speech execution system here striving inefficiently to achieve some underlying invariant goal, but with one in which the physical correlates of words can be radically reshaped from token to token. Note that some of the sources of variability referred to above are environmental and anatomical in origin and would therefore be expected to apply broadly similarly across all languages and all speakers. But in many cases (fine-grained) variability has been shown to differ systematically across languages, accents, and speakers of

---

[2] Local (p.c.) has pointed out that Lindblom's notion of adaptive variability resonates strongly with the view emerging from Conversation Analysis (e.g. Schegloff 1988) that turns at talk (and therefore their phonetic shape) are 'recipient designed'.

the same accent (e.g. Keating 1984; Fourakis and Port 1986; Docherty 1992; Cohn 1993; Kingston and Diehl 1994; Cho and Ladefoged 1999; Scobbie *et al.* 1999; Thomas, forthcoming, and see the findings of our own work described below), suggesting that such patterns of performance reflect learned behaviour and are not simply due to environmental factors or the passive by-product of execution by the vocal apparatus.

Our overall research goal is to understand the patterns of performance that characterize native speakers, and, by extension, what features have to be acquired by children to enable them to produce and comprehend speech like native speakers. As just indicated, there is now a considerable amount of evidence suggesting that language-specific (and, therefore, learned) aspects of speech are present down to a very fine-grained level of analysis, although there have been very few attempts to track how performance features of this sort emerge as part of phonological acquisition[3] (a project currently being undertaken by the present authors is addressing precisely this question—see Section 3 below). This research impinges directly on the 'where' and 'what' of phonology, since, in a sense, what children learn (and what mature speakers have learned) is an ability to produce and comprehend the systematic sound patterns of their native language, and the knowledge that underlies that is precisely what many phonologists would see as central to their own field.

Our own recent work has been concerned with one particular dimension of non-invariance, that which would normally be termed sociophonetic variation; that is to say, with aspects of speech production that vary as a function of social factors associated with a speaker or group of speakers. The methodology for this research has been inspired generally by the work of Labov and the school of variationist sociolinguistics that has arisen in his wake (Labov 1990; 1994, Chambers 1995). What research in this vein has amply demonstrated is that strong correlations can be found between (i) patterns of speech production, (ii) social factors characterizing individuals and groups of speakers, and (iii) stylistic and situational factors arising from the context in which an utterance is produced. We present an example from our own work in Table 5.1.

This table shows the percentage realization of five different variants of (t) in word-final pre-vowel position (e.g. in sequences such as *get it, lot of*) by thirty-two speakers of Tyneside English (four per group, with each group classified by class, age, and gender). The table shows the frequency of occurrence of the five variants that are produced in this context by our informants. In accounting for this pattern of variation, lexical and social factors are as important as phonological ones (Docherty *et al.*, 1997). In particular, there is clearly strong social differentiation

---

[3] Most work on acquisition is focused on acquisition of segmental phonemic contrasts and does not place a lot of attention on the developing patterns in the realization of those contrasts; yet, if we are to understand how all the learned aspects of speech come to be acquired, this is an area that merits investigators' attention (cf. Local 1983).

Table 5.1. Percentage realizations (to the nearest integer) of (t) in word-final pre-vowel position, by speaker group, Tyneside corpus

Speaker group	Variant					
	ɹ	t̞	t	ʔt	ʔ	n
Working class						
older females	40	18	27	12	2	404
older males	15	35	7	42	2	178
young females	21	39	5	20	13	402
young males	3	59	4	23	12	230
Middle class						
older females	12	27	39	20	2	366
older males	6	32	5	53	4	398
young females	2	42	5	17	34	383
young males	1	46	4	27	23	305

Note: n = number of tokens analysed.
Source: Docherty *et al.* (1997).

present as a function of class, age, and gender in respect of the patterns that are found.[4]

A key conclusion that arises from work on sociophonetic variation is that it appears to be impossible to exclude a social and/or situational dimension from a systematic account of these observations. That is to say, the patterns of variation observed cannot be comprehensively accounted for by appealing exclusively to phonological factors such as segmental context or the influence of the prosodic hierarchy. This has two implications. The first is that accounts of speech production will have added validity if they can take this social dimension into consideration; for example, given the findings shown in Table 5.1, an account of the complex alternations of word-final pre-vowel (t) in Tyneside English based on data derived from a group of young middle-class men would be likely to draw very different conclusions from one whose observations are based on the speech of older working-class women. The second is of more general import: our findings illustrate that systematic properties of speech production are determined not simply by the need to achieve lexical contrast. For example, it seems that speakers not only produce lexical items in sufficiently distinct form that their message can be successfully conveyed to listeners, but in doing so are simultaneously using the same vocal apparatus to signal aspects of their social identity. This is a reflection of

[4] The social effects identified here are overwhelmingly supported by statistical evidence (variation in linguistic variables with respect to social variables was analysed in this study using log-linear models). The variation inherent in the figures in Table 5.1 can be well accounted for by independent effects of age, gender and class, in decreasing order of importance (although all significant at $p < 0.001$). For further details, see Docherty *et al.* (1997).

a more general property of speech communication; as pointed out by Laver (1994), systematic properties of speech production have a range of functions in speech communication: lexical contrast, signalling pragmatic meaning, indexical information, and so on. Furthermore, these functions are overlaid one upon the other in that they make use of exactly the same motor planning and execution mechanisms.

As pointed out at the start of this section, an interest in understanding the systematic properties of speech production brings us into direct contact with phonological theory. Recall the first section of Kenstowicz's definition: 'Phonology is the component of our linguistic knowledge that is concerned with the physical realization of language. Possession of this knowledge permits us to realize words and the sentences they compose as speech ... knowledge of the pronunciation of words must be stored in memory' (1994: 2). In the following section we consider in more detail the question of how phonology stands in the face of the variable aspects of speakers' performance that we have exemplified above.

4. PHONOLOGY AND SPEECH PRODUCTION

4.1. *The status of data in phonology*

From the earliest days of Generative Phonology, phonology has had a rather schizophrenic approach to speech production (and there is ample evidence for a continuing uncertainty in this regard within the other contributions to this volume—see Section 5). In the opening sequence of *SPE* Chomsky and Halle (1968: 3) are at pains to point out that grammar is about specifying the correspondence between 'ideal phonetic form[s]' and sets of sentences, and that work in this vein (attempting to elucidate the properties of linguistic competence) should not be confused with 'what the speaker-hearer actually does', since this is not exclusively a function of the grammar but is influenced by other non-linguistic domains such as memory and attention and the bio-mechanical properties of the vocal organs. However, it is clear that one of the key elements of the construction of phonological theory (and *SPE* is no exception) is a set of observations that are in some sense an account of speaker performance. Textbooks and articles on phonology are replete with data which act as a trigger for discussion and development of theory. While some aspects of phonological theory are susceptible to testing by probing native-speaker intuition (for example, testing for permissible phonotactic combinations, acceptable truncations, syllabifications, rhyming, and so on), phonology relies to a significant extent for its validation on transcribed corpora of data. Indeed it is arguably much more dependent on corpora of this sort than other areas of grammatical analysis that tend to rely to a greater extent on native speaker grammaticality judgements.

In pursuing our argument in this chapter we would like to highlight a number of characteristics that are found to apply to a large part of the data used in phonological theorizing. Typically the data are a segmentally transcribed set of lexical or morphological alternations. Normally a very small corpus is used. This corpus is frequently obtained from a third-party source and is drawn from an unspecified number of speakers. Furthermore, there is usually no statement as to the reliability of the transcription nor about how the data were sampled; for example, it is typically not clear whether it is citation forms that have been elicited, or connected speech that has been analysed. It is, moreover, only in recent years (e.g. Browman and Goldstein 1992; Clements 1992) that there has been any degree of acknowledgement that segmental IPA-style transcriptions may not have any reality for anyone other than the transcriber. For example, Browman and Goldstein's model of Articulatory Phonology suggests that in speech production speakers manipulate the duration and magnitude of (quasi-)independently controllable articulatory gestures. Browman and Goldstein's approach would suggest that a segmental transcription is merely an external imposition on a fundamentally non-segmental activity. Likewise, as proponents of a form of Motor Theory of speech perception, they would very likely suggest that the objects of speech perception are those very same gestures. This view of conventional transcription is yet to have a widespread impact on the field, although there is no doubt that work in Laboratory Phonology (Pierrehumbert *et al.*, this volume) is highlighting that there may be much of interest and relevance to phonology in aspects of speech production that can only be observed outside the constraints of an auditory transcription.[5]

We can exemplify this general situation with a brief analysis of the data presented in Kenstowicz's (1994) text book (we should emphasize that Kenstowicz's volume is not particularly exceptional in this; this single volume is referred to chiefly because of the ample illustration of this point that it provides, and we could cite many other examples over the years that could all be criticized in the same way—e.g. Schane 1973, Hyman 1975, Lass 1984, Giegerich 1992, Carr 1993, Harris 1994, Roca and Johnson 1999, chapters in Goldsmith 1995, and a multitude of articles that have appeared in *Phonology* or in the Rutgers Optimality Archive). Kenstowicz's volume contains references to an admirably broad range of languages, and does a thorough job of citing sources (many of which are reports of original fieldwork). But, crucially from our point of view, the data are uniformly presented as a given; that is, there is no discussion of the nature of the material, the reliability with which it was transcribed, its degree of stability, the characteristics of the speaker or speakers, or of the community that the speaker(s) belong(s) to. For example, for any particular exemplar within a database it would be impossible to know if the target lexical item is consistently produced as it is transcribed by a single speaker, or by all speakers of the language/accent in all contexts and situations; that is, the information that we would need to do this is incomplete (see Simpson (1999), who questions the validity of Maddieson's (1984) UPSID database

[5] This is not to underestimate what can be achieved with detailed phonetic transcription (see Kelly and Local 1989 for exemplification of the sort of insights which can be achieved by very careful auditory analysis).

on similar grounds). These 'phonological facts' are subsequently marshalled in illustration (or in support) of particular lines of theory.

Our discussion is touching on difficult territory here, because there is a sense in which any account of speech is an abstraction away from what speakers are actually doing. Any instrumental acoustic investigation, for instance, requires considerable interpretation, which is dependent on how analysis parameters are set by the investigator. None the less, there is scope for compiling corpora of data that reflect to a greater or lesser extent the systematic properties of speech production and that have greater or lesser generalizability. Instrumental analysis, for example, gives a fine-grained multi-parameter perspective that in some cases can penetrate beyond the limits of the human auditory system. Likewise, a socially sensitive sample such as that which we have used in our own work moves some way towards capturing the fact that systematic patterns of speech can in some cases be identified only if the social dimensions of variation are considered. However, by not encapsulating any key dimensions of variability, the sort of data typically employed by phonologists reflect only a subset of the properties of speech production, and consequently there is substantial distance between the sort of data employed by phonologists in arguing for a particular theoretical position and the characteristics of utterances produced by communities of speakers in spoken communication.

It could be argued that our criticism here has a certain straw man quality, on the grounds that phonology is a theory that is (at least partly) about knowledge of speech sounds and not an account of properties of speech production, and has a primary focus on the manner in which sounds are used to contrast lexical items as opposed to other functions implemented within speech. It seems to us, however, that, while phonologists tend to eschew any dealings with 'non-linguistic' aspects of speech (for the reasons set out in *SPE* and referred to above), they do none the less present their data as being in some sense what speakers do. This is reflected in the following quotes from some of the earlier generative period, but we do not perceive the situation to have changed in the intervening years:

Phonology is concerned with the sound structure of language ... Of course, general phonological theory cannot be divorced from what happens in specific languages, since the theory evolves from experience with real linguistic data. Therefore, when discussing theoretical points we will refer to examples from various languages.   (Schane 1973: p. xv)

when approaching the sound system of a language, it is necessary to study not only *the physical properties of the attested sounds (that is, how they are made and what their acoustic correlates are)*, but also the grammatical properties of these sounds.   (Hyman 1975: 1, emphasis added)

Since it seems that the data used by phonologists do reflect a need to ground theory in what it is that speakers actually *do*, the question that remains then is how legitimate it is to present as relevant to phonology only *some* of the things that speakers do, whilst selectively filtering out many other properties of speech that differ across languages, accents, speakers, and contexts, and are therefore part of the individual's knowledge of native-language sound patterns. We return to this point in Section 5 of this chapter.

As this discussion might suggest, we feel a good deal of uncertainty as to how the data in phonology are to be interpreted. They are plainly not an adequate description of speaker performance. They are many steps removed from the actual performance that they are meant to represent. We are, therefore, forced to the conclusion that, however phonologists conceive of the data that they are using in triggering theoretical discussion, they are not building theories on thorough descriptions of the systematic characteristics of the performance of speakers. (Even work under the banner of Laboratory Phonology, while faring a little better in this regard, typically makes use of data that are one or more steps removed from natural speech production (see Vogel 1992; Docherty, forthcoming).) Having said this, many phonologists do seem to treat their corpora as accounts (albeit partial) of things that speaker-hearers do. This situation is disconcerting to investigators who are interested in understanding the systematic characteristics of speech production and who, at each turn, encounter greater complexity and patterns of activity that render the data sets used by many a phonologist ever more abstract and removed from actual speech performance. Most importantly it raises a question mark about the extent to which phonology really is engaging with the physical realization of speech, or the pronunciation of words by individual speakers—that is, about the extent to which it can adequately live up to Kenstowicz's assertion that 'phonology ... is concerned with the physical realization of language'.

Our uncertainty about the role of data in phonology is exacerbated by some aspects of the way the data are employed. Laboratory Phonology apart, it is unusual for phonologists to gather 'new' data in support of a theoretical position, and they rely largely instead on pre-existing accounts (with all of the inherent problems that this involves as mentioned above). More seriously, perhaps, we perceive a connection between a reliance on pre-existing accounts and a situation where there is a tendency for theoretical stances to be sustained in the absence of supporting data.

An example of this is the way in which the phoneme has been used over the years as a theoretical construct. While in recent years representations based on the phoneme have been relatively disfavoured in phonology, they were for many years the mainstay of phonological theory despite the fact that little independent supporting evidence could be adduced in their favour (indeed, many years of work in acoustic and articulatory phonetics served to demonstrate the overwhelming difficulty of reconciling a phonemic representation of an utterance with its phonetic realization). A quote from Halle (1964: 325) illustrates the sort of thinking that we wish to highlight here: 'the inability of instrumental phoneticians to propose a workable segmentation procedure ... has not resulted in the wholesale abandonment of the phoneme. Only a few easily frightened souls have been ready to do without the phoneme.' This illustrates that, from a relatively early stage in the development of Generative Phonology, there has been a readiness to sustain some basic theoretical constructs in the absence of firm experimental validation, and, indeed, in the presence of considerable data suggesting that the particular stance may be difficult to sustain. We have given an old example here, but the general issue remains valid today, and we discuss a more recent example of this in the following section. In other words, it appears that, while phonology may be (at least partially) about the physical realization of speech sounds, phonological theory for many years evolved along a path that has been relatively unperturbed by many insights gained about the real complexities of natural speech. It is interesting to note, however, that the adherence to a phonemic view of phonology did eventually succumb in some quarters to the weight of evidence from speech production that many systematic features of phonological alternation were best handled in non-linear fashion. This adds weight to our own argument in this section: if this aspect of speech production can impact on the nature of phonological representations, why cannot other aspects? What is the principle that determines what aspects of speech production are relevant to phonology and what are not? The most likely answer to this question is that phonology is interested only in lexically contrastive aspects of speech. This, however, reflects a somewhat restricted view of 'knowledge of speech sound patterns', and explicitly excludes many aspects of sound patterning that speakers clearly do have knowledge of.

Later in the same article referred to above, Halle argues for the validity of his approach, pointing out that it is possible to postulate theoretical constructs for which it is not (yet) possible to gather direct evidence. This 'theory-driven' approach (described by Halle, but practised fairly widely within phonology) gives phonology a different style of discourse from that which applies in many other areas of empirical investigation. It contrasts, for example, quite sharply with the approach that tends to be taken by Labovian sociolinguistics, as can be seen if we highlight a number of features of work carried out in this latter tradition. First, its theoretical base is initially relatively unconstrained.[6] Hypotheses and theoretical insights arise from quantitative analysis of a substantial body of data normally gathered for the purpose. A key feature is that any description that is offered must be accountable to the data, which in turn are normally a sizeable sample systematically collected from one or more speech communities. By accountability what we mean is that not only are occurrences of a particular variant noted but also other sites where it can occur are identified. The analysis then focuses not only on instances of that variant but on all the variants that occur in these sites. A sample such as this allows a range of distributional regularities to be specified. One

---

[6] Although, clearly, some assumptions are built in to work in this vein, particularly about what the likely social dimensions of variation might be, and some have suggested that this work has a rather questionable faith in the homogeneity of variance within the socially defined groups of speakers (see Mufwene 1994: 205).

particularly important consequence of this is that data that appear initially to be irregular or randomly distributed may nevertheless turn out to exhibit theoretically suggestive regularities in their sociolinguistic distribution—that is, this would suggest that we are dealing with some form of patterned behaviour that is learned by those speakers, as opposed to being an aspect of speech that varies in a less constrained fashion.

The point of comparing this approach to developing theory with that most commonly adopted in phonological studies is to emphasize the 'data-driven' nature of this work (that is, the only theories that can be sustained are those that are supported by accountable empirical observations of a representative sample of speakers). This contrasts sharply with the 'theory-driven' approach to phonology outlined by Halle, and puts into focus the concerns we have raised above about the impoverished nature of the data typically invoked by phonologists. Ohala (1986*a*, for example) discusses the different types of evidence that are brought to bear in the pursuance of phonological theory, and draws a conclusion similar to our own. He suggests that phonologists have access to a number of valuable sources of data, but that experimental studies have a clear advantage in 'their potential for providing crucial evidence which helps to differentiate between competing hypotheses' (1986*a*: 12).

In general, then, we are forced to the conclusion that phonological theorizing is not particularly responsive to the goal of descriptive adequacy (if by this latter term we mean the extent to which the data that are used as the input to theory are a faithful representation of the systematic properties of speaker performance). Any auditory or instrumental description of speech is some way removed from the features of actual speaker performance, but the data typically called upon to justify theoretical positions in phonology do not capture some significant (and easily observable) aspects of speakers' performance. There is a strong sense in which the theoretical discourse has proceeded in the absence of a resolution of some key issues such as the non-invariance problem. We suggest that, while phonology might indeed seek to be an account of speakers' knowledge of the sound patterns of their native language, there is not a good mapping between the representations of phonological theory and the learned characteristics of native-speaker performance. We return to these issues in Section 5.

4.2. *Competence and speakers*

Our work on variability, particularly of the sociophonetic kind, leads us to address a further point that is at the heart of the question about what phonology is seeking to achieve. Kenstowicz notes that 'knowledge of the pronunciation of words must be stored in memory'. One of the key assumptions of phonological theory in relation to this is eloquently expressed elsewhere in this volume by Myers: referring to the 'Uniqueness Hypothesis', Myers points out that most phonologists have implicitly assumed that 'For every linguistic expression, there is one and only one phonological representation' (p. 260). Schools of phonology differ with respect to the precise make-up of these unique representations, but typically they are componential structures comprised of lexically contrastive elements (phonemes, features, geometrical representations, gestures, elements).

This assumption clearly runs into difficulty if it is projected onto speech production and perception. Immediately, variability in performance rears its head as a 'problem'—that is, as an obstacle to the transmission of an invariant target form by the speaker to an invariant percept by the listener.[7] In response to this, investigators (following the lines laid out by *SPE*) have suggested that speakers/ listeners acquire complex rules for deriving surface forms and develop sophisticated skills in abstracting from an abundantly variable input (note that not everyone would agree that derivation is an online cognitive process, but then this does beg the question of what it actually is). However, it is fair to say that over fifty years of work in this area (using the early spectrographic studies as our point of reference) have failed to deal comprehensively with the mismatch between invariant phonological representations and variable phonetic realizations. The non-invariance 'problem' remains a problem, and variation has been cast as 'noise' in the signal that 'gets in the way' (Pisoni 1997). Recall, however, that, as pointed out in the previous section, phonological research over the years has proceeded relatively unperturbed in the face of this rather significant but unresolved issue, and, as Myers explains, 'uniqueness' is a pervasive assumption.

We would like to contrast this state of affairs with an alternative view offered by multiple trace models of lexical representation. Multiple trace models of lexical representation (Pisoni 1997: 25 ff.—sometimes referred to as exemplar models) assume that lexical representation is composed not of maximally redundant abstract representations, but of memory traces of tokens of words that have been heard/recognized. Johnson (1997: 146) describes the basic operation of this model as follows:

In exemplar models of perception (Estes 1993, Hintzman 1986, Nosofsky 1986, 1988, 1991, Nosofsky, Kruschke & McKinley 1992) a perceptual category is defined as the set of all experienced instances of the category. That is, no abstract categories are posited. The process of categorization then involves comparing the to-be-categorized item with each of the remembered instances of each category, and categorization is based on the sums of similarity over each category. Hintzman (1986) demonstrated that a model of this sort behaves as if categorization is based upon category prototypes, although category abstraction is produced at decision time rather than during acquisition.

A key feature of this approach is that variability in the stimulus is directly

---

[7] Given more space, it would be relevant to consider the position of phonology regarding the extent to which, whatever the nature of language-specific phonological knowledge, it is shared by all speakers of that language or accent; i.e. while English speakers may differ in their token-to-token phonetic realization of words, all speakers would have the same 'underlying representation' for each lexical item regardless of the extent to which it may vary in context in actual speech production. When one encounters expressions such as the 'phonology' of English or Japanese, the impression is certainly given that this is the case.

encoded in the lexical representation. As pointed out by both Johnson and Pisoni, this places greater demands on memory,[8] but it dispenses with the non-invariance 'problem' at a stroke, and, as we suggest below, in doing so it poses a challenge to the view that speakers' knowledge of the phonological structure of their lexicon is embedded exclusively in a set of unique representations for lexical items.

The evidence that seems most persuasive in rendering this a reasonably plausible theory of lexical representation comes from studies that show that aspects of the signal that are conventionally viewed as being unconnected to speech perception or word recognition (such as speaker characteristics, gender, accent, speaking rate, even the listeners' stereotypes, and so on) do appear to have a role in decoding the linguistic properties of the speech signal. For example, Pisoni (1997) describes a programme of experimentation looking at the effects of stimulus variability on speech perception, leading to the conclusion that 'details of the perceptual analysis of words are not lost ... they become an integral part of the mental representation of words in memory' (p. 21). Strand and Johnson (1996) showed that gender stereotypes influenced listeners' categorization of tokens on a nine-step [s]–[ʃ] continuum, suggesting that 'higher-level relatively complex social expectations might have an influence on such low-level basic processes as phonological categorization of the speech signal' (Strand 1999: 93).

This model also seems to be in tune with findings from studies that suggest that in phonological acquisition children do not seem to discriminate between those features that appear to have a significant social marking function and those that are less socially marked (and that, given an *SPE*-view of phonology, have a role that might be more directly related to conveying lexical contrast). The overall picture from the recent variationist literature is succinctly summarized by Chambers (1995: 158): 'sociolinguistic competence ... develops very early. There are no studies documenting a time gap between the acquisition of linguistic competence and the development of sociolinguistic competence. In fact there is no reason to consider them different to one another. When children acquire their mother tongues, they evidently acquire the local variants and the norms of their usage too.' More recently, Roberts and Labov (1995) and Roberts (1997) have shown that 3 year olds in Philadelphia reproduce complex patterns of vowel and consonant realisation, some of which are undergoing change in the local adult community. Roberts (1997) furthermore found statistically significant differences between 3-year-old boys' and girls' usage of particular variants. Roberts and Labov (1995: 110) conclude that the 3-to-4-year age range is 'a critical period for the acquisition of dialectal norms of the speech community, just as it is for language learning in general'. Some results of our own work (Foulkes *et al.* 1999) are also

---

[8] But both Johnson and Pisoni note that the demand made on memory is probably not excessive. Note too that Linguistics has in the past fifty years or so been heavily influenced by Information Theory; as pointed out by Anderson (1985: 13), 'Those who (like Jakobson) identified the phonological form of an utterance with its potential information content were thus led to require the elimination of predictable information from phonological forms ...'.

relevant here. Our previous work (Docherty and Foulkes 1999) revealed that a pre-aspirated variant of pre-pausal (t) was an innovative form in Tyneside English, strongly correlated with social class and gender, emerging most clearly in the speech of young working-class women speakers. In a subsequent developmental project, our aim has been to investigate the extent to which fine-grained accentual features of this sort can be acquired by even very young children (in the age range 2–4 years) in the process of acquiring their native phonology. Fig. 5.1 shows the frequency with which ten working-class Tyneside children (a subset of the full sample of data, which is still in the process of being collected and analysed) produce a pre-aspirated variant for voiceless stops in pre-pausal position. The findings are not uniform across all speakers but what they do clearly demonstrate is a significant frequency of occurrence of the pre-aspirated pattern in the speech of most of the children. These findings and those of the other investigators mentioned above are supportive of the multiple-trace account in so far as they suggest that children are not simply dispensing with fine-grained features of the signal that are not crucial for lexical contrast—that is, the learned aspects of speech (at least at this stage of development) appear to include features that have a function that is probably not primarily 'linguistic'. And it is not too surprising that this might be the case, for how could children know, *a priori*, what is a *socio*phonetic feature in the ambient language and what is not? Indeed, there is some evidence that variation might have a functional role in phonological learning, which would make it even more important that it is not discarded. Pierrehumbert *et al.* (this volume) cite a number of strands of evidence from first- and second-language acquisition that suggest that 'uniformity impedes the process of language acquisition, and that variability facilitates it' (p. 292).

One issue that is raised by multiple-trace models of lexical representation is whether the statistical information that is amassed will over time lead language-acquirers to reason that there may be abstract categories underlying the complex representations that they have amassed, and the question then is whether those categories might bear any resemblance to categories posited in theoretical models of phonology. This is a matter discussed by Vihman and Velleman (this volume), who conclude that this indeed might be the case, and that innate predispositions may be invoked in carrying out this task. This issue is also tackled by Kuhl and Iverson (1995). Crucially they point out that even if an abstract category representation does emerge from the multiple-trace representations, this is not mutually exclusive with those multiple traces being retained—that is, abstract representation is not necessarily incompatible with a representation which embodies variation. Furthermore, if the work by Pisoni, Johnson, and Strand is on the right track, it would seem implausible for information that might assist with speech perception and word recognition to be discarded.

While the multiple-trace model offers in principle a solution to the difficulties presented by phonetic non-invariance, there is still much to be done in testing its full implications for models of lexical representation. Not least of these is the fact

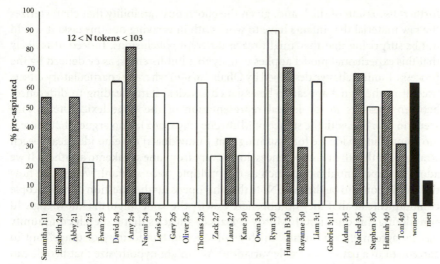

Fig. 5.1. Relative frequency of pre-aspiration in pre-pausal (t) produced by twenty-six Tyneside children aged between 2;0 and 4;0

Note: Bars show the percentage of tokens per child that have pre-aspiration compared to the findings for a group of adult male and female speakers of the same variety of English. The adult bars are not strictly comparable, since they are from a previous study (Docherty *et al.* 1997), but they are given here to allow for a general comparison between the adult and child patterns.

that it needs to be measured up against existing experimental evidence (see Fitzpatrick and Wheeldon, this volume) that would appear to support the view that lexical representations are in fact phonetically underspecified. There are various aspects of the model that require further investigation. First, what is the nature of the parameterization of the traces, and does the parameterization bear any resemblance to the features/prototypes/categories employed by phonologists? Secondly, how are aspects of the signal that are truly 'noise' (for example, environmental noise) distinguished from those aspects of the signal that reflect activity of the speaker's vocal organs? Thirdly, what are the roles of context and lexical probabilities in recognizing and learning that a diverse set of acoustic forms are associated with a single lexical item? And, finally, how does the memory trace representation inform speech production (for example, what is the nature of the goal in word production if its lexical representation is a network of diverse auditory traces)?

In relation to the subject matter of the present volume, a key implication of the multiple-trace model is not only that individual speakers will have many memory traces of the same lexical item, but also that all speakers should not necessarily be expected to acquire the same representations for individual lexical items. If the development of the phonological aspects of lexical representation is largely driven by exposure to the ambient language (see Vihman and Velleman, this volume, for further discussion of this), and, given the enormous variability that characterizes the raw material that infants have to work with in carrying out this task, it would not be surprising that they might reach different conclusions. Indeed, it is likely that this experiential model applies equally to adult listeners, as evidenced by the process of sound change described by Ohala (1986*b*) whereby coarticulatory effects present in the signal appear to be assigned a lexical status leading to differences between speakers in the lexical representation of the same lexical item. This scenario is in line with the stance of Mufwene (1994: 208), who argues that there is 'no compelling evidence for assuming that [individuals] develop identical speech strategies or that their competences do not vary from one speaker to another'. If we adopt an experiential model such as the multiple-trace account, we can see how this would come to be the case. Note that this opens up the question of how people communicate at all if they do not share exactly the same linguistic knowledge. In considering this question, J. Milroy (1992: 90) suggests that a speech community has an 'agreement on norms which results not in "uniformity of usage" but in agreement of a pattern of stable variation'. We might hypothesize that people can communicate when they have linguistic knowledge that is shared above a certain threshold (presumably because the input that they have received in acquiring their native language has equally had a core of shared features).

So, where does this discussion leave us with regard to where and what is phonology? The conventional view of 'uniqueness' is not fatally undermined simply by the presence of an alternative account in the form of multiple-trace models. But it is challenged by the fact that the alternative account is supported by a growing quantity of independent evidence, whereas the position held by many phonologists is apparently sustained in the face of the non-invariance problem remaining unresolved (and, in the eyes of the multiple-trace protagonists, it is irresolvable, because it is only a problem if you assume invariant lexical representations). We revisit this matter in Section 5 below.

There seem to be two conclusions. Either, one of these two models of lexical representation is to be preferred over the other because it offers greater explanatory power (although, given what we have said above about 'data' in phonology, it is not obvious that the benchmark for evaluating explanatory power is common to the two approaches), or we are dealing with theories that are in completely different domains, but purporting to be modelling the same 'entity'—speaker-listeners' knowledge of sound patterning. We turn to this question in the final section.

5. LINGUISTIC THEORY AND SPEECH PERFORMANCE

In this chapter we have argued that phonological theory stops short of providing an account of all of the learned aspects of speech; while it has within its scope a focus on knowledge of pronunciation, it is clear that speakers 'know' much more about this than is—or could be—encapsulated within phonological theory.

Furthermore, it largely does not (as a matter of principle) attempt to account for functional aspects of speech that are not related to lexical contrast, but that are nevertheless encoded systematically and simultaneously by a speaker and that call upon the very same vocal apparatus. In illustrating this situation, we have also drawn attention to emerging evidence that the lexical representation of words may not be 'unique' in the way suggested by phonology and that the non-invariance 'problem' may be something of an artefact of a particular way of approaching phonology.

It is important to acknowledge that we are far from being alone in finding it difficult to reconcile theoretical work on phonology with the evidence on performance variation (e.g. Weinreich *et al.* 1968, Lass 1976, Guy 1994, Kemmer and Israel 1994, Pierrehumbert 1994, many chapters in the Hinskens *et al.* (1997) volume, and in those by Perkell and Klatt (1986) and Johnson and Mullenix (1997)). Despite the long-standing nature of this concern, the difficulty remains.

We suspect this difficulty is driven to a considerable extent by what we perceive as a degree of inconsistency within phonology about the extent to which it is considered legitimate to engage with broader theoretical domains other than that provided by UG. Chomsky (1995) has argued for 'knowledge without grounds' as being one of the key features of UG (reminiscent of the stance taken at the start of SPE referred to earlier), and yet elsewhere seems to admit that there must be some grounding of phonology: 'The information provided by L has to be accommodated to the human sensory and motor apparatus. Hence UG must provide for a phonological component that converts the objects generated by the language L to a form that these 'external' systems can use: PF, we assume. If humans could communicate by telepathy, there would be no need for a phonological component …' (Chomsky 1995: 221).

Relatively few phonologists discuss the empirical foundations of the material they present (hence one of the motivations of this volume), but, as already indicated, none the less they do by and large make heavy appeal to some aspects of speech performance in validating particular theoretical constructs (recent developments in Optimality Theory are no exception to this). At the very least this suggests that there has to be a point of contact with theories with a performance orientation. On the other hand, a much more radical position is proposed by Hale and Reiss (this volume), who advocate a substance-free phonology. One is left to wonder what the evidence would be for such a theory of phonology, and the situation this depicts is reminiscent of that described by Ohala (1995: 715):

One of the fundamental tasks of phonology is to establish how different linguistic messages are conveyed by sound. Whether it is lexical differences or grammatical function, distinct messages must have distinct physical encodings … Well-established methods exist for discovering the physical correlates of different linguistic messages in cases where they are uncertain or disputed. Although such studies are often regarded as having purely phonetic, not phonological interest, this is a mistake: without having an 'anchor' in the real world, phonology risks having its claims apply only in an imaginary universe of little interest to those outside the narrowly circumscribed world of autonomous phonology.

Burton-Roberts and Carr (both this volume) argue strongly for UG to be substance free, but, since they cannot see how phonology could possibly be substance free (a point with which we would agree), they take the line that phonology cannot therefore be a dimension of the radically internal and innate grammar as conceived by Chomsky.

One factor that seems to underlie this uncertainty is that phonology is simultaneously trying to look in two directions; towards UG and towards specific languages and accents. There is a clear tension here; to the extent that a theory is a better account of Language (in general) it may be a less acceptable account of a specific language, and vice versa. On the other hand, languages/accents/lects are all instances of Language and there is no doubt that the study of individual languages has been crucial in informing us of some of the properties that are shared by all languages (the notions of markedness, and naturalness come to mind in this respect).[9]

From our own perspective, we are unconvinced by the arguments for a completely autonomous phonology. While there may be an innate predisposition for acquiring a phonology (any phonology), the facts of phonological acquisition suggest strongly that speaker-hearers' knowledge of the sound patterning of their native language is driven by their exposure to those sounds in the first place. Furthermore, it seems difficult to conceive of speaker-hearers having knowledge of phonology that is not in some way applied in the processes of speaking and listening.

We think there is much to be gained by looking at phonology within a broader context, one that seeks to determine the cognitive, motor, perceptual, and developmental processes that account for the complex sound patterns of human language and languages (taking language in its broadest sense to encompass not simply lexical contrast but all of the other communicative functions that language covers). As an inseparable element of this, it is important to determine how the fact that speech is acquired and used within a fundamentally social context impacts on our understanding of these processes. This is a research agenda that explicitly appeals to extralinguistic factors (and to the insights of other related disciplines). The question is, where does phonology fit within this theory? Part of this overall theory must be an account of what speakers acquire and know about the sound patterning of their native language. It would be perfectly sensible to take as a starting hypothesis that some of the constructs of phonological theory may well be relevant in understanding speech processing; see Fitzpatrick and Wheeldon (this

---

[9] We must acknowledge here that the view that we are presenting of the relationship between Language and languages reflects one of the two possible ways of specifying this relationship identified and discussed at length by Burton-Roberts (this volume). Burton-Roberts labels this approach as the 'generic' conception of this relationship, and he contrasts it with the 'realist' or 'naturalistic' approach according to which Language 'has a reality independent of languages'.

volume) and Nolan (1982), who points out that some of the best hypotheses we have about the speech-production mechanism are those that are provided by phonological theory—not to mention the now substantial evidence that linguistic structure can govern the phonetic shape of words (see Shattuck-Hufnagel and Turk (1996) for an overview of this work), and the abundance of work in psycholinguistics demonstrating the apparent role of different types of representation in speech processing (Cutler 1986, 1992). Crucially, where there is evidence of phonological structure influencing performance (for example, truncations, speech errors[10]), then the onus within this approach would be on providing independent evidence of how these structures are present in the processing chain, as opposed to simply assuming that the phonological analysis is actually part of the processing chain.

The question for phonological theory and those who formulate it is whether, when all is said and done, they see their work embedded in a broader theoretical framework of this sort. If phonology cannot be conceived of as part of a broader model of speech communication, as we suspect many of its practitioners would wish to argue, then we remain pessimistic about the extent to which the impasse which we have identified in this chapter will be overcome. If it can, however, then we would welcome further exploration of the extent to which phonology captures individuals' knowledge of speech sound patterning in the broadest sense. For example, it may well be that contrast-related patterning is handled differently in memory from patterning related to other functions (although the evidence from work on multiple-trace models of representation and our own findings regarding phonological acquisition suggests this may not be the case); but the point is that this is an empirical issue and it will only be possible to sustain any theoretical stance on a foundation of a sufficient and adequately interpreted body of data.

REFERENCES

Abbs, J. (1986), 'Invariance and Variability in Speech Production: A Distinction between Linguistic Intent and its Neuromotor Implementation, in J. Perkell and D. Klatt (eds.), *Invariance and Variability in Speech Processes* (Hillsdale, NJ: Lawrence Erlbaum), 202–19.

Anderson, S. (1985), *Phonology in the Twentieth Century* (Chicago: University of Chicago Press).

Burton-Roberts, N. (this volume), 'Where and What is Phonology? A Representational Perspective'.

Browman, C. P. and Goldstein, L. (1992), 'Articulatory Phonology: An Overview', *Phonetica*, 49: 155–80.

Carr, P. (1993), *Phonology*, (London: Macmillan).

—— (this volume), 'Scientific Realism, Sociophonetic Variation, and Innate Endowments in Phonology'.

Chambers, J. K. (1995), *Sociolinguistic Theory* (Oxford: Blackwell).

---

[10] See Mowrey and MacKay (1990) for interesting counter-evidence.

Cho, T. and Ladefoged, P. (1999), 'Variation and Universals in VOT: Evidence from 18 languages, *Journal of Phonetics*, 27: 207–29.

Chomsky, N. (1995), *The Minimalist Program* (Cambridge, Mass.: MIT Press).

—— and Halle, M. (1968), *The Sound Pattern of English* (New York: Harper & Row).

Clements, G. N. (1992), 'Phonological Primes: Features or Gestures?', *Phonetica*, 49: 181–93.

Cohn, A. (1993), 'Nasalization in English: Phonology or Phonetics', *Phonology*, 10: 43–81.

Cutler, A. (1986), Phonological Structure in Speech Recognition, *Phonology*, 3: 161–78.

—— (1992), 'Psychology and the Segment', in G. J. Docherty, and D. R. Ladd (eds.), *Papers in Laboratory Phonology* II (Cambridge: Cambridge University Press), 290–5.

Docherty, G. J. (1992), *The Timing of Voicing in British English Obstruents* (Berlin: Foris).

—— (forthcoming), 'On the Interpretation of Speakers' Performance: Commentary on Papers by Zawaydeh, Silverman, Hayward *et al.*, and Tajima and Port', in J. Local, R. Ogden, and R. Temple (eds.), *Papers in Laboratory Phonology VI* (Cambridge: Cambridge University Press).

—— and Foulkes, P. (1999), 'Derby and Newcastle: Instrumental Phonetics and Variationist Studies', in P. Foulkes and G. J. Docherty (eds.), *Urban Voices: Accent Studies in the British Isles* (London: Arnold), 47–71.

—— —— Milroy, J., Milroy, L., and Walshaw, D. (1997), 'Descriptive Adequacy in Phonology: A Variationist Perspective', *Journal of Linguistics*, 33/2: 275–310.

Estes, W. K. (1993), 'Concepts, Categories and Psychological Science', *Psychological Science*, 4: 143–53.

Fitzpatrick, J. and Wheeldon, L. (this volume), 'Phonology and Phonetics in Psycholinguistic Models of Speech Perception'.

Foulkes, P. and Docherty, G. J. (1999) (eds.), *Urban Voices: Accent Studies in the British Isles* (London: Arnold).

—— —— and Watt, D. (1999), 'Tracking the Emergence of Structured Variation: Realizations of (t) by Newcastle children', *Leeds Working Papers in Linguistics and Phonetics*, 7: 1–25.

Fourakis, M. and Port, R. (1986), 'Stop Epenthesis in English', *Journal of Phonetics*, 14: 197–221.

Giegerich, H. (1992), *English Phonology: An Introduction* (Cambridge: Cambridge University Press).

Goldsmith, J. A. (1995), (ed.), *The Handbook of Phonological Theory* (Oxford: Blackwell).

Guy, G. (1994), 'The Phonology of Variation', in K. Beals, J. Denton, R. Knippen, L. Melnar, H. Suzuki, and E. Zeinfold (eds.), *Papers from the 30th Meeting of the Chicago Linguistic Society*, ii. *Papers from the Parasession on Variation* (Chicago: Chicago Linguistic Society), 133–49.

Hale, M. and Reiss, C. (this volume), 'Phonology as Cognition'.

Halle, M. (1964), 'On the Bases of Phonology', in J. Fodor and J. Katz (eds.), *The Structure of Language: Readings in the Philosophy of Language* (Englewood Cliffs, NJ: Prentice-Hall), 324–33.

Harris, J. (1994), *English Sound Structure* (Oxford: Blackwell).

Hinskens, F., Hout, R. van, and Wetzels, L. (1997), (eds.), *Variation, Change, and Phonological Theory* (Amsterdam: John Benjamins).

Hintzman, D. L. (1986), '"Schema Abstraction" in a Multiple-Trace Memory Model', *Psychological Review*, 93: 411–28.

Hulst, H. van der (this volume), 'Modularity and Modality in Phonology'.

Hyman, L. M. (1975), *Phonology, Theory and Analysis* (New York: Holt, Rinehart and Winston).

Johnson, K. (1997), Speech Perception without Speaker Normalization, in K. Johnson and J. W. Mullennix (eds.), *Talker Variability in Speech Processing* (San Diego, Calif.: Academic Press), 145–65.

—— and Mullenix, J. (1997), (eds.), *Talker Variability in Speech Processing* (San Diego, Calif.: Academic Press).

Keating, P. A. (1984), 'Phonetic and Phonological Representation of Stop Consonant Voicing', *Language* 60: 286–319.

Kelly, J. and Local, J. (1989), *Doing Phonology* (Manchester: University of Manchester Press).

Kemmer, S. and Israel, M. (1994), 'Variation and the Usage-Based Model', in K. Beals, J. Denton, R. Knippen, L. Melnar, H. Suzuki, and E. Zeinfeld (eds.), *Papers from the 30th Meeting of the Chicago Linguistic Society*, ii. *Papers from the Parasession on Variation* (Chicago: Chicago Linguistic Society), 165–79.

Kenstowicz, M. (1994), *Phonology in Generative Grammar* (Oxford: Blackwell).

Kingston, J. and Diehl, R. (1994), Phonetic Knowledge, *Language*, 70: 419–54.

Klatt, D. H. (1986), 'The Problem of Variability in Speech Recognition and in Models of Speech Perception', in J. Perkell and D. Klatt (eds.), *Invariance and Variability in Speech Processes* (Hillsdale, NJ: Lawrence Erlbaum), 300–19.

Kuhl, P. K. and Iverson, P. (1995), 'Linguistic Experience and the "Perceptual Magnet" Effect', in W. Strange (ed.), *Speech Perception and Linguistic Experience: Theoretical and Methodological Issues* (Baltimore: York Press), 121–54.

Labov, W. (1986), 'Sources of Inherent Variation in the Speech Process', in J. Perkell and D. Klatt (eds.), *Invariance and Variability in Speech Processes* (Hillsdale, NJ: Lawrence Erlbaum), 402–23.

—— (1990), 'The Intersection of Sex and Social Class in the Course of Linguistic Change', *Language Variation and Change*, 2: 205–54.

—— (1994), *Principles of Linguistic Change*, i. *Internal Factors* (Oxford: Blackwell).

Ladd, D. R. (1996), *Intonational Phonology* (Cambridge: Cambridge University Press).

Lass, R. (1976), *English Phonology and Phonological Theory* (Cambridge: Cambridge University Press).

—— (1984), *Phonology* (Cambridge: Cambridge University Press).

Laver, J. (1994), *Principles of Phonetics* (Cambridge: Cambridge University Press).

Lindau, M. (1975), 'Features For Vowels', *UCLA Working Papers in Phonetics*, 30: 1–155.

Lindblom, B. (1986), 'On the Origin and Purpose of Discreteness and Invariance in Sound Patterns', in J. Perkell and D. Klatt (eds.), *Invariance and Variability in Speech Processes* (Hillsdale, NJ: Lawrence Erlbaum), 493–510.

—— (1990), 'Explaining Phonetic Variation: A Sketch of the H & H Theory', in W. Hardcastle and A. Marchal (eds.), *Speech Production and Speech Modelling* (Dordrecht: Kluwer), 403–39.

Local, J. K. (1983), 'How Many Vowels in a Vowel?', *Journal of Child Language*, 10: 449–53.

Maddieson, I. (1984), *Patterns of Sounds* (Cambridge: Cambridge University Press).

Milroy, J. (1992), *Linguistic Variation and Change: On the Historical Sociolinguistics of English* (Oxford: Blackwell).

Milroy, L., Milroy, J., Docherty, G. J., Foulkes, P., and Walshaw, D. (1999), 'Phonological Variation and Change in Contemporary English: Evidence from Newcastle upon Tyne and Derby', *Cuadernos De Filología Inglesa De La Universidad De Murcia*, 8: 35–46.

Mowrey, R. and MacKay, I. (1990), 'Phonological Primitives: Electromyographic Speech Error Evidence', *Journal of the Acoustical Society of America*, 88: 1299–312.

Mufwene, S. (1994), 'Theoretical Linguistics and Variation Analysis: Strange Bedfellows?', in K. Beals, J. Denton, R. Knippen, L. Melnar, H. Suzuki, and E. Zeinfeld (eds.), *Papers from the 30th Meeting of the Chicago Linguistic Society*, ii. *Papers from the Parasession on Variation* (Chicago: Chicago Linguistic Society), 202–17.

Myers, S. (this volume), 'Boundary Disputes: The Distinction between Phonetic and Phonological Sound Patterns'.

Nolan, F. (1982), 'The Role of Action Theory in the Description of Speech Production', *Linguistics*, 20: 287–308.

Nosofsky, R. M. (1986), 'Attention, Similarity, and the Identification-Categorization Relationship', *Journal of Experimental Psychology: General*, 115: 39–57.

—— (1988), 'Exemplar-Based Accounts of Relations between Classification, Recognition, and Typicality', *Journal of Experimental Psychology: Learning, Memory, and Cognition*, 14: 700–8.

—— (1991), 'Tests of An Exemplar Model for Relating Perceptual Classification and Recognition Memory', *Journal of Experimental Psychology: Human Perception and Performance*, 17: 3–27.

—— Kruschke, J. K., and McKinley, S. C. (1992), 'Combining Exemplar-Based Category Representations and Connectionist Learning Rules', *Journal of Experimental Psychology: Learning, Memory, and Cognition*, 18: 211–33.

Ohala, J. J. (1986a), 'Consumer's Guide to Evidence in Phonology', *Phonology*, 3: 3–26.

—— (1986b), 'Phonological Evidence for Top-Down Processing in Speech Perception', in J. Perkell and D. Klatt (eds.), *Invariance and Variability in Speech Processes* (Hillsdale, NJ: Lawrence Erlbaum), 386–96.

—— (1995), 'Experimental Phonology', in J. A. Goldsmith (ed.), *Handbook of Phonological Theory* (Cambridge, Mass.: Blackwell).

Pandeli, H. (1993), 'The Articulation of Lingual Consonants: An EPG Study', Ph.D. dissertation (Cambridge University).

Perkell, J. and Klatt, D. (1986), (eds.), *Invariance and Variability in Speech Processes* (Hillsdale, NJ: Lawrence Erlbaum).

Pierrehumbert, J. B. (1994), 'Knowledge of Variation', in K. Beals, J. Deaton, R. Knippen, L. Melnar, H. Suzuki, and E. Zeinfeld (eds.), *Papers from the 30th Meeting of the Chicago Linguistic Society*, ii. *Papers from the Parasession on Variation* (Chicago: Linguistic Society), 232–56.

—— Beckman, M., and Ladd, D. R. (this volume), 'Conceptual Foundations of Phonology as a Laboratory Science'.

Pisoni, D. B. (1997), 'Some Thoughts on "Normalization" in Speech Perception', in K. Johnson and J. W. Mullennix (eds.), *Talker Variability in Speech Processing* (San Diego, Calif.: Academic Press), 9–32.

Roberts, J. (1997), 'Acquisition of Variable Rules: A Study of (-t, d) Deletion in Preschool Children', *Journal of Child Language*, 24: 351–72.

—— and Labov, W. (1995), 'Learning to Talk Philadelphian', *Language Variation and Change*, 7: 101–12.

Roca, I. and Johnson, W. (1999), *A Course in Phonology* (Oxford: Blackwell).

Schane, S. (1973), *Generative Phonology* (Englewood Cliffs, NJ: Prentice-Hall).

Schegloff, E. (1988), 'Discourse as an Interactional Achievment II: An Exercise in Conversation Analysis', in D. Tannen (ed.), *Linguistics in Context: Connecting Observation and Understanding* (Norwood, NJ: Ablex).

Scobbie, J. M., Hewlett, N., and Turk, A. (1999), 'Standard English in Edinburgh and Glasgow: The Scottish Vowel Length Rule Revealed', in P. Foulkes and G. J. Docherty (eds.), *Urban Voices: Accent Studies in the British Isles* (London: Arnold), 230–45.

Shattuck-Hufnagel, S. and Turk, A. (1996), 'A Prosody Tutorial for Investigators of Auditory Sentence Processing', *Journal of Psycholinguistic Research*, 25: 193–247.

Simpson, A. (1999), 'Fundamental Problems in Comparative Phonetics and Phonology: Does UPSID Help to Solve Them?', in J. Ohala, R. Hasegawa, M. Ohala, D. Granville, and A. Bailey (eds.), *Proceedings of the XIV International Congress of Phonetic Sciences* (distributed on CD-Rom by the Regents of the University of California), 349–52.

Strand, E. (1999), 'Uncovering the Role of Gender Stereotypes in Speech Perception', *Journal of Language and Social Psychology*, 18: 86–99.

—— and Johnson, K. (1996), 'Gradient and Visual Speaker Normalization in the Perception of Fricatives', in D. Gibbon (ed.), *Natural Language Processing and Speech Technology: Proceedings of the 3rd KONVENS Conference, Bielefeld, October 1996* (Berlin: Mouton), 14–26.

Thomas, E. (2000), 'Spectral Differences in /ai/ Offsets Conditioned by Voicing of the Following Consonant', *Journal of Phonetics*, 28: 1–25.

Trubetzkoy, N. S. (1969), *Principles of Phonology* (Berkeley and Los Angeles: University of California Press) (translation by C. Baltaxe of *Grundzüge der Phonologie* (Goettingen: Vandenhoeck and Ruprecht, 1958).

Vihman, M. M. and Velleman, S. (this volume), 'Phonetics and the Origin of Phonology'.

Vogel, I. (1992), 'Comments on Chapters 3 and 4', in G. J. Docherty and D. R. Ladd (eds.), *Papers in Laboratory Phonology II* (Cambridge: Cambridge University Press), 124–7.

Weinreich, U., Labov, W., and Herzog M. (1968), 'Empirical Foundations for a Theory of Language Change', in W. P. Lehmann and Y. Malkiel (eds.), *Directions for Historical Linguistics* (Austin, Tex.: University of Texas Press), 95–188.

6

Phonology and Phonetics in Psycholinguistic Models of Speech Perception

JENNIFER FITZPATRICK AND LINDA R. WHEELDON

1. INTRODUCTION

The relationship between psychological and linguistic theory has never been clear-cut. Indeed, following the unsuccessful attempts to demonstrate the psychological reality of transformational grammar, developments in these disciplines have been more parallel than interactive. However, in recent years, increasing use has been made of many ideas from generative phonology by psycholinguists interested in the processes underlying our comprehension of spoken language. In this chapter we will examine and evaluate the developing relationship between linguistic and psychological approaches to the representations and processes underlying the comprehension of spoken words.

The structure of this chapter will be as follows. We will begin in Section 2 with a discussion of the different aims of psychologists and linguists in relation to the description of language structure and process and the extent to which these aims could or indeed should coincide. That is, is it necessarily the case that those representations that best capture a speaker's underlying knowledge of the sound systems of their language are the same as those stored or generated during the comprehension of a spoken utterance?

Section 3 will give an introduction to early psycholinguistic models of language perception. In particular, we will focus on the role of phonological and phonetic representations in psycholinguistic models of spoken-word recognition. These models will be discussed in relation to linguistic theory. Here, the question of interest is which assumptions, representations, and processes have been adopted from phonetic and phonological theory and how do they relate to the purely psychological aspects of the models. While early models of spoken-word recognition were happy to adopt morphological, syntactic, and semantic

Our thanks to Aditi Lahiri, Henning Reetz, Michael Wagner, and the editors of this volume for valuable comments on this paper.

representations more or less directly from linguistic theory, they largely sidestepped those issues that had to do with the relationship between acoustic-phonetic representations of the speech signal and stored lexical-phonological representations. More recently, however, psycholinguistic modelling of early speech recognition processes has increased dramatically in its linguistic sophistication and models are emerging that promise to provide a framework for the solution of some perennial problems faced both by psycholinguistic models and by automatic speech recognition systems. One such model, the FEATURALLY UNDERSPECIFIED LEXICON (FUL) MODEL will be described in some detail in Section 4, and experimental evidence will be discussed in Section 5. The chapter will conclude in Section 6 with an evaluation of the success of the psychology–linguistics relationship to date and some suggestions for the way forward.

2. PSYCHOLOGICAL AND LINGUISTIC MODELS OF LANGUAGE

2.1. *The early days: syntactic theory*

Attempts to sort out the relationship between psychology and linguistics began in earnest with developments in the field of syntax. Early psycholinguistic research focused on generative grammar. In *Syntactic Structures* Chomsky (1957) proposed that each sentence has a computational derivation comprising a kernel structure and transformations for changing that structure. The possibility that such underlying mechanisms might be psychologically real posed a challenge to behaviourism as an empirical approach to language behaviour, and a new school of cognitive psychologists set about developing experimental methods to determine to what extent the principles and constructs proposed in theoretical linguistics are psychologically valid. Research that attempted to demonstrate the behavioural relevance of hierarchical phrase structures and surface phrase structures met with some success (Fodor and Bever 1965; Blumenthal 1967). However, evidence in support of the psychological validity of transformations was not forthcoming (Fodor and Garrett 1967; Bever 1970). Such failures led to a general abandonment of the idea that abstract models proposed by linguistics need map onto observed language behaviour.

Chomsky's own solution to the division of labour between linguistics and psychology rested on the distinction he drew between linguistic competence and linguistic performance. According to Chomsky, the work of linguistics is to detail linguistic competence, or the knowledge that people have of the grammar of their language. In contrast, the proper focus of psychology is to explain performance, or the way in which people use their linguistic competence in the perception and production of spoken language. Indeed, Chomsky's grammars could never be interpreted as performance models. The central role is given to an autonomous, generative syntactic component from which both meaning and form can be derived. Therefore, the order of processes in the grammar cannot be mapped, in any straightforward fashion, onto the order of processes required for speech production or perception that must progress from meaning to sound and vice versa. Chomsky (1967) makes it clear that his grammar is not a performance model but a model of the mental grammar that is tapped into during language use. However, even this proposal for the relationship between grammar and language use has failed to bear fruit in terms of an integrated model of linguistic knowledge and language perception or production. Perhaps unsurprisingly, a grammar that describes the relationship between meaning, sound, and syntax without taking account of their temporal relationship during language use is unlikely to generate those structures or processes required by cognitive models of language processing. More recently, lexical approaches to grammar have proved more useful to psychologists in providing representations and processes that can be incorporated into testable models of language processing (see e.g. Gazdar 1981; Bresnan and Kaplan 1982; Langacker 1987).

2.2. *Phonological theory and language processing*

In recent years phonological theory has undergone its own generative revolution. In early generative phonology, following *The Sound Pattern of English* (*SPE*) (Chomsky and Halle 1968), rules were complex and representations simple; the only units of phonological representation posited were segments made up of unordered sets of features developed from the distinctive feature theory of Jakobson, Fant, and Halle (1952). In the 1970s much of the interest in phonology shifted from rules to representations, and there followed a boom in hierarchical phonological structure, including segmental slots, autosegmental features, hierarchical feature structure (feature geometry), metrical constituents such as syllables, feet, and prosodic words, subconstituents of the syllable (onset-rhyme for some, moras for others), and phonological domains such as the phonological phrase and the intonational phrase. These structures figure in a wide variety of linguistic phenomena, including, but not limited to, tone and intonation, vowel harmony, segment length, feature dependencies and assimilations, stress, prosodic morphology, and phrasal phonology.

As the phonological representations became richer, in many respects they became sparser where underspecification was adopted (for an overview, see Steriade 1995). Both rules and representations were claimed to be more highly constrained under Lexical Phonology/Morphology (LPM) (see Kiparsky 1982, 1985; Mohanan 1986, 1995). LPM did more than replace *SPE*'s awkward boundary symbols with levels; it made predictions about the behaviour of lexical and postlexical rules, it constrained rule application, placed restrictions on the abstractness of underlying representations and the opacity of derivations, and banned predictable information from underlying representations.

Rules also became increasingly replaced by constraints following discussions of 'conspiracies' (Kisseberth 1970), natural phonology (Stampe 1980), markedness, and preferences. Constraints either were mixed with rules in constraint-violation-and-repair systems (Paradis 1988; Myers 1991) or replaced them entirely in non-derivational systems (Declarative Phonology: Bird 1990; Scobbie 1991; Optimality Theory: McCarthy and Prince 1993; Prince and Smolensky 1993).

Psycholinguistics is just beginning to catch up with this theoretical revolution. As will be seen in the next section, early phonological psycholinguistic investigations were predominately focused on phonemes/segments/letters, but the rediscovery of the syllable in phonology sparked a large interest (Forster 1979; Mehler *et al.* 1981; Cutler *et al.* 1986; Cutler and Norris 1988; Church 1987). The phonological word has been much discussed in the production literature (Levelt 1989; Levelt and Wheeldon 1994; Wheeldon and Lahiri 1997; Levelt *et al.* 1999) but largely ignored in perception. Investigations of intonation have been struggling to determine intonational categories and assign meaning to contours, but all the experiments are offline (e.g. Gussenhoven and Rietveld 1997) and do not tap into the intonational lexicon in the same way that psycholinguistic experiments tap into the mental (word) lexicon.

The focus of this chapter is the modelling of speech perception processes. In particular, the process by which we map from the acoustic speech signal to some representation of words in our MENTAL LEXICON. Within this field psychologists have only just begun to take full advantage of the recent developments in phonological theory. Nevertheless, it is already clear that major benefits are accruing from a more linguistically sophisticated approach. There are a couple of reasons why phonological theory may be proving more immediately tractable than syntactic theory to psychologists. In addition to the necessity of taking into account the ordering of processes necessary for a particular linguistic behaviour, psycholinguistic models of language processing must provide an account of the temporal properties of human linguistic performance. An adequate cognitive model of human behaviour must explain the speed with which a given behaviour is accomplished and why certain contexts can have facilitatory or detrimental consequences for performance. Generative phonology has provided clearer models for potential mappings from phonological to psychological ordering of processes. In addition, as we will demonstrate below, phonological theory provides clearly testable predictions concerning the relationship between the representation of linguistic form and observable language behaviour.

3. PSYCHOLINGUISTIC MODELS OF SPOKEN WORD RECOGNITION

Psycholinguistic models tend to concentrate either on issues of processing—whether comprehension involves autonomous, serial processes or interactive, parallel processes—or on issues of representation—what levels of linguistic representation are relevant for comprehension and what linguistic units speakers use to access the lexicon. These two aspects are discussed in Section 3.1 and Section 3.2, and, as we will see, most models fail to provide a unified account of both.

3.1. Issues of processing

Early psycholinguistic models were heavily influenced by linguistics in so far as the levels and units of mental representations of linguistic form incorporated were derived directly from linguistic theory. All theories assumed a long term-memory store of linguistic knowledge comprising separate processing systems of phonological, morphological, syntactic, and semantic representations and rules. However, the main aim for psycholinguists (very much along Chomskian guidelines) was to detail the processes by which this information was accessed and used during the recognition of spoken words. The important questions focused on processing and architecture. To what extent can the comprehension process be broken down into autonomous subprocesses? To what extent do these processes interact? And what computational architectures can best model these processes?

Many psychologists first assumed that the distinct knowledge systems proposed by linguists could be translated directly into computationally independent or autonomous processing components. Forster's SEARCH MODEL (1976, 1979) embodies these assumptions. It proposes that linguistic information is processed in an entirely autonomous and serial fashion. The Search Model assumes that for each word we store lexical, syntactic, and semantic information. However, in Search, three autonomous linguistic systems encode and process these levels of representation. Initially, auditory information is passed onto a lexical processor, which matches it against stored phonetic lexical representations one by one until a match is found. Only once a match is found can lexical information be passed onto the syntactic processor, which attempts to build a syntactic structure. Finally, syntactic information is passed onto the message generator, where a conceptual structure is generated. Forster's model assumes, therefore, that information flows in one direction only and that higher level syntactic or semantic information cannot affect processing at the level of lexical form.

However, serial, autonomous models were soon challenged by experimentally derived performance data detailing the speed and accuracy of speech processing in a number of laboratory tasks. In spoken-word monitoring tasks response times to words spoken in normal sentence contexts are approximately 250 ms from word onset—far too early for the acoustic information itself to be sufficient to specify uniquely the word in question (Marslen-Wilson and Tyler 1980). Moreover, subjects who can repeat speech back at delays of approximately 250 ms show evidence that sentential context can affect their interpretation of the input (Marslen-Wilson 1973). The need to explain such data led to the generation of more interactive processing models. Morton's (1969, 1982) LOGOGEN MODEL postulated a recognition device or logogen for each word in the mental lexicon. A logogen stores all levels of linguistic information for a given word and becomes activated by any appropriate phonological and sentential information derived from the processing incoming speech signal. All kinds of information (phonological, morphological, syntactic, and semantic) are monitored for simultaneously by all logogens in parallel. Matching information activates all appropriate logogens in parallel until one crosses a threshold level of activation and fires. At this point the word represented by that logogen is recognized. The Logogen Model therefore functions in a highly parallel and interactive fashion in that it places no constraints on how and when different kinds of linguistic information affect word recognition. Although the Logogen Model is not explicit about either the nature of the information represented or its weighting in the recognition process, many of the basic assumptions in the Logogen Model have been incorporated into interactive activation computer models such as TRACE (McClelland and Elman 1986). In this model the representation of a word is distributed over a network of simple processing units or nodes. Separate levels of nodes represent distinctive features, phonemes, and words. Every word node is linked to the nodes for the phonemes it comprises at the level below, and in turn every phoneme node is linked to its distinctive feature nodes. The links between levels of representation are bidirectional and pass activation. In addition, all nodes within a level of representation are connected by bidirectional links, but these links spread inhibition. Similar to the Logogen Model, nodes are activated by matching information in the incoming signal. When a given node reaches its threshold of activation, it spreads either activation or inhibition to all nodes connected with it. A word is said to be recognized when its activation level reaches a criterial level of activation compared to the sum of the activation levels of all other units (the Luce choice rule (Luce 1959)). Unlike the Logogen Model, TRACE is a highly explicit model in both representation and processing terms. Input to this model consists of idealized acoustic feature values across different time slices.

The COHORT MODEL (Marslen-Wilson and Tyler 1980; Marslen-Wilson 1984, 1987; Lahiri and Marslen-Wilson 1991, 1992) incorporates both autonomous and interactive processing features. This model assumes that word recognition involves a process of narrowing-down from an initial set of candidate words. According to the Cohort Model, the activation of an initial set of candidate words is based entirely on whether their stored lexical-phonological representations match with the first 150 ms of the incoming speech signal. This matching process results in a cohort of candidate words that share initial phonemes. As soon as the initial cohort is delimited, all kinds of linguistic information can be used in parallel to eliminate candidate words. Words can be rejected if they mismatch with continuously incoming acoustic-phonetic information but also if they mismatch with the available syntactic or semantic structure being generated for the utterance. Word recognition occurs when only one candidate remains in the cohort.

3.2. Issues of levels and units of representation

In psycholinguistic models the two perceptual processes that involve the lexicon are lexical access and word recognition. Lexical access refers to the initial mapping of the incoming acoustic signal onto lexical representations stored in the mental lexicon and word recognition occurs when a single lexical entry is selected.

Phonetic processes and representations played no real part in early psycholinguistic models of spoken-word recognition. Klatt's (1979) LEXICAL ACCESS FROM SPECTRA (LAFS) MODEL was largely ignored by psychologists. In the LAFS Model spoken-word recognition is accomplished based on acoustic information alone. However, this model proposes the parallel matching of acoustic information in the form of power spectra directly against stored prototype lexical representations consisting of diphone power spectra sequences (see also prototype models, as in Estes 1994). The problem of how we map from the continuously varying context-dependent acoustic signal to discrete linguistic units has proved highly intractable over the last thirty years (Liberman *et al.* 1967; Studdert-Kennedy 1974; Stevens and Blumstein 1981). Psychologists essentially sidestepped the problem of explaining what information listeners extract from the acoustic signal to access the lexicon. The detailing of this process was considered the realm of psychoacoustics and acoustic phonetics. Instead it was assumed that some intermediate representation consisting of abstract phonological information mediates between the acoustic signal and the lexicon. The issue addressed by psycholinguistics was then given a prelexical phonological representation of the speech input, how are the lexicon accessed and the appropriate word selected? Some debate occurred as to the nature of the linguistic units generated by early acoustic-phonetic processes. In particular, syllables were proposed as access units that mediate between the acoustic input and the lexicon (discussed below). However, the general assumption following Chomsky and Halle (1968) was that the access representation consisted of linear strings of discrete phonemes (see Pisoni and Luce 1987 for a review).

Despite having avoided the issue of acoustic-phonetic non-invariance, the psycholinguistic models outlined above provide no real account of how phonological variation is dealt with during speech perception. One view expressed in the literature is that variation is 'noise', in part because it leads to a loss of information (see the discussion in Church 1987). For instance, in English flapping neutralizes the distinction between /t/ and /d/ to [ɾ], palatalization neutralizes /s/ and /ʃ/, reduction of unstressed vowels to schwa neutralizes a number of vowels. Another view is that, since regular variation (allophonic as well as neutralizing) is context sensitive, it reveals useful cues about prosodic and morphosyntactic structure, which can aid in processing (Lehiste 1960; Christie 1974; Church 1987). To deal with variation, one extreme is to pack as much information into the lexicon as possible, storing every variant pronunciation of a word, while the other extreme is to put as little information into the lexicon as possible, letting the grammar take care of variation. The latter approach allows for (at least) two possibilities: one is to 'undo' the variation before accessing the lexicon, the other is to access the lexicon immediately.

Generative phonologists tend to think in terms of generating/production rather than processing/perception.[1] This is not a trivial point, since perception is not simply production reversed. Psycholinguistic models of language production (Levelt 1989; Levelt and Wheeldon 1994; Levelt *et al.* 1999), sketched in (2), correspond more or less to the GENERATIVE PHONOLOGY MODEL in (1). But psycholinguistic models of perception, three of which are sketched in (3), vary in their fundamental assumptions about what levels and units of representations are involved in perception, as summarized in (4).

(1) Generative phonology model

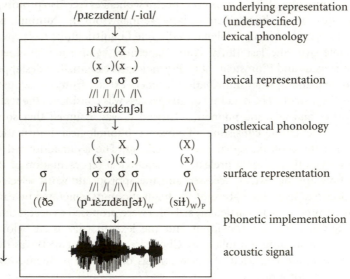

(2) Psycholinguistic model of production

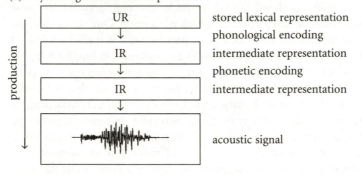

---

[1] But see Burton-Roberts (this volume) and Carr (this volume) for discussions on whether 'generate' is to be equated with 'produce'.

(3) Psycholinguistic models of perception

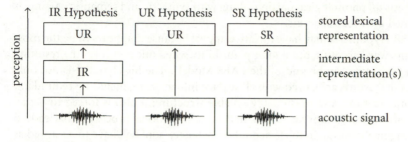

(4) Lexical access

(*a*) *The IR Hypothesis*:
The acoustic signal is analysed in terms of some intermediate abstract phonological unit (segments, syllables, or strong syllables), and this access unit is used to access the lexicon.

(*b*) *The UR Hypothesis*:
The features extracted from the acoustic signal are mapped directly onto the underlying, underspecified representations of words. The access unit is the feature.

(*c*) *The SR Hypothesis*:
The information extracted from the acoustic signal is mapped directly onto the surface representations of words, which are fully specified with all phonetic and phonological information.

The IR and UR Hypotheses share the assumption that the mental representation of a lexical item (in the psycholinguistic sense) corresponds to the abstract, phonologically underspecified underlying representation of that item (in the linguistic sense). In contrast, the SR Hypothesis assumes that the mental representation of a lexical item corresponds to its surface representation.

The notion of an intermediate representation, (4*a*), has received a great deal of interest in psycholinguistics. Early versions of the Cohort Model assumed that the incoming acoustic-phonetic information was analysed into linear strings of phonemes that were matched against lexical representations with a similar phonological structure. More explicit versions of (4*a*) proposed syllables (Forster 1979; Mehler *et al.* 1981; Church 1987) or strong syllables (Cutler *et al.* 1986; Cutler and Norris 1988; Norris 1994) as access units that mediate between the acoustic input and the lexicon. In contrast, (4*b*), later versions of the Cohort Model (Lahiri and Marslen-Wilson 1991, 1992), including the FUL Model, assume that distinctive features extracted from the acoustic signal are used to access the lexicon, bypassing any type of intermediate representation. This novel use of features as access units unifies processing and representation in a single model. The IR Hypothesis initially seems plausible, because it mirrors the production process, and it is assumed that listeners build abstract structure—phonological, syntactic, semantic—when processing an utterance. However, under debate is at what stage in the perception process this abstract structure is built. Under the IR Hypothesis *some* phonological parsing is performed *before* lexical access, while under the UR Hypothesis *all* phonological parsing, along with syntactic and semantic parsing, is performed *after* lexical access.

The SR Hypothesis may have intuitive appeal because it appears to be the most straightforward account, but it loses plausibility when one considers the resulting lexicon (the same can be said of the LAFS Model). The SR Hypothesis not only assumes that words are stored with all surface information, including redundant, allophonic features and presumably syllable structure; it also is forced to list all variant pronunciations of each word. In the case of optional processes, this leads to surprising proliferation in the lexicon. For instance, 'son' will have to be stored as [sʌn] ~ [sʌm] ~ [sʌŋ]. The grammar must also be active to tell the listener which variant is viable in which context ([sʌm bɹɔt] could be either 'some brought' or 'son brought', [sʌm keɪm] could only be 'some came'), meaning the representations are duplicating the work of the grammar. The SR Hypothesis need not take a stand on whether there is an abstract underlying representation, although one reason for making this hypothesis is the assumption that there is no UR.

The IR Hypothesis was assumed in a series of experiments demonstrating the 'syllable effect', discussed in Section 5.1. The UR Hypothesis was assumed in a set of experiments that led to the FUL Model. This model is first described in detail in Section 4, after which the experimental evidence is discussed in Sections 5.2 and 5.3. The SR Hypothesis was assumed in a related experiment, also discussed in Section 5.2.

4. THE FUL MODEL

The Featurally Underspecified Lexicon Model is intended to be a model of both human speech perception (Lahiri and Jongman 1990; Lahiri and Marslen-Wilson 1991, 1992) and automatic speech recognition (Reetz 1998; Lahiri 1999; Lahiri and Reetz 1999, forthcoming). This is a knowledge-based recognition model, as opposed to a purely statistical model based on Hidden Markov Models (HMMs) or neural nets.[2] The model is sketched in Fig. 6.1.

4.1. Lexical access vs. parsing

This model makes a crucial division of labour between lexical access and parsing. Lexical access is the first stage in perception, where features are extracted from the acoustic signal and mapped directly onto the lexicon. Parsing is the second stage, where the candidate set (the set of cohorts) activated by the lexicon is parsed in terms of morphological, syntactic, semantic, and hierarchical phonological structure (syllables, feet, phonological phrasing, and so forth).

[2] Statistical models are purely mathematical and do not necessarily have any knowledge or understanding of language. Analogously, a weather forecasting HMM needs no knowledge of meteorology, only a set of statistics of day-to-day weather patterns. See Reetz (1998) for a detailed discussion.

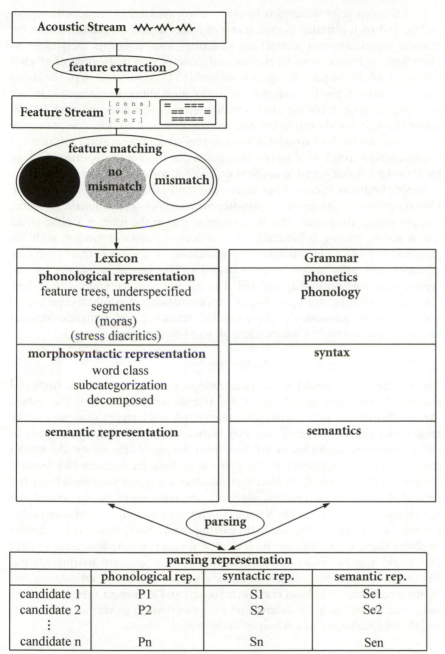

Fig. 6.1. The FUL Model of perception and recognition

Lexical access is initiated solely by information available in the acoustic signal, and the lexicon is activated as soon as one or more features are extracted from the acoustic signal. Abstract hierarchical structure, from segments to syllables to phonological phrases, syntactic phrases, and semantic structure—none of which is directly visible in the acoustic signal—has nothing to do with this step. The access unit is the feature, and the system never 'waits' for additional information before accessing the lexicon (unlike models with intermediate representations). Lexical access through feature extraction and matching is unidirectional, so, once the acoustic stream has been converted into a feature stream, the acoustic information is unavailable during lexical access. This means that there is no opportunity to 'go back' to the acoustic signal to confirm or look for additional information.

Parsing begins as soon as one or more word candidates are found in the lexicon. Here the grammars are invoked to hypothesize all higher-level syntactic, semantic, and phonological structure that is not represented in the lexicon. Unlike initial lexical access, parsing is bidirectional. The lexicon works in tandem with the grammar to posit a new candidate representation or reject a current candidate whenever new information becomes available. Like lexical access, the parsing representation is continually updated. The parsing representation is the whole enchilada, including full phonological representation (metrical structure, prosodic phrasing, intonation). The prosodic, syntactic, and semantic analyses operate in parallel to, but independent of, word recognition.

4.2. The acoustic stream and the feature stream

The first step in the model is feature extraction, whereby the acoustic front end analyses the incoming acoustic signal and translates it into features. The feature 'stream', like the acoustic stream, is not segmented, and feature values need not be temporarily aligned, meaning they may be overlapping. No attempt is made to extract segments, diphones, or syllables from the signal (the closest the system comes to positing segments at this point is to look for segment-like features [consonantal] and [vocalic]). Note that this does not mean these aspects are not part of the perception process: segments are represented in the underlying representations of words in the lexicon, and hypotheses about syllables and other prosodic structures are relegated to the parsing stage. Each feature is either present or absent (here the features are implemented as unary/monovalent/privative, but they could also be binary or multivalued), but not gradient or quantitative. Features are defined according to distinctive feature theory with articulatory and acoustic correlates (Jakobson *et al.* 1952; Stevens and Blumstein 1981; Lahiri *et al.* 1984). Each language has a different set of oppositions in its segment inventory, and thereby makes use of a subset of the universal features.

4.3. *Access units and levels of representation*

The decision to use the feature as the access unit in the FUL Model was motivated by the difficulty in identifying segments (let alone syllables) in the acoustic signal. Following unsuccessful attempts to locate segments in the signal, diphones in the LAFS Model (Klatt 1979, see also 1989) were proposed, but also proved difficult. Features were proposed in the LEXICAL ACCESS FROM FEATURES (LAFF) MODEL (Stevens 1992), which developed into the ACOUSTIC LANDMARKS MODEL (Stevens *et al.* 1992), whereby certain featural cues or 'landmarks' are used to identify segments. The idea of the FUL Model is that, since not all features are available simultaneously in the signal (for example, manner information might be available before place information), and since feature information is often overlapping, the listener does not wait to have all featural information linked to a particular segment before accessing the lexicon. Segments are represented in the lexicon and constructed in the parsing representation by the listener, but they are not analysed in the acoustic signal.

Underspecification and the ternary logic matching in the FUL Model account for regular phonological variation (such as nasal assimilation, vowel nasalization, aspiration, flapping, or final devoicing; deletions and prosodically motivated insertions can also be accounted for, but other insertions might prove more difficult) without having to 'undo' these processes before accessing the lexicon. The result is that there is no need for an intermediate organizational level between the acoustic signal and the lexical representation.

4.4. *Underspecification in the lexicon*

The lexicon contains abstract underlying phonological representations with segments and features that are underspecified and hierarchically organized. Non-distinctive information such as redundant and allophonic features and syllable structure is not represented. Moras may be represented only for contrastive length and stress diacritics for unpredictable stress. Lexical entries are morphologically decomposed (at least partially—the items that might be listed separately include suppletive morphology like 'go~went' and stem alternations like 'life~lives'; unproductive morphology like much of what is found at Level I in English; variations of function words like 'going to'~'gonna' and 'have'~'v').

Underspecification is not arbitrary erasure of information for the purposes of saving ink, or 'data compression'. Eliminating predictable information from the lexicon is phonologically motivated. This includes not just particular feature values, but all suprasegmental information that is not distinctive in a given language, such as moras in languages with no distinctive length, tones in non-tonal languages, and syllables in any language.

4.5. Matching with a ternary logic

Lexical access involves matching the features extracted from the signal, which are a full set of universal features, with the lexical features, which are a language-specific subset of those features and which may be underspecified. Because of underspecification, the matching process involves a ternary logic, as shown in (5).

(5)	Signal feature	Lexical feature	Matching condition
(a)	F	F	match
(b)	F		no mismatch
(c)	F	X	mismatch $(F \rightarrow \neg X)$
(d)		F	
(e)			

Candidates with a MISMATCH are rejected, while candidates with either a MATCH or a NO MISMATCH are selected, but crucially ranked in this order. Each candidate is scored for its goodness of fit in terms of the number of possible matches between the signal and the lexicon, where a match counts towards the score but a no mismatch does not. If a feature is not found in the signal (5d,e), regardless of whether it is found in the lexicon or not, the matching condition is silent and the score is unaffected. The formula for each segment is:

$$\text{score} = \frac{\text{number of matching features}^2}{(\text{signal features} * \text{lexical features})}$$

An example is given in (6), where FG is found in the signal and is compared with lexical items (6a–e). F mismatches X. Notice how (6a), a perfect fit, is a better match than (6b–d).

(6)	Signal features	Lexical features	Matching condition	Match score	Rank
(a)		FG	2 match	$2^2/(2*2) = 1$	1st
(b)		FGH	2 match	$2^2/(2*3) = 2/3$	2nd
(c)	FG	F	1 match, 1 no mismatch	$1^2/(2*1) = 1/2$	3rd
(d)			2 no mismatch	$0^2/(2*0) = 0$	4th
(e)		GX	1 match, 1 no mismatch, 1 mismatch	rejected	

Some mismatches for English are listed in (7).

(7)

Signal feature	Lexical feature	Matching condition
[high] [low]	[low] [high]	mismatch mismatch
[labial] [dorsal]	[dorsal] [labial]	mismatch (consonants) mismatch (consonants)
[coronal]	[dorsal]	mismatch
[coronal]	[labial]	mismatch

The mismatch [high] $\to \neg$ [low] means that, if [high] is found in the signal, all candidates specified for [low] constitute a mismatch (for example, [bɪd] mismatches /bæd/). Vowels like /u/ are both [labial] and [dorsal], but consonants may only have one place feature, so the [labial] $\to \neg$ [dorsal] and [dorsal] $\to \neg$ [labial] mismatches are restricted to consonants. The feature [coronal] is not present in the lexicon—that is, is unspecified—so there exists no mismatch of the form [dorsal] $\to \neg$ [coronal] or [labial] $\to \neg$ [coronal]. This is crucial to the understanding of processes such as nasal assimilation (8–10). Underlying /n/ is unspecified for place, so any surface place will be a no mismatch, while /m/ is specified for [labial], so any other surface place will constitute a mismatch. Note that the feature [coronal] is not computed in the matching score: it is not found in the lexicon, it can never count towards the number of lexical features found, so it is not added to the number of signal features found. (The identity of the segments [n], /m/, and so on in the following is for the reader's convenience.)

(8) Nasal assimilation in English

/n/	$\to$	[n]	indecent, in Toronto		/m/	$\to$	[m]	some beans
	$\to$	[m]	impossible, i[m] Boston			$\not\to$	[n]	*so[n] tea
	$\to$	[ŋ]	i[ŋ]complete, i[ŋ] California			$\not\to$	[ŋ]	*so[ŋ] carrots

(9)

	Signal features	Lexical features	Matching condition	Match score	Rank
(a)	[m] [cons nas lab]	/m/ [cons nas lab]	3 match	$3^2/(3{*}3) = 1$	1st
(b)		/n/ [cons nas]	2 match 1 no mismatch	$2^2/(3{*}2) =$ 2/3	2nd

(10)

	Signal features	Lexical features	Matching condition	Match score	Rank
(a)	[n] [cons nas cor]	/m/ [cons nas lab]	2 match 1 mismatch	rejected	
(b)		/n/ [cons nas]	2 match 1 no mismatch	$2^2/(2{*}2) = 2$	1st

4.6. Less is more

Reetz (1998) demonstrates that underspecification actually increases the robustness of the automatic speech recognition system. A fully specified lexicon requires every feature to be set correctly in order to identify a phoneme. The underspecified model prevents viable candidates from being unintentionally deselected owing to misanalysed or ambiguous signal information (common for vowel height, for instance), information missing from the signal (deletion), additional information in the signal (insertion), or changed information in the signal (assimilation, coarticulation, and so forth).

The broad feature definitions in the acoustic front end and the underspecification in the lexicon would appear to lead to an explosion of word candidates. But even with an enlarged candidate set, it often turns out that many phonetically plausible candidates that the acoustic front end submits to the matching process simply are not found in the lexicon. No acoustic front end is foolproof: inter- and intra-speaker variation, postlexical assimilations, fast-speech phenomena, and problems with the signal such as external noise and poor transmission or recording quality all result in deviations from the idealized form. But human listeners, while also not foolproof, are usually able to overcome these deviations in the signal with relative ease because of their knowledge of the lexicon and the grammar. An approach that has too strict restrictions at the level of acoustic analysis and a fully specified lexicon will sabotage the whole perceptual process by disregarding candidates far too quickly. The motto of this model is to 'let the lexicon do the work'.

Further, the parsing of an utterance operates in parallel to lexical access. That is, syntax, semantics, pragmatics, and phonology all work to reject or make less plausible numerous potential interpretations of utterances. Many conceptions of automatic speech recognition systems assume a bottom-up approach, whereby a complete phonetic and phonological analysis of the incoming speech stream is handed over to syntactic and semantic modules. But this is surely not what human listeners do. There are also integrated top-down and bottom-up systems, of which the FUL Model is but one example. And, as discussed earlier, models of human perception that assume that some larger unit like the syllable is the access unit to the lexicon are forced to wait for some organizational analysis of the incoming signal stream before accessing the lexicon.

5. EXPERIMENTAL EVIDENCE

5.1. The syllable effect

The IR Hypothesis is the subject of a series of influential experiments beginning with Mehler *et al.* (1981), who discovered a 'syllable effect' in French. In a monitoring task, French subjects were instructed to monitor a stimulus (presented auditorily) for a fragment (the target, presented visually), and reaction times for the detection of the target were measured. The results are summarized in (11), with a sample stimulus-target set.

(11) French

| | | stimulus | |
		CV- pa-lace	CVC- pal-mier
target	CV pa	faster	
	CVC pal		faster

Subjects were faster at detecting the target when it corresponded to the first syllable of the stimulus (for instance, *pa* is identified faster in *pa-lace* than in *pal-mier*). Mehler *et al.* came to the conclusion that the syllable is a unit of speech processing, specifically that syllabic segmentation precedes lexical access and the syllable is an access unit to the lexicon. In particular, they were arguing against the segment as an access unit, as in the Cohort Model.

Cutler *et al.* (1986) repeated these experiments for English subjects listening to English stimuli (for instance, target *ba* or *bal*, stimulus *balance* or *balcony*), French stimuli, and nonsense stimuli, but found no syllable effect. They did, however, find a syllable effect with French subjects listening to English stimuli. They revised the earlier claim to say that speech segmentation strategies are language specific: French listeners syllabify, English do not, because 'syllabification would not be used when the phonological structure of the language in question would render it inefficient' (p. 395). This rests on their claim that French has clear, regular syllable structure and syllable boundaries but English does not (because it has more syllable types and ambisyllabicity), and thus French is easier to syllabify. But this is not really true. If anything, English has clearer syllable boundaries because it has many more cues to syllable structure through postlexical processes, including aspiration, flapping, glottalization, l-velarization, and r-deletion (contra the 'noise' view discussed in Section 3.2). The fact that French subjects showed a syllable effect regardless of the language they are hearing underscores the point that syllables are not part of the acoustic signal; they are an organizing unit of the language. Moreover, it suggests that the syllable effect is not part of lexical access, since French subjects are not tapping into their mental lexicon when listening to English (the subjects were not fluent in English).

Cutler and Norris (1988) continued this line of experimentation using English real words for targets and nonsense words for stimuli, as in (12).

(12) English

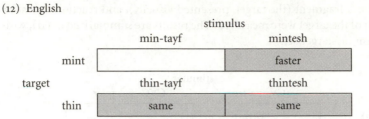

Here the target *mint* was detected faster in *mintesh* than in *mintayf*, while the target *thin* had equal reaction times in *thintayf* and *thintesh*. Their conclusion is that the syllable is indeed a unit of speech processing in English, but under a more elaborated account than before. First, they distinguish between 'segmentation', detection of boundaries in the signal, and 'classification', identification of units existing at a prelexical level of representation. English listeners segment, but do not necessarily classify, the signal into syllables, whereas French listeners presumably do both. Secondly, lexical access is initiated at segmentation boundaries, and for English the access unit is the strong (that is, stressed) syllable. Their account of (12) is that since *mintàyf* consists of two strong syllables, it is segmented as *min-tayf* and lexical searches are begun on *min* and *tayf*, whereas *mintesh* consists of a strong syllable and a weak syllable, it is not segmented, and a single lexical search is performed on *mintesh*. The detection latency in *mintayf* is due to the fact that the target *mint* is not a constituent in *min-tayf* because it crosses a segmentation boundary. In the second pair, since the target *thin* does not cross a segmentation boundary in either *thin-tàyf* or *thíntesh*, there should be no difference in reaction times. Note that it is not entirely convincing that the strong syllable, as opposed to any syllable, is relevant here. It is quite likely that the [t] in *mintesh* is ambisyllabic, which means that the target *mint* corresponds to the first syllable of *mintesh* but not of *mintayf*.

Cutler and Norris argue that initiating lexical access at every segment involves a lot of wasted effort owing to the large number of lexical searches. Having the syllable as the access unit reduces the number of lexical searches and thereby the number of futile access attempts. While this may be an advantage for computer processing, why this should be advantageous for human processing is unclear, since there is no evidence that speakers cannot handle this. Moreover, at best (12) provides evidence that listeners segment the two stimuli differently, but it provides no evidence that lexical access is initiated at segmentation boundaries—that is, that the strong syllable is an access unit. On the other hand, a consequence of this and other IR models is that the listener must 'wait' until they have enough information from the signal to build the access unit before consulting the lexicon, since, in order to build abstract structure, information later in the signal must be available. If the access unit is the syllable, then when a consonant is identified the system must wait until it has identified one or more following segments in order to determine whether this consonant is a coda or an onset, and only then is lexical access initiated. If the access unit is a strong syllable, the system must wait until it has identified one or more following syllables, since stress and rhythm are relational, meaning it is not possible to know if something is a strong syllable until a weak syllable has been heard.

The syllable effect in French has not only been replicated by other researchers in other Romance languages; it has also been found in Dutch (Zwitserlood *et al.* 1993), which, like English, is a Germanic language with ambisyllabicity. Zwitserlood *et al.* found clear evidence for a syllable effect (but not a strong syllable effect), and found that ambisyllabic consonants are analysed by the subjects as closing the first syllable. While they agree with Cutler *et al.* (1986) that processing routines are language specific, they disagree with the conclusion that segmentation plays a role in lexical access. Rather than being part of an intermediate representation between the signal and the lexicon, segmentation into syllables belongs to the parsing stage (see also Frazier 1987).

Frauenfelder (1998) also argues that the syllable effect in processing is open to other interpretations. His attempts to replicate the syllable effect in French—both with more rigorous experimental designs to counter some criticisms of the original experiments and with the original stimuli but using subjects with other dialects of French—have failed. He suggests that detection tasks do not tap into lexical processes, but rather involve metalinguistic or late cognitive components, and thus that syllabification may be relevant in defining segmentation units but not classification units.

In summary, while the syllable effect had a large influence on the construction of perception models, later interpretations have resulted in models that do not require segmentation into syllables prior to lexical access.

5.2. *Allophonic and contrastive features: [nasal]*

Lahiri and Marslen-Wilson (1991, 1992) investigated vowel nasalization in English and Bengali. In English vowel nasalization is allophonic—vowels are nasalized postlexically before nasal consonants, e.g. [bæ̃n]—and is therefore not represented in the lexicon. However, vowels also need not be represented underlyingly as [−nasal], and in fact they may not according to underspecification theory, which assumes that only distinctive, non-redundant information is represented in the lexicon. In Bengali, on the other hand, vowel nasalization is phonemic and therefore represented lexically. Nasalization is only distinct before oral consonants, as in *bad* [bɑd] 'difference', *bād* [bɑ̃d] 'dam', but not before nasal consonants, as in *ban* [bɑ̃n] 'flood', *[bɑn]. A crucial assumption is that words like *ban* are not lexically represented with the feature [nasal] on the vowel, even though it has this feature on the surface and even though Bengali has the feature [nasal] as a distinctive feature in the lexicon: Bengali *ban* looks exactly like English *ban*.

(13)

	English		Bengali		
UR	/bæd/	/bæn/ | [nasal]	/bɑd/	/bɑ̃d/ | [nasal]	/bɑn/ | [nasal]
SR	[bæd] bad	[bæ̃n] ＼.| [nasal] ban	[bɑd] 'difference'	[bɑ̃d] | [nasal] 'dam'	[bɑ̃n] *[bɑn] ＼.| [nasal] 'flood' *does not exist*

In a set of gating experiments, subjects heard portions of words like those above in sequences gated from the beginning of the word. In a lexical decision task, subjects responded with what word they thought they heard at each gate. The cases of interest are those gates prior to the final consonant, such as English [bæ], excised from *ban*, represented henceforth as [bæ(n)]. The purpose of the experiment was to see how subjects would interpret vowel nasalization without knowing the identity of the following consonant: upon hearing [bæ(n)], would subjects use the nasal information for lexical access and respond with mostly or only with *ban* (or *bang, band*, and so on), or would subjects ignore the nasality and respond with *bad* (or *bag, back*, and so on) as well?

The process of word recognition involves comparing the incoming acoustic signal (in the experiment the stimulus) to the lexicon (represented by the subject's response). According to the UR Hypothesis, as spelled out in the FUL Model, lexical candidates are evaluated according to 'goodness of fit', as shown in (14). Candidates are rejected only when a feature mismatch occurs (for example [coronal] in the signal is a mismatch with [dorsal] in the lexicon), which does not happen in this experiment.

If the feature [nasal] is not found in the signal (14a), there is nothing to map to the lexicon so the matching condition is silent, but the ranking of candidates is determined according to overall goodness of fit. Both oral and nasal vowels are candidates, with oral ranked higher than nasal because the number of (other) matched features is higher (for simplicity the only other feature computed is [vocalic]). If the feature [nasal] is found in the signal (14b), both oral and nasal vowels are candidates, also ranked by the matching condition. Nasal candidates, where the signal feature finds a match in the lexicon, are better than oral candidates, where the feature is absent, resulting in a no mismatch condition. Oral candidates are none the less viable, because the no mismatch condition reflects the fact that surface nasal vowels can correspond to underlying oral vowels.

(14) Evaluating [nasal] in Bengali

	Signal features	Lexical features	Matching condition	Match score	Rank
(a)	[ɑ] [voc]	/ɑ/ [voc]	1 match	$1^2/(1*1) = 1$	1st
		/ã/ [nasal voc]	1 match	$1^2/(1*2) = 1/2$	2nd
(b)	[ã] [nasal voc]	/ɑ/ [voc]	1 match 1 no mismatch	$1^2/(2*1) = 1/2$	2nd
		/ã/ [nasal voc]	2 match	$2^2/(2*2) = 1$	1st

The results of the experiment on Bengali triplets are given in (15), where shading indicates the ranking of the candidates according to the UR Hypothesis in (14) and the percentages indicate the summary of subjects' responses over all gates up to vowel offset (see Lahiri and Marslen-Wilson (1991, 1992) for details of word frequency and confidence ratings).

(15) Bengali triplets (UR Hypothesis)

		response		
		CVC /bad/	CṽC /bãd/	CVN /ban/
	CV(C) [ba(d)]	80.3%	0.7%	13.4%
stimulus	Cṽ(C) [bã(d)]	33.2% no mismatch	56.8% match	5.2% no mismatch
	CV(N) [bã(n)]	23.5% no mismatch	63.0% match	7.9% no mismatch

Subjects responded to oral stimuli ([ba(d)]) overwhelmingly (80.3%) with CVC words (*bad, baʃ, bari*), occasionally (13.4%) with CVN words (*ban, baŋla*) and almost never (0.7%) with CṽC words (*bãd, bãk*). According to the UR Hypothesis, *bad* and *ban* are better candidates than *bãd* because the first two are represented underlyingly with an oral vowel. The ratio of *bad* responses to *ban* responses reflects the distributional facts of the language, where of words with underlyingly oral vowels, 81% are CVC and 19% CVN.

Subjects responded to nasal stimuli [bã(d)] and [bã(n)] most often with *bãd*, less often with *bad*, and least often with *ban*. The bias towards *bãd* in the results indicates that subjects indeed interpreted the feature [nasal] as an underlyingly nasal vowel rather than as ambiguous between underlying nasal vowel and a surface nasalized vowel. Under the UR Hypothesis, *bãd* is a perfect match and therefore the best candidate. The other two are possible candidates because there is no mismatch, but less good. Here *bad* responses outnumber *ban* responses in roughly the same ratio as before, as explained by distributional facts.

The SR Hypothesis makes different predictions (16). Ohala and Ohala (1995) repeated the Bengali and British English experiment with Hindi and American English. Their results were largely similar to Lahiri and Marslen-Wilson's (modulo some changes in the experimental design), but they reinterpret the results as only partially supporting the UR Hypothesis and partially supporting the SR Hypothesis, which they support.[3]

(16) Bengali triplets (SR Hypothesis)

		response		
		CVC /bad/	CṼC /bãd/	CVN /bān/
	CV(C) [ba(d)]			
stimulus	CṼ(C) [bã(d)]	no mismatch	match	match
	CV(N) [bã(n)]	no mismatch	match	match

The results in (15) show that CVN patterns with CVC, which is in accord with the UR Hypothesis, whereas the SR Hypothesis wrongly predicts that CVN patterns with CṼC. There are two asymmetries between CVN and CṼC responses. First, for the oral stimuli *ban* responses outnumbered *bãd* responses, while for nasal stimuli the opposite is true. Second, *ban* was given as a response about twice as often to oral stimuli as to nasal stimuli, indicating subjects interpret [ba(d)] as *ban* more often than they interpret [bã(d)] or [bã(n)] as *ban*, while the opposite is true for *bãd*. The SR Hypothesis predicts there should be no asymmetry anywhere between *bãd* and *ban* and that the ratios of responses should reflect distributional facts, neither of which is correct.[4]

The next step is to consider how subjects would interpret [nasal] if there is no possible CṼC response due to a lexical gap. One Bengali doublet is *ʃib* 'Siva', *ʃim* 'flat bean' (no word begins with **ʃĩ*). The results and the UR and SR Hypotheses are given in (17) and (18).

(17) Bengali doublets (UR Hypothesis)

		response		
		CVC /ʃib/	*CṼC	CVN /ʃim/
	CV(C) [ʃi(b)]	82.6%	0.0%	14.7%
stimulus	CV(N) [ʃĩ(m)]	64.7% no mismatch	17.0%	15.6% no mismatch

[3] Ohala and Ohala's (1995: 43) summary of the predictions the UR Hypothesis makes according to Lahiri and Marslen-Wilson (1992) is misleading, since it lists only the *best* candidates as predicted responses instead of *all* predicted responses. Secondly, the English doublets should indeed be identical to the Bengali doublets (but see their discussion, p. 55).

[4] According to Ohala and Ohala (1995: 56), 'what makes a vowel non-distinctively nasal (in Bengali and Hindi) is the presence of a following nasal consonant'. It might also be thought that that orthography has an effect: CṼC words are represented in the standard orthography with a nasal diacritic while CVN words are not, as in Bengali বাদ *bad*, বাঁদ *bãd*, বান *ban*. But neither of these statements is quite correct, since CṼN occurs in morphologically complex words, as in ছোঁন *tʃʰõ-n* 'touch-3P.HON', cf. ছোঁবে *tʃʰõ-b-e*, 'touch-FUT-3P'. Moreover, there is much variation in Bengali spelling.

(18) Bengali doublets (SR Hypothesis)

		response CVC [ʃib]		CVN [ʃĩm]
	CV(C) [ʃi(b)]			
stimulus	CVN [ʃĩ(m)]	no mismatch		match

Subjects responded to oral stimuli ([ʃi(b)]) nearly identically as in the triplets, with CVC words outnumbering CVN words according to distributional facts. Subjects responded to nasal stimuli ([ʃĩ(m)]) most often with *ʃib*, less often with *ʃim*, and surprisingly with a variety of CṼC words. These were either non-words (*ʃĩb*), similar words that matched for [nasal] but differed for some other feature (*ʃẽk* 'toast-IMP.2P'), or loanwords (Hindi *sĩʃna* 'irrigate'). These results also indicate that subjects were trying to interpret the feature [nasal] as an underlyingly nasal vowel, even if there was no easy choice available (*ʃĩC*), and even though there was a CVN choice available. Under the UR Hypothesis, the recognition process tries to match [nasal] with an underlying feature; if a perfect match CṼC is not available, either one of the CVC or CVN no mismatch candidates is chosen (which is missing one feature), a phonetically similar word is chosen (which errs in one or more features), or a nonsense or loanword is chosen.

The subjects' reluctance to produce a CVN response strikes a major blow to the SR Hypothesis, which predicts a majority of CVN responses. Ohala and Ohala admit the SR Hypothesis has no explanation for the CṼC responses.

The next step is to turn to English, where vowel nasalization is allophonic and therefore not in the underlying representation. Since [nasal] in vowels is not found in the lexicon, it does not contribute to the computation of the match score in (19) as it does in Bengali (see the discussion of [coronal] in Section 4.5).

(19) Evaluating [nasal] in English

	Signal features	Lexical features	Matching condition	Match score	Rank
(a)	[æ] [voc]	/æ/ [voc]	1 match	$1^2/(1*1) = 1$	1st
(b)	[æ̃] [nasal voc]	/æ/ [voc]	1 match 1 no mismatch	$1^2/(1*1) = 1$	1st

English doublets resemble the Bengali doublets, but the UR Hypothesis predicts that English and Bengali listeners interpret [nasal] differently.

(20) English doublets (UR Hypothesis)

		response CVC /bæd/ 'bad'	CVN /bæn/ 'ban'
	CV(C) [bæ(d)]	83.4%	16.6%
stimulus	CV(N) [bæ̃(n)]	59.3% no mismatch	40.7% no mismatch

(21) English doublets (SR Hypothesis)

		response	
		CVC [bæd] *bad*	CVN [bæn] *ban*
stimulus	CV(C) [bæ(d)]		
	CV(N) [bæ̃(n)]		match

Subjects responded to oral stimuli ([bæ(d)]) just as the Bengali subjects did, and they responded to nasal stimuli ([bæ̃(n)]) similarly, without, of course, the CṼC responses. The SR Hypothesis expects listeners to match the [nasal] feature in CV(N) stimuli to the nasalized vowel, and predicts a strong bias towards CVN, which was not found. The fact that they gave both oral and nasal responses to both oral and nasal stimuli suggests they are not matching [nasal] in the signal to the vowel. Under the UR Hypothesis, the only thing listeners can do with [nasal] is assign it to a nasal consonant, so that, when they hear a nasalized vowel, they can predict an upcoming nasal consonant.

The SR Hypothesis cannot account for all the results in these experiments, while the UR Hypothesis can.[5]

5.3. *Neutralization of a feature: [voice]*

Further evidence for the UR Hypothesis, specifically that regular phonological alternants of morphemes are not stored in the lexicon, is provided by an experiment on voicing assimilation in Dutch (Lahiri *et al.* 1990). Dutch has voicing contrasts like those in (22a), which are neutralized by final devoicing, as in (22b), and are also subject to both progressive and regressive voicing assimilation in certain environments (which are postlexical, optional, and dialect specific), leading to variations like those in (22c).

(22)	(a)	kusen	/kœsən]/	[kœsən]		'to kiss'
		kiezen	/kizən/	[kizən]		'to choose'
	(b)	kus	/kœs/	[kœs]		'kiss'
		kies	/kiz/	[kis]		'choose!'
	(c)	(ik) kus haar	/kœsdər/	[kœstər]$_w$~[[kœz]]$_w$ dər]$_w$	'(I) kiss her'
		(ik) kies haar	/kizdər/	[kistər]$_w$~[[kiz]]$_w$ dər]$_w$	'(I) choose her'

The UR Hypothesis assumes each verb has one underlying form (evident in (22a)), which is either specified or unspecified for [voice]. Lexical access is as in (23) (for simplicity, matching [voice] counts as 1 match, and matching all other features, which do not interest us here, counts as 1 match). Both [kœs] and [kœz] map to /kœs/, but [kœs] 'fits' better because it more closely matches the features of

---

[5] The UR Hypothesis does not claim that listeners are not aware of surface representations; it only makes a claim about what is involved in lexical access during perception. Lahiri (p.c.) points out that listeners do indeed pay attention to surface representations, given facts about language change. For example, postlexical vowel nasalization and coalescence may eventually result in lexically nasalized vowels: /VN/ → [ṼN] > /ṽ/.

the UR. Similarly, both [kis] and [kiz] map to /kiz/, but only [kiz] constitutes a perfect fit.

(23) Evaluating [voice] in Dutch (UR Hypothesis)

	Signal	Lexicon	Matching condition	Match score	Rank
(a)	[kœs]	/kœs/	1 match	$1^2/(1*1) = 1$	1st
(b)	[kœz] [voice]	/kœs/	1 match 1 no mismatch	$1^2/(2*1) =$ $1/2$	1st
(c)	[kis]	/kiz/ [voice]	1 match	$1^2/(1*2) =$ $1/2$	1st
(d)	[kiz] [voice]	/kiz/ [voice]	2 match	$2^2/(2*2) = 1$	1st

The SR Hypothesis assumes that both surface variants for each verb are stored in the lexicon, and lexical access would match forms as in (24).

(24) Evaluating [voice] in Dutch (SR Hypothesis)

	Signal	Lexical	Matching condition	Match score	Rank
(a)	[kœs]	[kœs]	1 match	$1^2/(1*1) = 1$	1st
(b)	[kœz] [voice]	[kœz] [voice]	2 match	$2^2/(2*2) = 1$	1st
(c)	[kis]	[kiz]	1 match	$1^2/(1*1) = 1$	1st
(d)	[kiz] [voice]	[kiz] [voice]	2 match	$2^2/(2*2) = 1$	1st

An experiment with auditory-auditory priming is summarized in (25). Priming tasks measure reaction times to words after they have been 'primed' by a semantically, phonologically, or morphologically related word—for example, *doctor* primes *nurse*, but *table* does not prime *nurse*. Here listeners were presented with a prime (the cliticized form [ɪk kœstər]) followed by a target (the imperative form [kœs]). Subjects performed a lexical decision task on the target, deciding if it was a word or a non-word. Of interest in such tasks is the amount of time it takes to recognize the word: either the reaction time of the test target can be the same as when primed by some unrelated control or some other test, showing no effect, or it can be faster, showing facilitation or priming, or it can be slower, showing inhibition or negative priming.

(25)

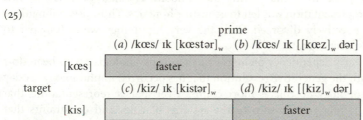

The target [kœs] was recognized faster when preceded by (25a) [ɪk kœstər] than by (25b) [ɪk kœzdər], while the target [kis] was recognized faster when preceded by (25*d*) [ɪk kizdər] than by (25*c*) [ɪk kistər], i.e. there was priming for (25*a*) and (25*d*). These differences can be accounted for only by the UR Hypothesis as shown in (23). There is facilitation of the target if the prime is identical to the underlying representation of the verb. The idea is that speakers must have recognized and parsed the prime, and the goodness of fit of the lexical item it found influenced the later recognition of another form of that same lexical item: a perfect fit in the prime (25*a,d*) facilitated recognition of the target later.

If, following the SR Hypothesis, both variants of each verb were represented in the lexicon, we would expect equal reaction times for (25*a,b*) and for (25*c,d*), showing no priming effects. If the match between the SR of the prime and target were relevant, or if the prosodic structure of the primes was relevant, we would expect priming for (25*a*) and (25*c*). The conclusion is that the UR must play a role in lexical decision tasks.

Further support for the UR Hypothesis has been shown by experiments on place of articulation in Bengali sibilants (Lahiri 1991), English consonants (Marslen-Wilson and Warren 1994) and English nasals (Gow 1999*a,b*; Lahiri and van Coillie 1999). See also Mohanan (1986: ch. 7) on lexical phonology and psychological reality, specifically how lexical representations, not surface representations, are relevant for speaker judgements, and Keating (1988), who argues that phonological underspecification can persist into the phonetics.

6. CONCLUSION

In this chapter we have examined the role of theoretical phonology in the development of psycholinguistic models of speech perception. This role has clearly been a central one. Early models derived their ideas about levels and units of representation directly from linguistic theory. However, the debate about the processing of this information centred on purely psychological issues to do with the speed of the availability of this information to the processing system. The phonological representation of words assumed by early models was influenced by *SPE* and consisted of linear strings of phonological segments. In consequence, most models assumed that phonological segments were first derived from the speech signal prior to contact with the lexicon. The job of deriving this phonological representation was left to acoustic phonetics. Thus, psycholinguistic models were effectively divorced from the very input they were designed to process—the speech signal.

Despite the early dependency on linguistic theory, psychologists have been slow to catch up with the generative revolution that has occurred in phonology. Today theoretical phonology postulates more complex yet sparser representations that have a much tighter relationship to the systems of rules and constraints that govern them. Importantly, the linguistic claims made about phonological representation have a direct impact on the kinds of psychological processes that can be postulated.

We have examined the current conflicting views about the role of abstract phonological representations in speech perception. Lexical access involves matching information from the acoustic signal to some stored representation in the mental lexicon, so the question we are faced with is what representation is used in each half of the matching equation. The first consideration is what information listeners extract from the acoustic signal and how they analyse it before accessing the lexicon. The IR Hypothesis assumes the listener analyses the acoustic signal in terms of some linguistic unit, such as the syllable, prior to lexical access. Such approaches presumably posit larger prosodic constituents after lexical access. The alternative is that higher-level structure plays no role in lexical access, and that the positing of prosodic structure is relegated to the parsing process, following lexical access, where all hypotheses about all abstract structure, phonological, syntactic, semantic, and so forth, are made. The second consideration is what stored representation is mapped to. The SR Hypothesis assumes the incoming signal is matched to the surface representation of words, while the UR Hypothesis assumes the signal is matched to the underlying representation. The experimental evidence, in our view, favours the latter. The FUL Model, while still in need of further development and experimental testing, provides a promising solution to many problems in human speech perception as well as automatic speech recognition.

REFERENCES

Bever, T. G. (1970), 'The Cognitive Basis For Linguistic Structures', in J. R. Hayes (ed.), *Cognition and the Development of Language* (New York: Wiley), 279–362.

Bird, S. (1990), 'Constraint-based Phonology', Ph.D. dissertation (University of Edinburgh).

Blumenthal, A. L. (1967), 'Prompted Recall of Sentences', *Journal of Verbal Learning and Verbal Behavior,* 6: 203–6.

Bresnan, J. and Kaplan, R. M. (1982), 'Introduction: Grammars and Mental Representations of Language', in J. Bresnan (ed.), *The Mental Representation of Grammatical Relations* (Cambridge, Mass.: MIT Press), pp. xvii–lii.

Burton-Roberts, N. (this volume), 'Where and What is Phonology: A Representational Perspective'.

Carr, P. (this volume), 'Scientific Realism, Sociophonetic Variation, and Innate Endowments in Phonology'.

Chomsky, N. (1957), *Syntactic Structures* (The Hague: Mouton).

—— (1967), *Language and Mind* (New York: Harcourt Brace Jovanovich).

—— and Halle, M. (1968), *The Sound Pattern of English* (New York: Harper & Row).

Christie, W. (1974), 'Some Cues For Syllable Juncture Perception in English', *Journal of the Acoustical Society of America,* 55: 819–21.

Church, K. (1987), 'Phonological Parsing and Lexical Retrieval', *Cognition,* 25: 53–69.

Cutler, A. and Norris, D. (1988), 'The Role of Strong Syllables in Segmentation for Lexical Access', *Journal of Experimental Psychology: Human Perception and Performance,* 14: 113–21.

Cutler, A., Mehler, J., Norris, D., and Segui, J. (1986), 'The Syllable's Differing Role in the Segmentation of French and English', *Journal of Memory and Language*, 25: 385–400.

Estes, W . K. (1994), *Classification and Cognition* (New York: Oxford University Press).

Fodor, J. A. and Bever, T. G (1965), 'The Psycholinguistic Reality of Linguistic Segments', *Journal of Verbal Learning and Verbal Behaviour*, 4: 414–20.

—— and Garrett, M. F. (1967), 'Some Syntactic Determinants of Sentence Complexity', *Perception and Psychophysics*, 2: 289–96.

Forster, K. I. (1976), 'Accessing the Mental Lexicon', in R. J. Wales and E. Walker (eds.) *New Approaches to Language Mechanisms* (Amsterdam: North-Holland), 257–87.

—— (1979), 'Levels of Processing and the Structure of the Language Processor', in W. E. Cooper and E. C. T. Walker (eds.), *Sentence Processing: Psycholinguistic Studies Presented to Merrill Garrett* (Hillsdale, NJ: Lawrence Erlbaum), 27–85.

Frazier, L. (1987), 'Structure in Auditory Word Recognition', *Cognition*, 25: 157–87.

—— (1995), 'Issues of Representation in Psycholinguistics', in J. L. Miller and P. D. Eimas (eds.) *Speech, Language, and Communication: Handbook of Perception and Cognition*, (2nd edn., San Diego, Calif.: Academic Press), 1–27.

Frauenfelder, U. (1998), 'Units of Speech Processing', talk given at the workshop on Lexical Representations in Language Comprehension, Maurach, Germany, 18 Dec.

Gazdar, G. (1981), 'Unbounded Dependencies and Coordinate Structure', *Linguistic Inquiry*, 12: 155–84.

Gow, D. W., Jr. (1999*a*), 'Assimilation and Anticipation in Continuous Spoken Word Recognition', MS, Massachusetts General Hospital and Salem State College.

—— (1999*b*), 'Does Phonological Assimilation Create Lexical Ambiguity?', MS, Massachusetts General Hospital and Salem State College.

Gussenhoven, C. and Rietveld, T. (1997), 'Empirical Evidence for the Contrast Between L* and H* in Dutch Rising Contours', in A. Botinis, G. Kouroupetroglou, and G. Carayiannis (eds.) *Proceedings of the ESCA Workshop on Intonation: Theory, Models and Applications* (Athens, Greece), 169–72.

Jakobson, R. C., Fant, G. C. M., and Halle, M. (1952), *Preliminaries to Speech Analysis: The Distinctive Features and their Correlates* (Acoustics Laboratory of the MIT, Technical Report, 13; Cambridge, Mass.: MIT Press).

Keating, P. A. (1988), 'Underspecification in Phonetics', *Phonology*, 5: 275–92.

Kiparsky, P. (1982), 'Lexical Morphology and Phonology', in Linguistic Society of Korea (ed.), *Linguistics in the Morning Calm* (Seoul: Hanshin), 3–91.

—— (1985), 'Some Consequences of Lexical Phonology', *Phonology Yearbook*, 2: 85–138.

Kisseberth, C. (1970), 'On the Functional Unity of Phonological Rules', *Linguistic Inquiry*, 1: 291–306.

Klatt, D. H. (1979), 'Speech Perception: A Model of Acoustic Phonetic Analysis and Lexical Access', *Journal of Phonetics*, 7: 279–312.

—— (1989), 'Review of Selected Models of Speech Perception', in W. Marslen-Wilson (ed.), *Lexical Representation and Process* (Cambridge, Mass.: MIT Press), 169–226.

Lahiri, A. (1991), 'Anteriority in Sibilants, *Proceedings of the XIIth International Congress of Phonetic Sciences, Aix-en-Provence, France*, Vol. 1 (Aix-en-Provence: Publications de l'Université de Provence), 384–8.

—— (1999), 'Speech Recognition with Phonological Features, in J. J. Ohala *et al.* (eds.) *Proceedings of the XIVth International Congress of Phonetic Sciences*, (Linguistics Department, University of California, Berkeley), 941–4.

—— and Van Coillie, S. (1999), 'Asymmetries in Feature Specification and Processing, MS, University of Konstanz.

—— and Jongman, A. (1990), 'Intermediate Level of Analysis: Features Or Segments?', *Journal of Phonetics*, 18: 435–43.

—— and Marslen-Wilson, W. (1991), 'The Mental Representation of Lexical Form: A Phonological Approach to the Recognition Lexicon', *Cognition*, 38: 245–294.

—— —— (1992), 'Lexical Processing and Phonological Representation', in G. J. Docherty and D. R. Ladd (eds.) *Papers in Laboratory Phonology II* (Cambridge: Cambridge University Press), 229–254.

—— and Reetz, H. (1999), 'The FUL Speech Recognition System', *Journal of the Acoustical Society of America*, 105: 1091.

—— —— (forthcoming), 'The FUL Speech Recognition System: A Linguistic Approach To An Old Problem', MS, University of Konstanz.

—— Gewirth, L., and Blumstein, S. E (1984), 'A Reconsideration of Acoustic Invariance For Place of Articulation in Duffuse Stop Consonants: Evidence from a Cross-Language Study', *Journal of the Acoustical Society of America*, 76: 391–404.

—— Jongman, A., and Sereno J. A. (1990), 'The Pronominal Clitic [der] in Dutch: A Theoretical and Experimental Approach', *Yearbook of Morphology*, 3: 115–27.

Langacker, R. (1987), Foundations of Cognitive Grammar (Stanford, Calif.: Stanford University Press).

Lehiste, I. (1960), 'An Acoustic-Phonetic Study of Internal Open Juncture', *Phonetica*, 5, suppl.

Levelt, W. J. M. (1989), *Speaking: From Intention to Articulation* (Cambridge, Mass.: MIT Press).

—— and Wheeldon, L. R. (1994), 'Do Speakers Have Access to a Mental Syllabary?', *Cognition*, 50: 239–69.

—— Roelofs, A., and Meyer, A. S. (1999), 'A Theory of Lexical Access in Speech Production', *Behavioural and Brain Sciences*, 22: 1–75.

Liberman, A. M., Cooper, F. S., Shankweiler, D. S., and Studdert-Kennedy, M. (1967), 'Perception of the Speech Code', *Psychological Review*, 74: 431–61.

Luce, R. D. (1959), *Individual Choice Behaviour* (New York: Wiley).

McCarthy, J. J. and Prince, A. (1993), 'Generalized Alignment', in G. Booij and J. van Marle (eds.), *Yearbook of Morphology*, 1993, 79–153.

McClelland, J. L. and Elman, J. L. (1986), 'The TRACE Model of Speech Perception', *Cognitive Psychology*, 18: 1–86.

Marslen-Wilson, W. D. (1973), 'Linguistic Structure and Speech Shadowing At Very Short Latencies', *Nature* (London), 244: 522–3.

—— (1984), 'Function and Process in Spoken Word Recognition', in H. Bouma and D. G. Bouwhuis (eds.), *Attention and Performance X: Control of Language Processes* (Hillsdale, NJ: Lawrence Erlbaum), 125–50.

—— (1987), 'Functional Parallelism in Spoken Word-Recognition', *Cognition*, 25: 71–102.

—— and Tyler, L. K. (1980), 'The Temporal Structure of Spoken Language Understanding', *Cognition*, 8: 1–71.

—— and Warren, P. (1994), 'Levels of Perceptual Representation and Process in Lexical Access: Words, Phonemes and Features', *Psychological Review*, 101: 653–75.

Mehler, J., Dommergues, J. Y., Frauenfelder, U., and Sequi, J. (1981), 'The Syllable's Role in Speech Segmentation'. *Journal of Verbal Learning and Verbal Behavior*, 20: 298–305.

Mohanan, K. P. (1986), *The Theory of Lexical Phonology* (Dordrecht: Reidel).

—— (1995), 'The Organization of the Grammar', in J. Goldsmith (ed.), *The Handbook of Phonological Theory* (Cambridge, Mass.: Blackwell), 24–69.

Morton, J. (1969), 'Interaction of Information in Word Recognition', *Psychological Review*, 76: 165–78.

—— (1982), 'Disintegrating the Lexicon: An Information Processing Approach', in J. Mehler, E. Walker, and M. Garrett (eds.), *On Mental Representation* (Hillsdale, NJ: Lawrence Erlbaum), 89–109.

Myers, S. (1991), 'Persistent Rules', *Linguistic Inquiry*, 22: 315–44.

Norris, D. G. (1994), 'Shortlist: A Connectionist Model of Continuous Speech Recognition', *Cognition*, 52: 189–234.

Ohala, J. J. (1992), 'Comments on Chapter 9' [discussion of paper by Lahiri and Marslen-Wilson], in G. J. Docherty and D. R. Ladd (eds.), *Papers in Laboratory Phonology II: Gesture, Segment, Prosody* (Cambridge: Cambridge University Press), 255–7.

—— and Ohala, M. (1995), 'Speech Perception and Lexical Representation: The Role of Vowel Nasalization in Hindi and English', in B. Connell, and A. Arvaniti (eds.), *Papers in Laboratory Phonology IV* (Cambridge: Cambridge University Press), 41–60.

Paradis, C. (1988), 'On Constraints and Repair Strategies', *Linguistic Review*, 6: 71–97.

Pisoni, D. B. and Luce, P. A. (1987), 'Acoustic–Phonetic Representations in Word Recognition', *Cognition*, 25: 21–52.

Prince, A. S. and Smolensky, P. (1993), *Optimality Theory: Constraint Interaction in Generative Grammar* (Rutgers Center for Cognitive Science, Technical Report 2; Rutgers University, New Brunswick, NJ).

Reetz, H. (1998), 'Automatic speech recognition with features', thesis, University of the Saarland.

Scobbie, J. M. (1991), 'Attribute-value phonology', Ph.D. dissertation (University of Edinburgh).

Stampe, D. (1980). *A Dissertation on Natural Phonology* (New York: Garland).

Steriade, D. (1995), 'Underspecification and Markedness', in J. A. Goldsmith (ed.) *The Handbook of Phonological Theory* (Cambridge, Mass.: Blackwell), 114–74.

Stevens, K. N. (1992), 'Lexical Access from Features', *Speech Communication Group Working Papers, Research Laboratory of Electronics, MIT*, 8: 119–44.

—— and Blumstein, S. E. (1981), 'The Search For Invariant Acoustic Correlates of Phonetic Features', in P. D. Eimas and J. L. Miller (eds.) *Perspectives on the Study of Speech* (Hillsdale, NJ: Lawrence Erlbaum), 1–39.

—— Manuel, S., Shattuck-Hufnagel, S., and Liu, S. (1992), 'Implementation of a Model For Lexical Access Based on Features', in J. J. Ohala (*et al.*) (eds.), *Proceedings of the 2nd International Conference of Spoken Language Processing (ICSLP 92)* (Banff, Canada), 1: 499–502.

Studdert-Kennedy, M. (1974), 'The Perception of Speech', in T. A. Sebeok (ed.), *Current Trends in Linguistics* (The Hague: Mouton).

Wheeldon, L. R. and Lahiri, A. (1997), 'Prosodic Units in Language Production', *Journal of Memory and Language*, 37: 356–81.

Zwitserlood, P., Schriefers, H., Lahiri, A., and van Donselaar, W. (1993), 'The Role of Syllables in the Perception of Spoken Dutch', *Journal of Experimental Psychology: Learning, Memory and Cognition*, 19: 260–71.

7

Phonology as Cognition

MARK HALE AND CHARLES REISS

1. FORM AND SUBSTANCE IN PHONOLOGY

This chapter attempts to ground phonology within psychology. That is, we are interested in phonology as a branch of the study of mental representation, the psychology of mind. In order to develop this 'phonology of mind' we need to understand the relationship between form and substance in linguistic representation. A coherent account of this distinction has yet to be proposed for either phonology or syntax. We attempt to contribute to this necessary enquiry in the domain of phonology by first defining 'form' and 'substance', and then critiquing some recent work that implicitly or explicitly touches on the relationship between the two. We will argue that current trends in phonology fail to offer a coherent conception of form and substance and are also inconsistent with basic principles of science. Since we are not proposing a complete alternative model of phonology, we invite the reader to reflect on how our proposals could be implemented or on how our assumptions (which we believe are widely shared in principle, if not in practice) should be modified.

It has proven quite useful for linguists to conceive of a grammar as a relationship between (i) a set of symbols—entities such as features and variables, constituents such as syllables, feet, NPs, and so on, and (ii) a set of computations—operations whose operands are drawn from the set of symbols, such as concatenation, deletion, and so on. The set of symbols and relations together describe the formal properties of the system. Relevant questions in discussing formal properties include 'Is the system rule and/or constraint based?'; 'Do operations apply serially or in parallel?'; and 'Are there limits on the number of operands referred to in the course of a given phonological computation?'

The issue of substance essentially arises only with respect to the set of symbols and the extent to which their behaviour in phonological computation is driven by

This chapter expands on Hale and Reiss (2000). We are grateful to audiences at the Montreal–Ottawa–Toronto Phonology Workshop 1998 at the University of Ottawa and at the Berkeley Phonology Laboratory, as well as to Noel Burton-Roberts, Morris Halle, Bill Idsardi, Madelyn Kissock, Afton Lewis, Jean-Philippe Marcotte, and Ida Toivonen for discussion and challenging criticism that improved the chapter. The authors' names appear in alphabetical order.

what they symbolize. For the sake of simplicity we restrict ourselves in this discussion to the set of phonological primitives known as distinctive features and to the representations that can be defined as combinations of distinctive features.

We will concentrate in this chapter on this notion of substance in phonological representation. In brief, the question we are interested in is the following:

(1) Do the phonetic correlates (that is, the substance) of a particular distinctive feature or feature bundle have any non-arbitrary bearing on how that feature or feature bundle is treated by the computational system?

It is trivial to show that languages differ in that their computational systems treat specific features or feature bundles differently—for example, Standard German has coda obstruent devoicing and English does not. From this we can conclude that languages *can* treat the same symbols differently. A more challenging problem arises when we find an apparent example of cross-linguistically universal, seemingly non-arbitrary treatment of a feature or feature bundle. In such cases we must ask ourselves the following:

(2) Is the observed pattern a reflection of substantive constraints on the computational system (that is, the grammar), or is the pattern due to other causes?

Other *a priori* plausible causes include, as we shall show in what follows, the process of language change, the nature of the language acquisition device, sampling errors, and so on. From the standpoint of grammatical theory, factors such as sampling errors are obviously uninteresting. However, language change and the nature of the learning path are also, strictly speaking, not part of grammatical theory. The modular approach to linguistics, and to science in general, requires that we both model the interactions between related domains, and also sharply delineate one domain from another. Occam's Razor demands that, in doing so, we avoid redundancy and the postulation of unnecessary factors.

Even before proceeding to our argument that generalizations that bear on patterns of phonetic substance are not relevant to phonological theory as we define it, we can see that there is potentially much to gain from this modular approach in that it posits that universal phonology should be studied not just across languages, but also across modalities. What is shared by the phonologies of signed and spoken languages? We believe that phonology consists of a set of formal properties (for example, organization into syllables and feet, feature spreading processes) that are modality independent and thus not based on phonetic substance. The goal of phonological theory should be to discover these formal properties. Failure to appreciate this goal has resulted in rampant 'substance abuse' in the phonological community.

We discuss various aspects of substance abuse in Sections 2–5. In Section 6, we offer a modest contribution to a substance-free phonology. In Section 7, we return to substance with a discussion of the putative phenomenon of phonetic enhancement in grammars. Section 8 ties together the preceding sections with arguments against functionalist 'explanation' in linguistics. We argue that *dysfunctionalist* reasoning fares as well as its better-known rival. Section 9 provides a concluding plea for a modular approach to the study of sound patterns in human languages.

2. THREE EXAMPLES OF SUBSTANCE ABUSE IN GRAMMATICAL THEORY

2.1. *Positional faithfulness in Beckman* (1997)

Beckman (1997) proposes the constraints in (3*a–b*) as members of the universal constraint set:

(3)(*a*) IDENT-σ_1(hi)
    A segment in the root-initial syllable in the output and its correspondent in the input must have identical values for the feature [high].
  (*b*) IDENT(hi)
    Correspondent segments in output and input have identical values for the feature [high].

As Beckman explains, this set of constraints allows faithfulness to a feature, like [high], to be maintained in some contexts, but not others, since the context-sensitive constraint (3*a*) can be ranked above a markedness constraint that is violated by, say, the presence of high vowels, *HIGH, which in turn is ranked above the general constraint in (3*b*). In other words, the ranking in (4) will allow surface high vowels only in root-initial syllables.

(4) IDENT-σ_1(hi) $\gg$ *HIGH $\gg$ IDENT(hi)

This is assumed to be a welcome result: 'The high ranking of positional faithfulness constraints, relative to both the more general IDENT constraints and markedness constraints, yields the result that features and/or contrasts in *just those positions which are psycholinguistically or perceptually salient* are less susceptible to neutralization than in other locations which are not protected' (Beckman 1997: 8; emphasis in original). Beckman (1997: 5) cites more than ten psycholinguistic studies to support her claim that word-initial material is more salient than medial or final material.[1] We believe that the correct conclusion to be drawn from this psycholinguistic evidence is the *exact opposite* of that which Beckman draws.[2] Encoding the findings of psycholinguistic experimentation in the grammar is a

---

[1] It is unclear whether this generalization would hold, say, in a language with non-initial stress. It is also unclear whether Beckman's extension of psycholinguistic findings concerning word-initial syllable to *root*-initial syllables is justified. However, we will assume, for purposes of this discussion, that Beckman has stated the relevant generalizations correctly.

[2] We wish to stress that we are not singling Beckman out for any reason except for the fact that her paper appeared recently in a widely read journal and is well written and clear in its arguments and assumptions.

mistake because it is possible to achieve the same empirical coverage without positing new mechanisms like positional faithfulness.[3] Consider the following alternative account.

We know that children acquire spoken language primarily on the basis of acoustic input from speakers in their environment, with Universal Grammar (UG) providing constraints on the hypothesis space.[4] We also know that phonological contrasts are best distinguished and recalled when occurring in certain positions. Imagine a child exposed to a language $\mathcal{L}_1$ that allows high vowels in all syllables—initial, medial, and final. Imagine further that $\mathcal{L}_1$ has initial stress and that stress is realized as relatively increased duration and intensity. Given this scenario, it is easy to see that a child constructing $\mathcal{L}_2$ on the basis of ouput from $\mathcal{L}_1$ could consistently fail to acquire a contrast between mid- and high vowels in relatively short, quiet syllables (those that are non-initial and thus unstressed), but succeed in acquiring this distinction in initial syllables, which are stressed and thus longer and louder. This type of relationship between $\mathcal{L}_1$ and $\mathcal{L}_2$ is known as 'sound change' (in particular, as a 'conditioned merger'). On the other hand, it is highly implausible that an acquirer would consistently fail to correctly analyse the mid/high contrast in longer, louder (stressed) syllables, yet successfully analyse the contrast in relatively short, quiet syllables. Note that this implausibility is independent of our view of the nature of UG.

We see, therefore, that the existence of positional faithfulness phenomena can be understood as merely reflecting the nature of the learning situation and not a reflection of any grammatical principle:[5]

(5) If the acoustic cues of a given contrast in the target language are correctly analysed by the acquirer in a context where they are relatively weak, they will also be analysed correctly in a context where they are relatively strong.

Note that (5) is essentially definitional, since the strength, or acoustic salience, of a contrast is just a measure of how easy it is to perceive. What is most important to understand is that the theory proposed here is not meant to *replace* a synchronic account of the data. So, the best synchronic analysis must somehow be able to generate vowel neutralization in noninitial syllables. (5) is meant to guide us in choosing a theory of grammar in which to couch that synchronic account, but (5) is not part of the grammar. Whatever theory of phonology one adopts, it must be able synchronically to generate the type of patterns that Beckman describes, but the predictions generated by the correct theory, qua phonological theory, need not replicate the predictions derivable from (5).

---

[3] For other arguments against context-sensitive faithfulness, see Reiss (1996: 315).

[4] It may be a useful idealization to assume that UG does not just constrain the learning path, but completely determines it. We suspect that such a position will prove most fruitful in sketching an explicit theory of acquisition, but justification for this goes beyond the scope of this chapter.

[5] This idea is discussed more thoroughly in Hale (forthcoming *b*).

By adopting the view of sound change proposed here, we see that many supposedly phonological tendencies, or markedness patterns, are actually emergent properties—that is, epiphenomenal. 'Positional faithfulness' is due, not to the nature of *phonology*, but to the 'sifting effect' of acquisition on the incidental, arbitrary nature of the phonetic substance. Since effects such as those observed by Beckman already have a coherent extragrammatical account within acquisition theory (and it is necessary, in any event, to have an acquisition theory), building positional faithfulness into a theory of universal phonology is a misuse, or abuse, of phonetic substance in theory construction.

2.2. /r/-insertion in McCarthy (1993)

McCarthy's (1993) discussion of intervocalic *r*-insertion in Massachusetts English is fairly well known, so an example should be sufficient for illustration. In this dialect, an underlying sequence like *Wanda arrived* is realized with a 'linking' [r]: *Wanda[r] arrived*. As McCarthy himself notes (and as discussed by LaCharité and Paradis 1993 and Halle and Idsardi 1997) 'r is demonstrably not the default consonant in English' (1993:189). That is, it is not the maximally unmarked consonant that an Optimality Theory (OT) account predicts would emerge in such a situation. In order to account for the insertion of [r] McCarthy proposes a special *rule* of *r*-insertion: 'a phonologically arbitrary stipulation, one that is outside the system of Optimality' (1993: 190). There are several problems with this proposal, many of which are insightfully discussed by Halle and Idsardi. However, we propose that one of their criticisms requires elaboration. Halle and Idsardi rightly point out that 'reliance on an arbitrary stipulation that is outside the system of Optimality is equivalent to giving up on the whole enterprise' (1997: 337), but these authors do not discuss what we consider to be the most important point: grammars do contain arbitrary processes. McCarthy's grammar has an arbitrary component (containing rules like *r*-insertion) and a non-arbitrary component (containing the substantive OT constraints). Such a theory is empirically non-distinct from the theory we propose below, which posits that *all* grammatical computations are arbitrary with respect to phonetic substance. This is because the set of phenomena predicted to exist by our theory (with only arbitrary processes) is identical to the set of phenomena predicted to exist by McCarthy's theory (with both non-arbitrary and arbitrary processes). Since McCarthy must adopt a model that allows arbitrary phenomena (like *r*-insertion), the addition to the theory of a special subcomponent to account for alleged 'non-arbitrary' phenomena violates Occam's Razor.

The diachronic source of *r*-insertion is transparent—the relevant dialects also exhibit *r*-deletion in codas, so insertion reflects rule inversion triggered by hypercorrection. Again, the diachronic facts do not make a synchronic account unnecessary, but they show us that basically idiosyncratic historical events affect specific grammars—and, in part, how they may do so.

2.3. *Structural constraints on non-structures*

Perhaps one of the most problematic cases of substance abuse we have come across is McCarthy's (1996) appeal to parameterized constraints to account for opacity effects in Hebrew spirantization by invoking the notion of constraint schema. McCarthy makes some reasonable simplifying assumptions in this first attempt:

> I will assume that every constraint is a prohibition or negative target defined over no more than two segments, α and β. That is, the canonical constraint is something like *{α,β}, with appropriate conditions imposed on α and β. These conditions are as follows:
>
> (i) a specification of the featural properties of α and β as individual segments;
> (ii) a specification of the linear order relation between α and β ($\alpha < \beta$, $\beta < \alpha$, or both in the case of mirror-image rules ...
> (iii) a specification of the adjacency relation between α and β (e.g., strict adjacency, vowel-to-vowel adjacency ...)
>
> The decomposition of the conditions imposed by a phonological constraint will be crucial in accounting for the range of opacity phenomena. Even more important, though, is this: each condition—the featural composition of α, the featural composition of β, linear order and adjacency—must also name the level (underlying, surface, or either) at which it applies. Correspondence Theory allows us to make sense of conditions applying at one level or the other. As a bookkeeping device, I will state the constraints in the form of a table ... (1996: 220)

We reproduce here the schema-based constraint that McCarthy proposes to account for Tiberian Hebrew post-vocalic spirantization.

(6) Constraint for opacity in Hebrew spirantization (McCarthy 1996: 223)

*	Condition	Level
α	V	Indifferent
β	[-son, -cont]	Surface
Linear order	$\alpha > \beta$	Indifferent
Adjacency	Strict	Indifferent

As McCarthy says. 'In correspondence terms, the meaning of this constraint is this: the constraint is violated if a surface stop β or its underlying correspondent is immediately preceded by a vowel' (1996: 223).

As pointed out in Reiss (1997), this powerful constraint type has several problems. First, it compromises the OT notion of a universal, innate constraint set by allowing apparently language-specific parameterized constraints. This may not be a serious problem, since it represents an attempt to define the form of possible constraints. In other words, McCarthy could be interpreted as presenting a theory in which the intensional description of the set of constraints is universal, but languages vary in which constraints they actually incorporate (based on evidence presented to the learner).[6]

Most relevant to our present purposes, however, is the fact that such constraints undermine implicit and explicit appeal to phonetic grounding of well-formedness constraints in McCarthy's work. For example, McCarthy and Prince (1995: 88) refer to a constraint *VgV as the 'phonologization of Boyle's Law'. It is incoherent to argue that a constraint is motivated by the facts of phonetics, when the structures that violate this constraint need not be surface structure strings. In fact, they need not exist as strings at *any level of representation*.

3. NEO-SAUSSUREANISM

The conclusion we wish to draw from the above examples and many others like them is that the best way to gain an understanding of the computational system of phonology is to assume that the phonetic substance (say, the spectral properties of sound waves) that leads to the construction of phonological entities (say, feature matrices) *never* reflects how the phonological entities are treated by the computational system. The computational system treats features and the like as arbitrary symbols. What this means is that many of the so-called *phonological universals* (often discussed under the rubric of markedness) are in fact epipheno-mena deriving from the interaction of extragrammatical factors such as acoustic salience and the nature of language change. It is not surprising that, even among its proponents, markedness 'universals' are usually stated as 'tendencies'. If our goal as generative linguists is to define the set of *computationally possible* human grammars, 'universal tendencies' are irrelevant to that enterprise.

We therefore propose extending the Saussurean notion of the arbitrary nature of linguistic signs to the treatment of phonological representations by the phonological computational system. Phonology is not and should not be grounded in phonetics, since the facts that phonetic grounding is meant to explain can be derived without reference to *phonology*. Duplication of the principles of acoustics and acquisition inside the grammar constitutes a violation of Occam's Razor and thus must be avoided. Only in this way will we be able correctly to characterize the universal aspects of phonological computation.

John Ohala (e.g. 1990) has done the most to demonstrate that many so-called markedness tendencies can be explained on phonetic grounds and thus should not be explained by principles of grammar. Examples discussed by Ohala include patterns of assimilation and the contents of phonemic inventories. For an extensive bibliography on this topic, see Ohala (1998). We differ from Ohala in our

---

[6] McCarthy does not explicitly make this argument, but it seems to us to be a better theory than the standard OT claim that all constraints are literally present in all grammars. Of course, adopting our suggested interpretation will force OT practitioners to revise their views on acquisition and, especially, *the emergence of the unmarked*. This view of OT would also make it much closer to a theory of learned rules.

use of the term 'phonology' (which for him covers *all* aspects of the sound systems of human language), but whole-heartedly endorse his approach.

3.1. *Substance in* The Sound Pattern of English

It is obvious that our proposal runs contrary to most of the discussion in chapter 9 of *The Sound Pattern of English* (SPE) (Chomsky and Halle 1968). This chapter starts out with an 'admission' that the theory developed in the earlier chapters is seriously flawed:

The problem is that our approach to features, to rules and to evaluation has been overly formal. Suppose, for example, that we were systematically to interchange features or to replace $[\alpha F]$ by $[-\alpha F]$ (where α is +, and F is a feature) throughout our description of English structure. There is nothing in our account of linguistic theory to indicate that the result would be the description of a system that violates certain principles governing human languages. To the extent that this is true, we have failed to formulate the principles of linguistic theory, of universal grammar, in a satisfactory manner. In particular, we have not made use of the fact that the features have intrinsic content.   (*SPE* 400)

Later in the chapter Chomsky and Halle themselves acknowledge that, with the above-quoted assertion, they are on the wrong track:

It does not seem likely that an elaboration of the theory along the lines just reviewed will allow us to dispense with phonological processes that change features fairly freely. The second stage of the Velar Softening Rule of English (40) and of the Second Velar Palatalization of Slavic strongly suggests that the phonological component requires wide latitude in the freedom to change features, along the lines of the rules discussed in the body of this book.   (*SPE* 428)

In other words, Chomsky and Halle ultimately recognize that the truly important parts of the phonology, in the sense of the ones that are unnatural, are those that cannot be derived from functional considerations of naturalness. This conclusion is echoed elsewhere: 'Where properties of language can be explained on such "functional" grounds, they provide no revealing insight into the nature of mind. Precisely because the explanations proposed here are "formal explanations", precisely because the proposed principles are not essential or even natural properties of any imaginable language, they provide a revealing mirror of the mind (if correct)' (Chomsky 1971: 44).

We propose that switching the feature coefficients as described in the first quotation might lead to the description of systems that are *diachronically* impossible human languages (ones that could never arise because of the nature of language change), but not to ones that are *computationally* impossible. The goal of phonological theory, as a branch of cognitive science, is to categorize what is a computationally possible phonology, given the computational nature of the phonological component of UG.[7]

3.2. *Computation versus transduction: A place for substance*

It is important to note that the preceding discussion is not meant to imply that the mapping of sound to features is arbitrary. It is only the treatment of phonological representations within the computation that is arbitrary. Articulatory and acoustic substance *are* related to the representations we construct, but not within the grammar. The nature of this relationship is part of the theory of *transduction*—the mapping between the physical and the symbolic (Pylyshyn 1984). As Bregman (1990: 3) points out, 'In using the word representations, we are implying the existence of a two-part system: one part forms the representations and another uses them to do such things as calculate ...'. Bregman is concerned with the auditory system that does not have an output module—in discussing language, we also need to model output transducers that map from surface (featural) representations to articulatory gesture. For our purposes, Bregman's distinction corresponds to speech perception (construction of featural representations, ultimately from auditory signals) and grammar, which performs symbolic computation. We know from the existence of visual and auditory illusions that the transduction process is not simple. The perceptual system does not just form a direct record of physical stimuli. As Bregman points out, we know that representations are being constructed, because only then could they be constructed incorrectly, leading to illusions.

Pylyshyn (1984) provides the following discussion: 'This, then is the importance of a transducer. By mapping certain classes of physical states of the environment into computationally relevant states of a device [e.g. a human], the transducer performs a rather special conversion: converting computationally arbitrary physical events into computational events. A description of a transducer function shows how certain nonsymbolic physical events are mapped into certain symbolic systems' (p. 152). Pylyshyn points out that the '*computationally relevant* states are a tiny subset of [a system's] physically discriminable states' and that the 'former are typically a complex function of the latter' (p. 150). In (7) we paraphrase Pylyshyn's criteria for a psychological transducer (pp. 153–4)—that is a transducer from physical signals to representations.

(7) Criteria for a psychological transducer
- The function carried out by a transducer is itself *non-symbolic*; it is part of the functional architecture of the system.
- A transducer is stimulus bound, operating independently of the cognitive system.
- The behaviour of a transducer is described as a function from physical events to symbols:

---

[7] This argument, as well as other ideas in this chapter, was anticipated by Hellberg (1980). See also Burton-Roberts, this volume, Section 5.

(*a*) The domain of the function (the input) is couched in the language of physics.

(*b*) The range of the function (the output) must be computationally available, discrete atomic symbols (for example, feature matrices).

(*c*) The transformation from input to output must follow from the laws of physics.

This is where issues of substance arise—the physical aspects of the acoustic signal serve as the input into the transducer function. From that point on, in the manipulations of the constructed symbolic representations, substance is irrelevant to computation. Only the *formal* properties of such representations are relevant to the computational system.

It is worth contrasting Pylyshyn's well-articulated modular approach to that of Prince and Smolensky (1993), who directly reject the kind of extreme formalist position we advocate here.

'We urge a reassessment of this essentially formalist position. If phonology is separated from the principles of well-formedness (the "laws") that drive it, the resulting loss of constraint and theoretical depth will mark a major defeat for the enterprise' (Prince and Smolensky 1993: 198, see also p. 3). This view of the goals of phonology stems from a failure to observe the critical transducer versus grammar distinction—that is, from extensive 'substance' abuse. It is also at odds with the well-established goals of cognitive science in general: 'if we confine ourselves to the scientific and intellectual goals of understanding psychological phenomena [as opposed to predicting observed behaviour] one could certainly make a good case for the claim that there is a need to direct our attention away from superficial "data fitting" models toward deeper structural theories' (Pylyshyn 1973: 48). As our discussion of markedness below will indicate, we do not believe that any 'principles of well-formedness' exist, aside from those that constrain the set of possible representations. That is, we find the evidence for markedness-based constraints to be unconvincing.

The 'principles of well-formedness' that Prince and Smolensky refer to and adopt as the basis of OT constraints are merely derived from the heuristic devices that constitute the intuitions of an experienced linguist. For example, we may intuitively believe that a sequence like [akra] will more likely be syllabified as [a.kra] rather than as [ak.ra] in a random sample of grammars, although both syllabifications are found, for example, in the Ancient Greek dialects. Lacking information to the contrary, it may be useful to assume that the more common syllabification is present in a new, unfamiliar language. This will allow the formulation of hypotheses that may then be tested, and the guess will turn out to be correct more often than not, if our intuitions have any basis. However, it is a mistake to assume that our intuitions reflect the nature of the system we are studying in any direct manner. The intuition that heavy things fall faster than light things is very useful when someone drops something from a window, but the intuition needs to be transcended to understand the workings of gravity. Heuristics are used by the analyst to make useful guesses about data, and guesses can be wrong. This is why OT constraints need to be violable, unlike all other scientific laws.

The pervasiveness of such 'data-over-principles' approaches to phonology can be appreciated by the following quote from an influential pre-OT paper: 'The goal of phonology is the construction of a theory in which cross-linguistically common and well-established processes emerge from very simple combinations of the descriptive parameters of the model' (McCarthy 1988: 84). By concentrating on what is 'common', rather than what is possible, phonology will provide (or rather has provided) plentiful material for descriptive work at some level of sophistication, but it is clear that no science should be concerned with making it particularly simple to express that which happens often. The goal of any science is to define a coherent domain of enquiry and to establish a common vocabulary for *all* events in that domain. This involves reducing the common *and* the rare events (for example, planetary motion and the Big Bang) to special cases of an abstract set of primitive notions. All of this suggests that, while a change of course for phonological theory was definitely needed in the early 1990s, OT has been a change in exactly the wrong direction.

3.3. Acoustophilia: a warning

Sapir (1925: 37) points out that 'it is a great fallacy to think of the articulation of a speech sound as [merely] a motor habit'. A corresponding error is committed in many of the studies (e.g. Flemming, forthcoming) that argue for the increased use of acoustic information to model human phonological computation. This work tends to establish units of analysis in terms of measurements taken over the acoustic signal itself. We believe that this technique shows the negative effects of 'acoustophilia'—the mental state arising from the deep and abiding satisfaction that comes from having *something* concrete to measure, in this case the acoustic signal. There is, we believe, a fairly serious difficulty with such an approach: we know with a great deal of confidence that human perception does not show the kind of direct dependency on the signal that the methodology of the acoustophiliacs requires.[8] This attitude towards the study of language echoes the overly positivist brand of empiricism adopted by the behaviourists, an attitude that was already discredited in the 1950s.

An example may make this clearer. Flemming (forthcoming) argues from an examination of F_2 interactions in an experimental setting that it is necessary to have the grammar generate a statistical pattern that forms a reasonable match to his experimental results. A parallel from the field of the cognition of vision would examine the properties of an image as measured with, for example, a photometer,

---

[8] Since phonetic substance provides the raw material for phonological theory construction, selective use of fine-grained acoustic data can give rise to insights into the nature of phonological computation. We recognize the significant body of work done on the phonetics/phonology interface with reference to acoustic studies. Keating (1988), which uncovers interesting phonetic regularities, but maintains a theory of phonology that makes no direct reference to this phonetic substance, is a brilliant example.

and require of us that our 'grammar of vision' generate a representation like that measured on the page. So, in Fig. 7.1, it would require—since the triangle we see is of precisely the same colour and brightness as the background (as can be verified by the use of a photometer)—that we construct a human visual system that does *not* see the triangle projecting from the page. This is of course the wrong result—the human visual system, given the input in Fig. 7.1, constructs a 'percept' that is very different from the patterns we might infer from photometric readings (see Hoffman 1998). The difficulty that this presents to more acoustically oriented approaches to *phonology* is fairly obvious: it is often claimed, on the basis of some physical measurement of the signal, that something is 'difficult' or 'easy' to perceive (auditorily), 'salient' or not so salient. Again, note that the edges and inside of the perceived triangle have absolutely no physical properties to distinguish them from the background. What the visual example in Fig. 7.1 shows us is that measurements taken over the raw data presented to the human auditory system should not be taken as direct evidence for what kind of data actually arrive at the *linguistic* processing system.

Fig. 7.1. Triangle constructed by visual system

Turning to the domain of auditory perception, it is a well-known result of psychoacoustics that the relationship between, say, intensity of a signal and *perceived* loudness is non-linear: doubling the physical intensity of a signal does not create a signal that is judged to be twice as loud. As we move further from the physical signal, to auditory perception and on to the construction of linguistic representations, things become even less clear. In particular, when several distinct and independent cues interact in the signal (as in the cases discussed by Steriade 2000), we cannot conclude without detailed and extremely difficult studies of the nature of auditory perception that we understand the way these cues interact to form an auditory percept. It is yet more difficult to determine how these auditory percepts get organized into *linguistic* (that is, featural, symbolic) representations. These topics will provide psychologically oriented phoneticians and their colleagues with challenging research projects for years to come. However, the questions and the answers we hope to get are only distally related to the subject matter of phonology.

Part of the confusion in this area stems from the fact that discussion of 'output' forms often fails to distinguish between the output of the grammar (a feature-based representation) and, say, the output of the speaker (an acoustic or articulatory event). As demonstrated most clearly by our ability to construct 3D representations based on a black-and-white pattern on a printed page, there is a vast gap between physical stimuli/outputs and the internal (cognitive) representations that relate to them. Therefore, even if phonologists had a metric of the complexity or difficulty inherent in interpreting or creating certain physical stimuli or outputs (which they do not), it is apparent that there is no reason to believe that such a scale would translate straightforwardly to a markedness scale for representations. There is no reason to believe that the *representation* of the act of pushing a bar of gold is more difficult or complex or marked than the representation of the act of pushing a feather (cf. Burton-Roberts, this volume).

4. EXPLANATORY INADEQUACY

What are the implications of our view that phonology should be all form and no substance? In particular, does this conclusion about the nature of phonological operands have any positive implications for phonological theory? We think that there is one clear conclusion to be drawn. Since, as we have argued, languages appear to vary in some arbitrary ways (for example, inserting [r] and not, say, [t]), it is necessary to develop a theory that allows for such variation. In other words, the child should be equipped with a universal computational system and a set of primitives that can be modified upon exposure to positive evidence. For this reason, we believe that current versions of OT, which assume a universal set of (phonetically) substantive constraints (for example, *VoicedCoda, Lazy, and so on) do not shed light on the nature of grammar. A set of constraint templates, with principles of modification from which the learner can construct the necessary constraint inventory for the target language, may prove to be more useful. Similarly, a rule-based theory equipped with a set of principles for defining possible rules would also allow for the type of stipulative, cross-linguistic variation we have argued is necessary. Note that, given an explicit theory of acquisition, such a 'nativism *cum* constructivism' view of phonology is well constrained: UG delimits the set of possible rules or constraints; the data determine which rules or constraints are actually constructed.

In order to appreciate the fact that positing the type of substantive constraint found in the OT literature adds nothing to the explanatory power of phonological theory, consider the situation in which a learner finds himself or herself. Equipped with an OT-type UG, a child born into a Standard German-speaking environment 'knows' that voiced coda obstruents are 'marked'. However, this child never needs to call upon this knowledge to evaluate voiced coda obstruents, since there are none in the ambient target language. In any case, by making use of positive evidence, the child successfully acquires a language like German. Born into an English-speaking environment, the child again knows that voiced coda obstruents are marked. However, the ambient language provides ample positive evidence that such sounds are present, and the child must override the supposed innate bias against voiced coda obstruents in order to learn English. So, this purported UG-given gift of knowledge is either irrelevant or misleading for what needs to be learned. Our substance-free theory of phonology shares with OT-type theories a reliance on positive evidence. The two theories have the same empirical coverage, since we also assume that both English and German are acquired. The difference is that we leave out of the genetic inheritance 'hints' that are irrelevant or misleading. We find our solution to be more elegant. Once again, note that this argument is equally applicable to markedness theories of all types, not just those couched within OT. Since markedness cannot have any bearing on learnability, it is probably irrelevant to any explanatorily adequate theory of grammar. We thus propose banishing markedness from consideration in future linguistic theorizing.[9]

5. DISCUSSION

The substance-abuse approach has been criticized for cognitive science in general by Pylyshyn (1984: 205 ff.). Pylyshyn describes a box emitting certain recurrent patterns of signals. He then asks what we can conclude about the nature of the computational mechanism inside the box, based on the observed pattern of output. The answer is that we can conclude nothing, since the observed patterns may reflect the nature of what is being computed (in his example, the output is a Morse Code rendering of English text, and the observed regularity is the 'i before e, except after c' rule), not the nature of the computer. In Pylyshyn's words, 'the observed constraint on [the system's] behavior is due not to its intrinsic capability but to what its states represent.' If we are interested in studying the phonology 'computer' then we need to distinguish a possible phonological computation from an impossible one. The set of attested phonological patterns and their distribution may be somewhat skewed by the sifting effect of language change. Real explanation of the nature of phonological computation requires us to see beyond such epiphenomena as 'markedness tendencies'.

---

[9] In fact, there are two distinct types of markedness in the phonological literature. This chapter is concerned with substantive markedness. Simplicity or evaluation metrics of the *SPE* symbol-counting type can be seen as measuring 'formal' markedness. We believe that the best approach to such formal requirements is to build them into the language acquisition device (LAD). Under this view, learners never compare extensionally equivalent grammars for simplicity or economy, they just construct the one that is determined by the LAD. There is, then, no reason to introduce the terms 'simplicity' and 'economy' into the theory, since they are contentless labels for arbitrary (i.e. not derivable) aspects of the LAD. For a concrete example of how we think the characterization of the LAD should be approached, see Hale and Reiss (forthcoming).

We believe that the current impregnation of the architecture of the phonological 'virtual machine' with phonetic substance represents a step backward for phonological theory. Phonologists should now call upon their impressive success in amassing descriptions of individual phonological 'programs' and aim for a more abstract, but deeper understanding of phonological computation.

Pylyshyn's example raises the question of whether constraints are appropriate elements for the construction of grammars at all. By defining grammars via constraints—that is, in negative terms—we are drawn into the problem of *inductive uncertainty*. In general, science works in terms of positive statements. A physical or formal system is defined in positive terms by a list of primitive elements, operations, relationships, and so on. The set of impossible chemical or physical processes, for example, is infinite, and so is the set of impossible linguistic structures.

Consider the question of hierarchical structure in syntax. Let us imagine that we want to express the claim that all structure is hierachically organized as a trait of UG. How should this proposal be formulated? If one seeks to characterize UG by listing constraints on the set of possible languages, then one might say something like 'Flat structure is not possible'. Since UG is instantiated in real brains, it must consist of a finite set of characteristic features. Note, however, that, using such negative constraints, we would actually need an infinite set of statements to characterize UG. This is because it is also the case that 'No language marks past tense by having the speaker eat a banana after uttering the verb', and 'No language requires that listeners look at a square to interpret iterativity', and so on are also true statements about human language. In other words, there is an infinite set of constraints on the set of possible languages.

These examples are, of course, preposterous, because in practice the constraints are stated in terms of a (usually implicit) universe of discourse. For example, the universe of discourse of linguistic theory does not include bananas, eating, seeing or squares. Therefore, a constraint is interpretable only in the context of a list of positive statements (such as a list of primitive elements like phonological distinctive features, and primitive operations like Move) that define the universe of discourse of any formal system.

We see, then, that a theory that formulates linguistic universals in terms of constraints must *also* contain a vocabulary of elements and operations in which those constraints are expressed, or to which they refer. This vocabulary of items and processes is presumably based on empirical observations and inferences. Consider a simpler alternative.

If our current hypothesis concerning UG is stated only in *positive* terms, without *negative* constraints, we can achieve a more economical model. The positive terms are just those entities and operations (features, deletions, insertions, Merge, Move, and so on) that have been observed empirically or inferred in the course of model construction. When faced with a phenomenon that is not immediately amenable to modelling using existing elements of the vocabulary, scientific methodology (basically Occam's Razor) guides us. We must first try to reduce the new phenomenon to a description in terms of the vocabulary we already have. If this can be shown to be impossible, only then can we justify expanding the vocabulary.

Thus, a 'constraining approach' to UG, stated in terms of what is disallowed, requires a set of constraints and a vocabulary that defines the universe of discourse in which the constraints are valid. The alternative proposed here requires only the vocabulary of possible entities and operations, along with the metatheoretic principle of Occam's Razor. The alternative is thus more elegant and should be preferred.

In more concrete terms this means that our theory of UG should consist of the minimum number of primitives that we need to describe the grammars we have seen. Note that we should not be influenced in our search by preconceived notions of simplicity. For example, if we know that we need hierarchical structure for some phenomena, but there exist other phenomena that are ambiguous as to whether they require flat or hierarchical structure, then we should assume that the ambiguous cases also have hierarchical structure. If our current theory of UG contains an operation that only generates hierarchical structure from the primitive elements, constraints against flat structure will be superfluous. In fact, positive statements like 'structures are organized hierarchically' and 'all branching is binary' are also superfluous to grammar modelling (assuming they are correct), since they are just a reflection of how structure-building operations work.

The approach advocated here seems to be consistent with that used in science in general. If a physicist observes a constraint on the behaviour of a particle, say, then he or she posits a set of properties for that particle from which the observed behaviour emerges. The constraint thus has the status of a derivative and not primitive aspect of the theory. The arguments given here for constraints *on* grammars can be extended to apply to constraints *in* grammars as well, but this discussion is beyond the scope of the current paper (see Reiss 1999).

The issue of 'substance abuse' is closely tied to the use of constraints in phonological theory. Despite the fact that phonologists tend to characterize current debate concerning OT as a question of 'rules versus constraints', this is misleading. Many rule-based analyses make use of constraints such as the Obligatory Contour Principle (OCP). Constraints in otherwise rule-based phonologies serve two main purposes. Either they define certain structures as disfavoured or ill-formed, and thus subject to modification by rule; or they are used to block the application of a rule just in case the rule's output would be disfavoured or ill-formed. Work by Paradis (1988) and Calabrese (1988) are typical of the use of constraints as diagnostics for repair of certain structures. The rule-based account of stress systems presented by Halle and Idsardi (1995) appeals to 'Avoidance Constraints' (pp. 422 ff.) that prevent the application of rules in cases where the rules' output would be a 'disfavoured' structure. The OCP has been invoked for both of these purposes in a number of papers, most notably McCarthy (1986) and Yip (1988), who makes the following remark: 'The main contribution of the OCP is that it allows us to separate out condition and cure. The OCP is a trigger, a pressure for change ...' (p. 74).

Given the problems with markedness theory alluded to above, note that, in the absence of a theory of disfavouredness, this approach is slightly circular: the only real evidence for the disfavoured status is that the posited rule appears to be blocked; and the reason for the blocking is that the resultant structure would be disfavoured. Halle and Idsardi point out that certain advantages derive from mixing rules with constraints in the analysis of individual languages. In general, the use of constraints allows us to formulate simpler rules. However, they note that a fully rule-based analysis is in principle always possible—Halle and Vergnaud (1987) is an example they cite. We propose that considerations of elegance for a theory of UG take precedence over elegance in the analysis of individual languages, and thus the Halle and Idsardi system, for example, should be adapted in a way that preserves its mathematical explicitness, while doing away with constraints on unattested structures. In general, a goal of future phonological research should be to take the idea of rule-based phonology seriously—by avoiding constraints altogether. Such an approach will offer a principled alternative to OT and other constraint-based models. In other words, rather than stating simple, but empirically inadequate rules, reinforced by an arsenal of language-particular or universal constraints, we should attempt to understand what kind of rules we actually need if we are to do without constraints. An example of this approach is discussed in the next section.

6. A RESULT IN THE FORMAL CHARACTERIZATION OF UNIVERSAL GRAMMAR

In order to show that there is progress to be made in the characterization of formal properties of UG consider a limited type of condition on rule application (or constraint applicability). Vowel syncope rules are found with (at least) all three of the following types of conditioning:

(8) Some conditions on vowel deletion rules (Odden 1988: 462)
   (*a*) Delete a vowel unless flanking Cs are identical.
   (*b*) Delete a vowel blindly (whatever the flanking Cs are).
   (*c*) Delete a vowel only if flanking Cs are identical.

Condition (*a*) can be restated as 'Delete a vowel if flanking Cs are *not* identical'. Thus, (*a*) demands non-identity and (*c*) demands identity of segments in Structural Descriptions (SDs). Phonological formalism must, therefore, have at least enough power to express conditions of non-identity and identity. These conditions may also be restricted to a given subset of phonological features, such as the set of Place features.

Autosegmental representation can represent (c) using linked structures—two C-slots may be linked to a single-feature tree or matrix. Alternatively, two slots may be explicitly linked to separate, but identical trees/matrices. However, (*a*), the requirement of non-identity, cannot be represented using just autosegmental notation. This is because non-identity can be due to a disagreement with respect to *any* feature, and autosegmental notation does not make use of variables. In order to represent conditions of non-identity, Reiss (1999) makes use of a system of Feature Algebra (FA) incorporating the existential and universal quantifiers. FA allows the formulation of conditions that have traditionally been notated as, say, $C_1 \neq C_2$ and $C_1 = C_2$. The conditions are stated here in prose form:

(9) Attested conditions of rule application
 (i) The NON-IDENTITY CONDITION (encompasses condition (*a*))
     There exists some feature F, such that C_1 and C_2 have opposite values for F.
 (ii) The IDENTITY CONDITION (encompasses condition (*c*))
     For all features F, C_1 and C_2 have the same value.

In both conditions the set of features over which non-identity or identity is computed may be a subset of the total feature set. For example, an identity condition may be applicable only to the set of Place features in a given rule.

Reiss (1999) applies the FA formalism to data presented by McCarthy (1987), Yip (1988) and Odden (1986, 1988) in their arguments concerning the status of the OCP as a principle of grammar. The use of FA notation has several benefits. First, it provides us with counter-arguments to Yip's claim that the effects of, for example, the IDENTITY CONDITION should not be built into SDs. Secondly, it allows us to evaluate the status of constraints like the OCP in the light of data conforming to the apparently contradictory conditions (*a*) and (*c*). Thirdly, the formalism helps us to discover that two other formally similar conditions are unattested.

(10) Unattested conditions on rule application
 (i) COMPLETE NONIDENTITY CONDITION
     For all features F, C_1 and C_2 have the opposite value for F.
 (ii) VARIABLE PARTIAL IDENTITY CONDITION
     There exists some feature F, such that C_1 and C_2 have the same value for F.

The COMPLETE NON-IDENTITY CONDITION would allow a rule deleting a vowel only if flanking segments have opposite values for, say, all Place features, or even for *all* features; for example, 'Delete a vowel in the environment $C_1\_\_C_2$ if C_1 is [−anterior, −labial, +dorsal] and C_2 is [+anterior, +labial, −dorsal], or C_1 is [+anterior, −labial, +dorsal] and C_2 is [−anterior, +labial, −dorsal], and so on.

The VARIABLE PARTIAL IDENTITY CONDITION would allow, say, a rule that deleted a vowel only if flanking consonants have the same value for *any* feature (perhaps in a given subset of features): 'Delete a vowel in the environment $C_1\_\_C_2$ if and only if C_1 and C_2 are both [αanterior], or [αlabial], or [αdorsal], and so on'.

It turns out that, while these two conditions are apparently unattested in phonology, they are used in the interpretation of binding relations. Thus a careful consideration of the formal requirements of UG can lead to interesting results. It should be satisfying enough to get a handle on what we know UG can do, what its formal properties are, without worrying about what it cannot. In this sense, positive characterizations of grammars are to be preferred to constraint-based ones.

7. THE MIRAGE OF ENHANCEMENT

A particularly illustrative combination of what we consider to be the misuse of substantive considerations and functionalism can be found in the literature on phonetic enhancement and the maximization of contrast (e.g. Stevens *et al.* 1986). For example, the tendency of three-vowel systems to contain the maximally distinct set /i,u,a/ is taken as a reflection of a phonological principle demanding the 'best' use of the available acoustic space. Like other claims concerning markedness and UG, this pattern is no more than a tendency. However, we can show that the view of markedness as an emergent property, outlined above, can give insight into this statistical pattern. Imagine a language $\mathcal{L}_1$ that had the four vowels /i,u,e,a/. Now we know that merger of acoustically similar vowels (such as /i/ and /e/) is a common diachronic process. It would not be surprising if a learner constructing $\mathcal{L}_2$ on the basis of data from speakers of $\mathcal{L}_1$ were to fail to acquire a slight distinction and end up with a three-vowel system containing /i,u,a/. However, it is much less likely that the learner would fail to acquire an acoustically more robust distinction like /u/ versus /a/ and end up with an inventory containing, say /i,u,e/.[10] So, vowels that are close together in the acoustic space are likely to merge diachronically. Vowels which are acoustically distant are not likely to merge diachronically. The observed pattern of maximal contrast is thus not built into the phonology, but is an emergent property of the set of observed phonological systems owing to the nature of diachronic sound change.

8. FUNCTIONALISM AND DYSFUNCTIONALISM

The rise of OT has been accompanied by a revival of functionalism in phonology. In fact, there is no necessary connection between OT as a theory of computation and functionalist reasoning, and an OT proponent might invoke what we call the National Rifle Association defence ('Guns don't kill people; people kill people'): computational theories are not inherently functionalist, people are functionalist. However, the ease with which functionalist ideas can be implemented in OT has clearly invited this 'functionalist' explosion and may bear on the question of whether or not the theory is sufficiently constrained or even constrainable. Note also that the 'logic' of functionalism (namely, that *all* phenomena are explicable by

---

[10] Note that 'phonetic substance' may itself indicate how weak the reasoning is in this case: English [i], as well as the other front vowels, is significantly lower than Danish [i]. Why is the 'maximization of contrast' not active at the phonetic level—precisely the level that provides the alleged 'substance' (perceptual distinctness, in this case) for the functionalist claim?

reference to competition between universal, but violable, principles) is identical to the logic of OT. In this section we briefly show that the 'substance' orientation of functionalism can be turned on its head to yield a theory that we will dub 'dysfunctionalism'.

Many functionalist theories of grammar can be summarized in almost Manichean terms as consisting of a struggle between the 'competing forces' of ease of articulation (what is presumed to be 'good' for the speaker) and avoidance of ambiguity (what is presumed to be 'good' for the hearer). As an example of the former, consider Kirchner's (1997: 104) constraint 'LAZY—Minimize articulatory effort'. For the avoidance of ambiguity, consider Flemming's (forthcoming) MAINTAIN CONTRAST constraints, which are violated by surface merger of underlying contrasts.

The interplay of what is 'good for' the speaker and what is 'good for' the hearer supposedly gives rise to the patterns we see in language: sometimes mergers occur and the speaker's output is 'simplified'—potentially creating a difficulty for the hearer; sometimes the speaker maintains distinctions, perhaps producing a more 'complex' output, thus avoiding ambiguity for the hearer.[11]

The problem with this theory is that functionalist principles can be replaced by their opposites, which we will call 'dysfunctionalist' principles, with no significant change in the set of grammars predicted to exist. Consider the following principles, proposed by a linguist with a different view of human nature than the functionalists have.

(11) Principles of dysfunctionalism
  OBFUSCATE: merge contrasts, use a small inventory of distinctive sounds, and so on.
  NO PAIN–NO GAIN: maintain contrasts, use a large inventory, generate allomorphy, and so on.

Merger, widely attested in the languages of the world, as well as the oft-proclaimed diachronic principle that 'change is simplification', will be accounted for by the (dys)functional requirement that one should OBFUSCATE. The failure of merger, equally well attested, and the generally ignored diachronic process of 'complexification', will be attributed to the effects of the NO PAIN–NO GAIN Principle. The competition of these two 'dysfunctionalist' principles will thus lead to the exact same results as the usually cited functionalist principles. While the ultimate question of whether human beings are fundamentally lazy, but helpful, or something seemingly more perverse is intriguing, it hardly seems as though investigation into such matters should form the foundation of a theory of

---

[11] Further evidence for the incoherence of the functionalist position is the fact that 'careless' speech can often lead to supposedly complex outputs such as the stop cluster in [pt]*ato* for *potato*. Onset stop clusters are not found in careful speech, so it is surprising, from a functionalist perspective, that they should be found precisely when the speaker is not putting forth greater articulatory effort.

phonological computation.[12] We propose, therefore, that functionalism provides no insight into the nature of grammar. Again, we propose leaching all substance out of phonology in order better to observe the abstract computational system.

The alternative—which seems to be the focus of many current developments in phonological theory—seems clear. Given a sufficiently rich and explicit theory of the human personality (giving us principles such as 'be lazy' and 'be helpful to the listener') and the human articulatory and perceptual systems ('phonetic' substance), phonology itself will turn out to be epiphenomenal. While this seems considerably less promising to us, it has clear implications for the research strategy that phonologists should adopt. Phonologists, under such a view, should focus their energies in two domains: phonetics and the empirical explication of fundamental features of the human personality ('laziness,' 'helpfulness,' and so on).

The anti-functionalist stance taken here is, of course, not new. For example, Halle (1975: 528), points out that, 'Since language is not, in its essence, a means for transmitting [cognitive] information—though no one denies that we constantly use language for this very purpose—then it is hardly surprising to find in languages much ambiguity and redundancy, as well as other properties that are obviously undesirable in a good communication code.' Halle suggests that it is more fruitful to conceive of language as a kind of mathematical game than to concern ourselves with the 'communicative functions' approach to studying language. The latter viewpoint led to such dead ends as the application of formal information theory to natural language.

CONCLUSIONS

We are advocating that phonologists, qua phonologists, attempt to explain less, but in a deeper way. As we hope to have indicated, empirical results provided by phoneticians and psycholinguists contribute to the development of a substance-free phonology, and we look forward to important cooperation with scholars in these fields. We recognize that only they can provide explanation for many (E-language) generalizations that are striking in their statistical regularity.[13] Since

---

[12] The authors would be happy to provide examples—drawn from the history of linguistic theory—of the evolutionary advantages of self-interested effort (NO PAIN–NO GAIN) and OBFUSCATE. We refrain for reasons of space, fully confident that the reader will have no difficulty generating ample evidence on his or her own.

[13] But see Engstrand (1997a,b) for arguments that the statistics may be misleading. For example, the purported markedness of /p/, as evidenced by its relative rarity in voiceless stop inventories, *vis-à-vis* /t/ and /k/, is probably illusory. The overwhelming majority of the languages in a database like UPSID (Maddieson 1984; Maddieson and Precoda 1989) lacking a /p/ are found in Africa. Similarly, the languages of Africa do not 'avoid' voiced velar stops, which are also commonly assumed to be marked (see Hale, forthcoming b). 'Thus, it cannot be concluded that velars and bilabials constitute underrepresented members of the respective voiced and voiceless stop series. Although this pattern is to be expected from proposed production and perception constraints, it is largely overridden by areal biases' (Engstrand 1997a: 1).

we believe that the focus of phonological theory should be on the cognitive architecture of the computational system, we also believe that the non-substantive aspects of OT have been tremendously important for the development of the field. The best of the OT literature is far more explicit about the nature of the assumed computational system than its predecessors often were. The mere existence of such a well-developed alternative to rule-based phonology is valuable, regardless of specific formal problems (for example, synchronic 'chainshifts') or the 'substance abuse' found in any particular implementation. However, we have also raised the question of whether constraints are appropriate entities for scientific modeling, since they must always be accompanied by a somewhat redundant positive characterization of a universe of discourse.

REFERENCES

Beckman, J. N. (1997), 'Positional Faithfulness, Positional Neutralisation and Shona Vowel Harmony', *Phonology*, 14: 1–46.

Bregman, A. (1990), *Auditory Scene Analysis* (Cambridge, Mass: MIT Press).

Burton Roberts, N. (this volume), 'Where and What is Phonology? A Representational Perspective'.

Calabrese, A. (1988), 'Towards a Theory of Phonological Alphabets', Ph.D. dissertation (MIT).

Chomsky, N. (1971), *Problems of Knowledge and Freedom* (New York: Random House).

—— (1986), *Knowledge of Language* (New York: Praeger).

—— and Halle, M. (1968), *The Sound Pattern of English* (New York: Harper & Row).

Engstrand, O. (1997a), 'Areal Biases in Stop Paradigms', in *Papers from Fonetik 97, The Ninth Swedish Phonetics Conference*, held in Umeå, 28–30 May 1997. Reports from the Department of Phonetics, Umeå University (PHONUM), iv. 187–190.

—— (1997b), 'Why are Clicks so Exclusive?' in *Papers from Fonetik 97, The Ninth Swedish Phonetics Conference*, held in Umeå, 28–30 May 1997. Reports from the Department of Phonetics, Umeå University (PHONUM), iv. 191–4.

Flemming, E. (forthcoming), 'Phonetic Detail in Phonology: Toward a Unified Account of Assimilation and Coarticulation', in K. Suzuki and D. Elzinga (eds.), *Coyote Papers , Proceedings of the Arizona Phonology Conference 5, Features in Optimality Theory*. University of Arizona, Tucson.

Hale, M. (forthcoming a), 'What is output?' in M. Halle, C. Reiss, and B. Vaux (eds.), *Phonology 2000* (Oxford: Oxford University Press).

—— (forthcoming b), *Theory and Method in Historical Linguistics* (Oxford: Blackwell).

—— and Reiss, C. (2000), 'Substance Abuse and Dysfunctionalism: Current Trends in Phonology', *Linguistic Inquiry*, 31: 157–69.

—— —— (forthcoming), 'Grammar Optimization', *Language Acquisition*.

Halle, M. (1975), 'Confessio Grammatici', *Language*, 51: 525–35.

—— and Idsardi, W. (1995), 'Stress and Metrical Structure', in J. A. Goldsmith (ed.), *Handbook of Phonological Theory* (Oxford: Blackwell).

—— —— (1997), 'r, Hypercorrection and the Elsewhere Condition', in I. Roca (ed.), *Derivations and Constraints in Phonology* (Oxford: Clarendon Press), 331–48.

—— and Vergnaud, J. R. (1987), *An Essay on Stress* (Cambridge, Mass.: MIT Press).

Hellberg, S. (1980), 'Apparent Naturalness in Faroese Phonology', *Nordic Journal of Linguistics*, 3: 1–24.

Hoffman, D. D. (1998), *Visual Intelligence* (New York: Norton).

Keating, P. A. (1988), 'Underspecification in Phonetics', *Phonology*, 5: 275–92.

Kirchner, R. M. (1997), 'Contrastiveness and Faithfulness', *Phonology*, 14: 83–111.

LaCharité, D. and Paradis, C. (1993), Introduction: The Emergence of Constraints in Generative Phonology and a Comparison of Three Current Constraint-Based Models', *Canadian Journal of Linguistics*, 38: 127–51.

McCarthy, J. (1986), 'OCP Effects: Gemination and Antigemination', *Linguistic Inquiry*, 17: 207–630.

—— (1988), 'Feature Geometry and Dependency: A Review', *Phonetica*, 45: 84–108.

—— (1993), 'A Case of Surface Rule Inversion', *Canadian Journal of Linguistics*, 38: 169–95.

—— and Prince, A. (1995), 'Faithfulness and Reduplicative Identity', in J. Beckman, L. Walsh-Dickey, and S. Urbanczyk (eds.), *University of Massachusetts Occasional Papers (UMOP)* 18 (Amherst), 249–384. Rutgers Optimality Archive, http://ruccs.rutgers.edu/roa.html.

—— (1996), 'Remarks on Phonological Opacity in Optimality Theory', in *Proceedings of the Second Colloquium on Afro-Asiatic Linguistics*. J. Lecarme, J. Lowenstamm, and U. Schlonsky (eds.), *Studies in Afro-Asiatic Grammar, Papers from the Second Conference on Afro-Asiatic Languages, Sophia, Antipolis, 1994* (The Hague: Holland Academic Graphics), 215–43.

Maddieson, I. (1984), *Patterns of Sounds* (Cambridge: Cambridge University Press).

—— and Precoda, K. (1989), 'Updating UPSID', *Journal of the Acoustical Society of America*, suppl. 1, Vol. 86, S19.

Odden, D. (1986), 'On the Obligatory Contour Principle', *Language*, 62: 353–83.

—— (1988), 'Antiantigemination and the OCP', *Linguistic Inquiry*, 19: 451–75.

Ohala, J. J. (1990), 'The Phonetics and Phonology of Aspects of Assimilation', in J. Kingston and M. Beckman (eds.), *Papers in Laboratory Phonology I* (Cambridge: Cambridge University Press).

—— (1998), 'A Bibliography of the Phonetics of Sound Change', Department of Linguistics, University of California, Berkeley.

Paradis, C. (1988), 'On Constraints and Repair Strategies', *Linguistic Review*, 6: 71–97.

Prince, A. and Smolensky, P. (1993), *Optimality Theory: Constraint Interaction in Generative Grammar* (Rutgers Center for Cognitive Science, Technical Report, 2; Rutgers Univesity, New Brunswick, NJ).

Pylyshyn, Z. (1973), 'On the Role of Competence Theories in Cognitive Psychology', *Journal of Psycholinguistic Research*, 2: 21–50.

—— (1984), *Computation and Cognition: Toward a Foundation for Cognitive Science* (Cambridge, Mass: MIT Press).

Reiss, C. (1996), 'Deriving an Implicational Universal in a Constrained OT Grammar', *NELS* 26: 303–17.

—— (1997), 'Unifying the Interpretation of Structural Descriptions', *West Coast Conference on Formal Linguistics*, 15: 413–27.

Reiss, C. (1999), 'Philosophical and Empirical Reasons to Ban Constraints from Linguistic Theory', MS Concordia University.

Sapir, E. (1925), 'Sound Patterns in Language', *Language*, 1: 37–51. Repr. in Martin Joos (ed.), *Readings in Linguistics* (Washington: American Council of Learned Societies, 1957), 19–25.

Steriade, D. (2000), 'Paradigm Uniformity and the Phonetics–Phonology Boundary', in M. B. Broe and J. B. Pietrehumbert (eds.), *Papers in Laboratory Phonology V* (Cambridge: Cambridge University Press), 313–34.

Stevens, K., Keyser, S. J., and Kawasaki, H. (1986), 'Toward a Phonetic and Phonological Theory of Redundant Features', in J. Perkell and D. Klatt (eds.) *Symposium on Invariance and Variability of Speech Processes* (Hillsdale, NJ: Lawrence Erlbaum).

Yip, M. (1988), 'The Obligatory Contour Principle and Phonological Rules: A Loss of Identity', *Linguistic Inquiry*, 19: 65–100.

8

Vowel Patterns in Mind and Sound

JOHN HARRIS AND GEOFF LINDSEY

Language is primarily an auditory system of symbols. In so far as it is articulated it is also a motor system, but the motor aspect is clearly secondary to the auditory. In normal individuals the impulse to speech first takes effect in the sphere of auditory imagery and is then transmitted to the motor nerves that control the organs of speech. The motor processes and the accompanying motor feelings are not, however, the end, the final resting point. They are merely a means and a control leading to auditory perception in both speaker and hearer . . . Hence, the cycle of speech . . . begins and ends in the realm of sounds.

(Sapir 1921: 17–18)

1. INTRODUCTION

The sound aspect of a linguistic sign provides the information that enables listeners and speakers to access the sign's lexical and grammatical meaning. The channel for this information is the speech signal, through which speakers transmit and monitor the information and listeners receive it. On the basis of this rather obvious point, it would be natural to conclude that phonological features—the code in terms of which the information is compiled—should be defined in terms of auditory imagery.

Yet for a generation the most influential brand of feature theory has been centred almost wholly on articulation. This is surprising; for, while articulations constitute a delivery system for linguistic information, they are not of themselves information-bearing. To echo Sapir: the perceptible form of a linguistic sign is essential and primary, the means by which it is produced secondary.

Consider an analogy from the realm of written signs. Countless disabled people have learned to read, despite lacking the mechanical wherewithal to write. Are such people illiterates? By no means. Only a bias towards production over perception, or some bogus egalitarianism in relation to these domains, would insist that they are. Who could learn to write without the ability to read? Only a trained ape—an illiterate ape.

We are indebted to Neil Smith, Bencie Woll, and the editors for their valuable comments on earlier drafts.

Even when the recent hegemony of articulatory features has been challenged, it has rarely been with anything like the whole-hearted commitment to the auditory-acoustic that characterized Jakobsonian feature theory (Jakobson *et al.* 1952). One response has been to make acoustic specifications parasitic on primarily articulatory features (see e.g. Clements and Hertz 1991). Another allows for acoustic features to coexist with an articulatory set (see Flemming 1995; Boersma 1998).

In work of this orientation, the auditory and the acoustic are often conflated, and for understandable reasons: they are more intimately linked with one another than either is with the articulatory. Just as optics deals with light processed by vision, so acoustics deals with sound processed by hearing. There is an acoustic-auditory chain consisting of waves in the air, disturbance in the middle ear, firings in the inner ear, and cognitive activations. It is possible to draw a distinction between disturbance external to the human body and response internal to the human body, the latter being strictly auditory. But note that even this distinction gets tricky at the interface: is the vibrating air within the ear canal part of the human body or not?

The crux of the matter is that in speech the acoustic entails the auditory-perceptual, by definition. The informational or signifying potential of variations in atmospheric pressure is realized when they produce disturbances in the ear that trigger central reponses. But the high degree of isomorphy between activity in the air and the ear-brain has no parallel in the relation between either of these domains and vocal-tract movements. Without air disturbance there is no ear disturbance; and without ear disturbance there is no information. But the informational force of air disturbances is quite independent of what produces them—be it a human vocal tract, a digital synthesizer, or a budgerigar.

In this chapter, taking the representation of vowel quality as our illustrative focus, we set out reasons for rejecting feature definitions based on articulation or raw acoustics. The alternative view we present is somewhat old-fashioned, owing much to the tradition of Saussure, Sapir, and Jakobson. It holds that the mental representation of speech sounds is constituted not of tongue heights, for instance—nor of formant heights, nor for that matter of basilar stimulation points. Rather it is constituted of information-bearing patterns that humans perceive in speech signals. The arguments on which this view is built are, we believe, fundamentally sound. However, they have hardly been heeded, still less countered, in the recent feature literature.

This conclusion, let us hasten to point out, does not lead us to deny that phonology has been shaped in some measure by the physical nature of the vocal apparatus. Other shaping influences include gravity and atmospheric pressure. However, none of these belongs in mental representation. Nor does the conclusion entail totally expunging from phonology all considerations traditionally regarded as phonetic, the type of austere view sometimes advocated in the literature, most recently by Hale and Reiss (2000, this volume). We address this point in Section 2.

While phonological categories qua mental objects cannot be the same as external acoustic events, we take the view that they must nevertheless stand in some non-arbitrary relation to them—hence the justification in referring to the categories, in the spirit of Saussure and Sapir, as auditory images.

We identify the set of categories constituted by sound images through the traditional phonological method of determining the manner in which sounds are organized into systems and natural classes. In Section 3, we briefly survey the salient patterns of organization displayed by vowel systems, both in their maximal form and when subject to positional neutralization. Section 4 suggests how the phonological categories that by hypothesis underpin these regularities can be construed as sound images, elementary patterns detectable in the acoustic signal. Our proposals rest on familiar phonetic findings but are novel in establishing the COMPOSITIONALITY of vowels: some vowels are literally made up of others. Section 5 considers and rejects various alternative proposals to explain vowel patterning in terms of vision, articulation, or raw acoustics. Section 6 concludes.

2. PHONOLOGY: MODULE OR EPIPHENOMENON?

Generations of academics and students have struggled over the conceptual distinction between phonetics and phonology. Of the two, phonetics probably yields more readily to succinct definition: 'the study of the physical aspects of speech' would be one attempt—though even this might exclude such phonetic domains of enquiry as psychoacoustics and the linguistic phonetics that presupposes an understanding of linguistic contrast.

In generative linguistic theory, phonology has classically been seen as a component of grammar, an independent cognitive module characterizing what humans know about linguistic sound patterns. However, linguists have long been nagged by the obvious fact that much of the sound patterning in language reflects constraints imposed by the physical nature of the organs of speech and hearing. Many generalizations traditionally considered phonological, such as the prefer-ence human language shows for voiceless over voiced obstruents, are clearly relatable to non-cognitive factors.

Which raises the fundamental question of whether there exists a core of immaculate phonology that can be exposed through phonetic cleansing. Answer-ing this question in the affirmative holds an obvious appeal for professional phonologists, who frequently take the existence of a pure phonology as a matter of necessity. In the words of Hale and Reiss (2000: 158), 'there must be a core of formal properties (e.g., organization into syllables and feet, feature spreading processes) that are modality independent [i.e. equally applicable to sign language] and thus not based on phonetic substance. The goal of phonological theory should be to discover this formal core.'

However, Occam's Razor works just as effectively on brains as it does on tongues and ears. Many phonological properties not amenable to functional-phonetic explanation are almost certainly shared with other domains. For instance, categoriality and arboreal structure (or, more generally, head-dependent relations) are shared with syntax. Moreover, it is even open to debate whether these are peculiar to Universal Grammar (UG), since both can plausibly be attributed to cognition in general. As for Hale and Reiss's own examples, feet and syllables seem to be required by our cognitive musical faculties. And it is hard to think of a human behaviour to which some analogue of feature spreading would not be applicable (again music would do as an example). The search for phonology's formal core may turn out to be about as successful as the quest for universal solvent or the world's edge.

An alternative view, not widely endorsed by generativists, is that phonology is epiphenomenal, a well-defined area of study but not one that corresponds to any specific organ of body or mind. A research strategy founded on this view does not *preclude* the possibility that there exist uniquely phonological forms of knowledge or behaviour but places the burden of proof on the demonstration of their existence. Explanation of linguistic sound patterns (and, depending on one's definition, gesture patterns in sign language) is initially to be sought in domains such as cognitive psychology, aerodynamics, neurology, and physiology, a research ethic maintained most prominently in the work of Ohala (see 1992 for references). Peculiarly phonological apparatus, on this view, should be appealed to only as an explanation of last resort.

Among the functionalist targets singled out for attack by Hale and Reiss are recent Optimality Theory (OT) treatments of positional vowel neutralization. Two main characteristics of this phenomenon demand explanation. Why do subsystems of vowel contrast vary in size according to the phonological context in which they occur? And why do reduced subsystems tend to mimic the maximal inventories of languages with simpler overall systems? A hermetically sealed phonological account would posit neutralization rules or constraints for the first characteristic, attribute the second to universal markedness preferences, and leave things at that. Functionalist OT accounts go further by proposing that each of the constraints that deliver these effects directly embodies some pressure applied by the physics of speech. Beckman (1997), for example, proposes a set of positional faithfulness constraints that, when ranked high enough, protect certain privileged contexts, such as word- and stem-initial syllables, from constraints that favour neutralization (see also Zoll 1998 for discussion and further references). The faithfulness constraints, she claims, are motivated by psycholinguistic evidence that demonstrates the perceptual salience of the relevant contexts. Flemming (1995) attributes the universal tendency towards unmarked patterning in both full and reduced systems to a preference for the maximal dispersion of contrasts in vowel space, compelled by phonological constraints that are grounded in auditory processing (cf. Lindblom 1986).

Critiques of this general functionalist approach centre on the question of why it should be necessary to duplicate in the grammar explanations of sound patterning that are independently required by general theories of sound change and language acquisition. On this point, the views of Ohala and of Hale and Reiss largely converge (see also Hyman, forthcoming). Indeed, it might even be said that the duplication is inherently contradictory. For example, it is not immediately obvious how positional asymmetries in vowel distribution can simultaneously 'arise from' grammar-internal constraints (Beckman 1997: 7) and be motivated by grammar-external speech functioning. The constraints in question could have at best some intermediate place in a chain of causation.

What has been conspicuous by its recent absence from this debate is any serious discussion of the very nature of the linguistically significant categories that code vowel contrasts. Much of the relevant literature simply takes the categories for granted—essentially the articulatory features inherited from *The Sound Pattern of English* (*SPE*) or an acoustic set based on the parameters of machine spectrography. It is our contention that both of these approaches are fundamentally flawed. They not only fail to establish a satisfactory bridge to auditory perception but also inadequately describe the nature of vowel systems and processes.

We present an alternative, compositional model in which the qualities *a*, *i*, *u*, which anchor vowel systems and which show up preferentially as neutralization reflexes, are simpler than other vowels—literally simpler, in terms of the signal patterns that are detected by speakers. That is, vowel neutralization can be shown to involve both a reduction in the complexity of phonological representations and a corresponding reduction in the amount of information that can be extracted from the signal.

We are quite prepared to accept that the compositional aspect of this account may ultimately prove amenable to explanation in terms of some combination of physiological, neurological, and cognitive facts that are not specific to language. Indeed, decisive evidence may eventually emerge to debunk the generativist notion of a fully modular phonology altogether. However, neither of these developments could relieve working phonologists of their duty to model as precisely as possible the speech pattern phenomena that call for ever deeper explanation.

In short, a Hjelmslevian programme of the kind advocated by Hale and Reiss is both too exclusive and too inclusive. It is too exclusive to the extent that it banishes auditory imagery from the mental representation of phonology, and too inclusive to the extent that it presupposes, contra Occam, a modular core which cannot be the null hypothesis.

3. VOWEL PATTERNS IN PHONOLOGY

It is a well-known fact that vowel systems across the world's languages show a clear predilection for triangular patterning built around the 'corner' vowels *a*, *i*, *u*. Recurrent extensions of this basic set include the canonical five-term system (the most favoured of all) and, through the addition of Advanced Tongue Root (ATR) contrasts, seven- and nine-term inventories (Crothers 1978; Maddieson 1984).

Typically of course, a language's maximal vowel inventory is not sustained in all phonological contexts. Positional neutralization of vowel contrasts produces two general patterns, which may occur singly or in combination in a given language. One can be described as centrifugal: vowels belonging to a contracted subsystem disperse to the far corners of vowel space. Textbook examples are provided by Modern Greek, Russian, and Tamil, where canonical five-term systems reduce to *a, i, u* in unstressed positions. The other pattern is centripetal, in which neutralization reflexes are drawn into central areas of vowel space. Languages exhibiting this type of reduction typically do so in conjunction with some part of the centrifugal pattern. Romance is particularly rich in examples—Catalan, Neapolitan Italian (Bafile 1997), Portuguese and Romansch (Kamprath 1987), to name a few.

The particular version of the pattern that occurs in Catalan results in a seven-term peripheral system contracting to *i, u, ə*, producing stress-conditioned alternations such as those below (Palmada Félez 1991):

(1) prím   'slim'   əprimár   'to slim'
     sérp   'snake'   sərpəntí   'winding'
     pέl   'hair'   pəlút   'hairy'
     gát   'cat'   gətέt   'kitten'
     ʎúm   'light'   ʎuminós   'luminous'
     gós   'dog'   gusέt   'puppy'
     pɔ́rt   'port'   purtuári   'of the port'

All of the languages just mentioned illustrate the manner in which the size and shape of vowel systems can vary as a function of stress. However, it would be far from the truth to assume that all cases of systemic contraction are conditioned in this way. This immediately renders problematic any attempt to explain vowel neutralization in terms of diminished perceptual salience resulting from reduced loudness and duration, a point we return to below. In some cases, the context to which the maximal inventory is tied is defined in purely morphological terms. The telling evidence comes from languages in which stress either is orthogonal to neutralization or is absent altogether. The full six-vowel system of Chumash, for example, is restricted to roots; in affixes, we find contraction to *a, i, u* (Applegate 1972). This distribution is quite independent of word stress, which typically falls on the penultimate syllable. Neutralization in the total absence of stress is found, for example, in Punu and Ruund (both Bantu), where canonical five-term systems contract to *a, i, u* in suffixes (Hyman 1999: 239).

A variation on the reductive neutralization theme is to be found in languages that combine it with assimilative neutralization. In such cases, certain vowels appear in a neutralization site only if they are harmonically supported by some other vowel occurring in a dominant nucleus. Pasiego Spanish provides an example in which stress is implicated (Penny 1969). Stress-free examples include Ibibio (Urua 1990) and the height-harmony pattern widely encountered in Bantu (Hyman 1998, 1999). In each of these cases, as with non-harmonic contraction, it is mid-vowels that are distributionally defective in the neutralization contexts.

A relatively simple example of the Bantu pattern is provided by Chichewa (Mtenje 1985): verb roots license a maximal five-vowel inventory (see (2)), while the basic vocalic content of suffix vowels is restricted to *a* (e.g. reciprocal *-an-*), *i* (e.g. applied *-il-*), and *u* (e.g. reversive *-ul-*). Mid-vowels do occur in suffixes, but only as alternants of high vowels lowered under the harmonic influence of a mid-root vowel (see (2)*b*).

(2)   Root   Root+applied
  (a) *pind-a*   *pind-il-a*   'bend'
      put-a   *put-il-a*   'provoke'
      bal-a   *bal-il-a*   'give birth'
  (b) *lemb-a*   *lemb-el-a*   'write'
      konz-a   *konz-el-a*   'correct'

Centrifugal patterns of vowel neutralization have always been something of an embarrassment to orthodox *SPE*-style features. Standard specifications organized around [±high], [±low], [±back], and [±round] fail to tease out the fact that the corner vowels form a natural class *vis-à-vis* mid. This is one of the shortcomings that spurred the development of an alternative model of vowel contrast in which the vowels a, *i*, *u* are treated as the embodiment of independent segmental elements (Anderson and Jones 1974 and subsequent work by many researchers—see Harris and Lindsey 1995 for references). This is the approach we adopt here, employing the labels [A], [I], and [U] for the categories, as distinct from their respective pronunciations *a*, *i*, *u*. The following section is devoted to a discussion of the definition of these categories. Mid-vowels are represented as compounds: *e* as [A, I], *o* as [A, U]. Thus mid-vowels are more complex than corner vowels by virtue of being composed of them.

This model allows for centrifugal vowel reduction to be characterized quite simply: representationally complex vowels are barred from the neutralization site.

Other types of vocalic process provide further support for compositionality. Perhaps the most graphic confirmation comes from vowel coalescence. In one recurrent pattern, two corner vowels collide through morphemic juxtaposition to yield a mid-vowel, as in Zulu *na-iŋkosi* > *neŋkosi* 'with the chief', *na-umuntu* > *nomuntu* 'with the person'. The phenomenon is straightforwardly represented as the compacting of two sequentially ordered elements into a single complex segment, [A]–[I] yielding [A, I] in the case of *a–i* > *e*. This account compares favourably with one based on articulatory features, in which one set of specifications has to be rewritten by another: in the case of *a–i* > *e*, [−high,

+low, +back]–[+high, −low, −back] is arbitrarily replaced by [−high, −low, −back].[1]

The AIU treatment of coalescence carries over directly to harmony. For example, height harmony consists in the spreading of [A] from a harmonic trigger to a vowel composed of [I] or [U] (cf. Goldsmith's (1985) analysis of the general Bantu pattern). Diphthongization is simply the reverse of this effect: examples such as *e > ai* and *o > au* (cf. the history of English) manifest the breaking-up of a complex vowel's components into a sequence of two simplex vowels.

To summarize: a range of phonological facts relating to the systemic, reductive, and assimilatory behaviour of vowels supports the conclusion that certain vowels are complex in the sense that they are composed of other vowels.

4. VOWEL PATTERNS IN THE SIGNAL

4.1. *Elemental patterns*

Guided by the phonological patterning just reviewed, we will now propose definitions of the categories [A], [I], and [U], which will allow us phonetically to model the composition of complex *e* and *o* in terms of simplex *a, i, u*.

Before getting down to the specifics, let us make explicit a close parallel we are seeking to draw with compositionality in consonants. There is a clear sense in which consonantal lenition—like vowel reduction, often neutralizing in effect—degrades phonetic information. Take, for example, the salient spectral discontinuities that provide cues to the phonological identity of a plosive in a VCV sequence, such as abrupt change in amplitude, noise burst, rapid formant transitions, and f0 perturbation. Fewer of these cues are present in lenited reflexes, none of them in a vocalized reflex. Elsewhere we have shown how this phonetic impoverishment can be related to a categorial reduction in phonological representations (Lindsey and Harris 1990; Harris and Lindsey 1995; Harris, forthcoming).

It is perhaps not clear that phonetic-informational asymmetries of this order are also to be found in vowel neutralization, especially when this is expressed in terms of standard features. That is, there is no immediately obvious sense in which the outputs of vowel reduction could be said to be informationally more impoverished than unreduced counterparts. For example, *SPE*-style tongue–body representations of mid peripheral *e* and centralized *ə* both require three feature values: [−high, −low, −back] versus [−high, −low, +back]. Specifications of this type grant equal informational status to all vowels.

Expression in terms of formant values also fails to suggest any informational

---

[1] As an alternative articulatory account, not directly expressible by means of *SPE*-type features, it might seem appealing to think of coalescence as reflecting a compromise between the extreme dorsal gestures involved in the production of opposing corner vowels. The implementation of this idea is problematic, based as it is on an impressionistic notion of tongue height that has no foundation in articulatory reality. We expand on this point below.

asymmetries. As is evident from Table 8.1, vowels that the phonology tells us are simplex have the same amount of formant-value information as vowels that the phonology tells us are complex.

Table 8.1. Ball-park formant frequencies of six vowels (adult male)

Vowel	F_1	F_2	F_3
i	300	2,200	3,000
e	500	1,800	2,700
a	700	1,200	2,500
o	500	900	2,400
u	300	600	2,300
ə	400	1,400	2,400

Quantal theory (Stevens 1972, 1989) might be turned to for an analysis that captures the special status of the corner vowels, specifically in terms of psychoacoustic salience related to formant convergence. However, this theory fails to account for the apparent compositionality relations that phonological patterning suggests—for example, the composition of *e* in terms of *i* and *a*. The quantal nature of the corner vowels derives from the salient manner in which F2 and F3 converge in *i* and F1 and F2 converge in both *a* and *u*. But this perspective actually obscures the compositionality of mid-vowels: *e*, for example, cannot have an F2 that is simultaneously merged with F3 (as in *i*) and with F1 (as in *a*). The quantal characteristics of *i* and *a* are in fact both missing from *e*.

We now present an alternative view of vowels, according to which speaker-hearers extract three basic patterns from vocalic speech signals. We consider the internalized form of these patterns—that is, the three basic auditory images—to be the elements that we notate as [A], [I], [U]. These three patterns will be shown to embody in a sense the quantal characteristics of the three corner vowels; but we go beyond quantal theory in suggesting that languages may use these patterns not only alone but also in combination.

These three elements are precisely analogous to those that speaker–hearers extract from obstruent speech signals, such as frication noise and abrupt amplitude-change (notated [h] and [?] respectively), and that likewise can occur both alone and in combination (Harris and Lindsey 1995). This approach allows us to demonstrate that the consequences of vowel neutralization are informationally parallel to those of consonant lenition.

Unlike *SPE*-style features, each pattern may occur alone in speech: the elements are independently pronounceable, requiring nothing akin to the filling-in of redundant features (Harris and Lindsey 1995). The solo pronunciations of the categories [I], [A], [U] are the three corner vowels *i, a, u*.

The elementary auditory images can be notated either with the capital-letter symbols [A], [I], [U] or, more transparently, with iconic symbols or with the mnemonics mAss, dIp and rUmp (see Fig. 8.1).

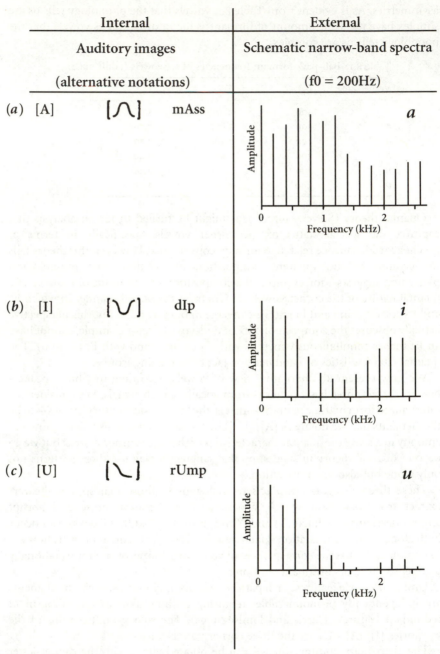

Fig. 8.1. The three basic elementary patterns (auditory images) for vowels and schematic spectra for three vowels, each of which exhibits only one elementary pattern

In the case of [A], the internal mental category (or auditory image) corresponds to a pattern in external signals consisting of a central energy mass with troughs at top and bottom of the vowel spectrum (that is, approximately 0–2.5kHz for men and 0–3kHz for women) (Fig. 8.1*a*). In [I], the mental category/auditory image corresponds to a converse pattern in the external signal, one in which energy is distributed to the top and bottom of the vowel spectrum with a trough or dip in between (Fig. 8.1b). In [U], the internal category/auditory image corresponds to an external marked skewing of acoustic energy to the lower half of the spectrum (over and above the −6dB per octave downward slope characteristic of all vowels (Fig. 8.1*c*)).

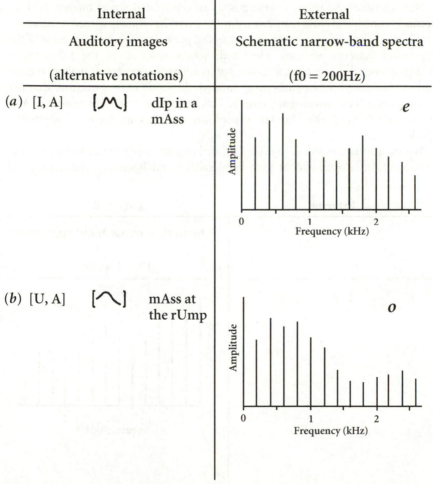

Internal	External
Auditory images	Schematic narrow-band spectra
(alternative notations)	(f0 = 200Hz)

(a) [I, A]   [ʍ]   dIp in a mAss

e

(b) [U, A]   [ʌ]   mAss at the rUmp

o

Fig. 8.2. Composite elementary patterns (auditory images) and schematic spectra for two vowels, each of which exhibits two elementary patterns: (*a*) *e*, (*b*) *o*

It is now possible to define *e* as comprising two of these patterns—namely dIp and mAss (see Fig. 8.2*a*). Acoustically, *e* shares with *i* the clear energy dip between F_1 and F_2. We model this as the presence of the elementary image, dIp. But, in *e*, F_1 and F_2 are closer together than in *i*, such that the vowel's energy is massed towards a central spectral region, with troughs at top and bottom of the frequency range. We model this as the presence of an elementary mAss pattern in addition to the dIp pattern. Both auditory images are activated by this vowel. By the same token, *o* exhibits a rUmp pattern, since its energy is markedly skewed to the lower part of the frequency range. On the other hand, the peak energy is far enough above the bottom of the frequency range to constitute a mAss, with troughs above and below (see Fig. 8.2*b*). Both auditory images are activated.

Now consider the signal characteristics of centralized vowel quality, such as occurs in centripetal reduction. Acoustically, schwa has equally spaced formants— that is, it exhibits no merged-formant spectral peaks (see Fig. 8.3). In terms of the key vowel patterns we have identified, schwa lacks all of the following: a mid-frequency dip in energy, a massing of its energy in the central spectral region, and a pronounced skewing of energy towards the rump of its spectrum. In other words, schwa is informationally empty. This is consistent with the notion in AIU theory that schwa is the phonetic expression of a nucleus devoid of segmental specification.

We are now in a position to offer a unified treatment of both centrifugal vowel neutralization (manifested in peripheral raising and lowering) and centripetal

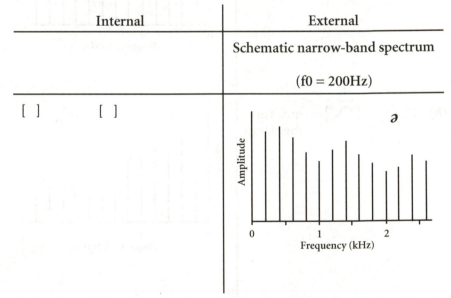

Fig. 8.3. Categorial non-representation and schematic spectrum of a schwa vowel exhibiting none of the three elementary patterns

reduction (centralization): both simultaneously involve a loss of internal categorial and external signal information.

4.2. *Internal–external isomorphy*

Let us now revisit the question of how the elements or auditory images proposed here differ from *SPE*-type features.

Over several decades' use, square brackets and plus/minus signs have taken on a kind of inherent authority, as if the physical expression of *SPE*-type features could be taken for granted. Let us dispel this assumption at once: acoustic cues to *SPE*-type features have not been well established. Formulae like '[+anterior]' remain what they always were—notational labels for conjectural generalizations over bodies of observed speech behaviour.

Like *SPE*-type features, elements are conjectural generalizations over data. But there are at least three differences. First, we believe elements capture generalizations more elegantly, such as the vowel neutralization facts outlined in Section 3. Secondly, elements may occur in isolation—that is, each is independently pronounceable without any need of redundancy fill-in machinery. Thirdly, elements allow far greater isomorphy between the conjectured internal objects and the external phenomena that cue them.

It is a reasonable assumption that the informational content of sounds is directly encoded in phonological representations. (In fact, there is a good case for saying that this is the whole point of phonological representations.[2]) In terms of the patterns defined here and motivated on the basis of phonological evidence reviewed in Section 3, corner vowels can be said to carry less information than mid-vowels. It makes sense to conclude that the proposed patterns correspond directly to phonological categories. Unlike orthodox feature theory, the model requires no adaptor mechanism to translate between a set of auditory-acoustic terms and a non-matching set of phonological terms. The isomorphism between the internalized vowel categories and external patterns in the signal that the AIU model establishes is unprecedented in the annals of recent feature history.

We feel justified in using our element terminology ambiguously, to refer (i) to the inner objects that, among other things, make up lexical addresses and (ii) to characteristics of external acoustic signals that cue the inner objects. A useful analogy can be drawn with astronomical constellations. What is Orion? Orion is an ambiguously used term referring both to a mental concept and to a grouping of physical stars—a physical object, in so far as it is perceived as such. We represent Orion on the page either with the word 'Orion' or with a stylized graphic of points

---

[2] This position is of course at variance with Hale and Reiss's (this volume) view of phonology as being modality independent (see also van der Hulst, this volume). However, taking phonology to be specifically targeted on speech does not prevent us from subsuming it under a grander study of all the modalities associated with language (including deaf sign and writing)—a branch of linguistic semiology that would concern itself with the informational content of all relevant perceptible physical media.

and lines somewhat resembling an optical or photographic impression of the physical sky. Our elements are analogous. Each is an ambiguously used term referring both to a mental object and to a patterning of acoustic energy—a physical object, in so far as it is perceived as such. We represent it on the page either with a capital letter or with an icon somewhat resembling an aural or spectrographic impression of the physical energy.

Thinking back to an *SPE*-type formula such as '[+anterior]' now highlights the difference between such objects and our elements. It has always been assumed that *SPE* features have both mental and non-mental referents. To be sure, the non-mental referent of, say, [+anterior] could be represented on the page by a stylized graphic, presumably a sketch of the front end of the mouth. But the front end of the mouth, we suggest, has no signifying value whatever.

5. ALTERNATIVE APPROACHES TO VOWEL PATTERNING

In this section, we consider and reject three alternatives to the account of vowel patterning presented in the previous section, one based on vision (Section 5.1), one on articulatory features (Section 5.2), and one on formant features (Section 5.3).

5.1. Vision

One way in which *a, i, u* might be considered simpler than *e* and *o* is in terms of lip shape, schematized in Fig. 8.4. Of the various labial configurations associated with the five canonical vowels, the three associated with *a* (box shape), *i* (slit shape), and *u* (round shape) can reasonably be considered maximally distinct. Plausibly, these vowels involve relatively simple processing in visual perception and, despite the apparently greater displacement of the lips from a rest position, articulation. Informally, the postures are respectively 'as open as possible', 'as spread as possible', and 'as rounded as possible'. Since *e* and *o* are intermediate between the three extremes of *a, i, u*, they may involve subtler and hence more complex visual processing.

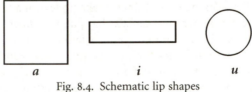

a i u

Fig. 8.4. Schematic lip shapes

One reason for at least considering the possibility that vision influences the patterns of vowel neutralization is that speech-reading by eye is known to play a role in speech perception, as demonstrated for example by the McGurk effect (McGurk and MacDonald 1976). The interaction of vision and audition is further demonstrated by more recent research showing that, when subjects see speech without hearing it, their auditory cortex is none the less activated (see e.g. Calvert *et al.* 1997).

Against this must be weighed the consideration that speech is entirely intelligible without visual input and that the congenitally blind acquire normal phonology. These facts demonstrate that vision could play no more than a subsidiary role in shaping the vowel patterns under discussion here, at best enhancing the primacy of *a, i, u*.[3]

5.2. *Articulation*

Researchers have sought to explain consonantal lenition in unstressed syllables as resulting from target undershoot, on the grounds that unstressed syllables are characterized by shorter duration and less extreme articulatory movements than stressed counterparts (see de Jong 1998 for recent discussion and references). Extended to vowel neutralization, this approach might be considered consistent with the occurrence of centripetal patterns of reduction: the trajectories followed by the tongue in the production of centralized reflexes are shorter than those followed in peripheral vowels (Fourakis 1990). But it makes completely the wrong prediction about centrifugal vowel neutralization. Given the more extreme dorsal manœuvres involved in the articulation of the corner vowels, it is mid-vowels that would be expected to show up as the preferred peripheral reflexes of neutralization, precisely the opposite of what we find.

In any event, this account fails to explain why the same neutralization effects can occur quite independently of stress prominence, as noted in Section 3 above.

This specific failing of the target-undershoot account is symptomatic of a more general inability of articulation-oriented approaches to model vowel neutralization adequately. One problem, already alluded to in Section 4, centres on the failure of articulatory features to express the informational asymmetries between neutralized and unneutralized vocalic reflexes.

The case for persisting with an articulation-based approach to vowel categorization has been made with renewed vigour in the recent literature, especially with regard to the use of scalar height features. If accepted, these must then be implicated in the specification of both centrifugal and centripetal vowel neutralization. Earlier advocacy of such features (e.g. Ladefoged 1971) was widely resisted, at least as phonological classifiers, on the grounds that they fail to capture the non-continuous behaviour of vowel–height contrasts in such phenomena as chain shifts, harmony, and, as we have already seen here, positional neutralization itself.

The upturn in the fortunes of scalar vowel height has coincided with the recent proposal that what counts as phonologically distinctive in a particular grammar emerges as a result of phonetically fine-grained features being coarsely chunked by

---

[3] Visual information is of course the very stuff of sign language. The elements of sign phonology are internalised visual patterns.

ranked constraints (Flemming 1995; Kirchner 1997; Hayes 1999). Kirchner (1997) assumes the existence of a unitary analogue dimension of tongue height that can be finely digitized for the purpose of feature classification. There is, however, no reason to take the articulatory reality of this dimension for granted.

Scalar vowel height categorizations are founded on the notion of 'the highest point of tongue'. In fact, enough is known about vowel production for us to conclude that this is no more than a descriptively convenient fiction. Vowel quality is determined by the overall volume and geometry of the vocal tract, themselves determined by a combination of factors—the positioning of the tongue by the extrinsic muscles, the shaping of the tongue by the intrinsic muscles, the positioning of the lower mandible, overall lip shape, the shape of the pharynx, and so forth (see Perkell 1997 for a literature summary). The mutually influencing nature of these dimensions is confirmed by the fact that there can be considerable variation in the way a particular quality is executed, not just across languages and speakers but also within the speech of a single speaker (see Lindblom *et al.* 1979 and, for further references, Lieberman and Blumstein 1988: 162 ff.). Nowhere in this overall scheme of vowel production is there evidence of an independent dimension of tongue height functioning as a unit of central control in speech.

In exploiting the concept of vowel height, phonologists have been guilty of the same misuse of pseudo-articulatory labels as is perpetuated in practical phonetics by the Cardinal Vowel system. Vowel 'heights' are to be taken no more literally than the 'slenderness' of vowels or the 'darkness' of laterals. Employing such notions as descriptive conveniences should not lull us into the misapprehension that these are real categories in phonology-to-speech mapping.

Much more fundamental, however, are the grounds for doubting whether an articulatory approach is the appropriate way to model not just vowel patterning but phonological categorization in general. The reasons are hardly a secret, although they have been largely ignored in the phonological literature since *SPE* made the switch away from Jakobsonian acoustic features. The main problem, as noted by Saussure, Sapir, and indeed Jakobson (1968) himself, arises from the fundamental asymmetry between speech production and auditory perception, by virtue of which the former is parasitic upon the latter.

It is well established that speech perception precedes speech production throughout the language acquisition of normally hearing infants. Moreover, the congenitally deaf do not learn to produce speech normally, while those born with even the severest obstacles to speech production will, in the absence of cognitive deficit, acquire normal speech perceptual ability. Further, when individuals become deaf after the acquisition of phonology, their speech production suffers immediately. So does that of hearing adults under conditions of distorted auditory feedback.

The conclusion towards which such facts inexorably point is that articulation has as its *raison d'être* the production of pre-existing auditory targets. In spite of this, among phonologists the notion has predominated that the phonetic definitions of phonological entities are primarily or exclusively articulatory. This view reaches its apotheosis in the work of Bromberger and Halle (1988, this volume), who claim that phonological forms represent articulatory intentions and that phonological derivation is an aspect of speech production itself.

The fact remains that the first and necessary experience of humans for the acquisition of phonology is the hearing of speech sounds.[4] Articulatory competence is secondary—developmentally and epistemologically.

5.3. Acoustics

Of course, acoustic or auditory feature definition has not been completely neglected in recent phonological theory. In phonetically driven constraint-based theory, for example, there have been moves to rehabilitate auditory-acoustic features, albeit only as co-occupants of the categorial roster with articulatory features—the validity of which continue to be taken for granted (see Flemming 1995; Boersma 1998).

Which returns us to the proposal of Beckman (1997), Flemming (1995), and others that positional vowel neutralization can be explained in terms of functional constraints originating in auditory processing. At least in languages where amplitude is one of the physical correlates of stress, unstressed syllables are less audible than stressed, especially in quiet speech or under conditions of background noise. Because of this, it would be reasonable to expect unstressed syllables to carry less functional load and thus exhibit fewer contrasts. However, like the articulatory-strength account touched on above, this fails to explain why neutralization also occurs independently of stress prominence. Moreover, even amongst languages in which vowel reduction is stress-conditioned there are some in which amplitude is apparently not one of the physical correlates involved; examples include Tamil and Malayalam (Mohanan 1986: 112).

The specific 'auditory' features that Flemming (1995) employs for the representation of vowel quality are in fact scalar categorizations of individual formant values. Like *SPE* articulatory features, these fail to give expression to the informational asymmetries between reduced and unreduced vowels. Compare, for example, how a mid-peripheral and a centralized vowel are characterized in terms of F1/F2 features of the type proposed by Flemming:

---

[4] Obviously, the hearing of speech sounds is not a prerequisite for the acquisition of sign language phonology, which presumably prerequires visual exposure to sign patterns. Regardless of modality, perception precedes production.

(3) (a) *e*   (b) ə

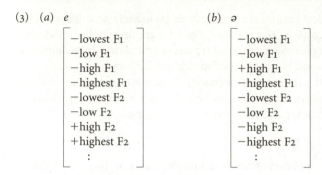

If every vowel is defined in terms of the frequency of individual formants, no vowel can be said to bear any more or less information than another.[5]

Several decades of acoustic-phonetic research have generated valuable numeric data detailing typical resonant frequencies in the speech of men, women, and children. But it would be misguided to assume that truly auditory representations in phonology should contain such data in relatively undigested form. The human listener is not equipped with a formant-tracking device. Vowel quality is perceived on the basis of gestalt spectral patterns rather than the precise centre-frequencies of formants (Lindblom 1986)—a point with which the element proposal in Section 4 is in obvious accord.

6. CONCLUSION

It is astonishing that mainstream generative interest in the way humans phonologically parse speech signals became sidelined once the Jakobson, Fant, and Halle (1952) feature set had been usurped by the articulatory set ushered in by *SPE*. With certain notable exceptions, recent phonological theory and speech-recognition technology have been virtually estranged, most phonologists retreating from acoustics and auditory perception to the reassurance of simplistic articulatory or pseudo-articulatory labels.

The enduring popularity of articulation-based features is hard to explain. It would probably be only mildly unfair to put it down to the stereotypical image of a speech chain that commences with an articulatory act or to the accident of pedagogical and technological history whereby elementary courses on phonetics begin with vocal-tract anatomy rather than with spectrography or the auditory system.

Persisting with articulatory features can only hinder progress in understanding

---

[5] This is not to say that the perceptually salient convergence of formants cannot be expressed by means of features such as those in (3). It can, specifically by conjoining pairs of constraints that refer to particular formant values (Flemming 1995: ch. 3). However, any pair of formant specifications can be potentially linked in this way, thereby missing the point that it is only certain combinations that contribute to the informational profile of vowels.

the sound facet of linguistic signs, surely the very essence of phonology. To repeat a point made earlier: linguistic information is projected by means of articulations but is not embodied in them. The information is constituted by sound patterns, which are extracted from the speech signal by listeners and used as targets by talkers.

The vowel patterns mAss, dIp, and rUmp are motivated firstly by phonological investigation, which identifies cross-linguistic regularities in vowel systems and processes. They are proposed as inner, mental objects—auditory images. Although our compositional analysis allows an unprecedented isomorphy between the internal and external aspects of speech, it should be emphasized that the elements are not physical phenomena inhering in sound waves. Rather, they constitute an aspect of the specifically human way with sound. We may reasonably assume that an organism different from ourselves would not parse human speech in like manner—just as the signals used by crickets, toads, and whales are semiologically opaque to us, when perceptible at all.

How does the compositional parsing of vowels arise? We remain open-minded about the explanatory factors that future research will identify, whether internal and/or external and, if internal, whether central or peripheral. It might be that mAss, dIp, and rUmp are components of UG—though the very isomorphy between these elements and the external environment would rule this possibility out if UG is viewed as a radically internal device that has evolved in isolation from the outside world (see Burton-Roberts and Carr, both in this volume). Alternatively, it might be that elements form part of some more generalized genetic endowment, or that they are posited *de novo* by learners through some interaction between external signals and general receptive capabilities.

Whether there turns out to be an immaculate phonological core or not, 'phonological theory' can always serve as a name for the enterprise that seeks to identify and explain patterning in speech sound.

REFERENCES

Applegate, R. B. (1972), 'Ineseño Chumash Grammar', Ph.D. dissertation (University of California, Berkeley).

Anderson, J. M. and Jones, C. (1974), 'Three Theses Concerning Phonological Representations', *Journal of Linguistics*, 10: 1–26.

Bafile, L. (1997), 'L'innalzamento vocalico in napoletano: Un caso di interazione fra fonologia e morfologia', in L. Agostiniani (ed.), *Atti Del III Convegno Internazionale della Società Internazionale di Linguistica e Filologia Italiana* (Naples: Edizioni Scientifiche Italiane), 1–22.

Beckman, J. N. (1997), 'Positional Faithfulness, Positional Neutralization and Shona Vowel Harmony', *Phonology*, 14: 1–46.

Boersma, P. (1998), *Functional Phonology: Formalizing the Interactions between Articulatory and Perceptual Drives* (LOT Dissertations, 11; The Hague: Holland Academic Graphics).

Bromberger, S. and Halle, M. (1988), 'Why Phonology is Different', *Linguistic Inquiry*, 20: 51–70.

—— —— (this volume), 'The Ontology of Phonology'.

Burton-Roberts, N. (this volume), 'Where and What is Phonology? A Representational Perspective'.

Calvert, G. A., Bullmore, E. T., Brammer, M. J., Campbell, R., Williams, S. C. R., Mcguire, P. K., Woodruff, P. W. R., Iversen, S. D., and David, A. S. (1997), 'Activation of the Auditory Cortex during Silent Lipreading', *Science*, 276: 593–6.

Carr, P. (this volume), 'Scientific Realism, Sociophonetic Variation, and Innate Endowments in Phonology'.

Clements, G. N. and Hertz, S. R. (1991), 'Nonlinear Phonology and Acoustic Interpretation', in *Proceedings of the XIIth International Congress of Phonetic Sciences* (Provence: Université de Provence), 1/5: 364–73.

Crothers, J. (1978), 'Typology and Universals of Vowel Systems', in J. H. Greenberg, C. A. Ferguson, and E. A. Moravcsik (eds.), *Universals of Human Language*, ii. *Phonology* (Stanford, Calif.: Stanford University Press), 93–152.

Flemming, E. S. (1995), 'Auditory Representations in Phonology', Ph.D. dissertation (Univesity of California, Los Angeles).

Fourakis, M. (1990), 'Tempo, Stress, and Vowel Reduction in American English', *Journal of the Acoustical Society of America*, 90: 1816–27.

Goldsmith, J. A. (1985), 'Vowel Harmony in Khalkha Mongolian, Yaka, Finnish and Hungarian', *Phonology*, 2: 251–74.

Hale, M. and Reiss, C. (2000), 'Substance Abuse and Dysfunctionalism: Current Trends in Phonology', *Linguistic Inquiry*, 31: 157–69.

—— —— (this volume), 'Phonology as Cognition'.

Harris, J. (forthcoming), 'Release the Captive Coda: The Foot as a Domain of Phonetic Interpretation', *Laboratory Phonology*, 6.

—— and Lindsey, G. (1995), 'The Elements of Phonological Representation', in J. Durand and F. Katamba (eds.), *Frontiers of Phonology: Atoms, Structures, Derivations* (Harlow: Longman), 34–79.

Hayes, B. (1999), 'Phonetically Driven Phonology: The Role of Optimality Theory and Inductive Grounding', in M. Darnell, E. Moravesik, M. Noonan, F. Newmeyer, and K. Wheatly (eds.), *Functionalism and Formalism in Linguistics*, i. *General Papers* (Amsterdam: John Benjamins), 243–85.

Hyman, L. M. (1998), 'Positional Prominence and the "Positional Trough" in Yaka', *Phonology*, 15: 41–75.

—— (1999), 'The Historical Interpretation of Vowel Harmony in Bantu', in J.-M. Hombert and L. M. Hyman (eds.), *Recent Advances in Bantu Historical Linguistics* (Stanford, Calif.: CSLI), 235–95.

—— (forthcoming), 'The Limits of Phonetic Determinism in Phonology: *NC revisited', in E. Hume and K. Johnson (eds.), *The Role of Speech Perception in Phonology* (New York: Academic Press).

Jakobson, R. C. (1968), *Child Language, Aphasia and Phonological Universals*, trans. A. Keiler (The Hague: Mouton).

—— Fant, G., and Halle, M. (1952), *Preliminaries to Speech Analysis: The Distinctive Features and their Correlates* (Acoustics Laboratory of the MIT, Technical Report, 13; Cambridge, Mass.: MIT Press).

Jong, K. de (1998), 'Stress-Related Variation in the Articulation of Coda Alveolar Stops: Flapping Revisited', *Journal of Phonetics*, 26: 283–310.

Kamprath, C. K. (1987), 'Suprasegmental Structure in a Raeto-Romansch Dialect: a Case Study in Metrical and Lexical Phonology', Ph.D. dissertation (University of Texas, Austin).

Kirchner, R. M. (1997), 'Contrastiveness and Faithfulness', *Phonology*, 14: 83–111.

Ladefoged, P. (1971), *Preliminaries to Linguistic Phonetics* (Chicago: University of Chicago Press).

Lieberman, P. and Blumstein, S. E. (1988), *Speech Physiology, Speech Perception, and Acoustic Phonetics* (Cambridge: Cambridge University Press).

Lindblom, B. (1986), 'Phonetic Universals in Vowel Systems', in J. J. Ohala and J. J. Jaeger (eds.), *Experimental Phonology* (Orlando, Fla.: Academic Press), 13–44.

—— Lubker, J., and Gay, T. (1979), 'Formant Frequencies of Some Fixed-Mandible Vowels and a Model of Speech-Motor Programming by Predictive Simulation', *Journal of Phonetics*, 7: 147–62.

Lindsey, G. and Harris, J. (1990), 'Phonetic Interpretation in Generative Grammar', *UCL Working Papers in Linguistics*, 2:355–69.

McGurk, H. and Macdonald, J. (1976), 'Hearing Lips and Seeing Voices', *Nature*, 264: 746–48.

Maddieson, I. (1984), *Patterns of Sounds* (Cambridge: Cambridge University Press).

Mohanan, K. P. (1986), *The Theory of Lexical Phonology* (Dordrecht: Reidel).

Mtenje, A. A. (1985), 'Arguments for an Autosegmental Analysis of Chichewa Vowel Harmony', *Lingua*, 66: 21–52.

Ohala, J. J. (1992), 'Bibliography', *Language and Speech*, 35: 5–13.

Palmada Félez, B. (1991), 'La fonologia del català I Els principis actius', doctoral dissertation (Universitat Autònoma de Barcelona).

Penny, R. J. (1969), 'Vowel-Harmony in the Speech of Montes de Pas (Santander)', *Orbis*, 18: 148–66.

Perkell, J. S. (1997), 'Articulatory Processes', in W. J. Hardcastle and J. Laver (eds.), *Handbook of Phonetic Sciences* (Oxford: Blackwell), 333–70.

Sapir, E. (1921), *Language* (New York: Harcourt, Brace & World).

Stevens, K. N. (1972), 'The Quantal Nature of Speech: Evidence from Articulatory-Acoustic Data', in E. E. David and P. B. Denes (eds.), *Human Communication: A Unified View* (New York: McGraw Hill), 51–66.

—— (1989), 'On the Quantal Nature of Speech', *Journal of Phonetics*, 17: 3–46.

Urua, E. E. (1990), 'Aspects of Ibibio Phonology and Morphology'. Ph.D. dissertation (University of Ibadan).

Zoll, C. (1998), 'Positional Asymmetries and Licensing', MS, MIT, ROA–282–0998.

9

Modularity and Modality in Phonology

HARRY VAN DER HULST

1. INTRODUCTION

In this chapter, I claim that the innate abilities that underlie phonology are neither modular nor modality specific. The phonology of a language emerges from the interplay between innate (linguistic and perhaps even more general cognitive) principles and formats and the phonetic domain of the language modality. I will propose an account of the formation of phonological primes, phonological structure, and phonetic implementation for both spoken and signed language that is based on such principles and formats. I then discuss differences (involving the notions segment and syllable) between the two kinds of phonology, which I explain as *modality effects*.

As a working definition, I define phonology (as a subdiscipline of linguistics) as the study of the perceivable form of language and its cognitive representation. The term 'phonology', when used as a name for a component of the internalized grammar of language users, refers to a cognitive reality only. These definitions make no reference to the notion 'sound' because, in my view, sound is just one of the media that make linguistic forms perceivable, the most obvious other medium being the visual image.[1]

Most students of phonology, and language in general, will agree that signed languages are, in fact, natural human languages just like spoken languages. As such, signed languages are acknowledged to have the property of dual patterning (or dual articulation), which means that (the cognitive representation of) the perceived form of signed utterances has an internal compositional organization

I wish to thank all those with whom I have collaborated on developing the approach to phonology that I take in this chapter. This includes my colleagues Colin Ewen, Norval Smith, Nancy Ritter, and Elan Dresher and my former and present Ph.D. students Claartje Levelt, Helga Humbert, Rob Goedemans, Els van der Kooij, and Onno Crasborn. Michael Studdert-Kennedy, Onno Crasborn, Nancy Ritter, and the editors of this volume offered helpful comments on an earlier draft of this chapter. Finally, I especially wish to thank Nancy Ritter for the many discussions that we had on the subjects covered in this chapter. Where I am full of doubt, she points me in the right direction.

[1] In this chapter, I will not discuss any form of tactile languages.

that is independent from its morphosyntactic organization, and its meaning. The latter aspect is often captured by referring to the 'arbitrary relationship' between form and meaning. In this chapter, I claim that the innate abilities that underlie phonology are neither modular nor modality specific. The focus, however, lies on examining the consequences of designing a phonological theory that covers both spoken and signed languages. This enterprise will lead me to pose questions regarding the nature and scope of phonological theory. Specifically, I will defend the idea that phonology is not different from syntax, and therefore not somehow 'outside UG' (see Burton-Roberts, this volume). On the contrary, I will develop a view on phonology and syntax that makes them fully parallel. I will also address the question as to what the difference is between phonology and phonetics, arguing against a full fusion of both modules. I will develop a view on the relationship between phonetic categories and phonological primes, on the one hand, and between phonological structure and phonetic implementation, on the other hand. With respect to the issue of sign languages, I will subscribe to the view that phonologies in that modality are essentially parallel to the phonologies of spoken languages and thus that phonological theory must generalize over both modalities.

The structure of this chapter is as follows. In Section 2, I discuss two widespread beliefs about phonology (involving modularity and modality) that I will question in this chapter. Section 3 provides a proposal for the compositional organization of both spoken and signed language phonology. Here I also discuss differences between these two kinds of phonology, which I explain as MODALITY EFFECTS. Section 4 offers a brief summary and my main conclusions.

2. ON MODULARITY AND MODALITY

In most conceptions of the subject, phonology both at the universal (innate) and language-specific (acquired) level is both modular and, at least implicitly, modality specific (specific to spoken language). In this section, following van der Hulst and Ritter (forthcoming), I argue that the innate abilities that are relevant to phonology are specific neither to phonology, nor to spoken language.[2] However, these principles are *instantiated* in language-specific phonologies and these instantiations *are* both modular and modality specific.

2.1 Modularity

In this section, I wish to argue that phonology is 'module free'. In other words, I reject the spirit behind the claim that 'phonology is different'. This claim has been defended most explicitly in Bromberger and Halle (1989). What they mean is that 'phonology is different from *syntax*' in that the former appeals to mechanisms like extrinsic rule ordering of a list of phonological 'transformations', an idea that

---

[2] Even though I use the first person singular pronoun in this section, the proposals are directly drawn from van der Hulst and Ritter (forthcoming).

generative syntax has moved away from many years ago. With this view, Bromberger and Halle implicitly take issue with theories of phonology such as Dependency Phonology (Anderson and Ewen 1987), Government Phonology (Kaye *et al.* 1985, 1990), and Head-Driven Phonology (Ritter 1995; van der Hulst and Ritter 1999; forthcoming), which make the opposite claim and argue that phonology and syntax are organized in parallel ways.[3] Anderson and Ewen (1987: 283–4) write: 'Quite simply, we expect, *ceteris paribus*, different levels to display the same basic structural properties. Conceptual economy demands no less.' They argue, in particular, that the recurrence of the notions of *headedness and dependency* in both syntax and phonology is a manifestation of what they call structural analogy (see also Taylor 1995 on this point). Clearly, structural analogy (unlike modularity) militates against the idea that the internal organization of the grammatical modules is entirely different. My view is that the Structural Analogy Hypothesis, and thus the idea that grammar recapitulates, rather than proliferates, structures and principles, is on the right track. The Structural Analogy Hypothesis does not, of course, imply that the actual phonology and syntax of specific languages are identical, or that there is only one component. We *do* have two different components, each accounting for the well-formedness of hierarchical constructs. Why, then, are the phonological and the syntactic constructs different? The answer is that both types of constructs take different sets of basic units as their starting point. In phonology, these basic units are phonetic categories, whereas in syntax the units are semantic categories. The notion of CATEGORY here means that the relevant units are (mental) concepts of real world phenomena, phonetic events, and, non-phonetic events, respectively.[4]

The two different domains of phonetic and non-phonetic events, being different in themselves, project different sets of categories, and this means that the structures (although not their structural properties), which must accommodate these categories, will be different too. Thus, the phonological and syntactic components will, in part, instantiate different (rules for) hierarchical structures, which (I claim) merely reflect differences in the domains from which the basic categories are formed. This is why we need two components.

The conception of grammar that I have committed myself to here can be diagrammatically represented as follows (I will refine the conception below):

---

[3] Michaels (1991) also capitalizes on the fact that phonology and syntax are structurally similar.

[4] See Jaeger (1980), Jaeger and Ohala (1984), and Miller (1995) for empirical discussions of phonological categorization, and of the structure of phonetic categories.

(1)

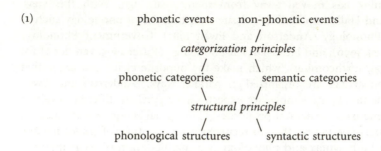

What *are* the categories in both domains? Following linguistic terminological practice, these units must be '-emes', and thus syntactemes and phonemes, respectively. Tradition, however, gives us the term 'word' instead of syntacteme, and I will follow this practice. The stock of words (the primes of syntax) constitutes the lexicon. The syntax of words involves several layers. First, words form phrases (XPs), then phrases are combined into (simple) sentences, and, finally, simple sentences form complex sentences.

So where is morphology? Again, I adopt a traditional point of view and assume that morphology deals with the internal form-meaning structure of words. Words thus have an internal syntax (morphology) and an external syntax (syntax).[5] The building blocks of morphology are, of course, morph*emes*. Hence morphemes rather than words are linguistic *labels* for basic semantic categories.

Can we make parallel distinctions for phonology? The basic building block, or the prime of phonology, is said to be the phoneme. If the phoneme is parallel to the word, as I suggest here, we expect to find a phoneme-internal organization that parallels morphology. Indeed, according to theories such as Dependency and Government Phonology, phonemes must be decomposed into buildings blocks, referred to as 'components' or 'elements', respectively (Schane 1984 calls them 'particles'). We can understand elements now as labels for basic phonetic categories, just like morphemes are labels for semantic categories. The inventory of phonemes that each language has constitutes, then, a 'lexicon of phonemes'.

What about features? Elements are phonological units, but they are not, as understood here, the same thing as features. Elements are building blocks, whereas features are attributes. One could argue, however, that elements (or rather the phonetic category that they represent) can be described in terms of phonetic features (that is, attributes), just like the semantic category represented by morphemes can be analysed into semantic features. Indeed, Kaye, Lowenstamm, and Vergnaud (1985) proposed that their elements were characterized in terms of set of phonetic features (like [±round], [±back] and so on). Since these features do not seem to play a direct role in phonology, Government Phonology

---

[5] I do not address here the different forms of morphology (that is inflectional, derivational, compounding).

subsequently abandoned them. Analogous, perhaps, is the debate as to whether semantic features (like [±animate]) are relevant to syntax. The features mentioned here (in both domains) can be seen as *content* (or *substance*) features. Morphemes, in addition, also have distributional features, like [±N] and [±V]. Where do these come from, and are there comparable distributional features for phonological elements? With respect to the latter question, the answer is that a feature like [±syllabic], and perhaps also [±consonantal] and [±sonorant], is probably equivalent to [±N] and [±V] in so far as the former features essentially encode whether an element (or the phoneme it heads) projects an onset or a rhyme, just like the syntactic features [±N, ±V] encode whether the morpheme (or the word it heads) projects a VP, NP, or other major phrase type. In fact, we can think of distributional features as diacritics that indicate how a particular unit in the inventory of elements or morphemes is restricted in its occurrence in the syntactic or phonological structural organization. Golston and van der Hulst (1999), in fact, argue that distributional features are to be eliminated as features of elements, since they are in essence structural, a claim that is equivalent to the minimalist idea that morphemes or words do not have inherent syntactic features.

Thus, it would seem, then, that phonology and syntax show a perfect structural analogy:

(2)

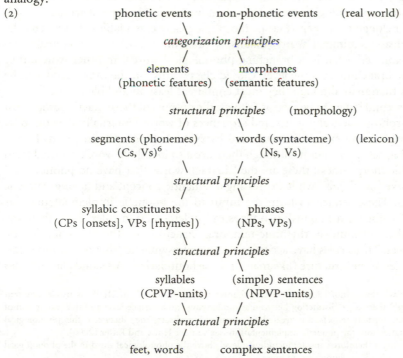

```
          phonetic events    non-phonetic events    (real world)
                        \       /
                    categorization principles
                        /       \
                 elements            morphemes
            (phonetic features)   (semantic features)
                        \       /
                    structural principles    (morphology)
                        /       \
         segments (phonemes)         words (syntacteme)    (lexicon)
              (Cs, Vs)⁶                   (Ns, Vs)
                        \       /
                    structural principles
                        /       \
         syllabic constituents          phrases
        (CPs [onsets], VPs [rhymes])    (NPs, VPs)
                        \       /
                    structural principles
                        /       \
              syllables        (simple) sentences
             (CPVP-units)        (NPVP-units)
                        \       /
                    structural principles
                        /       \
          feet, words        complex sentences
```

⁶ I use the labels C and V for consonant and vowel. Below CP and VP stand for onset and rhyme constituent, respectively.

Two further issues need to be dealt with. How do phonology and syntax come together, and how does phonetic (and semantic) interpretation (or implementation) come about?[7]

With respect to the first issue, I adopt the traditional position that overt (that is, audible) morphemes are listed in the lexicon with phonological a form. Inaudible (so-called zero) morphemes also exist. Logically, the next smallest phonological form would be a single element, such as the element *nasal* or *high* (*tone*), characterizing, for example, an inflectional morpheme. More typically, however, morphemes are provided with phonological forms that are constituted by units higher up in the phonological hierarchy, that is complete (or near complete, so-called archi-)phonemes, syllabic constituents, syllables, feet, and words.

Following van der Hulst and Ritter (1999), I adopt the view that the phonological word is a *bounded* constituent (maximally comprising two feet), like feet are maximally bisyllabic. Thus, we expect that morphemes typically do not exceed a certain size (that is, four syllables). This seems correct, in general. In English, however, a morpheme like *hippopotamus* exceeds that size, so it must consist of more then one phonological word.[8]

I will furthermore assume then that the lexicon is constrained in the following way: all syntactic words are phonological words. The issue of what constitutes a well-formed phonological word depends, however, on the type of syntactic word. Words belonging to open (that is, morphologically extendable) classes typically are at least a minimal word (that is, a branching foot) and maximally two (bis)yllabic feet (that is, a branching phonological word); in other words, they must be branching at some level. Closed class words, on the other hand, can be smaller than that, although they must contain at least an audible rhyme.[9]

The second issue can be seen as follows: the outputs of the syntactic component are morphosyntactically structured sequences of words (internally structured by morphology, and externally structured by syntax). Most of these words have a phonological specification, although there are also inaudible words (formed from inaudible morphemes); these are the 'abstract' words that have no phonological form (like 'small' *pro*), while expressing a semantic concept and having syntactic features. These sequences form the input to the phonetic implementation (or interpretation). I distinguish two types of implementation rules. First, there are rules that attribute a rhythmic-temporal structure to the morphosyntactic sequences. These rules have access to the morphosyntactic (that is, grammatical) properties of the structure (like major phrase boundaries). A second class of rules

---

[7] An issue that is not addressed in this chapter is that of 'levels'. In HDP (as in Government Phonology) there is no distinction between an underlying and a surface level and thus no notion of derivation. Opacity effects are treated in terms of a discrepancy between the phonological representation and the phonetic implementation; see van der Hulst and Ritter (2000).

[8] One might therefore consider including a level above the phonological word in the phonological hierarchy—that is, a phonological phrase.

[9] See Dresher and van der Hulst (1998) for an explanation of this difference between open and closed class words.

implements the phonological elements. These rules are context-sensitive in that elements are implemented with reference to other (locally accessible) elements, and the head-dependent relations that form part of the phonological structure.

Thus, by including the first category of implementation rules, I incorporate into phonetic implementation the kind of grouping rules that have been proposed for forming the prosodic hierarchy.[10] By regarding the 'grouping rules' as a special class, we prevent rules that the interpretation of the phonological elements can be sensitive to grammatical information as well.

We can, of course, talk about phonetic implementation only if we conceptualize this implementation in terms of a phonetic model of the actual production and perception of linguistic utterances. This model is *not* a part of the phonology, although it may 'look like' it, in that it will probably make use of units that are somewhat similar to elements, syllables, feet, and larger groupings. Thus, we get a distinction between phonological structure and phonetic structure. Elsewhere (van der Hulst 1999*b*), I have argued that so-called structure paradoxes arise when phonological structures and phonetic structures turn out to be non-isomorphic (as they often do). Such situations are experienced by linguists as problematic only if both structures are, erroneously, placed within the same component, in which case we have a real contradiction. If, on the other hand, the non-isomorphic structures are located in different components, there is an apparent contradiction (that is a paradox) only. To give one example, ambisyllabic consonants (which form an embarrassment for theories of phonological structure that typically do not allow overlapping constituents) exist in my view only in the phonetic structure. The option of delegating certain structural proposals to the phonetic representation not only prevents structural contradictions, it also keeps phonological structure in line with syntactic structure, as required by the structural analogy hypothesis.[11]

Parallel to phonetic implementation, I assume a semantic implementation that likewise operates on the output sequences of the syntactic component:

(3)   Phonological Component—morphemes, words (lexicon, morphology)

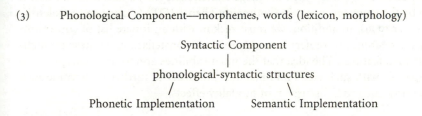

Syntactic Component

phonological-syntactic structures

Phonetic Implementation   Semantic Implementation

---

[10] Note that I make a theoretical distinction between a phonological hierarchy (formed in the phonological component) and a prosodic hierarchy (formed in the phonetic interpretation component).

[11] At the level of primes, we might say that so-called gestures (as used in Articulatory Phonology, (Browman and Goldstein 1989)) form, as phonetic units, the phonetic counterpart of phonological elements. (See Clements 1992.)

With respect to the relationship between phonology and phonetics, we have here argued that the former is, in some sense, connected to phonetics 'on two sides'. At the deepest level, phonological elements are labels for mental categories of phonetic events, while at the most surface level phonological structures (being encapsulated in the syntactic structures) receive an implementation in terms of (a model of) real world phonetic events.

In this section, then, I have argued for a set of module-free abilities that enable the language learner to construct a grammar:

(4)   (a) Categorization
       (b) Structure building
       (c) Implementation

Each of these abilities specifies a set of principles or formats to construct (in the course of acquisition) the two components, syntax and phonology,[12] including for each the relevant set of basic categories and implementation system.[13]

Differences, then, between the two components are a consequence of the fact that the domains from which the basic categories are formed are different. However, this being said, I have not subscribed to the viewpoint that 'phonology can be reduced to phonetics'. On the contrary, the three parts in (4) have nothing to do with phonetics. To this I should add that they also have nothing to do with phonology *per se*. What we call 'phonology' arises from the interplay of these general abilities and the specific domain to which they are applied. In my view, the language-specific categorization of phonetic events, phonological structure, and phonetic implementation *emerge* in the process of language acquisition.

This view is totally different from the view of Halle and Bromberger, and, in fact, most other work in generative phonology. Proponents of generative phonology attribute phonological categories and phonological structures to an innate system (Universal Grammar (UG)). Thus, one prevailing idea is that there is a list of innate, phonetically defined *phonological features* (often organized in a hierarchical tree structure) from which language learners allegedly make a choice that is driven by the language input. In Optimality Theory (OT) (Prince and Smolensky 1993; Kager 1999), in addition, we must reckon with an innate list of constraints that make reference to preferred or dispreferred constellations of these phonetically defined features. The idea that the innate abilities are not module specific is incompatible with such views on innateness. In order to further undermine such views, I now turn to a discussion of modality effects.

---

[12] I refer to van der Hulst and Ritter (1999; forthcoming) for an extensive proposal concerning the general, non-modular principles that account for the well-formedness of phonological structures and 'processes'.

[13] I ignore here two huge issues. First, if we say that semantic and phonetic categories result from categorization principles, we seem to imply that these categories as such are not innate. This is controversial, especially with regard to semantic categories or concepts. Secondly, we might wonder whether the abilities in (4) are specific to language or are, in fact, of a more general cognitive nature.

2.2 *Modality*

With reference to the model sketched in the preceding section (see 2), I claim, of course, that there is no innate set of phonological 'features'. The claim that whatever is innate, is not intrinsically defined in phonetic terms, is further supported by referring to the existence of sign languages. I assume that deaf-language learners construct a grammar, including a phonology, in the process of language acquisition, being guided by the same innate cognitive abilities that guide hearing people in constructing their grammar. Then, surely, whatever these abilities are, it must follow that they cannot be modality specific, in the sense of being exclusively specialized in the production and perception of the speech signal.

Thus, it follows that the relevant innate abilities must be A-MODAL (modality free, modality neutral), as well as being A-MODULAR,[14] creating for the phonology, a system of phonetic categories, a combinatory calculus for building representations and an implementation system. The argument developed in the preceding section, that innate abilities and principles are not intrinsically phonetic, is complemented by the present argument that these abilities must generalize over the phonetics of both spoken and signed languages.

Returning now to the working definition of phonology we can be more precise and define phonology as the study of the phonological instantiations of the abilities in (4), as well as of these abilities themselves. In covering the abilities themselves, phonology (as a discipline) overlaps with the discipline of syntax that (as per the Structural Analogy Hypothesis) also studies these same abilities, in addition to their syntactic instantiations. Phonology, I conclude, includes categorization (normally totally ignored in so far as the end result is simply postulated as a list of features or elements), structure (uncontroversially included by all phonologists in some form or other, often rather unrestricted though), and phonetic implementation (normally presupposed and/or referred to Laboratory Phonology).

3. CATEGORIZATION, STRUCTURE, AND IMPLEMENTATION IN PHONOLOGY

3.1. *Spoken language*

3.1.1. Introduction

This section sketches a theory of categorization, phonological structure, and phonetic implementation, up to and including the level of the syllable. This theory, called RADICAL CV PHONOLOGY (RcvP) has been developed in a series of articles (van der Hulst 1988*a*,*b*, 1989, 1994*a*,*b*, 1995*a*, 1996*c*, 1999, forthcoming *b*). RcvP reconstructs mostly well-known and widely accepted ideas about phonological

---

[14] See Sandler (1993*b*) for a discussion of modularity in the context of sign languages.

primes and their phonetic correlates, as found in works on binary feature theories (Hyman 1973; Keating 1987), or in theories based on unary components (Anderson and Ewen 1987), elements (Kaye *et al.* 1985), or particles (Schane 1984). Likewise, RcvP incorporates ideas about segment-internal (class node) organization, various forms of 'complex' segments (Clements 1985; Sagey 1986), and syllable structure (notably Anderson and Ewen 1987; Kaye *et al.* 1990). A full-blown presentation of the theory is offered in van der Hulst (forthcoming *b*).[15] RcvP embodies the ideas presented in Section 2.1 in offering an account of phonology that is based on general principles and formats, that are not specific to the construction of the phonological module. Their independence of modality is discussed in Section 2.2.

With respect to phoneme structure, I adopt the idea that a phoneme has a tripartite design (Clements 1985), here modelled as a headed X-bar structure. Each node represents a class

(5)

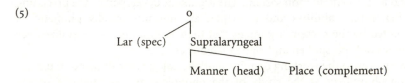

MANNER forms the head of the phoneme because manner properties (here taken to include major class distinctions) determine the external syntax of segments—that is, their distribution in the syllable. Precisely for this reason it is justified to consider *manner* primes as a class (on a par with place and laryngeal primes). The argument that *manner* primes do not form a functional unit in ('dynamic') phonological insertion, deletion or movement processes (whether correct or wrong) does not invalidate their unity as a class if we consider the ('static') distributional regularities. Laryngeal (tone and phonation) is arguably the 'outer shell' of the phoneme, the most suprasegmental (that is mobile or moveable) and, at the same time, most optional class, which motivates its specifier status. Thus place must then, as the complement, form a unit supralaryngeal together with *manner*.

RcvP acknowledges that the X-bar scheme represents a universal non-modular structural scheme that is instantiated in those cases where *unlike* categories are combined to form a complex expression (see Dresher and van der Hulst (1998); van der Hulst and Ritter (1999, forthcoming).

In each of the three classes we find an array of possible elements (in fact, as we will see, exactly *two* elements, encoding *four* phonetic categories or features). A major goal of RcvP is to propose that the set of phonetic categories can be derived from general principles, rather than being postulated in the form of an (innate) set of distinctive features. These general principles, in a sense, can be regarded as principles that guide the categorization of the space of (linguistically relevant) phonetic events into mental phonetic categories. The principles impose a structure on the phonetic substance, a structure, however, that recapitulates itself in other domains, both above the syllable and, I presume, in the syntactic component. Hence, these principles are a-modular. When we discuss sign language phonology, we will learn that these principles are also a-modal.

As we will see, the principles of RcvP allow two syllabic constituents, corresponding to the traditional onset and rhyme. Instead of using the labels O(nset) and R(hyme), I use the labels 'C' and 'V' instead (see n. 16). Both syllabic constituents can be branching and non-branching:

(6)   C   C   V   V
                            | \ | \

Following Dependency Phonology (DP) (Anderson and Ewen 1987), Government Phonology (GP) (Kaye *et al.* 1985, 1990), and Head-Driven Phonology (HDP) (van der Hulst and Ritter 1999, forthcoming), I assume that all constituents (phonological and syntactic) are binary and headed. Head positions are indicated by a vertical line, dependent positions by a slanting line. This implies that the maximal syllable is as in (2):

(7)   Syllable
                            / |
                            C   V
                            \   \

As is apparent from (7), I adhere to the widespread idea that the rhyme is the head of the syllable. This makes sense for two reasons. First, the structure of rhymes (or their heads) determines the external syntax of syllables—that is, their role in foot structure. Quantity-sensitive and sonority-driven stress is dependent on the complexity of rhymes and the ('sonority') properties of rhymal heads, respectively (see Dresher and van der Hulst 1998). Secondly, rhymes form the obligatory units in the syllable. Note that onsets and rhymes are universally head-initial, while the syllable itself is universally head-final.

3.1.2. The phoneme

In each of the three class nodes of the phoneme, we find a set of phonetic categories. These categories are encoded in terms of phonological elements. As stated, rather than simply listing the relevant categories and elements, I will propose to derive them from a parsing strategy, which I view as a form of categorization. This strategy follows the spirit of Jakobson's (1968) idea that phonological contrast arises from a polarization principle. First we assume that the whole phonetic space that is available for phonemes constitutes the value of one element. At this point there is, in fact, no phonological contrast, and only one type of phonological utterance is possible. Its phonetic value is variable, but favours those phonetic events that later, when the space has been cut up in a variety of categories, turn out to be the value of unmarked elements (I discuss the notion of markedness below). Thus, a child might utter [pa], [ta], or [da], the prototypical syllables, but, even though she seems to produce a /p/, /t/, /d/, and /a/, she really produces the unit /syllable/, which is paradigmatically distinctive with silence at best.

The next step involves acquiring a syntagmatic contrast between onset and rhyme. This appears to happen before the development of paradigmatic distinctions that we associate with distinctive features. In order to make the first paradigmatic contrast, the child locates, within the phonetic space of both onset and rhyme two extreme (that is, maximally dispersed) categories, and then, if the need for further distinctions arises, she takes each of the phonetic subspaces and divides them again. How often division can be applied seems an empirical rather than a formal matter, although I will argue below that the reason for limiting division to maximally two times (as I will demonstrate is the case) may be theoretical.

There is, or must be, a step in between the syntagmatic division into onset and rhyme, and the division of each of these into paradigmatically contrastive categories. Accepting the intrasegmental structure in (5), we must assume that the formation of contrastive phonetic categories takes place per class node. Hence the categorization of the whole speech space into a *laryngeal*, *manner*, and *place* must intervene. It seems intuitively obvious that the division into *laryngeal*, *manner*, and *place* is formally different in kind from the division of, say, stricture into obstruent and sonorant. Rather than involving a binary split producing two polar categories of the same kind, it produces three categories that are different in kind. I have suggested that the possibility of imposing an X-bar scheme on this tripartite categorization is not an accident. The tripartite specifier–head–complement structure is, I proposed, another example of an a-modular (and a-modal) structure that (together with binarity and headedness) dictates that structure in (5). Thus, the X-bar design is both a structural principle and a principle that drives, or limits, the categorization of the phonetic space.

I will now turn to the categorization of class nodes. The specific proposals that I incorporate into RcvP for the division of the phonetic spaces corresponding to *laryngeal*, *manner*, and *place* are not at all unlike typologies of features that are available in the literature, although the particular combination of typologies is unique to this theory. That I can rely on existing proposals, of course, only strengthens my case. I have no desire to ignore empirically well-founded proposals for (partial) feature sets. Nor do I attempt to repeat, in this chapter, the empirical motivation for these proposals. My goal, rather, is to organize (and, in some sense, formally motivate) these proposals within an integrated theory of phonological structure.

3.1.3. Manner and syllable structure

In this chapter (for reasons of space), I will discuss only *manner* distinctions, while, at the same time, explaining the basic line of thinking, including notational issues. The RcvP treatment of *place* and *laryngeal* distinctions can be found in van der Hulst (forthcoming *b*). The typology in (8) is close to the one that I eventually will propose for the *manner* class:

(8)

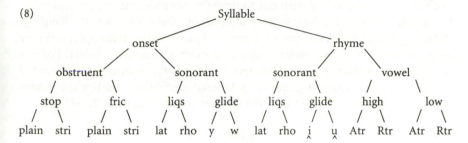

My use of terminology is perhaps not completely unquestionable. The problem is, of course, that there is no full agreement on terminology in our field. The term 'sonorant' is used here in two different ways—that is, in opposition with 'obstruent' (the traditional use) and in opposition with 'vowel'. The same holds for the term 'glide'. Some, in fact, will avoid this term altogether and refer to /y/ and /w/ as 'approximants', and to /i̯/ and /u̯/ as 'semi-vowels'. Note, incidentally, that (as in the case of glides) terms such as 'lateral' and 'rhotic' refer to rather different phonetic events, depending on whether we look at onsets or rhymes. From my point of view, all terms in (8) are 'pre-theoretical' anyway, so I will not worry about terminological matters at this point. My concern is with the specific categorization that is implied in (8).

The typology in (8) seems to involve the following more or less traditional binary features:

(9)　　　　[±syllabic]
　　　　　　[±sonorant], [±consonantal] (or [±vocalic])
　　　　　　[±continuant], [±approximant], [±low] (or [±high])
　　　　　　[±strident], [±lateral], [±round] (or [±back]), [±ATR]

With respect to calling all these features 'manner features', at least four issues arise here. First, the feature [approximant] has not been so widely used. Clements (1990) introduces the feature to separate nasals from, what he calls, glides. For want of a better name, I use the feature here to separate liquids from glides. A related issue is that liquids, like glides, occur twice. These apparent duplications, however, simply reveal that the distinctions made in (8) are distinctive *within* the syllabic constituents, or subconstituents (that is, head or dependent position). It will become clear in a moment that the two lower levels in the structure in (8) encode the 'true' manner distinctions that are required per syllabic position. Secondly, no mention is made of nasality. I will not discuss nasality in this chapter (see van der Hulst, forthcoming *b*). Thirdly, it would seem that some of the distinctions involve *place* rather than *manner*. This is especially so for the distinction between /y/ and /w/, and between /i̯/ and /u̯/. To interpret these distinctions as *manner* will turn out to have the advantageous consequence that the property of *place* can be restricted to heads of syllabic constituents. Fourthly, collapsing height and ATR into a manner (a dimension involving aperture) may seem strange at first. A similar proposal is made in Clements (1991). For the moment, I will step over these points and continue to focus, in this section, on the method, the line of reasoning, and the notational conventions. Putting such issues aside, then, we can repeat (8) with the features as annotations in the structure:

(10)

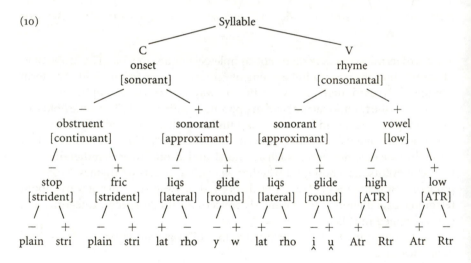

Assuming that the terminal layer of this structure gives us all and only the segment classes that we wish to distinguish (manner-wise), we notice immediately that, for economy reasons, we *could*, in principle, represent all distinctions with just three binary features, one for each decision layer below the onset/rhyme split. A consequence would be that each feature would have several phonetic interpretations, depending on the domain (in terms of higher-level decisions) it operates in. We would then also have to make a choice with respect to 'name' the three features, making perhaps arbitrary decisions; for example:

(11) [+sonorant] means *sonorant* for onsets and *vowel* for rhymes
      [−sonorant] means *obstruent* for onsets and *sonorant* for rhymes
      [−continuant] means *stop* for obstruents, *liquid* for sonorants and glide, and *high* for vowels
      [+continuant] means *fricative* for obstruents, *approximant* for onset sonorants, *semi-vowel* for rhyme sonorants, and *low* for vowel

This method leads to terminological friction (that is, rhymal sonorants are [−sonorant]). Especially, at the lowest level, a choice seems semantically arbitrary, also because the plusses and minuses for the original features do not seem to line up in the correct way. Hence it is difficult to replace [strident], [lateral], [back], and [ATR] by one of them. The problem is not dependent on the distribution of plusses and minuses, because, after all, the assignment of specific values is simply dependent on the 'name' of the feature. Had we chosen the feature name [high], rather than [low], the assignment of plusses and minuses would be reversed. An alternative would be to replace plusses and minuses by markedness values such as 'm' and 'u' (as in Chomsky and Halle 1968: ch. 9). This approach might succeed if one worked out the appropriate markedness theory. Seemingly, I will adopt another route, although, as we will see, I am, in fact, incorporating a theory of markedness in the RcvP notation. Instead of making arbitrary decisions about feature names, I will simply use a *single* terminology for all levels in the typology, thus achieving even greater economy. Instead, however, of choosing one *binary feature*, I will adopt two unary labels—that is, C and V—because these adequately express that in each opposition, we basically encounter the type of contrast that we also make for the syntagmatic contrast between onset and rhyme—that is, essentially a contrast between a closure and non-closure state:[16]

(12)

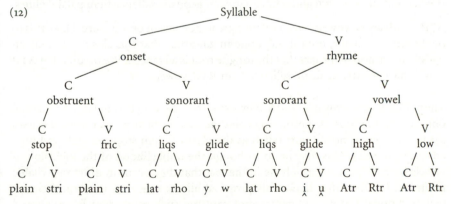

[16] At this point, C and V are still just classificatory labels. Later in this section, I will make the conceptual change of regarding C and V as two *phonological elements*. In the end, it will turn out that the labels C and V simple stand for *head* and *dependent*. Whether C or V is the head depends on the domain within which the distinction is made; see below.

Including the onset/rhyme division, C clearly refers, from an articulatory point of view, to (relative) closure in the oral cavity at the first three levels. At the lowest level, however, we encounter a seemingly heterogeneous collection of oppositions.

Strident. In the opposition strident/plain (or *mellow*) for fricative, one might object to taking stridency to be the V (that is relative open) choice; indeed Anderson and Ewen (1987: 166) give non-strident fricative an extra C. In the case of strident stops, however, which I take to be affricates (following Jakobson *et al.* 1952, Jakobson and Halle 1956), stridency *does* involve non-closure. In the case of fricatives, on the other hand, V foremost expresses the extra acoustic energy that strident fricatives have. If, then, in the end, the C/V opposition is taken to represent a head-dependency relation, expressed in terms of acoustic salience (and its articulatory correlates), rather than simply relative stricture or aperture, the problem with stridency involving an extra obstruction rather than lesser constriction does not exist anymore.

Lateral. Anderson and Ewen (1987: 163) give lateral an extra C, because, as they say, laterals have an extra, secondary central closure. Rhotics do not have this closure, although they have a *repeated closure* (with the tip of the tongue or with the uvula). The critical difference, then, is that the closure for lateral is persistent. Most so-called sonority scales will, as expected, have rhotics as more sonorous than laterals.

Round. Why would front unrounded glides be more closed ('more C') than back rounded glides (assuming that both are of the same height)? Apparently we have to pay attention here to what happens in the oral cavity. Front glides have a palatal constriction in the oral cavity, while rounded glides have a dorsal constriction. We predict that labial-dorsal glides have a greater acoustic salience than palatal glides.

ATR. Advanced vowels have a relative greater degree of oral closure. I take this to be the decisive factor, even though one might argue that this closure is really an epi-phenomenon of the fact that the tongue root is advanced. We predict that ATR vowels have greater acoustic salience than RTR vowels.

The phonetic polysemy of C and V is evident from the structure in (12). A potential objection to the proposed economy could be that we now predict natural classes for which there is no support (such as the class of plain stops, lateral, and high advanced vowels). This may be so, although the unlikelihood of the inclusion of vowels in this class may simply lie in the fact that they occur in different syllabic positions. On the other hand, this proposal allows reference to natural classes that traditional feature systems cannot capture, such as strident fricatives and rhotic liquids (in processes of rhoticization). In this chapter, I do not discuss (counter-)evidence for the RcvP proposals that involve syntagmatic phonological processes, the focus being on paradigmatic distinctiveness.

We can 'transform' the typological structure in (12) into a syllable template (somewhat *à la* Kiparsky 1979) by reversing all the branches under the rhyme node, so that the left-to-right ordering of segment types on the lowest level reflects a sonority curve (see also Farmer 1979):

(13)

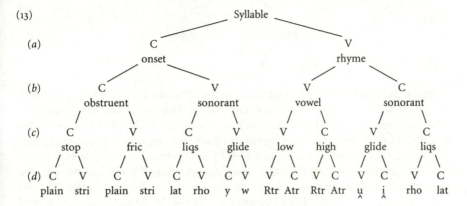

We see that the typology of manner categories has a depth of three layers (excluding the onset/rhyme split). As a first step towards proposing phonological manner elements, let us represent manner segment types in terms of chains of Cs and Vs:

(14)(*a*) *Manner*: onsets

(*b*) *Manner*: rhymes

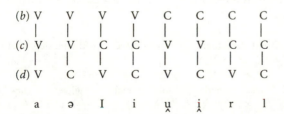

The syntagmatic contrast (encoded in syllabic structure) extends over the first two layers—that is, the onset/rhyme split and the further division into branching onsets branching rhymes:

(15)

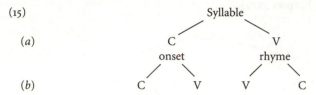

(a)

(b)

At this point, we observe a redundancy in the notation. Layer (b) is incorporated in (14) as well as in (15); hence it occurs twice. This raises the questions as to whether layer (b) must be understood as belonging to the phoneme or to the syllable? A crucial consideration for taking this level to encode a phoneme-internal property is that sonorants can form onsets by themselves. If we strip level (b) from the segment-internal paradigmatic specification, then the distinction between stops and laterals disappears, and hence the distinction between a simple onset with either a stop or a lateral also becomes inexpressable. To avoid this, and indeed stripping level (b) from the phoneme structure, I propose that a syllable that starts with a liquid is really empty-headed, just like a so-called syllabic liquid may be taken to correspond to an empty-headed rhyme (van der Hulst and Ritter 1999):

(16)

We thus explain a parallelism: syllabic liquids acquire phonetic properties of vowels by being more sonorous, while liquids that form onsets by themselves acquire properties of obstruents by having a more forceful articulation.

By adopting this approach, I delegate the distinctions between obstruent and sonorant, and between vowel and glide, to the realm of syllable structure. This being the case, we end up with the following system of manner distinctions in each of the four syllabic positions:

(17)

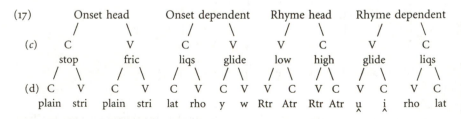

Thus, in each syllabic position the phonetic space that is available to manner is categorization in accordance with the following template:

(18)

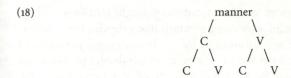

Note that this (paradigmatic) categorization is identical to the (syntagmatic) categorization that we have attributed to syllable:[17]

(19)

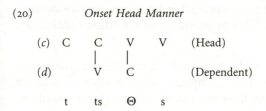

I propose that the template in (18)/(19) *is* the template for categorization of phonological spaces. Its driving principle is binary polarization (or dispersion).

I will now make the theoretical step from categorization to phonological elements by proposing that, in fact, we need only *two phonological elements* to represent all the relevant phonetic categories. These elements will (following DP) simply be called 'C' and 'V', a choice that was anticipated by the use of the C/V labels that I used thus far. We need only two elements, instead of four, if we adopt the fundamental DP idea that elements can occur by themselves or can be combined, and that, if combined, elements enter into a head-dependency relation (the levels refer back to 13 and 14):

(20)   *Onset Head Manner*

(*c*)	C	C	V	V	(Head)
		|	|		
(*d*)		V	C		(Dependent)
	t	ts	Θ	s	

---

[17] An implication of the proposals for manner and syllable structure is that syllabic complexity is more limited than what is usually assumed. First, there are no monosyllabic long vowels. A branching rhyme can only be a diphthong, a vowel followed by a liquid l or r, or a nasalized vowel. The nasal option, introduced in Section 3.1.6, could materialize as a true nasal in case an onset consonant follows it from which the nasal glide snatches the consonantal place properties (Humbert 1995). We might perhaps wish to allow the rhyme dependent (that is, coda) to be empty to accommodate geminates. In any event, the present model does not allow obstruents or (unassimilated) nasals in coda position; see van der Hulst and Ritter (1999), van der Hulst (forthcoming *b*).

A 'flat' shorthand for these representations will sometimes be used:

(21)   C   Cv   Vc   V

The idea that phonetic categories can be encoded by single elements and by combinations, in a sense, explains why categorization has a depth of two layers. More categories could not be accommodated by the fundamental principle of binary combination that only allows the structures in (20). Indeed, I propose that dependency structures (formed by combining units of the same type, like elements) are limited to those in (20).[18]

Being able to occur as a head or a dependent, each element has a dual interpretation (van der Hulst 1988*a*). However, since every element can occur in four syllabic positions, elements actually have eight phonetic interpretations:

(22)

		onset head	dependent	rhyme head	dependent
C	*head*	stop	liquid	high	liquid
	dependent	mellow	lateral/y	ATR	lateral/i̯
V	*head*	fricative	glide	low	glide
	dependent	strident	rhotic/w	RTR	rhotic/u̯

Note that the interpretations in both 'syllabic dependent' positions are identical, at least in terms of the traditional labels that I have been using. In phonetic reality, the rhyme dependent (or coda) occurrences of sonorants are much weaker than the onset dependent occurrences. The syllabic head positions, however, bring out more significant differences. This is exactly what one would expect, if head positions enforce the phonetic realization that best serves the syntagmatic contrast within the syllable.[19]

Let me point out at this juncture that the notation that is used here expresses two important concepts that remain unexpressed in traditional feature systems: markedness and enhancement. I will briefly comment on how these concepts are expressed in the notation.

Markedness. We might say that each choice that repeats the identity of the category that it splits represents the *unmarked* option. In the dependency notation with elements, this same idea returns: if the dependent is identical to the head, the dependent is unmarked. Thus obstruents are unmarked onsets, stops are unmarked obstruents, and plain stops are unmarked stops. On the vowel side, we see that retracted, low vowels are unmarked vowels. Markedness could be

[18] Recall that the three-level X-bar structure is reserved for combinations of units of a different type. Also, to avoid confusion, the structures in (14) represent paths of the typology in (13) and not dependency structures of elements.

[19] The proposal here does not imply that every syllabic position will have the same number of phonological contrasts in a particular language. Contrastive manners for each language must be specified (and learned) per syllabic position.

expressed in an 'ink-saving' way by adopting the convention that, in a situation of *contrast*, the unmarked symbol is suppressed, being predictable in terms of the following universal redundancy rule (with E ranging over C and V):

(23) Universal Redundancy Rule

Thus, for example, mannerwise we refer to 'C' and 'V' instead of 'Cc' and 'Vv' for stops and vowels, respectively (see (20) and (21)).

Enhancement.   This notion, introduced in Stevens and Keyser (1989), is related to markedness. For example: stridency is said to enhance fricativeness. In terms of the structure in (12) this means that enhancement involves the redundant addition of an unmarked element. At the vowel side, we see that is it correctly predicted that, in the absence of an ATR contrast, low vowels are retracted, while high vowels are advanced. It would seem, then, that in the *absence of contrast*, rule (23) can operate as well, now, as a *Universal Enhancement Rule*.

3.1.4. Conclusions

By deriving the set of phonological primes from the basic structural principles of head-dependency and binarity, RcvP avoids the arbitrary list-character of most feature theories. RcvP, then, is compatible with the idea that the phonological component of UG does not contain an arbitrary list of features (possibly grouped in an arbitrary number of feature classes) from which individual languages make a choice, but rather a module-free 'parsing strategy' (determined by general structural principles) for dividing phonetic spaces into a well-defined set of categories. This approach is supported by the fact that the number of syllabic positions as well as distinctions (per class) that is needed for the analysis of spoken languages does not seem arbitrary; they all result from the same parsing template.

Strictly speaking, RcvP recognizes only *two* phonological elements. As shown in van der Hulst (forthcoming *b*), C and V are also used in the place and laryngeal class. The two elements have a variety of phonetic interpretations, depending, first, on the dominating class node, secondly, on the occurrence in an onset or a rhyme, and, thirdly, on being a head or a dependent. In achieving maximal economy, RcvP exploits the use of structure in guiding the phonetic implementation of phonological elements.

We can extend RcvP into higher levels of organization in the lexical phonology, up to the phonological word. Foot structure is obviously binary and the head–non head relationship holds here as well. The word can also be seen as a binary constituent (see Section 2.1). We would not be inclined to encode the head-dependent relationship in terms of Cs and Vs. Rather we would simply use the labels H(ead) and D(ependent). This merely indicates that we should use those labels at the lower levels as well. The C/V-labelling reflects the segmental/syllabic 'origin' of RcvP (see n. 16).

In fact, the foot and word structure together reiterate the characteristic parsing template:

(24)

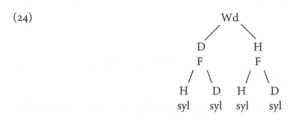

The location of heads at the level of feet might also be universally fixed (see van der Hulst, forthcoming), while headedness at the word level is parametric.

As I argued earlier, the abstract (a-modular, a-modal) RcvP approach makes all the more sense if one considers the existence of sign languages. Learners of those languages also construct a phonology, being guided, I assume, by the same UG that hearing learners put to use. Clearly, a list of actual features (such as [consonantal], [coronal], and so on) will not be very helpful in constructing the phonology of a sign language. Let us now investigate, then, whether RcvP also produces an adequate set of phonetic distinctions and phonological elements for sign language phonology.

3.2. Sign Language

If RcvP is an a-modal theory, its principles must be appropriate for constructing a phonological organization for sign languages. In this case, we do not have the advantage of being able to rely on a long tradition of proposals for feature sets and higher constructs. If linguistics is a young (and, some would say, immature) discipline, then sign linguistics has just been born. It essentially started in 1960 with the publication of Stokoe (1960), anticipated by earlier work that recognized the linguistic, communicative status of signing (e.g. Tervoort 1953). As might be expected from explorative proposals for feature sets, there has been a strong focus on the great richness of phonetic diversity of signs, and much less on phonological distinctiveness. As a consequence, most proposals for feature sets involve rather large sets of features, minutely encoding many phonetic details, and giving the impression that the feature structure of signed languages is much richer than that of spoken languages.

Having said this, I do not wish to underestimate the enormous advances that have been made in the short period of forty years by a relatively small group of linguists. In the early 1970s we find foundational work in Klima and Bellugi (1979), reflecting the research of a group of influential researchers. In addition, several very detailed dissertations on the phonology of American Sign Language (ASL) appeared around that time, and throughout the 1980s (e.g. Friedman 1976; Battison 1978; Mandel 1981; Sandler 1989; for overviews, see Wilbur 1987, Crasborn *et al.*, forthcoming). In the mid-1990s, when I started applying RcvP to SIGN PHONOLOGY, having little insight into the subject matter based on personal empirical research, I could interpret detailed models that by that time had been proposed for sign languages in terms of the principles of (polar) binarity and headedness, and by using unary elements (e.g. Liddell and Johnson 1989; Sandler 1986, 1989; see Brentari 1998 for an extensive overview and proposals in this area). The first results can be found in van der Hulst (1993*a*, 1995*b*,*c*, 1996*a*,*b*). The model proposed there has been empirically tested and developed in subsequent and ongoing research (Crasborn, forthcoming; van der Kooij, forthcoming). Here I discuss a proposal that is in the line of this type of work.

Since the pioneering work of Stokoe (1960), signs are said to be composed of NON-MANUAL properties and MANUAL properties. The former *can* play a role at the level of lexical distinctions, but seem more active at the post lexical level.[20] Here, I have no proposals concerning non-manual categorization of phonological elements. Manual properties involve a characterization of the HANDSHAPE, the MOVEMENT of the hand, and a LOCATION (where the action takes place). Battison (1978) added ORIENTATION (of the hand) as a fourth manual property. Each unit in (25) can be instantiated by a finite set of values, features, or elements:

(25)

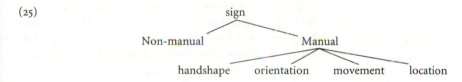

Stokoe put forward the idea that the difference between a sign (for example, meaning CAT) and the English word *cat*, was that the former was essentially a simultaneous event, whereas the latter had a temporal organization. Thus, the basic elements of a sign (*movement, handshape, location*, and so on), which he called 'cheremes' (and later phonemes) were noticed by Stokoe to be linearly unordered, whereas the phonemes of speech are linearly sequenced. Note, however, that the structure in (25) seems to have formal properties that make it look like the structure of single phonemes in spoken language (see 5). After all, the class units that make up a phoneme are not linearly ordered either. Hence, if one would compare (25) to single phonemes it would seem that the difference between spoken and signed languages is not whether or not use is made of linear order, but rather that monomorphemic words in sign language appear to be monoseg-mental (van der Hulst 1995*a*), whereas words in spoken languages (except for some closed class words—for example, certain prepositions or pronouns) are typically

---

[20] Non-manual properties at the postlexical level encode distinctions that, in spoken languages, are often encoded in terms of intonational tones (boundary tones, pitch accents). The functional correspondence between *non-manual* and *laryngeal* is supported here by a formal correspondence in terms of their place in the phonemic structure.

polysegmental. I will return to this issue below. First let us look at some more history (see also Corina and Sandler 1993).

After Stokoe's ground-breaking work, later researchers (e.g. Suppala and Newport 1978; Newkirk 1981; Liddell and Johnson 1984) felt that it was necessary to be able to make reference to the beginning and end point of the movement of signs, for example, for morphological inflectional purposes, or to express assimilations involving a switch in the beginning and end point of the movement (for a discussion of the arguments, see Sandler 1989 and van der Hulst 1993*a*). Without *formally recognizing* the beginning and end point in the linguistic representation it would be impossible to formulate rules that refer to these entities. These considerations led to the adoption of some kind of skeleton to which the other units of the sign associate in an autosegmental fashion (as explicitly proposed in Sandler 1986). Most researchers (Liddell and Johnson 1989; Sandler 1989, 1993*a*; Perlmutter 1992; Brentari 1998) proposed a skeleton that represented not only the INITIAL LOCATION and FINAL LOCATION, but also an INTERMEDIARY MOVEMENT:

(26)   L   M   L

Several researchers have assigned a central perceptual status to the movement unit (see Perlmutter 1992; Corina and Sandler 1993; Sandler 1993*a*; Brentari 1998 for relevant discussions) and it then seemed obvious to refer to the LML sequences as analogous to a CVC-syllable (see Chinchor 1979; Coulter 1982). Following up on these earlier ideas, Perlmutter (1992) explicitly compares the M to the vowel in speech and also adds a moraic layer to the representation.

The model that was proposed in van der Hulst (1993*b*), however, denies movement as a unit on the skeleton, following several other researchers (e.g. Stack 1988; Hayes 1993; Wilbur 1993), and replaces the LML-SKELETON by a bipositional XX-SKELETON. Having reduced the skeleton to two positions, we could, as I suggest here, interpret these positions as the syllabic onset/rhyme (offset) structure of the sign, assuming here without argument that the second position in the skeleton is the most salient one (on this claim, see Brentari 1998 and van der Kooij, forthcoming).

Before we turn to the question as to how we can understand the autosegmental relation between the skeleton (with or without a movement unit) and the primes that specify the 'content' of signs, we have to go into more detail concerning the required set of primes. As mentioned, I will limit myself to the manual part of (25). (What follows is discussed in more detail in Crasborn forthcoming, Crasborn *et al.* forthcoming, and van der Kooij, forthcoming.)

Place.   In order to indicate where a movement starts and where it ends, we need to assign place specifications to the skeletal positions. However, these specifications (whatever they are) do not exhaust the specification of place, since it appears that each individual movement (limiting ourselves to monomorphemic signs) is restricted to occur within a certain area—for example, in front of the chest, or in front of the upper or lower part of the face, or alongside the lower arm of the non-articulating hand, and so on. Sandler (1986) therefore proposes to distinguish between two notions of place. Here I refer to the restricted area as 'location' (for example, *chest*, *head*, *arm*, and so on) and to the specific beginning and end within these areas as 'settings' (for example, high, low and so on). The specification for location takes scope over the whole sign, while the setting values bear on the initial and final skeletal position. Here, I have no proposal to make for the categorization of place, which would hopefully develop along the lines of the schema in (19) (see (27) below). I will return to setting values below.

Handshape and orientation.   On the basis of joined behaviour in assimilation processes, Sandler (1986, 1989) proposed that *handshape* and *orientation* (of the hand) form a class that I will here call ARTICULATOR (following Brentari 1998). With reference to *handshape*, as with *place*, we also find properties that remain constant throughout the signs, as well as properties that can change. One constant property is FINGER SELECTION (*fingsel*). *Fingsel* refers to the fingers that are 'foregrounded' (selected), as opposed to the 'backgrounded' (non-selected) (see Mandel 1981: 81–4). Mostly, foregrounded fingers are the EXTENDED FINGERS, while backgrounded fingers are folded, and for our present purposes I will simply adopt this simplification (see Sandler 1989; Kooij, forthcoming, for a detailed discussion). *Fingsel* involves three finer class nodes. First, there is a node (*fing*) that bears on the four fingers, allowing the extension of [one] or [all] fingers.[21] Secondly, we specify the SIDE of the hand in case less than all the fingers are selected as [radial] or [ulnar] (thumb and pinky side, respectively). Thirdly, we can specify the selection of the THUMB separately as [in] or [out]. During the articulation of a (monomorphemic) sign, the specifications of all three *fingsel* nodes are constant. *Fingsel* does not fully determine the *handshape*, however. The selected fingers occur in a certain CONFIGURATION (*config*). *Config* also has three finer class nodes. First, we consider here the bending of the fingers in terms of FLEXION (*flex*) of the finger joints. We distinguish between the joints that connect the fingers to the hand ([base]), and the two 'higher' finger joints, jointly ([non-base]). A second dimension of *config* is APERTURE—that is, an [open]–[close] relationship between the thumb and the selected fingers. Thirdly, selected fingers can be SPREAD [open] or held against each other [close]. Of these three nodes, flex must remain constant, while both aperture and spreading can change.[22]

Turning now to *orientation*, it turns out that the value for this node may change—that is, a sign can involve a rotation of the underarm such that, for example, the palm faces the signer at the beginning while the back of the hand faces

---

[21] Henceforth, I use square brackets to indicate relevant phonetic categories. An interpretation in terms of elements follows in the text below.

[22] Dynamic spreading/non-spreading can be found in the sign for SCISSORS (in ASL and many other sign languages). This dynamic aspect may simply be an iconic trait of signs in this particular semantic field.

her at the end of the sign. I will refer to the values of orientation as [neutral] and [non-neutral]. The neutral value specifies the 'natural' (that is most 'comfortable') position of the underarm wherever the hand is placed.[23]

With this much detail, we can state precisely what remains constant and what may vary in the articulation of a monomorphemic sign. *Place*, *fingsel*, and *flex* are constant. Dynamic aspects of the manual part of the sign may involve *setting*, *orientation*, *aperture*, and perhaps (but very marginally) *spreading*. Figure (27) summarizes the categorization of the sign in class nodes, and of the class nodes in phonetic categories. Italicized nodes may involve a potentially dynamic specification, which I discuss below:[24]

(27)

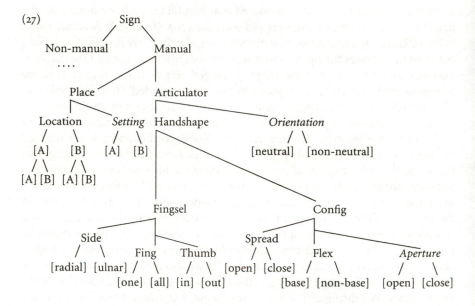

Although I have not motivated that here, we see that all nodes within the *handshape* unit are categorized in terms of two polar categories—that is, no further division seems necessary. At this juncture, (27), with all its distinctions, represents our best hypothesis (and partly: guess) with respect to what the phonologically relevant categories for sign language are. If we now equate each category (that results from a binary split of the relevant phonetic space) with an element, this implies that no combination (including head-dependency) of elements is required in most cases. We suspect that things will be more

---

[23] Perhaps, orientation changes should also include flexion and sideward movements of the wrist. It is also possible that such changes are really (reduced) path movements.

[24] I have not discussed here the distinction between one- and two-handed signs. In two-handed signs, the two hands cannot operate independently. Both hands are either copies of each other, or one of the hands is the place of articulation for the other; see van der Hulst (1996*b*).

complicated for *place* and we know that in the case of the node *Fing* we encounter a more complex situation, since, as said, there are in fact more options for finger selection than just [one] or [all]. Handshapes can also have two or three foregrounded fingers. Hence the elements corresponding to [one] and [all] can enter into combinations (and dependency relations). I will not, however, discuss, these combinations, and their interpretation here (see van der Hulst 1995c, 1996a; van der Kooij, forthcoming). The categorization of each phonetic subspace into polar categories is precisely what we expect given the principles of RcvP. That in most cases the division of the phonetic space is limited to two categories indicates, perhaps, that a more detailed parsing is less likely to occur in more 'refined' classes.

So how do we name the elements? Our first inclination is simply to extend the use of the C and V. It does not seem sensible, however, to use these labels, which betray their spoken language origin and bias. Rather, we might directly make use of a head-dependent labelling. In all cases, I assume that one of the elements is unmarked and thus a head (see Crasborn *et al.*, forthcoming; van der Kooij, forthcoming, for further discussion). The head choice is phonetically manifested as the more salient phonetic category. Thus, we would expect that the categories [all], [out], and [open] are heads. The choice seems less clear for the nodes *side* and *flex*.

Turning from elements to structure, we note that, in the spirit of RcvP, the structure in (27) is headed at every level. Given the (perceptual) centrality of the articulator, I have represented *non-manual* and *place* as dependents. Within place, location is taken to be the head, because it encodes the major place distinctions, with *setting* making subdistinctions. Within *handshape*, I take *fingsel* to be the head, since *config* clearly modifies the selected fingers, and within each of these nodes I have proposed to regard the property that is crucially defining the handshape as the head—that is, *fing* and *flex*. Notice that, if this is correct, invariance (that is, being constant across the sign) is a diagnostic property of heads. I realize that all these decisions need further motivation and I remind the reader of the tentative nature of this proposal.

Let us now turn to the dynamic aspects. There appear to be three types of movement:

(28)   *Types of movement*
   (a) Path movement
   (b) Aperture change
   (c) Orientation change

Path movement is movement of the articulator as a whole. We represent it in terms of *setting* values under the *place* node.

'Movement' of *orientation* is called orientation change, which is brought about by rotation of the underarm. Finally, movement in the *aperture* node is called aperture change.[25] Orientation change and aperture change have also been called 'local changes' as opposed to the 'global path movement'.

Each of these dynamic events may occur by itself and be the only movement of the sign. Path movement may also be combined with either aperture or orientation change. In that case the *global* path movement is called 'primary', while the other local movement is called 'secondary'. The beginning and end state of primary and secondary movements must coincide (as discussed in Perlmutter 1992).

The typology of movements for *orientation* and *aperture* is simple. In fact, for *orientation*, as said, we need an element that denotes the [neutral] state and one that represents the [non-neutral] state (but see n. 23). The beginning state of the sign is either neutral or non-neutral, while the end state (if there is an orientation change) is the opposite. For *aperture* we have the choices [open] and [close]. Again the beginning state can be either, while the end state (if there is an aperture change) is the opposite. A path movement can be specified in terms of polar settings on the three cubic axes (vertical, horizontal, and away from the signer), the 'movement' (if present) being the transition between a beginning and an end state:[26]

(29) Orientation [neutral]–[non-neutral]
      SelFing   [open]–[close]
      Config   [high]–[low], [ipsi]–[contra], [distant]–[proximate][27]

With these features we can represent movements as branching structures:

(30)   Node
                             /   \
                          [A]   [B]

The variable 'Node' in (30) can be *setting*, *orientation*, or *aperture*. So where do we locate the elements for [A] and [B] in the formal representation? The obvious locus for these elements is the X-positions on the skeleton. However, since we can have branching feature specifications for *setting*, *orientation*, and *aperture*, it would seem that we really have three skeletons:

---

[25] Aperture change is also sometimes subsumed under HAND-INTERNAL CHANGE, another type of hand-internal change being WIGGLING, which I have left out of consideration here.

[26] In some cases, however, the movement seems too complex to be understood as simple interpolation between the settings assumed here (for example, involving diagonal, curved, circular, or zigzag paths). This probably means that the categorization of the place space is more complex than what we have assumed here. It is also possible that some of these more complex paths are due to iconicity (see Section 4.3).

[27] [ipsi] means 'side of the articulating hand'; [contra] refers to the opposite side. Distant-proximate is probably the same as no-contact—contact (for example with the body).

(31)

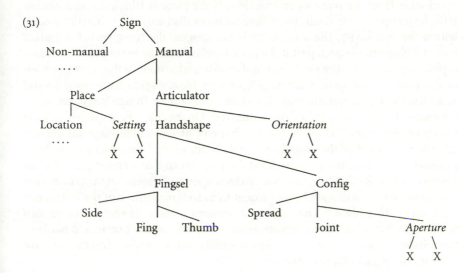

The understanding here is that the initial and final X (that is, onset and rhyme) in each case is synchronized in the phonetic implementation of the sign. By locating the primes that determine a dynamic event on the 'onset' and 'rhyme' slots we derive that their ordering is crucial because syllabic constituents *are* linearly ordered. If the branching structures were a proper part of the content specification of the sign, we would have to introduce linear order (not needed so far) at that level. It is more satisfying that we can keep the content structure free from linear order, and introduce linear order not until the syllabic organization starts. A consequence of the proposal here is that, in some sense, a sign with two movements is bisyllabic, the syllables being simultaneous. This conclusion converges with ideas expressed in Wilbur (1993) and Brentari (1998).

With respect to branching setting there may actually be an interesting alternative. Since *fing* is the ultimate head of the articulator, we might also decide to make the setting values dependent on this node. The conceptual advantage of that move would be that all movement would then be formally *movement of the articulator*. Below, we will see that we can then also achieve a unified notion of *manner of articulation* for both spoken and sign structure.

3.3. A comparison between spoken and signed language

3.3.1. The articulator and manner

An important difference between signing and speech is that in speech the articulator does not have distinctive properties.[28] The speech articulator is

---

[28] See Studdert-Kennedy and Lane (1980) for an intriguing comparison making some of the same points that I make here.

predictable from the place of articulation. If the place is labial, the articulation is the lower lip or lower teeth (the difference is not distinctive).[29] When the place is within the oral cavity, the articulator is the tongue, the front part if the place is dental/alveolar, the back part if the place is velar[30] and the lower part if the place is pharyngeal. This is why we do not find an articulator node in the representation of the phoneme of spoken languages, or why phonologists have come to use articulator and place terminology almost interchangeably. In sign languages, as we have seen, the articulator is far from redundant. On the contrary, it can have a wide variety of properties.[31] Thus, where the phoneme of spoken language has *manner* (that is, movement of the articulator) as its head, we find the *articulator* in head position in the structure of signs. This does not mean that sign language has no *manner*. In fact, for sign language, we can look upon movement (of the articulator) as manner, since, as in speech, movement *is*, in fact, movement of the articulator with respect to a place.[32] The difference between manner in speech and in sign seems to be that, while, in the former, manner is partly in the content and partly in the syllabic structure, manner in sign is wholly in the syllabic structure (I have lined up the parallel parts of the structures):

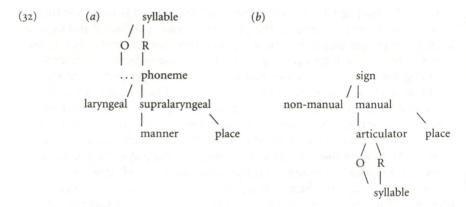

The extra architecture that the sign phoneme has apparently lies in the structure of the articulator, which, in fact, recapitulates the general X-bar template three

---

[29] The difference between bilabial and labiodental fricatives can be understood as a difference in manner—that is, stridency.

[30] The difference between velar and uvular, I assume, is one of complex or double articulation. Palatals also involve double articulation.

[31] It follows that sign language phonologies may, for that reason, have more phonologically relevant phonetic distinctions than spoken language phonologies.

[32] One might argue that an additional difference between sign and speech articulators is that signing has two articulators—that is, two hands. However, even though a distinction between one-handed and two-handed signs can be distinctive, the choice of which hand to use in one-handed signs cannot be used distinctvely. In this sense, then, the mind recognizes only one articulator.   .

times. In the next section, I will explore the notions of segment and syllable in both modalities in greater detail.

3.3.2. The segment and the syllable

Sign linguists have been investing a lot of energy in asking whether the sign is a syllable or a segment (see Corina and Sandler 1993; Wilbur 1993; van der Hulst 1995a; Brentari 1998). Several researchers, indeed, have suggested that the morphological simple sign is like a syllable (e.g. Chinchor 1978; Coulter 1982; Perlmutter 1992).[33] I have here arrived at the conclusion that this is, in fact, correct, and the two structures in (32) illustrate this. Sign language syllables are, in a sense, all 'CV' (that is, simple OR) syllables. In both cases, the total structure comprises both the syllabic and the phonemic structure. The structure in (32b), however, seems to imply that, in the structure of signs, certain portions of the phonemic class node structure dominate the syllabic structure. This is not just a consequence of designing the diagram. In sign language, most elements (except potentially those for *setting*, *orientation*, and *aperture*) have scope over the whole sign. In the syllabic organization of spoken language, however, the syllabic onset/rhyme division takes precedence over the distribution of elements, that, as a consequence, have scope over the onset or rhyme only. In spoken language, the syllable is suprasegmental, while in signed language the segment is suprasyllabic.

Let us now, subsequently, try to understand why the speech syllable is primarily a syntagmatic sequencing syllabic structure and, secondarily, per syllabic position a paradigmatic structure involving features or elements, while the sign syllable (in the spirit of Stokoe 1960 stated) seems primarily a paradigmatic featural structure that spreads out over a secondary sequencing structure. I wish to suggest that this difference is a true modality effect.

I believe that the reason for the difference lies in a crucial difference between auditory and visual perception. Not being an expert in perception, I none the less venture to suggest that the perception of signs is more 'instantaneous' than the perception of auditory speech input. The latter reaches the ear sequentially, in temporal stages. If this is so it does not come as a surprise that the temporal, syntagmatic organization of speech is perceptually salient and takes precedence over the paradigmatic organization. Turning to the sign syllable, Stokoe was right in saying (and seeing) that the notion of time-span is perceptually less important in the visual signal. Consequently, it does not seem plausible to assume that the structure of signs would depend foremost on separating the beginning and end phase of signs. Rather, the paradigmatic structure takes precedence over the syllabic, syntagmatic division in onset and offset (rhyme). The temporal structure of signs comes in as secondary structure, giving rise to the bipositional skeleton as a kind of afterthought.

---

[33] Often suggesting that the syllable = morpheme = word relationship in sign is like that in Chinese languages.

We can understand the difference in terms of Goldsmith's (1976) notions of vertical and horizontal slicing of the signal:

(33) Speech   Signing

    vertical (syntagmatic)   horizontal (paradigmatic)
    | |
    horizontal (paradigmatic)   vertical (syntagmatic)

I now wish to point to a difference between monomorphemic words in spoken languages and in signed languages that involves the monosyllabicity of signed words, as opposed to the typical polysyllabicity of spoken words.

In spoken languages, the need for going beyond simple CV words lies in wanting to have a sufficiently large number of semantic distinctions in the lexicon, without having to go into morphology. Thus spoken languages either elaborate the syllabic structure, allowing branching onsets and rhyme, and/or utilize polysyllabic units such as feet and prosodic words. A third option lies in invoking a complex tone system in terms of rhymal laryngeal distinctions.

We have seen that the notions of branching onset or branching rhyme do not apply to sign languages. Also it seems that most basic words are, syntagmatically, monosyllabic.[34] One does not typically encounter the additional layer of foot structure. I would like to suggest that this is so because of the availability, in sign, of the articulator (which is distinctively missing in speech). I noted that the articulator in signed languages, unlike that in spoken language, is a richly compositional unit. This means that lexical elaboration of the formational possibilities can easily be found in combining the extensive set of *handshapes* with every combination of *orientation*, *place*, and all the types of *movement*. We might add several other ways in which the compositional world of signs is richer than that of speech units. First, the type of manner (that is, movement) that is allowed in speech towards the constriction target is always predictable—that is, it is the shortest path. In sign, however, we note that movement of the whole hand (between an initial and a final state) can be performed in a variety of ways (straight, arced, circular, and so on). It seems to be the case that such differences are indeed used contrastively.[35] Secondly, sign language uses *iconicity* as a means of differentiating signs. From a functional point of view, then, there is simply less reason to complicate the structure of lexical entries by allowing for combinations of syllables into feet and beyond. The phonetic space that is available to the manual aspect of signing is more elaborate than the supralaryngeal aspects in speech, and

---

[34] Recall that signs with two movements can be regarded as being polysyllabic.
[35] I say this, realizing that I do not really have a well-developed set of really contrastive possibilities in any sign language.

this, combined with the other extra means mentioned, apparently, allows a rich enough inventory of monomorphemic words (or morphemes).[36]

4. SUMMARY AND CONCLUSIONS

In this chapter I have started out by developing an understanding of phonology that is both non-modular and modality free. In its non-modularity, phonology is not *different* from syntax, but rather, as per the Structural Analogy Hypothesis, *identical*. Thus, UG is just as much 'phonology free' as it is 'syntax free'. My view on the relationship between 'phonology' and 'phonetics' is that phonology emerges from the interaction between general categorization and structural principles and formats, and the specific phonetic domain of the modality. The primes of phonology (that is, the elements) are cognitive categories of phonetic (articulatory and perceptional) events that arise in the process of language acquisition. Phonological representations are phonetically implemented in terms of (a model of) the articulatory and acoustic properties of speech and sign events.

I continued by sketching models of both spoken language phonology and sign language phonology that, indeed, seem to be based on such principles. My account of sign phonology is, of necessity, more speculative (and theory-driven) than the account of spoken language, which is based on a long and rich tradition of feature theories. None the less, I subscribe to the view that sign languages have a phonology, just like spoken languages, and that the phonological component in both modalities is the result of the same innate abilities.

Finally, I discussed a number of specific differences between the phonologies of signed and spoken languages, trying to explain these differences in terms of modality-effects.

REFERENCES

Anderson, J. M. and Ewen C. (1987), *Principles of Dependency Phonology* (Cambridge: Cambridge University Press).

Battison, R. (1978), *Lexical Borrowing in American Sign Language* (Silver Spring, Md.: Linstok Press).

Brentari, Diane (1998), *A Prosodic Model of Sign Language Phonology* (Cambridge, Mass.: MIT Press).

Bromberger, S. and Halle, M. (1989), 'Why Phonology is Different', *Linguistic Inquiry* 20/1: 51–70.

Browman, C. P. and Goldstein L. (1989), 'Articulatory Gestures as Phonological Units', *Phonology*, 6: 201–51.

---

[36] Sign languages do not make abundant use of non-manual distinctions at the lexical level. In this sense (and to the extent that we can compare *non-manual* to *laryngeal*), sign languages are quite unlike Chinese languages.

Burton-Roberts, N. (this volume), 'Where and What is Phonology? A Representational Perspective'.

Chinchor, N. (1978), 'The Syllable in ASL', Paper presented at the MIT Sign Language Symposium, Cambridge, Mass.

Chomsky, N. and Halle, M. (1968), *The Sound Pattern of English* (New York: Harper & Row.

Clements, G. N. (1985), 'The Geometry of Phonological Features', *Phonology Yearbook*, 2: 225–52.

—— (1990), 'The Role of the Sonority Cycle in Core Syllabification', in J. Kingston, and M. Beckman (eds.), *Papers in Laboratory Phonology I: Between the Grammar and Physics of Speech* (Cambridge: Cambridge University Press), 283–333.

—— (1991), 'Vowel Height Assimilation in Bantu Languages', in K. Hubbard (ed.), *Berkeley Linguistic Society 17S: Proceedings of the Special Session on African Language Structures* (Berkeley: Berkeley Linguistic Society), 25–64.

—— (1992), 'Phonological Primes: Features or Gestures', *Phonetica*, 49: 181–93.

Corina, D. and Sandler, W. (1993), 'On the Nature of Phonological Structure in Sign Language, *Phonology*, 10: 165–208.

Coulter, G. (1982), 'On the Nature of ASL as a Monosyllabic Language,' paper presented at the Annual Meeting of the Linguistic Society of America, San Diego, Calif.

Coulter, G. (1993) (ed.), *Current Issues in ASL Phonology* (New York: Academic Press).

Crasborn, O. (forthcoming), 'Phonetic Implementation of Phonological Categories in Sign Language of the Netherlands', doctoral dissertation (Holland Institute of Generative Linguistics, University of Leiden).

—— van der Hulst, H., and van der Kooij, E. (forthcoming), *Phonetic and Phonological Distinctions in Sign Languages* (Holland Institute of Generative Linguistics, University of Leiden).

Dresher, E. and van der Hulst, H. (1998), 'Head-Dependent Asymmetries: Complexity and Visibility', *Phonology*, 15: 317–52.

Farmer, A. L. (1979), 'Phonological Markedness and the Sonority Hierarchy', in K. Safir (ed.), *Papers on Syllable Structure, Metrical Structure and Harmony Processes* (MIT Working Papers in Linguistics, 1; MIT, Cambridge, Mass.), 172–7.

Friedman, L. (1976), 'Phonology of a Soundless Language: Phonological Structure of ASL', doctoral dissertation (University of California, Berkeley).

Goldsmith, J. A. (1976), 'Autosegmental Phonology', doctoral dissertation (published, New York: Garland Publishing, 1979). (MIT, Cambridge, Mass.).

Golston, C. and van der Hulst, H. (1999), 'Stricture is Structure, in B. Hermans, and M. Oostendorp (eds.), *The Derivational Residue in Phonological Optimality Theory* (Amsterdam: John Benjamins), 153–74.

Hayes, B. P. (1993), 'Against Movement', in G. Coulter (ed.), *Current Issues in ASL Phonology* (New York: Academic Press), 213–26.

Hulst, H. van der (1988a), 'The Dual Interpretation of |i|, |u| and |a|', *North East Linguistic Society*, 18: 208–22.

—— (1988b), 'The Geometry of Vocalic Features', in H. Van Der Hulst and N. Smith (eds.), *Features, Segmental Structure and Harmony Processes* (Dordrecht: Foris), 77–126.

—— (1989), 'Atoms of Segmental Structure: Components, Gestures and Dependency', *Phonology*, 6: 253–84.

—— (1993a), 'Units in the Analysis of Signs', *Phonology*, 10: 209–41.

—— (1993b), 'Les Atomes de la Structure Segmentale: Composants, gestes, et dépendances', in B. Laks and A. Rialland (eds.), *Architecture des représentations phonologiques* (Paris: CNRS Editions), 255–90.

—— (1994a), 'Radical CV Phonology: the Locational Gesture', *UCL Working Papers in Linguistics*, 6: 439–77.

—— (1994b), 'An Introduction To Radical CV Phonology', in S. Shore, and M. Vilkuna (eds.), *SKY 1994: Yearbook of the Linguistic Association of Finland* (Helsinki: Suomen Kielitieteellinen Yhdistys), 23–56.

—— (1995a), 'Radical CV Phonology: The Categorial Gesture', in J. Durand and F. Katamba (eds.), *Frontiers of Phonology* (Essex: Longman), 80–116.

—— (1995b), 'Head-Dependency Relations in the Representation of Signs', in H. Bos and T. Schermer (eds.), *Sign Language Research 1994. Proceedings of the 4th European Congress on Sign Language Research. Munich 1–3 September 1994* (Hamburg: Signum Press), 11–38.

—— (1995c), 'The Composition of Handshapes', *Trondheim Working Papers*, 23: 1–17.

—— (1996a), 'Acquisitional Evidence for the Phonological Composition of Handshape', in Ch. Koster, and F. Wijnen (eds.), *Proceedings of Gala 1995.* (Groningen: Center for Language and Cognition), 39–56.

—— (1996b), 'On the Other Hand', in H. van Der Hulst and A. Mills (eds), *Issues in the Phonology of Sign Language*, theme issue of *Lingua*, 98: 121–44.

—— (1996c), 'Radical CV Phonology: The Segment–Syllable Connection', in J. Durand and B. Laks (eds.), *Current Trends in Phonology: Models and Methods*, (Manchester: European Studies Research Institute), 333–63.

—— (1999a), 'Features, Segments and Syllables in Radical CV Phonology', in J. Rennison and K. Kühnhammer (eds.), *Phonologica 1996: Syllables!?* (The Hague: Holland Academic Graphics), 89–111.

—— (1999b), 'Issues in Foot Typology', in M. Davenport and S. J. Hannahs (eds.), *Issues in Phonological Structure* (Amsterdam: John Benjamins), 95–107.

—— (forthcoming a), 'Structure Paradoxes in Phonology'.

—— (forthcoming b), *Principles of Radical cv Phonology*.

—— and Ewen, C. (1991), 'Major Class and Manner Features', in P. Bertinetto *et al.* (eds.), *Certamen Phonologicum II* (Turin: Rosenberg and Sellier), 19–42.

—— and Mills, A. (1996), 'Issues in Sign Linguistics: Phonetics, Phonology and Morpho-syntax', in H. G. Van Der Hulst and A. Mills (eds.), *Issues in the Phonology of Sign Language*, theme issue of *Lingua*, 98: 3–18.

—— and Ritter, N. A. (1999), 'Head-Driven Phonology, in H. van der Hulst, and N. A. Ritter (eds.), *The Syllable: Views and Facts*, (Berlin: Mouton/De Gruyter), 113–67.

—— —— (2000), 'No Sympathy for Opacity', in S. Billings, J. Boyle, and A. Griffith (eds.), *Chicago Linguistic Society*, 35/1: *The Main Session*, 153–73.

—— (forthcoming), *The External Syntax of Segments*.

Humbert, H. (1995), *Phonological Segments: Their Structure and Behaviour*, (HIL Dissertations, 12; The Hague: Holland Academic Graphics).

Hyman, L. M. (1973), *Phonology: Theory and Analysis* (New York: Holt, Rinehart & Winston).

Jaeger, J. (1980), 'Categorization in Phonology: An Experimental Approach', doctoral dissertation (University of California, Berkeley).

—— and Ohala, J. (1984), 'On the Structure of Phonetic Categories', in C. Brigman and M. Macaulay (eds.), *Berkeley Linguistic Society 10* (Berkeley: Berkeley Linguistic Society), 15–26.

Jakobson, R. (1968), *Child Language, Asphasia and Phonological Universals*, trans. A. Keiler (The Hague: Mouton).

—— and Halle, M. (1956), *Fundamentals of Language* (The Hague: Mouton).

Fant, C. G. M. and Halle M. (1952), *Preliminaries to Speech Analysis: The Distinctive Features and their Correlates* (Acoustics Laboratory of the MIT, Technical Report, 13; Cambridge, Mass.: MIT Press).

Kager, R. (1999), *Optimality Theory* (Cambridge: Cambridge University Press).

Kaye, J., Lowenstamm J., and Vergnaud, J.-R. (1985), 'The Internal Structure of Phonological Elements: A Theory of Charm and Government', *Phonology Yearbook*, 2: 305–28.

—— —— —— (1990), 'Constituent Structure and Government in Phonology', *Phonology*, 7: 193–231.

Keating, P. A. (1987), 'A Survey of Phonetic Features', *UCLA Working Papers in Phonetics*, 65: 124–50.

Kiparsky, P. (1979), 'Metrical Structure Assignment is Cyclic', *Linguistic Inquiry*, 10: 421–41.

Klima, E. and Bellugi, U. (1979), *The Signs of Language* (Cambridge, Mass.: Harvard University Press).

Kooij, E. van der (forthcoming), 'Phonological Complexity in Sign Language of the Netherlands', doctoral dissertation (Holland Institute of Generative Linguistics, University of Leiden).

Liddell, S. K. (1984), 'THINK and BELIEVE: Sequentiality in American Sign Language', *Language*, 60: 372–99.

—— and Johnson R. (1989), 'American Sign Language: The Phonological Base', *Sign Language Studies*, 64: 197–277.

Mandel, M. (1981), 'Phonotactics and Morphophonology in American Sign Language', doctoral dissertation (University of California, Berkeley).

Michaels, D. (1991), 'Movement Rules in Phonology', in P. Bertinetto *et al.* (eds.), *Certamen Phonologicum II* (Turin: Rosenberg and Sellier), 63–80.

Miller, J. (1995), 'On the Internal Structure of Phonetic Categories: A Progress Report', in J. Mehler and S. Franck (eds.), *Cognition on Cognition* (Cambridge, Mass.: MIT Press), 333–48.

Newkirk, D. (1981), 'On the Temporal Segmentation of Movement in American Sign Language', MS Salk Institute of Biological Studies, La Jolla, Calif. (Published in *Sign Language and Linguistics*, 1–2 (1998), 173–211).

Perlmutter, D. M. (1992), 'Sonority and Syllable Structure in American Sign Language', *Linguistic Inquiry*, 23: 407–42.

Prince, A. S. and Smolensky P. (1993), *Optimality Theory: Constraint interaction in Generative Grammar*, Rutgers Center For Cognitive Science; Technical Report 2, (Rutgers University, Piscataway, New Jersey).

Ritter, N. A. (1995), 'The Role of Universal Grammar in Phonology: A Government Phonology Approach To Hungarian', doctoral dissertation (New York University).

Sagey, E. C. (1986), 'The Representation of Features and Relations in Non-Linear Phonology', doctoral dissertation (MIT, Cambridge, Mass.).

Sandler, W. (1986), 'The Spreading Hand Autosegment of American Sign Language', *Sign Language Studies*, 50: 1–28.

—— (1989), *Phonological Representation of the Sign: Linearity and Non-Linearity in ASL Phonology*. Dordrecht: Foris Publications.

—— (1993*a*), 'Linearization of Phonological Tiers in ASL', in G. Coulter (ed.), *Current Issues in ASL Phonology* (New York: Academic Press), 103–29.

—— (1993*b*), 'Sign Language and Modularity', *Lingua*, 89: 315–51.

—— (1993*c*), 'The Sonority Cycle in American Sign Language', *Phonology*, 10: 243–80.

Schane, S. (1984), 'The Fundamentals of Particle Phonology', *Phonology Yearbook*, 1: 129–55.

Shapiro, M. (1972), 'Explorations into Markedness', *Language*, 48: 343–64.

Stack, K. (1988), 'Tiers and Syllable Structure in American Sign Language: Evidence from Phonotactics', MA Thesis (University of California, Los Angeles).

Stevens, K. N. and Keyser S. J. (1989), 'Primary Features and their Enhancement in Consonants', *Language*, 65: 81–106.

Stokoe, W. C. (1960), *Sign Language Structure* (Silver Spring, MD.: Linstok Press; 2nd edn. 1978).

Studdert-Kennedy, M. and Lane, H. (1980), 'Clues from the Differences between Signed and Spoken Language', in U. Bellugi and M. Suddert-Kennedy (eds.), *Signed and Spoken Language: Biological Constraints on Linguistic Form* (Wernheim: Verlag Chemie GmbH), 29–40.

Supalla, T. and Newport, E. (1978), 'How Many Seats in a Chair? The Derivation of Nouns and Verbs in American Sign Language', in P. Siple (ed.), *Understanding Language through Sign Language Research* (New York: Academic Press), 91–132.

Taylor, J. (1995), *Linguistic Categorization. Prototypes in Linguistic Theory* (2nd edn., Oxford: Oxford University Press).

Tervoort, B. T. M. (1953), 'Structurele analyse van visueel taalgebruik binnen een groep dove kinderen', doctoral dissertation (University of Amsterdam).

Trommelen, M. (1983), *The Syllable in Dutch: With Special Reference to Diminutive Formation* (Dordrecht: Foris).

Wilbur, R. B. (1987), *American Sign Language: Linguistic and Applied Dimensions* (2nd edn., Boston: Little/Brown).

—— (1990), 'Why Syllables? What the Notion Means for ASL Research, in S. Fischer, and P. Siple (eds.), *Theoretical Issues in Sign Language Research* (Chicago: University of Chicago Press), 81–108.

—— (1993), 'Syllables and Segments: Hold the Movement and Move the Holds!', in G. Coulter (ed.), *Current Issues in ASL Phonology* (New York: Academic Press), 135–68.

10

Boundary Disputes: The Distinction between Phonetic and Phonological Sound Patterns

Scott Myers

1. TWO KINDS OF SOUND PATTERN

Speech has two aspects. On the one hand, speech is a physical event: a continuously varying frequency spectrum, and a continuous flux in the state of the vocal tract. On the other hand, speech can be examined in terms of the discrete psychological categories of sound that humans insist on imposing on that physical continuum.

Sound patterns are to be found in both aspects of speech. A PHONOLOGICAL PATTERN is the distribution of a psychological sound category. PHONOLOGY is the theory of such patterns. A PHONETIC PATTERN is the distribution of physical quantities associated with a sound category. The theory of such patterns is PHONETICS.

The critical property distinguishing the two sorts of pattern is GRADIENCE. A phonetic pattern is gradient, while a phonological pattern is categorical (Pierre-humbert 1980, 1990; Keating 1988a, 1996). A categorical pattern is the distribution of a given class of sounds according to where it can occur in relation to other sound classes, as in the examples in (1) from English.

(1) (a) A short vowel (e.g. ɪ, ɛ, ɑ, ʊ, ə) never occurs in prevocalic position.
    (b) A long vowel (e.g. iː, eɪ, oʊ, uː) never occurs before [ŋ].

A categorical pattern is best expressed in terms of category labels, such as 'short' and 'long'. The classes involved are discrete: any entity either belongs to a given class or it does not. There are no gradations between categories.

A phonetic pattern lies in the statistical distribution of the measurable physical and psychological quantities. Examples of this sort of pattern in English are given in (2).

The research reported here was supported by grant SBR–9514481 from the National Science Foundation. I thank the editors of this volume for helpful comments on an earlier draft.

(2) (*a*) A vowel in a phrase-final syllable is on average 35% longer than a comparable vowel in another phrase position (Klatt 1976: 1217).

    (*b*) A vowel before a voiceless consonant has on average 61% of the duration of a comparable vowel before a voiced consonant (Chen 1970: 38).

Such a pattern is best expressed in terms of real numbers. The pattern lies in the fact that the mean value of the measurement under one condition is significantly different from that in another condition. They are gradient because there are many values that deviate from the means in both directions.[1]

The distinction between gradient phonetic patterns and categorical phonological patterns has been drawn throughout the history of phonology. Sapir (1925) and Trubetskoy (1939) argued for the importance of phonological patterns as distinct from gradient physical patterns, providing evidence that sound patterns cannot be understood without reference to the psychological notions of phoneme and contrast. Chomsky and Halle (1968) proposed that the grammar of a language is purely symbolic, and that the mapping from the categorical surface representation to the gradient continuum of phonetic measurements is universal and relatively trivial. Pierrehumbert (1980) argued, on the other hand, that the grammar of a particular language must include both a phonological and phonetic component, since there are language-particular sound patterns that are quantitative rather than categorical. Further enlightening discussion of the distinction is to be found in such works as Hockett (1955: 14), Pierrehumbert (1990, 1991, 1994*a*), Liberman and Pierrehumbert (1984), Keating (1985, 1988*a*, 1996), McCarthy (1986), Ohala (1990, 1998), and Cohn (1993).

There is a consensus in the literature that such a distinction exists,[2] but it remains a difficult task to determine whether a particular sound pattern is best described in terms of gradient physical measurements, or discrete psychological categories. The two modes of description are flexible enough that with enough effort either one can accommodate any pattern.

Given enough categories, one can describe any pattern in terms of discrete

---

[1] The term 'gradience' is sometimes used in a somewhat different sense in work in phonology. McCarthy and Prince (1993), for example, refer to 'gradient' violations of ALIGN constraints, for cases in which a violation is registered for each element that separates the edges of the two categories to be aligned. There is a kind of quantification here, but it is critical that it is quantification over categories. In the sense in which I am using the terms then, such a constraint is categorical and phonological, since it deals only in categories. The same terminological distinction holds of the quantification over categories in such work as Pierrehumbert (1993, 1994*b*), Berkley (1994), and Frisch *et al.* (1997). This work raises important questions about the nature of phonological patterns, but does not blur the boundary between such patterns and phonetic ones.

[2] One exception to the general consensus that there is a real distinction is Browman and Goldstein (1990*a*). These authors propose that categorical and gradient patterns lie in the eye of the beholder, categorical patterns being the macroscopic effects and gradient ones being the more microscopic ones. However, the examples they provide of categorical patterns suggest that they are only referring to cases in which a gradient pattern can lead to a change in transcription, as opposed to cases below the threshold of identifiability by a transcriber. They provide no means to express truly categorical patterns such as those in (1).

categories. One could, for example, restate the pattern in (2a) in categorical terms by defining the longer phrase-final counterparts of short vowels as 'medium-long' vowels, and the longer counterparts of long vowels as 'extra-long'. Then one could state the pattern as complementary distribution, as in (3).

(3) Medium-long and extra-long vowels occur only phrase finally.
    Short and long vowels occur only elsewhere.

Likewise, since sound categories are always associated with actual sounds, one can take the mean of some measured physical property of those sounds to stand for the category in a quantitative description. Thus, if we find that a long vowel is on average 54 ms longer than the corresponding short vowel (based on the measurements of Peterson and Lehiste 1960), then we could in principle restate the pattern in (1a) as in (4).

(4) A vowel before a vowel is 54 ms longer than elsewhere.

How then can we compare these pairs of models to determine whether a given pattern is phonetic or phonological? We generally compare models in terms of (a) *fit*—how well each model fits the facts, (b) *complexity*—how much machinery we require to attain that degree of fit, and (c) *generality*—how broad a range of cases the model covers. But we cannot compare in this way a statement about the distribution of speech categories, like (1a), to a statement about the distribution of acoustic measurement values, like (4). The two sorts of statement are evaluated in different ways.

In determining the fit of a statement of a phonological pattern, phonologists generally talk about how many exceptions it has. To determine how much machinery it requires, they count how many rules or constraints it contains, and how many stipulations are required to state each of these. A phonologist can argue that one phonological model is better than another by showing that it covers more facts, or that it requires less machinery to cover the same number of facts.

The rules are different with a quantitative model. The fit of the model can be stated precisely in terms of statistical measures such as R^2 or standard error. One model has a better fit than another if it has significantly less error as measured in one of these ways. The complexity of the machinery required depends on how many variables the model contains. If two models have the same degree of fit, but one has more variables, we favour the simpler one.

In order to compare two such different approaches to the same set of facts, one must state the two models in such a way that they can be evaluated in the same way. This can be done by adding to the phonological model an algorithm for mapping its outputs to actual physical values. This is simply a matter of being explicit as to the meaning of the categories one posits. Having done so, one then has two quantitative models of physical measurements, which one can compare on the basis of the usual rules for quantitative models. Such a model—one that includes a mapping of speech categories to measurable physical events—I will refer to as a *complete* model (cf. Pierrehumbert 1991). The two complete models to be compared differ just in whether the pattern in question is expressed in the distribution of categories, or in the mapping of categories to measurement values.

For example, to produce complete models corresponding to the statements in (1*a*) and (4) about the length of vowels before other vowels, we need to state a phonetic interpretation of the categories 'long vowel' and 'short vowel'. What we would find is that vowels such as [u:] and [ʊ] differ not only in duration in English, but also in quality (for example, tenseness). In one complete model, corresponding to (1*a*), we can build these quality distinctions into the mapping from the categories *long* and *short* to measurable acoustic values. If we then state, as in (1*a*) that all prevocalic vowels belong to the category *long*, it will follow that such vowels will have both the quality and the duration characteristics of long vowels. But in the complete model corresponding to (4), in which we are saying that the restriction on prevocalic vowels lies in phonetic realization, we would have to add a specification of these quality distinctions to our specification of the duration effect of prevocalic position. Both duration and quality properties would thus be stated twice, once for the category of long vowels, and again for the category of short vowel in prevocalic position. The latter complete model thus could achieve the same fit as the former only at the cost of additional variables. We should, therefore, favour the model in which the pattern is treated as a distribution of categories.

Similar considerations would weigh against treating final lengthening as a categorical effect, as in (3). The proposed categories 'medium-long' and 'extra-long' need to receive some sort of phonetic interpretation in a complete model. By adding these categories to the inventory of English, one has added to the complexity of the phonological component of the complete model, but there is no compensating simplification of the phonetic component, since there still needs to be a special interpretation for these categories that occur only in one position. The simpler complete model, then, will be the one in which the contextual effect lies wholly in the context-sensitive mapping from categories to acoustic events.

Only by comparing complete models, then, can we determine whether a pattern is phonetic or phonological. This chapter discusses some of the implications of making this determination. A more complete demonstration of how such a comparison works is provided in Section 2, using the example of a pattern in f0 in the Bantu tone language Chichewa. Making the distinction between phonetic patterns and phonological ones correctly is important, since it determines which patterns must be accommodated within phonological theory. In Section 3, I offer some examples illustrating how the classification of a single sound pattern can have consequences for phonological and phonetic theory. Section 4 decribes the methodological implications of this line of research. Section 5 is a discussion of the correspondence between phonetic and phonological patterns which makes the distinction so challenging. In Section 6, I offer suggestions as to further properties, beyond gradience, which distinguish phonetic from phonological patterns. Section 7 is a conclusion and an overview.

2. A COMPARISON OF PHONETIC AND PHONOLOGICAL APPROACHES TO F0 TIMING IN CHICHEWA

According to the careful tone transcriptions of Kanerva (1989), a lexical (that is, non-intonational) high tone in Chichewa (Bantu, Malawi) is disallowed in phrase-final position. A lexical high tone that would be expected to occur in phrase-final position is realized instead on the second half of the phrase-penultimate syllable, as illustrated in (5) and (6) (Kanerva 1989: 59). The phrase-penultimate vowel is always long; all other vowels are short.

(5) (a) mle^{n}dó uuyu
        'this visitor'
    (b) mleé^{n}do
        'visitor'
(6) (a) pezá nyaama
        'find the meat!'
    (b) peéza
        'find!'

In non-final position in the phrase, as in (5a) and (6a), the words *mlendo* and *peza* have a high tone on the final syllable. But in phrase-final position, as in the isolation forms in (5b) and (6b), these words have a high tone on the penultimate mora of the phrase, so that the lengthened penult syllable has rising tone. To account for this shift, Kanerva (1989: 58) proposes a phonological rule retracting a high tone from phrase-final position.

An alternative view would be that the high tone is not shifted to a non-final tone-bearing unit, but rather that the f0 peak realizing the high tone occurs relatively early relative to the phrase-final syllable. Steele (1986), Silverman and Pierrehumbert (1990), and Prieto, van Santen, and Hirschberg (1995) found that an f0 peak occurred earlier in a word- or phrase-final syllable than in a syllable further from the edge of such a prosodic domain. An earlier f0 peak in phrase-final position could be induced by the intonational boundary tone on the phrase-final syllable, since f0 peak delay is reduced if another f0 target immediately follows (Silverman and Pierrehumbert 1990; Arvaniti *et al.* 1998).

Thus, there are two hypotheses regarding the distinction between final and non-final position. According to Kanerva's phonological analysis, a phrase-final syllable cannot bear a high tone, and any potential phrase-final high tone occurs instead in the penultimate syllable. According to the phonetic alternative, a high tone can occur in phrase-final position, but it occurs earlier relative to that syllable than in other positions.

To distinguish the two hypotheses, we must first decide how to determine on the basis of phonetic data which syllable a given tone is associated with. In the original formulation of autosegmental phonology, Goldsmith (1976) proposed that association of a tone with a vowel is phonetically interpreted as meaning that the two are simultaneous. Sagey (1988) amended this proposal, suggesting instead that the phonetic instantiations of two elements associated with each other must merely overlap in time.

Neither proposal specifically addressed phonetic data, and neither is realistic as a proposal about phonetic timing. For example, if the f0 peak is taken to be the phonetic instantiation of a high tone, it generally does not overlap at all with the phonetic instantiation of the syllable it is associated with, but rather occurs early in the following syllable (Silverman and Pierrehumbert 1990). Similarly, Browman and Goldstein (1990b) point out that the peak of glottal spreading in an aspirated stop is timed to occur just after the end of the closure for that stop. The phonetic literature abounds with evidence that the various acoustic cues for a segment need not be either simultaneous or overlapping (e.g. Liberman *et al.* 1967).

Browman and Goldstein (1990b) propose that autosegmental association between phonological elements *a* and *b* is to be interpreted as stating that there is a regular phasing relation between the phonetic realizations of *a* and *b*. In other words, if two things are associated, then one can predict the timing of the phonetic realization of one based on the timing of the phonetic realization of the other. This definition is consistent with the regularities of interarticulator timing (Browman and Goldstein 1990b; Huffman 1993; Sproat and Fujimura 1993). Applied to tone, it implies that we can tell which syllable a high tone is associated with by finding which syllable provides the best prediction of the timing of the f0 peak (cf. Ladd, forthcoming). This test is applied in Myers (1999) to the issue of which syllable a high tone is associated with in Chichewa.

Three speakers of Chichewa produced the following two sentences, which are identical except for the final word. In these transcriptions, I have abstracted away from the tone retraction at issue.

(7) (a) Mlónda   ámaiwála   kuɲééɲa.
          watchman   he-forgets to-goof-off
          'The watchman forgets to goof off'
     (b) Mlónda   ámaiwála   mwaaná.
          watchman   he-forgets child
          'The watchman forgets the child'

The sentences were produced as a statement and as a question, and at three different loudness levels (soft, normal, loud). Speaking rate was a self-selected 'normal' one. The first 20 tokens of each sentence in each condition were selected for measurement, yielding 20 tokens × 2 sentences × 2 sentence types × 3 loudness levels = 240 total tokens. For details of the methods, see Myers (1999).

The measure of f0 timing was *relative peak delay*, which is the peak delay (time of the onset of the f0 peak minus the time of the onset of the syllable) divided by the duration of the syllable. This has been found to be the most robust measure of f0 timing across speaking rates (Silverman and Pierrehumbert 1990).

The f0 peak occurred in the penult syllable, whether the high tone was underlyingly final (*Mwaná*) or non-final (*Kuɲéɲa*), as indicated by the relative peak delay with respect to the penult syllable, summarized in Table 10.1. For all speakers, the mean values of relative peak delay are less than 1 for both underlying position classes, indicating that the f0 peak was generally attained within the penult syllable.

Table 10.1. Means of relative peak delay for each underlying position class (by speaker)

Speaker	Final (*Mwaná*)	Non-final (*Kuɲéɲa*)
SM	0.95	0.49
CJ	0.32	0.29
DJ	0.35	0.39

To compare a gradient phonetic analysis of this pattern with the phonological one, we compare two classes of quantitative models, both using multiple linear regression. In the first class of model, the PHONOLOGICAL MODELS, the assumption is that the high tone in both the final and the penult tone classes is associated with the phrase-penultimate syllable—that is, the high tone of *mwaná* is shifted to the penult. In these models, the timing of the f0 peak is predicted on the basis of the penult syllable, regardless of the underlying position of the high tone. The dependent variable is *syllable 1 peak delay* (peak delay relative to the penult syllable), and the independent variables are *position* (coded 0 for penult, 1 for final), *sentence type* (0 for statement, 1 for question), and *syllable 1 duration* (duration of the penult syllable). If these models are successful in predicting the location of the f0 peak, this supports the phonological account of high tone retraction, as posited by Kanerva (1989).

In the second class of model, the PHONETIC TIMING MODELS, the assumption is that the high tone remains in underlying position, so that the H in *kuɲéɲa* is associated with the penult, and that of *mwaná* is associated with the final syllable. In these models, the timing of the f0 peak is predicted on the basis of the penult syllable for penult high tones and the final syllable for final high tones. The dependent variable in these models is *syllable n peak delay*, which is *syllable 1 peak delay* for penult high tones (*kuɲéɲa*) and *syllable 2 peak delay* (peak delay relative to the final syllable) for final high tones (*mwaná*). The crucial independent variable is *syllable n duration*, which is the duration of the penult syllable for penult high tones and the final syllable for final high tones. The other independent variable is sentence type, as in the phonological models.

Because the dependent variables in the two models are different, it would be inappropriate to compare R^2 values between them. Instead, we compare the absolute value of the residual, which is the amount by which the predicted value differs from the actual value for each token. We can compare the two sets of residuals using a paired t-test.

By this measure, the phonological models outperformed the phonetic timing models for all three speakers. The results are laid out in Table 10.2. The average of the amount by which each model was off was considerably less in the phonological models than in the phonetic timing models (third column), and this difference in fit was significant according to the paired t-tests (fourth column). Thus the more accurate prediction of the timing of the f0 peak takes as its reference value the duration of the penult syllable, not the syllable to which the high tone belongs underlyingly. The penult, then, must be the syllable with which the high tone is associated, according to the phonetic test proposed above. See Myers (forthcoming) for an analysis of this pattern within Optimality Theory (OT), including the difference in the location of the f0 peak between speaker SM and the other two speakers.

Table 10.2. Comparison of models of peak delay (by speaker)

Speaker	Regression equation	Mean absolute residual (ms)	Paired t-test
SM	Phonological model $S_1P = ((0.47\ P + 0.55) \times S_1dur) - (9.33\ T) - 11.35$	15.6	$t_{237} = -15.3$, $p < 0.01$
	Phonetic timing model $S_nP = (0.95\ S_ndur) + (9.24\ T) - 177.09$	51.2	
CJ	Phonological model $S_1P = ((0.03\ P + 0.35) \times S_1dur) - (12.42\ T) - 7.56$	19.3	$t_{217} = -9.0$, $p < 0.01$
	Phonetic timing model $S_nP = (1.79\ S_ndur) + (54.71\ T) - 430.56$	44.4	
DJ	Phonological model $S_1P = ((-0.04\ P + 0.42) \times S_1dur) - (1.49\ T) - 7.13$	12.7	$t_{179} = -9.4$, $p < 0.01$
	Phonetic timing model $S_nP = (1.49\ S_ndur) - (33.79\ T) - 236.77$	38.2	

An explicit comparison of two complete models has allowed us to decide between a phonetic analysis and a phonological one for a particular pattern of f0. Such a comparison would not have been possible on the basis of tonal transcription data alone, since such data would not have allowed us to see a gradient pattern if it had been there.

3. WHY THE DISTINCTION MATTERS

Experience has shown that identifying a particular pattern as phonetic or as phonological can have important consequences for phonetic and phonological theory. Examples of such cases are provided in this section.

3.1. Tone spread in Japanese

The first explicit comparison of complete models to determine whether a pattern was phonetic or phonological was in Pierrehumbert and Beckman (1988), in the context of a study of accent in Japanese.

Haraguchi's classic (1977) study of Japanese accent crucially assumes Gold-smith's (1976) Well-Formedness Condition, according to which every vowel must have a tone. If a vowel does not receive tone otherwise, it was assumed, it would get a tone by spread (Goldsmith 1976) or default tone insertion (Pulleyblank 1986). In Haraguchi's analysis, an unaccented word in Japanese receives the default melody LH, which is mapped to vowels so that each vowel bears a tone. Thus the unaccented form *miyako-ga* 'capital city - NOMINATIVE' is represented as in (8) (Haraguchi 1977: 7):

(8) mi ya ko ga
    | \ | /
    L   H

Pierrehumbert and Beckman (1988), on the other hand, claimed that unac-cented phrases in Japanese have a sparser tonal structure, with the intonational phrase tone H on the second mora of the phrase, a L% boundary tone at the beginning of the next phrase, and no tones in between. Thus their representation for the form in (8) would be as in (9):

(9) mi ya ko ga
    |
    H   L%

This representation violates the Well-Formedness Condition, since it includes toneless syllables.

Pierrehumbert and Beckman demonstrated that the f0 contour in such unaccented phrases displays a straight line interpolation from the f0 peak corresponding to the high phrasal tone to the low value of the boundary L% at the beginning of the next phrase. They varied the length of the phrase and found that the slope of the straight line depended on the length of the toneless portion, being steeper when the distance between H and L% was shorter. The f0 values of the toneless syllables were clearly transitional, in that they depended on the f0 values of surrounding targets, and the amount of time elapsed between them. Pierrehum-bert and Beckman tried various quantitative models on the basis of the fully specified representation as in (8), but found that such models were less successful in describing the realization of tones in Japanese.

Pierrehumbert and Beckman thus showed, on the basis of a comparison of complete models, that the relevant pattern in Japanese is a phonetic one of interpolation, rather than a phonological one of high tone spread. This finding is of general interest, because it established that not every syllable has a tone in surface representation, contrary to Goldsmith's Well-Formedness Condition. Other instrumental studies have confirmed the point that the surface representation is underspecified (Pierrehumbert 1980; Keating 1988*b*; Davison 1992; Cohn 1993; Huffman 1993; van Bergem 1994; Choi 1995; Myers 1998). Such findings provide evidence against the assumption in some recent work that phonological representations are fully specified (e.g. Smolensky 1993; Calabrese 1995; Beckman 1997).

3.2. *Tone spread in Chichewa*

According to Mtenje (1987) and Kanerva (1989), a high tone in Chichewa that is not in the last three syllables of a phrase spreads one syllable to the right, as in the transcriptions in (10) from Kanerva (1989). It is important to note that the penultimate vowel of a phrase is always lengthened, and all other vowels are short.

(10) (*a*) mtsíkána   uuyu
           girl   this
           'this girl'
     (*b*) mtsíkaana
           'girl'

In (10*a*) the high tone of *tsí* is spread onto the following syllable *ká*. In (10*b*), on the other hand, the high-toned syllable is among the last three syllables of the phrase, so the high tone does not spread and *ka* surfaces without a tone.

This is typologically an unusual case of tone spread. Spread of a high tone rightward onto the next syllable is very common across languages, but there is no other case in the literature in which this spread depends on a count of syllables from the end of the phrase. Such a pattern would represent a violation of the generalization that a phonological process can be conditioned only by elements that are structurally adjacent to the target (Poser 1982; McCarthy and Prince 1986; Odden 1994). The pattern thus represents an anomaly in the typology of tone spread patterns, and a violation of locality principles.[3]

However, recent instrumental work suggests that this tone spread pattern is illusory. Myers (forthcoming) finds that the main difference in f0 between a high tone in phrase–penultimate position and one in an earlier position lies in the timing of the f0 peak. F0 generally begins rising at the beginning of a high-toned syllable, and the f0 peak is not attained until early in the next syllable. However, in

---

[3] Kanerva (1989) posits a dysyllabic foot at the end of the phrase, and formulates spread one mora to the right, with the condition that the target mora not be in the final foot. But this formulation has the same non-local character as Mtenje's, since determining whether the target mora is in the final foot requires reference to that foot, even if the target is at the other end of the phrase.

the case of the penultimate and final syllables, the f0 peak is attained early in that syllable. The general delay of the f0 peak has been noted in English (Silverman and Pierrehumbert 1990), Spanish (Prieto *et al.* 1995), Modern Greek (Arvaniti *et al.* 1998), and other languages. However it has also been noted that such peak delay is markedly reduced in the case of lengthened syllables (Silverman and Pierrehumbert 1990). This would fit the case of Chichewa penultimate and final syllables, which are both longer than comparable syllables in the phrase.

Thus, according to the phonological account of this pattern, a high tone before the last three syllables of the word must be associated with moras in two different syllables, while a high tone in the last three syllables is associated with just one mora. According to the alternative phonetic account, a high tone in either position is associated with just one mora, and the difference lies in the timing of the f0 peak.

In an experiment designed to test the two accounts, two speakers produced the sentence in (11), where the transcription abstracts away from the tone spread at issue.

(11) Mlónda   ámayenéra   kuɲééɲa.
     watchman   must   goof-off (infinitive)
     'The watchman must goof off'

Measurements of relative peak delay, as above in Section 2, for the italicized syllables: the lengthened penultimate *ɲée*, and the unlengthened preantepenultimate *né*. For details of methodology, see Myers (1999).

The results are summarized in Table 10.3. Relative peak delay is greater than 1 for the medial syllable *né*, indicating that in this case the f0 peak occurred after the end of that syllable. It is, on the other hand, less than 1 for the penultimate syllable, indicating that the peak in this case was well within that syllable. The t-tests reported in the third column of the table indicate that these differences were significant for both speakers.

Table 10.3.

Speaker	Medial	Penult	Paired t-test
SM	1.39	0.53	$t_{239} = 68.0$, $p < 0.01$
CJ	1.10	0.36	$t_{239} = 76.6$, $p < 0.01$

This typologically unexceptional pattern of f0 timing can be mistaken for tone spread. When the f0 peak is delayed, f0 is rising throughout the high-toned syllable, and does not begin to fall until well into the next syllable. It is thus easy for transcribers to hear raised pitch on both syllables, and this is the transcription found not only in Mtenje (1987) and Kanerva (1989), but also in my own fieldnotes from Malawi. However, I found that the f0 peak was not more extended in duration in the prepenultimate syllable than in the penultimate syllable, so it would be inaccurate to have the tone associated with two timing units in one case and with one timing unit in the other case.

Phonological theory does not have to allow for this anomalous case of tone spread, because the facts are better accounted for in terms of phonetic timing. Finding that the pattern is phonetic rather than phonological has the important consequence of removing a potential counter-example to the claim that phonological relations are local.

3.3. *Lip rounding in Turkish*

Boyce (1990) is a valuable study comparing patterns of lip rounding in Turkish and English. In Boyce's experiment, Turkish and English speakers produced nonsense words of the form *kVC(C)(C)Vk*, where *V* is either *u* or *i*, and the medial consonants are *k*, *t*, or *l*. Lip rounding was measured using an optical-electronic tracking system and EMG. Boyce found that in *kuCCuk*, Turkish speakers kept their lips rounded throughout the medial consonant cluster, producing one lip rounding gesture for the whole medial *VC(C)(C)V* string. English speakers, on the other hand, produced two distinct lip rounding gestures for the two rounded vowels, relapsing to an unrounded posture during the cluster.

These are interesting and important results. But I would take issue with Boyce's interpretation of the distinction between Turkish and English as an instance of two distinct language-particular coarticulation strategies. She concludes that 'current models of coarticulation are insufficient' to handle both cases, and that different articulatory strategies must be in force in the two different languages.

But this analysis fails to connect these data to the fact that Turkish is a language with rounding harmony and English is not. In Turkish, successive high vowels must generally agree in rounding (Clements and Sezer 1982). In a non-linear representation of Turkish, this is represented by requiring that one [+round] specification spread over the string in question, as in (12*a*).[4]

(12) (*a*)   [+round]

$$\text{V C C V}$$

(*b*) [+round]   [+round]

$$\text{V C C V}$$

In such a representation, there would only be one target requiring lip rounding, so one would expect only one extended lip rounding gesture as the realization. English does not show the harmony pattern, and so would not have such a representation. In English, each vowel would have its own [round] specification, as in (12*b*), leading one to expect distinct rounding gestures.

It is not clear from these data that there is any relevant difference between Turkish and English beyond the difference in phonological representation entailed

---

[4] It is immaterial for the point at hand whether or not the [+round] specification is associated just with the vowels, or also with the intervening consonants, as proposed by Ní Chiosaín and Padgett (1998).

by a non-linear approach to the vowel harmony pattern. In particular, there does not seem to be any strong reason to deduce that the languages differ also in coarticulatory strategy. Thus, treating this pattern as a phonological one would remove an argument that coarticulatory strategies vary arbitrarily from language to language. This clears the way for treating coarticulation in a maximally general way, as an instance of biomechanical economy (Lindblom 1983, 1990).

4. METHODOLOGICAL IMPLICATIONS

The cases we have considered have all involved a tone pattern. But there have also been a number of non-tonal patterns that had been thought to be phonological, but that have been found on examination of instrumental data to be better analysed as phonetic implementation: for example, vowel nasalization in English (Cohn 1993), apical stop deletion in English (Browman and Goldstein 1990*b*), lateral velarization in English (Sproat and Fujimura 1993), vowel assimilation in Marshallese (Choi 1995), and vowel assimilation in Igbo (Zsiga 1997).

Each such case brings into question phonologists' present reliance on transcription data. A transcription is inherently categorical, since it involves a human listener classifying what he or she is hearing according to the categories of a phonetic alphabet. A gradient pattern cannot be expressed in a transcription, and so must either be ignored or translated into categorical terms. A phonological theory based solely on transcription data is bound to be distorted by the inclusion of gradient phonetic patterns. The Japanese and Chichewa cases above show that such distortions can lead to unnecessary complications in phonological theory.

The likelihood of such an error depends on the domain. Tone categories, for example, are so variable and context sensitive in their realization that tonal transcriptions are necessarily quite abstract. Beginning to transcribe tone in a new language, one has to learn from scratch what the tones sound like in that language, which amounts to learning how to compensate for a particular pattern of phonetic implementation. Thus it is not surprising that there are such errors in the domain of tone. Generalizations about tone patterns based solely on transcription data are likely to be subject to this sort of error, as are generalizations about other very context-sensitive categories such as length and stress.

Allophonic patterns are also likely candidates for gradient analysis (Liberman and Pierrehumbert 1984: 228). When one considers the cases of complementary distribution in English that one discusses in beginning phonology classes, it is striking how many of them turn out on close analysis to be non-categorical: nasalization of a vowel before a nasal (Cohn 1993), dark versus clear /l/ (Sproat and Fujimura 1993), aspiration and flapping (Browman and Goldstein 1992). This raises the question of whether there are any cases of allophony that are truly categorical in nature.

On the other extreme, there seem to be no gradient patterns that bear any resemblance to reduplication or other patterns of prosodic morphology

(McCarthy and Prince 1986, 1995). Instrumental analysis of these patterns would presumably yield little useful information beyond what is provided by the transcription.

We do not know in advance whether a given pattern is phonetic or phonological, so we must always consider both possibilities. This would mean that we must compare complete models whenever we investigate a sound pattern, which requires that we gather carefully controlled quantitative data. The only way to get this kind of data is to adopt the experimental methodology that has long been common practice in phonetics (Liberman 1983; Liberman and Pierrehumbert 1984; Ohala and Jaeger 1986; Kingston and Beckman 1990; Ohala 1990; Pierrehumbert 1991). A phonologist must work like a phonetician in order to see what is phonological and what is not. This approach has been aptly named 'Laboratory Phonology'.

Precisely because the distinction between phonetic and phonological patterns is important and difficult, one must question the usefulness of the distinction between phonetics and phonology as professional disciplines. Since it requires substantial quantitative analysis of instrumental data to determine whether one is dealing with a phonetic pattern or a phonological one, one has to be prepared at the outset of a study to deal with either.

Besides making our factual basis more reliable, such an approach would also make our theories simpler and more coherent. If we can effectively rid all phonetic patterns from the set of patterns our phonological theory has to account for, we will presumably be left with something that makes more sense than the set of patterns we look at today. We have seen above some examples where a pattern that is anomalous as an instance of phonology makes sense as an instance of phonetics, and vice versa.

5. CORRESPONDENCE BETWEEN PHONETIC AND PHONOLOGICAL PATTERNS

The main reason that it is difficult to distinguish between phonetic and phonological patterns is that there are extensive correspondences between the two. The pervasive phonological phenomenon of assimilation, for example, corresponds to the universal phonetic phenomenon of coarticulation (Cohn 1993; Zsiga 1995; Majors 1998). Both involve an overlap of a gesture belonging to one segment with gestures belonging to another segment, the difference being that assimilation is categorical and coarticulation is gradient.

Indeed, all of the most widely distributed phonological processes correspond in some detail to phonetic patterns. Phonological closed syllable shortening corresponds to the fact that vowels in closed syllables are generally shorter in duration than vowels in open syllables (Maddieson 1985). Phonological vowel reduction and consonant lenition correspond to phonetic undershoot (Lindblom 1963, 1990). Ohala (1983) demonstrates that many common phonological patterns in the distribution of voicing and nasality have their origins in aerodynamic and physiological constraints.

One way to account for this systematic correspondence is to assume that the constraints that define phonological patterns are drawn from constraints on articulation, perception, and processing of speech sounds (Stampe 1980; Archangeli and Pulleyblank 1994; Steriade 1995; Myers 1997; Hayes 1999). But, for our present purposes, what is important about this correspondence is that it makes distinguishing phonetic patterns from phonological ones much more difficult than it would be otherwise. If there were no such thing as coarticulation, we might be left wondering why assimilation was so common, but we would know at a glance that, if a pattern involved a sound becoming similar to its context, it must be phonological assimilation. Owing to the correspondence, there is no short cut that avoids a quantitative analysis of the pattern to determine whether it is categorical or gradient.

6. A CHECKLIST OF CONDITIONING FACTORS

I have been discussing the distinction between gradient and categorical sound patterns. It would be useful to have a checklist of additional properties that correlate with either gradience or categoricalness, and so provide independent clues as to whether a pattern is phonetic or phonological. Such a checklist must at this point necessarily be provisional, since there are still too few quantitative studies of sound patterns to allow firm cross-linguistic generalizations. Nevertheless, it might be useful to consider what tentative generalizations can be made on the basis of the literature to date, even if they are doomed to be revised once more quantitative studies have been done.

6.1. *Common ground*

Some factors are common to both sorts of pattern. Both phonetic and phonological patterns depend on phonological categories. Different phonological categories have different realizations, and they also have different distributions. Whether a consonant is [+voice] or [−voice] will play a role in how it is realized, but it will also restrict where that consonant can occur in a word in a given language.

Phonological domains such as the phonological word and phonological phrase are also phonological categories relevant to both phonetics and phonology. Phonological alternations are generally restricted to some such domain (Selkirk 1980; Nespor and Vogel 1986). But recent work has shown that gradient phonetic patterns are also sensitive to categories such as phonological word, phonological phrase, intonational phrase, and utterance. Fougeron and Keating (1996a) have shown that stop closures are articulated more forcefully (as indicated by percentage of contact in electropalatograms) in phrase-initial than in phrase-medial position. Further evidence of phonetic patterns sensitive to phonological phrasing is provided by Wightman *et al.* (1992), Pierrehumbert and Talkin (1992), Sproat and Fujimura (1993), and Fougeron and Keating (1996b, 1997).

The inventory of phonological categories, including the categories of the prosodic hierarchy, are the common vocabulary of phonetics and phonology. Other factors are relevant exclusively to phonetics or exclusively to phonology, and these are of particular interest in the present context because they can be seen as clues for identifying a pattern as phonetic or phonological. The following sections give a partial inventory of these sorts of characteristic factors.

6.2. Factors in phonological patterns

6.2.1. The Uniqueness Hypothesis

One assumption that has long been held implicitly by many phonololgists is one that, if true, would go a long way towards clarifying the distinction between phonetic and phonological patterns. It is stated in (13).

(13) THE UNIQUENENESS HYPOTHESIS
      For every linguistic expression, there is one and only one phonological representation.

A linguistic expression is a morpheme, word, phrase, sentence, or any other meaningful syntactic unit of the language. According to the Uniqueness Hypothesis, the syntactic (and morphological) representations in a language are in one-to-one correspondence with the phonological representations.

The first part of the hypothesis is that there is at least one phonological representation for every linguistic expression. This means that there are no 'unpronounceable' expressions. For every grammatical word or sentence, there is a pronunciation. There are no words or sentences that are ruled out for phonological reasons.

The second part of the hypothesis is that there is at most one phonological representation for each expression. Every morpheme, word, and sentence consists phonologically of a particular configuration of sound categories. If two utterances have distinct phonological representations, then they must differ syntactically in terms of what morphemes they include or how they are put together.

Phonologists have long assumed something like this hypothesis, at least as a strong tendency. We talk about what *the* underlying or input representation for a form is, as if it was obvious that there is only one. One of the challenges in any phonological analysis is taken to be figuring out what single input can be mapped to all the outputs observed in different contexts. In both derivational models and non-derivational ones such as Optimality Theory (OT), the convention is rigorously maintained that each expression has a unique underlying/input representation. In the normal case, each expression is also assumed to have a unique surface representation, the exceptional case being that of 'optional rules' or 'free variation'.

As an English speaker, I know the word *dog*. One thing I know about it is how to pronounce it in my dialect. My intuition is that there is only one word *dog*, although this word can be used to refer to quite different sorts of animals, and although it can be produced in quite different ways under different speaking conditions. There's only one entry in my long-term memory for this item.[5]

This seems like a plausible assumption. Depending on how fast one is speaking or how much emphasis one puts on that particular word, the vowel in *dog* can vary from a low back vowel to something much higher and more central. The stops can sometimes be produced without complete closure. The degree of voicing varies strongly as a function of where the word occurs in the utterance. But it would be impossible to have a different representation of *dog* for each of these different situations. There is no limit on the number of different situations a word can be produced under, so there would be no limit on the number of *dog* items. We would not have space in memory for more than one word in our vocabularies.

Lacerda (1995) and Johnson (1997) have presented compelling evidence in support of an exemplar-based lexical representation for words, composed of the memory traces of every single instance of the item that the person has heard. Such a representation is well suited to accounting for such phenomena as frequency effects in lexical access, speaker normalization, and changes in norms over time. However, the exemplar approach does not entail that there have to be separate phonological representations corresponding to each instance of an item that has a memory trace. First, Johnson (1997) points out that there is not space in memory for a literal recording of each instance of an item, and suggests that instead each instance can be seen as contributing to the weights in one unified neural net representation of the item. Secondly, the memory trace of an instance does not itself contain any sound categories. Rather, the sound categories are a labelling associated with portions of that trace. What the Uniqueness Hypothesis demands is merely that there be a single category labelling for all the instances of a given item.

If the Uniqueness Hypothesis holds, the same phonological representation must be involved any time a given expression is used by a speaker. It follows that any differences we do observe in various productions by the same speaker of the same expression must be due to something outside the representation and so outside phonology. One can produce the same utterance at different rates, at different levels of loudness, and with different degrees of emphasis and carefulness. These factors must be outside the representation, then, in the system of realization.

If the Uniqueness Hypothesis holds, it puts useful limits on phonological patterns and the factors that can play a role in phonological patterns. It rules out

---

[5] Note that the Uniqueness Hypothesis is consistent with morphophonemic alternation. The plural marker is *-iz* after a sibilant (*roses*), *-s* after a voiceless consonant (*cats*), and *-z* elsewhere (*dogs*). There are four distinct expressions here: the plural marker, and the three different plural nouns. Each of the four expressions has a phonological representation, and it is not relevant to the Uniqueness Hypothesis that the plural nouns contain different exponents for the plural morpheme. What is crucial for the hypothesis is the assumption that the various forms of the suffix must be derived from a single form /-iz/.

phonological patterns that are sensitive to aspects of the actual speaking situation such as rate and speaking style.

At this point, I know of no clear counter-evidence to this hypothesis. It might be possible to use standard experimental paradigms from the lexical access literature to probe whether each lexical entry has just a single phonological entry. Priming, for example, is the facilitation of word identification (as measured in response time) triggered by the previous presentation of a related form (e.g. Stanners *et al.* 1979). If there are different entries for fast-speech versions and slow-speech versions of a lexical entry, for example, one might expect that a version at the same rate would be more efficient at priming identification than a version at a different rate. Another sort of counter-evidence to the hypothesis would be a finding that a rate-sensitive pattern is better analysed in categorical terms than in gradient terms. At present, I know of neither sort of counter-evidence.

6.2.2. Morphosyntactic category

Phonological patterns can be sensitive to morphological or syntactic categories: the distinction between noun and verb, for example, or distinctions among different tenses. The syntactic representation of an expression is by definition held constant over different realizations of that expression, so reference in phonology to syntactic categories is consistent with the Uniqueness Hypothesis. On the other hand, phonetic patterns are insensitive to such information.

In English, for example, the stress pattern for nouns is different from that of verbs and adjectives in being shifted one syllable to the left (Chomsky and Halle 1968; Hayes 1982). In an unaffixed verb, stress falls generally on the final syllable if heavy (*obéy*), otherwise the penult (*astónish*). In a simple noun, on the other hand, stress falls on the penult if heavy (*Arizóna*), otherwise on the antepenult (*América*). An analysis of English word stress must distinguish nouns from other categories.

Smith (1997) notes that in some Japanese dialects (such as that of Tokyo) the position of accent is contrastive in nouns, but predictable in verbs and adjectives. She proposes that there is a class of Faithfulness constraints restricted to nouns, and that this Noun Faithfulness can be ranked independently of general Faithfulness. In Japanese, Noun Faithfulness dominates constraints on tone alignment, mandating that underlying contrasts in accent position be preserved. But the tone alignment constraints in turn dominate general Faithfulness for tone position, subordinating any potential underlying contrasts to the alignment pattern in non-nouns. An analysis of this pattern requires reference to the distinction between nouns and other categories.

In Chichewa, a high tone within a verb stem is placed on the stem-final syllable or the stem-penult, depending on which tense it is (Kanerva 1989; Myers and Carleton 1996). A high tone belonging to the root morpheme or the subjunctive marking occurs on the final syllable of the stem, as in (14a) and (14b), respectively. In most other tenses, any high tone is placed on the stem-penultimate syllable, as in (14c). The stem is demarcated in all these examples by square brackets.

(14) (*a*) [tambalal-á]   (The root *tambalal* is high-toned.)
        stretch - out - legs - FINAL VOWEL
        'stretch out your legs!'
    (*b*) ti-[sangalats-é]   (The root *sangalats* is toneless.)
        we - please - SUBJUNCTIVE
        'let's please'
    (*c*) ndí-ma-[sangalál-a]   (The root *sangalal* is toneless.)
        I - habitual - be-happy - FINAL VOWEL
        'I am happy'

The placement of high tones in Chichewa must be sensitive to the different inflectional categories within the verb.

In contrast to these phonological patterns, there are no gradient phonetic patterns that distinguish among morphosyntactic categories. The realization of a noun is never distinguished from the realization of a phonologically comparable verb. There is no coarticulation pattern restricted to a given verb tense. There is thus no evidence that morphosyntactic category is information that is available to the phonetic implementation component.

6.2.3. Morphemes

Phonological patterns are frequently sensitive to morphemes and the boundaries between them. Some phonological patterns, known as morpheme structure constraints, apply only within a morpheme. Examples include the restrictions on consonantal roots in Arabic (McCarthy 1988; Pierrehumbert 1993; Frisch *et al.* 1997), such as the requirement that no two adjacent consonants in such a root be identical.

Other phonological patterns are restricted so that they apply only to combinations of two morphemes, and never within a morpheme. In Basque, for example, word-final *a* is raised to *e* if it occurs after a high vowel (Hualde 1989). This raising applies if the conditioning high vowel and the target vowel are in different morphemes, as in (15*a*), but not if they are within the same morpheme, as in (15*b*).

(15) (*a*) mutil-*e*   cf. giʃon-*a*
        boy - DEFINITE   man - DEFINITE
        'the boy'   'the man'
    (*b*) muɣa
        'limit'

Many such cases are discussed in the literature on derived environments and strict cyclicity (Kiparsky 1982*a*,*b*; Cole 1995).

Phonetic patterns, on the other hand, are oblivious to morphemes and morpheme boundaries. Coarticulation, for example, does not distinguish mono-morphemic forms from derived forms. There is no evidence in the phonetic literature that morpheme boundaries play a role in phonetic implementation.

6.2.4. Lexical item

Phonological patterns can also be sensitive to lexical identity—that is, which particular lexical item is involved. Many phonological patterns have lexical exceptions, and knowing the pattern can involve knowing which items it does not apply to. Patterns vary in their generality from absolutely exceptionless all the way to 'lexically triggered' cases where the forms participating in the pattern are outnumbered by the non-participating forms.

In Turkish, for example, vowels within a word must generally agree in backness, and in particular the vowels in affixes must agree with the closest vowel in the root (Clements and Sezer 1982). The vowel of the plural suffix - *l*ʸ*er* ~ -*lar* in (16), for example, agrees with the root vowel in backness.

(16) (*a*) ip-lʸer
        rope - PLURAL
        'ropes'
     (*b*) pul-lar
        stamp - PLURAL
        'stamps'

But there is a small class of disharmonic suffixes that fail to show this agreement. The second vowel of the progressive suffix -*Iyor*, for example, is the back vowel *o* regardless of what vowel precedes it, as seen in (17).

(17) (*a*) gʸelʸ-iyor-um
        'I am coming'
     (*b*) bak-ɨyor-um
        'I am looking'

An analysis of Turkish vowel harmony, or any other phonological pattern with lexical exceptions, must include a distinction between those lexical items that are included in the pattern and those that are excluded.

On the other hand, there are no such exceptional lexical items in a phonetic pattern (Keating 1996). There are no lexical exceptions to coarticulation. Likewise, the generalization in (2*b*), that a vowel in English is longer before a voiced consonant than before a voiceless one, holds across the vocabulary without exception.

6.3. *Factors in phonetic patterns*

6.3.1. Gradient factors

Phonetic patterns are gradient not only in the effect—the phonetic measure that is being predicted—but also in the factors that condition that effect. Thus f0 realization of a high tone, for example, can be affected not only by the category of the tones around it, but also by the f0 values of those tones (Pierrehumbert 1980;

Liberman and Pierrehumbert 1984; Pierrehumbert and Beckman 1988). In the sequence HLH, the second H is generally lower than the first, a phenomenon known as DOWNDRIFT or CATATHESIS. How much lower the second H is can be predicted on the basis of the f0 value of the first H. Thus the realization of a phonological element can be affected by the quantitative measures of the realizations of other elements in the representation.

The distribution of a phonological element, on the other hand, cannot be affected by such information. No pattern of tone distribution is sensitive to the exact f0 value of the context. This would be a number particular to a particular production of an expression, so it could not be relevant to the long-term mental representation of that expression according to the Uniqueness Hypothesis.

6.3.2. Speaking rate

The rate at which one is speaking can strongly affect how an expression is realized. Overlap of successive gestures is greater at faster rates (Gay 1981; Byrd 1994). Temporally defined contrasts such as voice onset time are always relative to the current rate of speech (Miller and Liberman 1979; Summerfield 1981; Wayland *et al.* 1994). Berkovits (1991) finds utterance-final lengthening in Hebrew only at faster rates.

According to the Uniqueness Hypothesis, rate could not play a role in phonology, since it varies from production to production of the same expression. I would claim that there are no clear cases of a categorical pattern that is sensitive to rate.

There are certainly many cases of patterns that are described as phonological that are restricted to 'fast speech' (Zwicky 1972; Hooper 1978; Stampe 1980). But these are all cases in which it was assumed without evidence that the pattern was categorical. Consider, for example, the pattern of schwa deletion, described on the basis of transcriptions by Zwicky (1972) and Hooper (1978). They note that the parenthesized schwa vowel in the following words is often not pronounced: *cam(e)ra, fam(i)ly, elab(o)rate*. Zwicky proposes that there are two phonological processes of schwa deletion, one for post-stress schwa and another for pre-stress, and he specified that the former rule applies 'in moderately fast or casual speech', while the latter applies 'in quite fast speech'. Browman and Goldstein (1990c), however, have presented evidence suggesting that such schwa deletion is not an independent process, but is a natural and inevitable consequence of gradient gestural overlap. If the consonant gestures surrounding the schwa overlap more, they tend to hide the schwa, with the limiting case being that the schwa is inaudible. There tends to be more of this hiding in faster speech because there is more gestural overlap in faster speech.

Bolozky (1977), surveying fast speech phenomena in Modern Hebrew, concludes that the overarching generalization is that segments tend to get more assimilated and reduced the faster the speech rate is. He argues against the assumption that there are distinct speeds (moderate, fast, very fast) with distinct blocks of phonological processes. Since assimilation and reduction are exactly what happens to segments under coarticulation, and we know that coarticulation is greater at faster rates, it would seem that the simplest hypothesis would be that the continuum of fast speech phenomena that Bolozky investigated can be attributed wholly to greater overlap between successive gestures at faster speech rates.

I would conclude, with McCarthy (1986) and Keating (1996), that the evidence available suggests that dependence on speech rate is one of the key properties distinguishing phonetic patterns from phonological patterns. If this generalization continues to survive scrutiny, then varying rate in one's experiments provides a relatively simple source of evidence as to whether the pattern one is investigating is phonetic or phonological.

6.3.3. Carefulness

Depending on the requirements of the listener, one can vary the carefulness of one's articulation from highly elliptical hypoarticulated speech to excruciatingly explicit hyperarticulated speech (Lindblom 1990). Towards the hyperarticulated end of this continuum, the speaker expends extra effort to ease the identification tasks of the listener. Moon and Lindblom (1994) show that, when speakers are required to speak 'more clearly', they readjust their articulation to reduce coarticulation and vowel reduction, and render their vowels more distinct from each other. Towards the hypospeech end, on the other hand, coarticulation and reduction run wild. Lindblom argues that the speaker keeps track of how much signal-independent information is available to the listener (for example, shared assumptions), and selects the level closest to the hypospeech end of the continuum that is compatible with the listener filling in the blanks and identifying the message.

Since one can produce the same expression in different speaking styles, the Uniqueness Hypothesis predicts that speaking style can play no role in phonology. As with speaking rate, there are frequent reports of phonological patterns that are restricted to 'casual', such as the schwa deletion discussed above, but no arguments have been produced that a categorical analysis of the pattern is superior to a gradient one. I would conclude, with Keating (1996), that dependence on speaking style distinguishes phonetic patterns from phonological ones.

6.3.4. Interspeaker anatomical differences

Different speakers have different vocal tracts and vocal folds in terms of shape and in particular size (Beck 1997). A longer vocal tract has lower resonant frequencies than a shorter one, all else being equal. Thus larger people with larger vocal tracts tend to have lower formant frequencies. Likewise, they tend to have longer vocal folds and so lower fundamental frequency ranges. The anatomy of the individual speaker thus accounts for a significant amount of the differences in speech measurements among speakers.

But these anatomical differences never play a role in categorical patterns. There are no vowel harmony patterns that are restricted to taller speakers, or tone patterns that are produced only by people with high-pitched voices. Speakers may differ from one another in the phonological patterns that they follow, but these differences can never be correlated with anatomical differences.

The absence of such information from phonology is predicted by the Uniqueness Hypothesis, since an expression can be produced differently by different people, yet still be counted by listeners as one and the same expression.

7. CONCLUSION

I have argued in this chapter that the relatively uncontroversial idea that there is a distinction between gradient phonetic patterns and categorical phonological ones brings with it some implications that have not yet enjoyed broad acceptance. First, transcriptions are not a reliable basis for phonological research, since they do not allow the researcher to determine whether the pattern being studied is gradient or not. Objective physical measurements are a more reliable basis for factual generalizations about sound patterns. Secondly, laboratory phonology is not one branch of phonological research, but simply the appropriate methodology for all of phonology. Thirdly, the distinction drawn between phonetics and phonology as fields of specialization retards progress towards understanding sound patterns. The most efficient means to bridge the current gap between the two cultures lies in collaborations between phoneticians and phonologists, as exemplified in Jakobson, Fant, and Halle (1952), or more recently in Hume, Johnson, Seo, and Tserdalis (1999).

REFERENCES

Archangeli, D. and Pulleyblank, D. (1994), *Grounded Phonology* (Cambridge: MIT Press).

Arvaniti, A., Ladd, D. R., and Mennen, I. (1998), 'Stability of Tonal Alignment: The Case of Greek Prenuclear Accents', *Journal of Phonetics*, 26: 3–25.

Beck, J. M. (1997), 'Organic Variation of the Vocal Apparatus', in W. Hardcastle and J. Laver (eds.), *The Handbook of Phonetic Sciences* (Oxford: Blackwell, 256–98).

Beckman, J. N. (1997), 'Positional Faithfulness, Positional Neutralization and Shona Vowel Harmony', *Phonology*, 14: 1–47.

Bergem, D. R. van (1994), 'A Model of Coarticulatory Effects on the Schwa', *Speech Communication*, 14: 143–62.

Berkley, D. (1994), 'Variability in Obligatory Contour Effects', in K. Beals, J. Denton, R. Knippen, L. Melnar, H. Suzuki, and E. Zeinfeld (eds.), *Papers from the 30th Meeting of the Chicago Linguistic Society*, ii. *Papers from the Parasession on Variation in Linguistic Theory* (Chicago: Chicago Linguistic Society), 1–12.

Berkovits, R. (1991), 'The Effect of Speaking Rate on Evidence for Utterance-Final Lengthening', *Phonetica*, 48: 57–66.

Bolozky, S. (1977), 'Fast Speech as a Function of Tempo in Natural Generative Phonology', *Journal of Linguistics*, 13: 217–38.

Boyce, S. (1990), 'Coarticulatory Organization for Lip Rounding in Turkish and English', *Journal of the Acoustical Society of America*, 88: 2584–95.

Browman, C. P. and Goldstein, L. (1990*a*), 'Representation and Reality: Physical Systems and Phonological Structure', *Journal of Phonetics*, 18: 411–24.

—— —— (1990*b*), 'Tiers in Articulatory Phonology, with Some Implications for Casual Speech', in J. Kingston and M. Beckman (eds.), *Papers in Laboratory Phonology I* (Cambridge: Cambridge University Press) 341–76.

—— —— (1990*c*), 'Gestural Specification using Dynamically-Specified Articulatory Structures', *Journal of Phonetics*, 18: 299–320.

—— —— (1992), 'Articulatory Phonology: An Overview', *Phonetica*, 49: 155–80.

Byrd, D. (1994), *Articulatory Timing in English Consonant Sequences* (UCLA Working Papers in Phonetics (86, Los Angeles: UCLA Phonetics Laboratory).

Calabrese, A. (1995), 'A Constraint-Based Theory of Phonological Markedness and Simplification Procedures', *Linguistic Inquiry*, 26: 373–463.

Chen, M. (1970), 'Vowel Length Variation as a Function of the Voicing of the Consonant Environment', *Phonetica*, 22: 129–59.

Choi, J. D. (1995), 'An Acoustic–Phonetic Underspecification Account of Marshallese Vowel Allophony', *Journal of Phonetics*, 23: 323–47.

Chomsky, N. and Halle, M. (1968), *The Sound Pattern of English* (New York: Harper & Row).

Clements, G. N. and Sezer, E. (1982), 'Vowel and Consonant Disharmony in Turkish', in H. van der Hulst and N. Smith (eds.), *The Structure of Phonological Representations (Part 2)* (Dordrecht: Foris), 213–55.

Cohn, A. (1993), 'Nasalization in English: Phonology or Phonetics', *Phonology*, 10: 43–82.

Cole, J. (1995), 'The Cycle in Phonology', in J. A. Goldsmith (ed.), *The Handbook of Phonological Theory* (Oxford: Blackwell), 70–113.

Davison, D. (1992), 'Parametric Variation in Pitch Realization of "Neutral Tone" Syllables in Mandarin', in *Proceedings of the Eighteenth Annual Meeting of the Berkeley Linguistics Society* (Berkeley: Berkeley Linguistics Society), 67–79.

Fougeron, C. and Keating, P. A. (1996*a*), 'Articulatory Strengthening in Prosodic Domain-Initial Position', *UCLA Working Papers in Phonetics*, 92: 61–87.

—— —— (1996*b*), 'Variations in Velic and Lingual Articulation Depending on Prosodic Position: Results for 2 French Speakers', *UCLA Working Papers in Phonetics*, 92: 88–96.

—— —— (1997), 'Articulatory Strengthening at Edges of Prosodic Domains', *Journal of the Acoustical Society of America*, 101: 3728–40.

Frisch, S., Broe, M., and Pierrehumbert, J. (1997), 'Similarity and Phonotactics in Arabic', Rutgers Optimality Archive, http://ruccs.rutgers.edu/roa.html.

Gay, T. (1981), 'Mechanisms in the Control of Speech Rate', *Phonetica*, 38: 148–58.

Goldsmith, J. A. (1976), 'Autosegmental Phonology', doctoral dissertation (MIT, Cambridge, Mass). (Published, New York: Garland Publishing, 1979.)

Haraguchi, S. (1977), *The Tone Pattern of Japanese: An Autosegmental Theory of Tonology* (Tokyo: Kaitakusha).

Hayes, B. (1982), 'Extrametricality and English Stress', *Linguistic Inquiry*, 13: 227–76.

—— (1999), 'Phonetically-Driven Phonology: The Role of Optimality Theory and Inductive Grounding', Rutgers Optimality Archive, in M. Darnell, E. Moravcsik, M. Noonan, F. Newmeyer, and K. Wheatly (eds.), *Functionalism and Formalism in Linguistics*, i. *General Papers* (Amsterdam: John Benjamins), 243–85.

Hockett, C. F. (1955), *A Manual of Phonology* (Indiana University Publications in Anthropology and Linguistics; Baltimore: Waverly Press).

Hooper, J. (1978), 'Constraints on Schwa-Deletion in American English', in J. Fisiak (ed.), *Recent Developments in Historical Phonology* (The Hague: Mouton), 183–207.

Hualde, J. (1989), 'The Strict Cycle Condition and Noncyclic Rules', *Linguistic Inquiry*, 20: 675–80.

Huffman, M. (1993), 'Phonetic Patterns of Nasalization and Implications for Feature Specification', in M. Huffman, and R. Krakow (eds.), *Nasals, Nasalization, and the Velum*, Phonetics and Phonology, 5 (San Diego, Calif.: Academic Press), 303–27.

Hume, E., Johnson, K., Seo, M., and Tserdalis, G. (1999), 'A Cross-Linguistic Study of Stop Place Perception', in J. Ohala, Y. Hasegawa, M. Ohala, D. Granville, and A. Bailey (eds.), *Proceedings of the XIVth International Congress of Phonetic Sciences* (Berkeley and Los Angeles: Linguistics Department, University of California), 2069–72.

Jakobson, R. C., Fant, G. C. M., and Halle, M. (1952), *Preliminaries to Speech Analysis: The Distinctive Features and their Correlates* (Acoustics Laboratory of the MIT, Technical Report, 13; Cambridge, Mass.: MIT Press).

Johnson, K. (1997), 'Speech Perception without Speaker Normalization', in K. Johnson and J. W. Mullenix (eds.), *Talker Variability in Speech Processing* (San Diego, Calif.: Academic Press), 145–65.

Kanerva, J. (1989), *Focus and Phrasing in Chichewa Phonology* (New York: Garland Press).

Keating, P. A. (1985), 'Universal Phonetics and the Organization of Grammars', in V. Fromkin (ed.), *Linguistic Phonetics* (Orlando, Fla.: Academic Press), 115–32.

—— (1988a), 'The Phonology–Phonetics Interface', in F. Newmeyer (ed.), *Linguistics: The Cambridge Survey*, i. *Linguistic Theory: Foundations* (Cambridge: Cambridge University Press), 281–302.

—— (1988b), 'Underspecification in Phonetics', *Phonology*, 5: 275–92.

—— (1996), 'The Phonology–Phonetics Interface', *UCLA Working Papers in Phonetics*, 92: 45–60.

Kingston, J. and Beckman, M. (1990), (eds.), *Papers in Laboratory Phonology I* (Cambridge: Cambridge University Press).

Kiparsky, P. (1982a), 'How Abstract is Phonology?', in P. Kiparsky (ed.), *Explanation in Phonology* (Dordrecht: Foris), 119–64.

—— (1982b), 'Lexical Morphology and Phonology', in Linguistic Society of Korea (ed.), *Linguistics in the Morning Calm* (Seoul: Hanshin), 3–91.

Klatt, D. H. (1976), 'Linguistic Uses of Segment Duration in English: Acoustic and Perceptual Evidence', *Journal of the Acoustical Society of America*, 59: 1208–21.

Lacerda, F. (1995), 'The Perceptual-Magnet Effect: An Emergent Consequence of Exemplar-Based Phonetic Memory', in K. Elenius and P. Branderud (eds.), *Proceedings of the 13th International Congress of the Phonetic Sciences* (Stockholm: KTH (Royal Institute of Technology) and Stockholm University), ii. 140–7.

Ladd, D. R. (forthcoming), 'Bruce, Pierrehumbert, and the Elements of Intonational Phonology', in Merle Horne (ed.), *A Festschrift for Gösta Bruce* (Dordrecht: Kluwer).

Liberman, A. M., Cooper, F. S., Shankweiler, D. S., and Studdert-Kennedy, M. (1967), 'Perception of the Speech Code', *Psychological Review*, 74: 431–61.

Liberman, M. (1983), 'In Favor of Some Uncommon Approaches to the Study of Speech', in P. MacNeilage (ed.), *The Production of Speech* (New York: Springer), 265–74.

—— and Pierrehumbert, J. (1984), 'Intonational Invariance under Changes in Pitch Range and Length', in M. Aronoff and R. Oehrle (eds.), *Language Sound Structure* (Cambridge: MIT Press), 157–233.

Lindblom, B. (1963), 'Spectrographic Study of Vowel Reduction', *Journal of the Acoustical Society of America*, 35: 1773–81.

—— (1983), 'Economy of Speech Gestures', in P. MacNeilage (ed.), *The Production of Speech* (New York: Springer), 217–45.

—— (1990), 'Explaining Phonetic Variation: A Sketch of the H&H Theory', in W. Hardcastle and A. Marchal (eds.), *Speech Production and Speech Modeling* (Dordrecht: Kluwer), 403–39.

McCarthy, J. J. (1986), 'OCP Effects: Gemination and Antigemination', *Linguistic Inquiry*, 17: 207–63.

—— (1988), 'Feature Geometry and Dependency: A Review', *Phonetica*, 43: 84–108.

—— and Prince, A. (1986), 'Prosodic Morphology', MS, University of Massachusetts, Amherst, and Brandeis University, Waltham.

—— —— (1993), 'Generalized Alignment', in G. Booij, and J. van Marle (eds.), *Yearbook of Morphology* 1993 (Dordrecht: Kluwer), 79–153.

—— —— (1995), 'Faithfulness and Reduplicative Identity', in J. Beckman, L. Dickey, and S. Urbanczyk (eds.), *Papers in Optimality Theory* (Amherst, Mass.: Graduate Linguistics Student Association), 249–384.

Maddieson, I. (1985), 'Phonetic Cues to Syllabification', in V. Fromkin (ed.), *Phonetic Linguistics* (Orlando, Fla.: Academic Press), 203–22.

Majors, T. (1998), 'Stress Dependent Harmony: Phonetic Origins and Phonological Analysis', Ph.D. dissertation (University of Texas, Austin).

Miller, J. and Liberman, A. (1979), 'Some Effects of Later-Occurring Information on the Perception of Stop Consonants', *Perception and Psychophysics*, 25: 457–65.

Moon, S.-J. and Lindblom, B. (1994), 'Interaction between Duration, Context, and Speaking Style in English Stressed Vowels', *Journal of the Acoustical Society of America*, 96: 40–55.

Mtenje, A. A. (1987), 'Tone Shift Principles in the Chichewa Verb: A Case for a Tone Lexicon', *Lingua*, 72: 169–209.

Myers, S. (1997), 'Expressing Phonetic Naturalness in Phonology', in I. Roca (ed.), *Derivations and Constraints in Phonology* (Oxford: Oxford University Press), 125–52.

—— (1998), 'Surface Underspecification of Tone in Chichewa', *Phonology*, 15: 367–91.

—— (1999), 'Tone Association and f0 Timing in Chichewa', *Studies in African Linguistics*, 28: 215–39.

—— and Carleton, T. (1996), 'Tonal Transfer in Chichewa', *Phonology*, 13: 39–72.

Nespor, M. and Vogel, I. (1986), *Prosodic Phonology* (Dordrecht: Foris).

Ní Chiosáin, M. and Padgett, J. (1998), 'Markedness, Segment Realization, and Locality in Spreading', talk presented at the Fourth Southwest Workshop on Optimality Theory, University of Arizona, 4–5 Apr.

Odden, D. (1994), 'Adjacency Parameters in Phonology', *Language*, 70: 289–330.

Ohala, J. J. (1983), 'The Origin of Sound Patterns in Vocal Tract Constraints', in P. F. MacNeilage (ed.), *The Production of Speech* (New York: Springer), 189–216.

—— (1990), 'There is no Interface between Phonology and Phonetics: A Personal View', *Journal of Phonetics*, 18: 153–71.

—— (1998), 'The Relation between Phonetics and Phonology', in W. Hardcastle and J. Laver (eds.), *The Handbook of Phonetic Sciences* (Oxford: Blackwell), 674–94.

—— and Jaeger, J. (1986), *Experimental Phonology* (Orlando, Fla.: Academic Press).

Peterson, G. E. and Lehiste, I. (1960), 'Duration of Syllable Nuclei in English', *Journal of the Acoustical Society of America*, 32: 693–703.

Pierrehumbert, J. B. (1980), *The Phonetics and Phonology of English Intonation* (Bloomington, Ind.: Indiana University Linguistics Club).

—— (1990), 'Phonological and Phonetic Representation', *Journal of Phonetics*, 18: 375–94.

—— (1991), 'The Whole Theory of Sound Structure', *Phonetica*, 48: 223–32.

—— (1993), 'Dissimilarity in the Arabic Verbal Roots', *Proceedings of the North East Linguistic Society*, 23: 367–81.

—— (1994*a*), 'Knowledge of Variation', in K. Beals, J. Denton, R. Knippen, L. Melnar, H. Suzuki, and E. Zeinfeld (eds.), *Papers from the 30th Meeting of the Chicago Linguistic Society*, ii. *Papers from the Parasession on Variation* (Chicago: Chicago Linguistic Society), 232–56.

—— (1994*b*), 'Syllable Structure and Word Structure: A Study of Triconsonantal Clusters in English', in P. Keating (ed.), *Papers in Laboratory Phonology III* (Cambridge: Cambridge University Press), 168–88.

—— and Beckman, M. (1988), *Japanese Tone Structure* (Linguistic Inquiry Monograph, 15; Cambridge, Mass.: MIT Press).

—— and Talkin, D. (1992), 'Lenition of /h/ and Glottal Stop', in G. Docherty and D. R. Ladd (eds.), *Papers in Laboratory Phonology II: Gesture, Segment, Prosody* (Cambridge: Cambridge University Press), 90–117.

Poser, W. (1982), 'Phonological Representation and Action-at-a-Distance', in H. van der Hulst and N. Smith (eds.), *The Structure of Phonological Representations (Part II)* (Dordrecht: Foris), 121–58.

Prieto, P., van Santen, J., and Hirschberg, J. (1995), 'Tonal Alignment Patterns in Spanish', *Journal of Phonetics*, 23: 429–51.

Pulleyblank, D. (1986), *Tone in Lexical Phonology* (Dordrecht: Reide).

Sagey, E. C. (1988), 'On the Ill-Formedness of Crossing Association Lines', *Linguistic Inquiry*, 19: 109–17.

Sapir, E. (1925), 'Sound Patterns in Language', *Language*, 1: 37–51; repr. in Martin Joos (ed.), *Readings in Linguistics* (Washington: American Council of Learned Societies, 1957), 19–25.

Selkirk, E. O. (1980), 'Prosodic Domains in Phonology: Sanskrit Revisited', in M. Aronoff and M.-L. Kean (eds.), *Juncture* (Saratoga, Calif.: Anma Libri), 107–29.

Silverman, K. and Pierrehumbert, J. (1990), 'The Timing of Prenuclear High Accents in English', in J. Kingston and M. Beckman (eds.), *Papers in Laboratory Phonology I* (Cambridge: Cambridge University Press), 72–106.

Smith, J. (1997), 'Noun faithfulness: On the Privileged Behavior of Nouns in Phonology', Rutgers Optimality Archive, http://ruccs.rutgers.edu/roa.html.

Smolensky, P. (1993), 'Harmony, Markedness, and Phonological Activity', Rutgers Optimality Archive, http://ruccs.rutgers.edu/roa.html.

Sproat, R. and Fujimura, O. (1993), 'Allophonic Variation in English /l/ and its Implications for Phonetic Implementation', *Journal of Phonetics*, 21: 291–311.

Stampe, D. (1980), *A Dissertation on Natural Phonology* (New York: Garland).

Stanners, R., Neiser, J., Hernon, W., and Hall, R. (1979), 'Memory Representation for Morphologically Related Words', *Journal of Verbal Learning and Verbal Behavior*, 18: 399–418.

Steele, S. (1986), 'Nuclear Accent f0 Peak Location: Effects of Rate, Vowel, and Number of Following Syllables', *Journal of the Acoustical Society of America*, 80, suppl. 1: S51.

Steriade, D. (1995), 'Neutralization and the Expression of Contrast', MS, University of California, Los Angeles.

Summerfield, Q. (1981), 'Articulatory Rate and Perceptual Constancy in Phonetic Perception', *Journal of Experimental Psychology: Human Perception and Performance*, 4: 621–37.

Trubetskoy, N. S. (1939), *Grundzüge der Phonologie (Travaux de Cercle Linguistique de Prague*, 7; Prague: Cercle Linguistique de Prague).

Wayland, S., Miller, J., and Volaitis, L. (1994), 'The Influence of Sentential Speaking Rate on the Internal Structure of Phonetic Categories', *Journal of the Acoustical Society of America*, 95: 2694–701.

Wightman, C., Shattuck-Hufnagel, S., Ostendorf, M., and Price, P. (1992), 'Segmental Durations in the Vicinity of Prosodic Phrase Boundaries', *Journal of the Acoustical Society of America*, 91: 1707–17.

Zsiga, E. (1995), 'An Acoustic and Electropalatographic Study of Lexical and Postlexical Palatalization in American English', in B. Connell and A. Arvaniti (eds.), *Papers in Laboratory Phonology IV* (Cambridge: Cambridge University Press), 282–302.

—— (1997), 'Features, Gestures, and Igbo Vowels: An Approach to the Phonology–Phonetics Interface', *Language*, 73: 227–74.

Zwicky, A. (1972), 'A Note on a Phonological Hierarchy in English', in R. Stockwell and R. Macaulay (eds.), *Linguistic Change and Generative Theory* (Bloomington, Ind.: Indiana University Press), 275–330.

11

Conceptual Foundations of Phonology as a Laboratory Science

JANET PIERREHUMBERT, MARY E. BECKMAN, AND D. R. LADD

1. INTRODUCTION

The term 'laboratory phonology' was invented more than a decade ago as the name of an interdisciplinary conference series, and all three of us have co-organized laboratory phonology conferences. Since then, the term has come into use not only for the conference series itself, but for the research activities exemplified by work presented there. In this chapter we give our own perspective on how research in laboratory phonology has shaped our understanding of phonological theory and of the relationship of phonological theory to empirical data.

Research activities within laboratory phonology involve the cooperation of people who may disagree about phonological theory, but who share a concern for strengthening the scientific foundations of phonology through improved method-ology, explicit modelling, and cumulation of results. These goals, we would argue, all reflect the belief that phonology is one of the natural sciences, and that all of language, including language-specific characteristics and sociolinguistic variation, is part of the natural world. In what follows, we explore the ramifications of this position for the relationship of data and methods to phonological theory; for the denotations of entities in that theory; and for our understanding of Universal Grammar (UG) and linguistic competence.

This chapter is a substantially reworked version of a position paper on laboratory phonology published in *Current Trends in Phonology I* (Durand & Laks 1996). For comments on previous drafts of this paper, we are grateful to Ann Bradlow, John Coleman, Jacques Durand, Jan Edwards, Stefan Frisch, Jen Hay, Patricia Keating, Chris Kennedy, John Kingston, and Moira Yip. Although none of them is likely to agree with everything we have said here, we have benefited greatly from their suggestions about both substance and exposition. We are particularly grateful to David Hull, for fruitful discussion of the philosophy of science, and to the readers of *Current Trends in Phonology I* and the audience at Current Trends in Phonology II, for their responses to the earlier version of this paper. Work on the paper was supported by NSF Grant No. BNS-9022484 to Northwestern University; and by an Ohio State University Distinguished Scholar award and NIH Grant No. 1 RO1 DC02932–01A2 to Mary Beckman. Part of D. R. Ladd's work on the chapter was carried out while a visiting scholar at the Max-Planck Institute for Psycholinguistics, Nijmegen.

2. WHO AND WHAT

The Conference in Laboratory Phonology series was launched at the Ohio State University in 1987 by Beckman and Kingston to provide a forum for people doing laboratory research in phonology. The proceedings of this meeting also inaugurated a book series from Cambridge University Press. Subsequent conferences were hosted by the University of Edinburgh, the University of California at Los Angeles, Oxford University, Northwestern University, and the University of York (UK), with the seventh conference to be held in 2000 at the University of Nijmegen. The conference has attracted people from very diverse intellectual backgrounds. American non-linear phonology has been well represented by scholars such as Clements, Hayes, Leben, McCarthy, Selkirk, Steriade, and Vogel; Articulatory Phonology by Browman, Fowler, Goldstein, and Zsiga; Declarative Phonology by Broe, Coleman, Local, and Scobbie, and Optimality Theory (OT) by Steriade and Gussenhoven. Many of the participants—such as Cutler, Kohler, Ladefoged, Marslen-Wilson, Munhall, Nolan, Shattuck-Hufnagel, Stevens, and Werker—are not associated with any particular school of phonological theory. About two-thirds of the participants are phonologists or phoneticians affiliated with linguistics departments. Most of the rest are affiliated with departments of psychology, electrical engineering and computer science, or communication sciences and disorders.

Despite the diverse backgrounds of the participants, a number of common goals and values have been reflected in the papers delivered at the conference. Papers have either reported experimental research on the mental representation of sound structure and its physical correlates, or else built on such research in a substantial way. The goal of such research is to address issues in phonology that are not effectively addressed using traditional types of data (namely, field transcriptions, informant judgements, and symbolic records of morphological alternations). The research presented at the meeting has drawn heavily on results and methodological advances in related sciences, including psychology, life sciences, and acoustics.

3. LINGUISTICS AND THE SCIENTIFIC STUDY OF LANGUAGE

Laboratory phonologists are scientists who use laboratory methods to discover and explain the sound structure of human language. Their philosophical stance is generally that of researchers in the mature sciences, such as biology and physics. Specifically, most laboratory phonologists have abandoned the doctrine of dualism. They view language as a phenomenon of nature, albeit a particularly complex one. Language as a cognitive system imputed to individuals is thus to be explained in terms of general facts about the physical world (such as the fact that the resonances of an acoustic tube are determined by its shape); in terms of specific capabilities of the human species that arose through evolution (including both gross anatomical properties, such as the position of the larynx, and neurophysi-ological properties); and in terms of the interactions of the organism with its environment during development. In this view, social interaction is subsumed under the same umbrella, as a phenomenon of nature. Human societies, like all other mammalian social groups, are natural collections of individuals. And social interactions form part of the natural environment for the species, which influence individual members through natural (physical) mechanisms, such as propagation of sound and light waves, physical contact, and pheromones.

On the basis of this viewpoint, we reject the traditional distinction between knowledge of natural phenomena and knowledge of social conventions (with social conventions differing from natural phenomena in being arbitrary).[1] We hold that social conventions *are* natural phenomena, so that there is no inconsistency in viewing language both as a social phenomenon and as a cognitive capability of the human species that is instantiated in individuals. Though social conventions vary considerably and surprisingly, so do the phenomena produced by many other physical systems, such as the weather. This does not mean that the variation is unbounded or that no relevant scientific laws can ever be formulated. Tools for building theories of such systems include statistics and stability theory, and we believe that these tools will play a significant role in our future theories of language.

Laboratory phonologists tend to believe that the scientific study of language both should and can progress. One reflection of this expectation is the long citation times for key works, such as Chiba and Kajiyama (1941) for perturbation analysis of vowel formants, and Fant (1960) for the linear acoustic theory of speech production. The idea that science progresses is very controversial in the philosophical literature. We would like to touch on this controversy because the relativists' position in it has been so influential amongst the leaders of generative linguistics. Much work by relativists, such as Kuhn (1962) and Feyerabend (1975), leaves the impression that shifts in scientific thinking are arbitrary outcomes of individual taste and power struggles within the scientific community. Espousal of Kuhnian thought has done much to glamorize conceptual upheavals within linguistics. Pullum (1991) acidly documents a climate in which authors of research

---

[1] The best-known type of arbitrariness in language is de Saussure's *l'arbitraire du signe*, or the apparently arbitrary association of lexemes (word sound patterns) with word meanings. *L'arbitraire du signe* bears some discussion in connection with the point we are making here. Clearly, the association of wordforms with word meanings is not determinate; different languages use extremely different lexemes for highly analogous concepts. Even onomatopoeic terms differ across languages. However, de Saussure was incorrect in assuming that any non-determinate relationship is arbitrary. In a stochastic system, non-determinacy still obeys laws, when the probability distributions of outcomes are examined. As online tools begin to make possible large-scale research into lexical structure, we expect that discoveries into the laws of lexeme-meaning associations will become available. For example, Willerman (1994) develops a model of why function words are disproportionately comprised of unmarked phonemes in many languages (cf. Swadesh 1971). In a similar vein, we would not be surprised to learn that basic-level categories are typically denoted by shorter words.

papers take no responsibility for either facts or theoretical claims presented in prior work. This situation often provokes indignation amongst phoneticians and psycholinguists, and can lead them to moralistic invocations of work by positivists, such as Carnap, who espouse the traditional ideal of progress in science. However, as Laudan (1996) points out, positivists tend to define progress so narrowly that even the most successful sciences fail to live up to their definitions. For example, the suggestion (by Putnam (1978) and others) that real science is strictly cumulative, with each new framework subsuming all of the successes of its predecessors, would leave humankind with no extant example of a real science, not even physics or chemistry. Naïve positivism is not a useful guide to productive scientific activity.

Our stance on this issue is a highly pragmatic one. Over its history, science has proved successful. A comparison between the state of scientific knowledge now and its state when it was closer to its beginnings (for example, at the time of Roger Bacon in the thirteenth century) reveals overall progress, in terms of the diversity of phenomena for which predictive theories exist, the detail and accuracy of the predictions, and the contributions of scientific knowledge to people's ability to thrive in their environment. Kuhn fails to explain the successes of science, by failing to explain how even two people—let alone humankind in general—can come to an agreement on matters such as the theory of electro-magnetism or the germ theory of disease. Recent work in the positivist tradition, such as Quine (1954/1966, 1960, 1961), also fails to account for the evident progress in science, through overemphasis on the logical underdetermination of scientific theories and the elusiveness of the ultimate truth. Therefore, we do not subscribe to either the relativist or the positivist position on science. We are more impressed by more recent work in philosophy of science, such as Hull (1988, 1989) and Laudan (1983, 1996), which treats science as an adaptive human activity. Both of these works reflect intimate familiarity with the everyday conduct of science, and seek to elucidate how scientists actually do cooperate to advance the state of human knowledge despite the logical and social impediments discussed by the relativists and the positivists.

Some of the hallmarks of successful scientific communities that Hull and Laudan discuss are particularly relevant to the laboratory phonology community. One is cooperation within a group of critical size and diversity. Like biological populations, scientific communities atrophy and ultimately fail if they are too small or too homogeneous. Achieving such critical size and diversity was a primary goal of the founders of the Laboratory Phonology conference series. A second hallmark of a successful community is maintenance of a common vocabulary—which can be used by opposing parties in an argument—even at the expense of gradual drift in both the meanings of technical terms and the empirical domain under discussion. As documented in Hull (1989), this was one of the chief reasons for the success of Darwinism over creationism. A third is the existence of 'auxiliary theories'—such as theories about how particular instruments work—which are also shared amongst people with different theories or research priorities. The laboratory phonology community has benefited from a plethora of auxiliary theories—covering matters from acoustic transmission to psychological distance, in areas from statistics and probability to physiology and neuroscience—which have permitted substantial agreement on the validity of experimental results and constructive debate about the relationship of these results to theory. Lastly, successful scientific communities recognize the value of mathematical formulation and use mathematics to make precise theoretical predictions. We develop this idea further in the next section.

4. FORMALISM AND MODELLING

Formalizing theories mathematically is a crucial step in making them predictive. The field of mathematics is generally divided into two major areas, discrete mathematics and continuous mathematics. Discrete mathematics includes logic and formal language theory. Continuous mathematics includes calculus. When generative linguistics was launched by Noam Chomsky and his mentor Zellig Harris, it relied exclusively on discrete mathematics. Chomsky is in fact responsible for important results in formal language theory, which are widely applied in computer science. Much of his early work makes natural language seem like computer languages, and poses for natural language the type of questions that arise in designing programming languages, compilers, and other discrete algorithms. The identification of formal linguistics with linguistics formalized by discrete mathematics persists to the present day.

We believe that the identification of formalism with discrete formalism is erroneous and is deeply misleading in its influence on research strategy. The laboratory phonology community uses both discrete mathematics and continuous mathematics. It continually debates and evaluates what type of formalism is most apt and incisive for what types of linguistic phenomena. One reason for this stance is the strong ties of the community to research in speech synthesis. About one-third of the authors of papers in the Laboratory Phonology books have worked on speech-synthesis systems, and many continue to be active in speech-synthesis research. The first speech synthesis was made possible by simultaneous breakthroughs in the acoustic theory of speech production and in the application of formal language theory to phonological description. The acoustic theory of speech production uses Laplace transforms (which belong to continuous mathematics) to model vocal tract transfer functions; Fant (1959) is noteworthy for its elegant discussion of how this particular tool supports deep understanding of the physical situation. The first comprehensive formalization of phonology—using discrete mathematics—is due to Chomsky and Halle (1968)—*The Sound Pattern of English (SPE)*—with key concepts already developed in Hockett (1953, 1954) and Chomsky (1964). These two ingredients—a well-behaved characterization of the speech signal and a comprehensive and mathematically coherent system for encoding the phonology—are prerequisites for any viable synthesis system.

Although the synthesis systems just sketched involve a discrete phonology and a continuous acoustic phonetics, subsequent and related work, which we review below, has substantially eroded this division of labour. The relevance of continuous mathematical tools for the classical question of phonology ('What is a possible language sound system?') is shown by work on phonetic grounding of phonology, by work on the role of statistical knowledge in adult phonological competence, and by work on the development of phonology in the child. There are thus both continuous and discrete aspects to the problems presented by language sound structure, even at the level of phonotactics and morphophonological alternations. We do not understand why most work in generative phonology declines to employ the tools of continuous mathematics.

It is widely recognized in the history and philosophy of science that formalization not only tests and consolidates theories; it also drives empirical exploration. Work on the articulatory and acoustic nature of phonological categories uses a methodology adopted from physics, in which the behaviour of the basic equations of the theory is explored with respect to issues such as stability, linearity, invertibility, and effects of boundary conditions. This exploration guides the selection of cases to be examined instrumentally. Cases in point include studies of the stability of vowel targets under natural and artificial perturbations (e.g. Lindblom, 1963; Lindblom *et al.* 1979; Maeda 1991; Edwards 1992); explorations of non-linearities in the articulatory-to-acoustics mapping (e.g. Keating 1984; Stevens 1989; Kingston 1990); and explorations of the invertibility of this mapping (e.g. Atal *et al.* 1978; Badin *et al.* 1995; Loevenbruck *et al.* 1999). The collected fruits of this research strategy have supported every one of the many Laboratory Phonology papers that interpret acoustic data or that use speech synthesis to create controlled stimuli.

There has been a similar give-and-take between formal models of the categorical aspects of sound structure, and empirical investigation. Almost all synthesis systems up through the 1980s used the phonological formalization of the *SPE* approach, because it was the only fully formalized model available. Its very exactness made it possible to identify the scientific penalties for ignoring non-local aspects of phonological representation. In the decade after it appeared, evidence about non-local dependencies was provided both by theoretical phonologists working on stress, tone, vowel harmony, and non-concatenative morphology (such as Goldsmith 1976; Liberman and Prince 1977; McCarthy 1985) and by experimentalists working on syllable structure, fundamental frequency, and duration (such as 't Hart and Cohen 1973; Klatt 1976; Bruce 1977; Fujimura and Lovins 1977; Bell and Hooper 1978; Harris 1978). This body of evidence in the end led to formal models of 'non-linear phonology'. Although the formalization of non-linear phonology by linguists was initially sketchy, limitations of the *SPE* approach for morphophonemic parsing and for synthesizing reflexes of prosodic structure and intonation drove efforts for more complete formalization. A formalization of non-linear intonational phonology, with related fundamental frequency synthesis algorithms, was published in Pierrehumbert and Beckman (1988). Additional work on formalizing non-linear phonology for purposes of segmental synthesis was carried out independently by Hertz (1990, 1991) and by Coleman and Local (Coleman 1992, 1994; Coleman and Local 1992). Other work on formalizing non-linear phonology includes Hoeksema (1985), Bird and Klein (1990), Kornai (1991), Scobbie (1999), Bird (1995), and Coleman (1998).

5. METHODS, FRAMEWORKS, AND ISSUES

The recent history of phonological theory has been marked by the invention of many frameworks, such as Lexical Phonology, Declarative Phonology, Government Phonology, and Optimality Theory. Frameworks are packages of assumptions about the fundamental nature of language, and the research strategy for empirical investigation is driven by top-down reasoning about the consequences of the framework. Frameworks correspond to paradigms in the Kuhnian view of science. One framework can replace another via a paradigm shift, if incorporating responses to successive empirical findings makes the prior framework so elaborate and arcane that a competitor becomes more widely attractive.

In contrast, laboratory phonology is not a framework. As we pointed out in Section 2, it is a coalition amongst groups of people, with some working in one or another of the various current frameworks, and others working in no phonological framework at all. As we mentioned in Section 3, the Kuhnian view of science is not prevalent among the members of the coalition as a whole, and our own view is that the Kuhnian attitude is at best an unhelpful guide to the conduct of laboratory work. Here we would like to develop some further consequences of this fact for the relationship among methodology, issues, and theories.

When a phonology student first embarks on experimental research, one of the most important lessons to assimilate is the need to operate both below and above the level of abstraction of a typical linguistic framework. On the one hand, the descriptive issues are extremely minute compared to those usually discussed by phonologists working in a particular framework. For example, a phonologist might begin with the observation that English, German, and Polish all exhibit a contrast between voiced and voiceless stops. In a laboratory experiment, the exact extent of the voicing, its statistical variation, and the dependence of these factors on structural position would all be at issue, as may be seen from the example of Keating (1984). An observation made in a few minutes in the field might suggest a hypothesis whose evaluation requires months of work in the laboratory.

On the other hand, almost any substantial fragment of a phonological framework turns out to be too specific and too rich in assumptions to be experimentally tested as such. For example, Feature Geometry packages together at least four assumptions that could in principle stand or fall separately (see

Clements 1985; McCarthy 1988). The articulatory characterization, rather than the acoustic or aerodynamic characterization, is implied to be primary. The inventory of relevant articulatory features and feature combinations is held to be finite and universal. The features are held to be organized into a tree (rather than a directed graph or a lattice). Subclassification and markedness are related to a single underlying mechanism. A single suite of laboratory experiments on features could not test all of these specific claims simultaneously. To develop a research programme in the general area of Feature Geometry, the laboratory researcher must instead identify and unbundle the framework's leading ideas.

Similarly, particular proposals about metrical or autosegmental theory, such as Goldsmith (1976), Liberman and Prince (1977), Selkirk (1984), Halle and Vergnaud (1987), and Hayes (1995), all package together many assumptions about the representation of phonological patterns and about the way that phonological representations interact in determining individual outcomes. No one has run experiments designed to test any of these frameworks; it would not be possible to do so. However, a comparison of these five frameworks brings out the fact that they make related, but not identical, claims about the kinds of non-local interactions that are available in natural languages. The interplay of local and non-local factors in speech production and perception is very much amenable to experimental investigation, as shown (for example) by Beckman, Edwards, and Fletcher (1992), Pierrehumbert and Talkin (1992), Choi (1995), and Smith (1995) for production; and Miller and Dexter (1988), Johnson (1990), Huffman (1991), and Ladd *et al.* (1994) for perception.

Given the rapid pace of change in theoretical linguistics, and the great expense and labour of laboratory research, the shrewd experimentalist will not devote an experiment to even the most central claim of any single linguistic framework. Instead, he or she will look for a topic that represents a source of tension across many frameworks, or that has remained unsolved by traditional methods over many decades.

One class of topics that lend themselves to advances using experimentation are *theoretical issues*. In using this term, we do not mean issues that arise as corollaries of the main assumptions of individual frameworks. Rather, we mean the issues that can be formulated after a deep and sustained effort to compare different frameworks. Issues at this level of abstraction that have been tackled using laboratory methods include: the interaction of local and non-local aspects of the cognitive representation of sound structure (e.g. Bruce, 1977, 1990; Kubozono 1992; Coleman 1994; also the references two paragraphs ago to the experimental investigation); the coherence and independence of putative levels of representation (e.g. Lindblom 1963; Harris 1978; Rialland 1994); the extent and objective consequences of underspecification (e.g. Pierrehumbert and Beckman 1988; Keating 1990a; Odden 1992; Choi 1995); the relation of qualitative and quantitative aspects of phonological competence (e.g. Keating 1984, 1990b; Pierrehumbert and

Beckman 1988). In fact, easily half of the papers in the Laboratory Phonology books have some connection to the issues just listed.

Methodological advances can be just as important as theoretical ones in the progress of science. Established sciences use diverse methods. As pointed out in Laudan (1983), people who disagree theoretically may still share methods. These shared methods are one reason why research paradigms in the established sciences are not as incommensurate as Kuhn claims, and they contribute to the cohesion of research communities that are diverse enough for long-term vitality. In addition, theories that unify results from many methods are more robust and more predictive, on the average, than those based on fewer methods, much as the five-prong chair base is more stable than the three-legged chair, which is in turn more stable than the one-legged chair. Overcoming the confining reliance of phonological research on the single method of internal reconstruction has been a high-priority goal for many laboratory phonologists. Research in this field uses an extreme diversity of methods, including: acoustic analysis of speech productions under various elicitation conditions in the field or the laboratory; judgements and reaction times obtained during identification, discrimination, or prototypicality ratings of natural or synthetic stimuli; direct measurements of articulator movements using electropalatography (EPG), X-ray microbeams, and other recently developed articulatory records; measurements of brain activity; statistical analysis of lexicons; longitudinal analysis of speech produced by children with speech disorders; novel word games; induction of speech errors; priming patterns in lexical decision and other psycholinguistic tasks; patterns of attention in babies.

Related to the idea of a method is the idea of an *auxiliary theory*. Auxiliary theories are established theories, whether broad or modest in scope, to which debate at the forefront of research can uncontroversially refer. Theories of how particular instruments work provide examples. Probably the single most important auxiliary theory in our field is the acoustic theory of speech production. This theory relates critical aspects of speech articulation to eigenvalues of the vocal tract, which can in turn be related to peaks in the spectrum. It is thanks to this theory that two researchers can compare the formant values of the vowels in their experiments, agreeing on observations such as 'The /i/ in Swedish is more peripheral in the vowel space than its closest counterpart in English'. Such agreement can in turn provide the basis for experimental work directed towards more abstract issues. For example, it provides the basis for current research on the role of general learning mechanisms in phonological acquisition (Kuhl et al. 1992; Guenther and Gjaja 1996; Lotto et al. 2000; Lacerda, forthcoming).

In connection with the goals of the present volume, we would like to point out that auxiliary theories help to provide denotations for phonological terms, along the lines suggested by Kripke (1972) and Putnam (1973) for scientific vocabulary in general. Putnam takes up the issue of the reference of scientific terms in common use, such as 'electricity' or 'vaccination'. As he points out, ordinary people do not in any deep sense understand the reference of these terms; however, the denotations are sufficiently established by access to experts who do have the requisite knowledge that they can also be everyday lay terms. In a similar sense, the denotation of the word 'vowel' is provided by the acoustic theory of speech production, and related work on vowel perception and the like. The denotation of the term 'articulatory gesture' is provided by the scientific community's present expertise in measuring articulatory events and relating them in a rigorously predictive way to their acoustic consequences. In so far as we know the denotation of the term 'syllable', it is provided by work such as Bell and Hooper (1978), Derwing (1992), and Treiman *et al.* (2000).

We would also like to adopt from the medical world the concept of a *syndrome*, defined (as in the *OED*) as 'a characteristic combination of opinions, behaviours, features, social factors'. In the history of the life sciences, discovery of a medical syndrome has repeatedly anticipated and shaped scientific theory by perspicuously uniting facts that point towards deeper conclusions. For example, the documentation of Broca's and Wernicke's aphasia syndromes led the way towards present neurolinguistic theory.

One of the major contributions of laboratory phonology to the field of phonology has been the careful documentation of syndromes in language sound structure. The diverse and opportunistic methodology of this community has permitted its documentation of syndromes to be both novel and thorough. One type of contribution is that a more accurate documentation of a previously reported syndrome can render moot a theoretical dispute by showing that the supposed facts driving the dispute are not true. For example, armchair impressions about the applicability of the English Rhythm Rule fuelled disputes in the various frameworks of metrical theory, such as Liberman and Prince (1977) and Hayes (1984). However, these impressions have been superseded by far more detailed instrumental studies, such as Shattuck-Hufnagel *et al.* (1994) and Grabe and Warren (1995). These studies both demonstrate that the Rhythm Rule applies in more contexts than reported in the previous phonological literature, and also suggest that the classic cases in English are as much a matter of accent placement as of stress or rhythm as such. This careful documentation of the syndrome at once vitiated Cooper and Eady's (1986) earlier scepticism and allowed laboratory phonologists to isolate those cases in which stress shift might be more purely a matter of rhythm (e.g. Harrington *et al.* 1998).

Documenting a new syndrome can raise new theoretical issues. For example, Pierrehumbert (1994*a*), Beckman and Edwards (2000), Frisch (2000), Treiman *et al.* (2000),) and Hay, Pierrehumbert, and Beckman (forthcoming), all document a syndrome relating lexical statistics, well-formedness judgements (which are opinions), and behaviours on various speech tasks. As discussed in Dell (2000), this syndrome reveals the limitations of an entire class of phonological frameworks, including all standard generative models.

A syndrome that has considerable theoretical importance at the present time is that of the semi-categorical process. Repeatedly, experiments have shown that facultative or phrase-level processes that are transcribed as categorical in the traditional literature actually require continuous mathematics if examined in detail. Browman and Goldstein (1990a) discuss examples in which putatively categorical fast speech rules are shown through X-ray microbeam studies to be cases of gradient gestural overlap. Both Silverman and Pierrehumbert (1990) and Beckman *et al.* (1992) show that lengthening and tonal realignment at prosodic boundaries are better handled by a quantitative description than by the phonological beat addition rules proposed in Selkirk (1984). Zsiga (1995) used electropalatagraphic data to show that the palatalization of /s/ in sequences such as *miss you* is not categorical, thereby contrasting with the categorical alternation found in pairs such as *confess, confession.* Silva (1992) and Jun (1994) use acoustic and electroglottographic data to evaluate a postlexical rule of lenis stop voicing proposed in Cho (1990). They show that apparent voicing at phrase-internal word edges is an artefact of the interaction of independent phonetic factors, which govern the precise timing of the laryngeal features in general.

One way of interpreting such results is as an indication that phonology proper covers less, and phonetic implementation covers more, than traditional approaches supposed. Papers from the first few Laboratory Phonology conferences suggest an implicit consensus in favour of this interpretation. More recently, however, many laboratory phonologists (including us) have begun to interpret these results differently. The steady encroachment of gradience into the traditional domain of phonology raises a number of more fundamental issues: how gradient processes are represented in the mind, how they relate to less gradient processes, whether any processes are truly categorical, and how categoriality—in so far as it exists—actually originates. We take up these issues in the next section.

6. CATEGORIALITY

Most, though not all, standard phonological frameworks presuppose a modular decomposition of phonology and phonetics in which one module (phonology) is categorical and free of gradient cumulative effects. Thus it is to be formalized using discrete mathematics. The other module (phonetics) has continuous variation, it exhibits gradient cumulative effects, and it is to be formalized using continuous mathematics. The two modules are related by a discrete-to-continuous mapping called the 'phonetic implementation rules'. Pierrehumbert and Beckman (1988) provide a very thorough development of this modular framework for the case of tone and intonation. Pierrehumbert (1994b), in a subsequent reassessment of her earlier stance, assigns it the acronym MESM (Modified Extended Standard Modularization).[2]

---

[2] The acronym MESM is an allusion to the syntactic framework of Revised Extended Standard Theory that Chomsky launched (Chomsky 1977) and subsequently abandoned in proposing first Government and Binding theory, and then Minimalism.

The MESMic approach is adopted, in different ways, in at least two chapters in the present volume (those by Myers and by Harris and Lindsey), as well as in Bromberger's earlier (1992) paper. Myers endorses MESM and seeks to develop its typological consequences. Bromberger (1992) takes the categorical entitles of phonology to be mental entities, and the continuous spatiotemporal events of phonetics to be in the world. Phonological entities thus denote classes of entities in the world, in the same way that words (such as 'dog') denote classes of physical objects in the world in the extensional treatments of semantics developed by philosophers such as Tarski and Quine. Other work developing the denotational relationship of phonology to phonetics includes Pierrehumbert (1990) and Coleman (1998). When embedded in this approach, phonetic implementation rules represent an explicit mathematical model of reference, within the limited domain of language sound structure, by encoding the expert scientific under-standing of the denotations of the elements of the description. Phonetic implementation rules can seem complicated and elaborate, and many speech researchers have held the hope that the right conceptual framework would render the mapping between phonology to phonetics direct and transparent. But this hope, we would argue, is not well founded. Although the relationship between a sound percept and a phonological category may seem very direct to an indi-vidual listener, it still presents to the scientist a dazzling degree of complexity and abstractness. It requires powerful mathematical tools to formalize this relationship.

To appreciate the problems with the assumption that it is possible to define a direct mapping that is somehow simpler or less abstract than phonetic implemen-tation, consider a layman's versus a scientist's understanding of the basic terms of colour perception. The percept of 'red' or 'green' may appear intuitively to be 'direct'. One might imagine that such colour terms correspond directly to particular light spectra. However, detailed experimental studies show that the correspondence is mediated by the exact frequency response of the cone cells in the retina, by the behaviour of the optical nerve in integrating responses from cone cells of different types, and by sophisticated higher-level cortical processing that evolved to permit constancy of colour percepts under varying conditions of illumination (Thompson *et al.* 1992). The colour terms of specific languages in turn involve a learned categorization of this perceptual space; just as with vowel inventories, this category system is neither arbitrary nor universal (Berlin and Kay 1991; Lucy 1996). A complete scientific model of the meanings of colour terms would need to describe the interaction of these factors. The intuitive 'directness' of our perceptions relates not to any particular simplicity in the scientific theory, but rather to the unconscious and automatic character of the neural processing involved.

The modularization of phonetics and phonology that was still assumed by most laboratory phonologists up through the early 1990s is no longer universally accepted, and we ourselves believe that the cutting edge of research has moved beyond it. A series of problems with MESM arises because the two types of representations it employs appear to be completely disparate. The approach thus fails to provide leverage on central problems of the theory, notably those relating to the *phonetic grounding* of phonology. It has been accepted since Jakobson, Fant, and Halle (1952) that phonological categories are phonetically grounded. However, every effort to detail this grounding comes up against an apparent paradox, arising from the fact that phonological categories are at once natural and language specific.

Phonological categories are natural in the sense that the actual phonetic denotation of each category shapes its patterning in the sound system. For example, as exhaustively documented by Steriade (1993) and Flemming (1995), neutralization of distinctive prenasalization or distinctive voicing typologically affects stops in unreleased positions, where bursts are not available as cues to the nasal contour or the voicing contrast. That is, the phonological rules that affect the stops (or, in a more modern formulation, the positional licensing constraints for the stops) reflect their actual phonetic character. Similarly, high vowels tend to participate in alternations with glides whereas low vowels do not. High vowels have a closer, or more consonant-like, articulation than low vowels and this phonetic property is what exposes them to being contextually interpreted as consonants.

The phonological categories are also natural in the sense that physical non-linearities—in both articulation and acoustics—have the result that phonetics is already quasi-categorical. These non-linearities appear to be exploited as the foundations of phonemic inventories. For specific proposals of this nature, see Stevens (1972, 1989), Browman and Goldstein (1990b), and Kingston and Diehl (1994).

But phonological categories are also language specific. Despite the similarities of the vocal apparatus across members of the species—and the ability of people of any genetic background to acquire any language—phoneme inventories are different in different languages. It is easy to think of languages that simultaneously display unusual phonemes while lacking certain typologically more typical phonemes. For example, Arabic displays an unusual series of pharyngeal consonants but lacks a /p/. More theoretically trenchant, however, is the fact that analogous phonemes can have different phonological characterizations in different languages. For example, the phoneme /h/ patterns with obstruents in some languages (such as Japanese, where it alternates with geminate /p/ and with /b/), but with sonorants in others. Some languages (such as Taiwanese) treat /l/ as a stop, whereas others (such as English) treat it as a continuant.

Experimental studies also show that there are no two languages in which the implementation of analogous phonemes is exactly the same. When examined in sufficient detail, even the most common and stereotypical phonetic processes are found to differ in their extent, in their timing, and in their segmental and prosodic conditioning.[3] For example, Bradlow (1995) shows that the precise location of Spanish vowels in the acoustic space is different from that for English vowels, even for typologically preferred point vowels. Laeufer (1992) shows that French and English differ in the extent of vowel lengthening before voiced stops (or vowel shortening before voiceless stops). Moreover, though the interaction of the effect with prosodic position is broadly similar for the two languages, there are also differences in detail relating to the allophonic treatment of syllable-final obstruents. Zsiga (forthcoming) demonstrates a difference between Russian and English in the extent of subcategorical palatal coarticulation across word boundaries. Caramazza and Yeni-Komshian (1974) demonstrate that Québecois and European French differ not only in the well-known assibilation of /d/ and /t/ before high vowels, but also in the modal VOT values of all voiced versus voiceless stops, including the dentals before non-high vowels. Hyman (forthcoming) discusses the strong tendency for a nasal to induce voicing of a following oral stop closure in nasal contour segments and in nasal-stop sequences (cf. Maddieson and Ladefoged 1993), but shows that, despite this tendency, some languages instead devoice stops after nasals.

Results such as these make it impossible to equate phonological inventories across languages; there is no known case of two corresponding phonemes in two languages having fully comparable denotations. Therefore phonological inventories exhibit only strong analogies. In fact, we would argue that there is no symbolic representation of sound structure whose elements can be equated across languages; the overwhelming body of experimental evidence argues against anything like Chomsky and Halle's (1968) phonological surface representation. In Chomsky and Halle (1968) and more recent work such as Chomsky (1993), Chomsky and Lasnik (1995), and Chomsky (1998), this representation (now known as 'PF' for 'Phonetic Form') is conceived of as symbolic, universal, and supporting a uniform interface to the sensorimotor system (Chomsky 1995: 21). Similar criticisms apply to the IPA if this is taken to be a technically valid level of representation in a scientific model (rather than the useful method of note-taking and indexing that it most assuredly is). The theoretical entities that can be absolutely equated across languages are the continuous dimensions of articulatory control and perceptual contrast. Languages differ in how they bundle and divide the space made available by these dimensions.

In view of such results, what is the character of the 'implicit knowledge' that the linguist imputes to the minds of individual speakers in order to explain their productive use of language? Obviously, anything that is language particular must be learned and thus represents implicit knowledge of some kind. Since languages

---

[3] Arguably, there are even no two idiolects in which the implementation of analogous phonemes is exactly the same. Here, however, we emphasize the systematic characteristics which are shared amongst members of a speech community, because these necessarily represent some kind of implicit knowledge that emerges during language acquisition. Idiolectal differences could result from idiosyncratic anatomical or neural properties.

can differ in arbitrarily fine phonetic detail, at least some of this knowledge is intrinsically quantitative. This should not come as a shock, since learned analogue representations are known to exist in any case in the area of motor control (e.g. Bullock & Grossberg, 1988; Saltzman and Munhall, 1989; Bailly *et al.* 1991). Although MESM asserts that the relationship of quantitative to qualitative knowledge is modular, this assertion is problematic because it forces us to draw the line somewhere between the two modules. Unfortunately, there is no place that the line can be cogently drawn. On the one hand, there is increasing evidence that redundant phonetic detail figures in the lexical representations of words and morphemes (see Fougeron and Steriade 1997, on French schwa; Bybee 2000, on word-specific lenition rates; Frisch 1996, on phonotactics). Thus phonology has a distinctly phonetic flavour. But, on the other hand, the detailed phonetic knowledge represents the result of learning, and therefore has a distinctly phonological flavour. Also non-linearities in the domains of articulation, acoustics, and aerodynamics mean that even the physical speech signal already has a certain categorical nature.

In short, knowledge of sound structure appears to be spread along a continuum. Fine-grained knowledge of continuous variation tends to lie at the phonetic end. Knowledge of lexical contrasts and alternations tend to be more granular. However, the sources of categoriality cannot be understood if these tendencies are simply assumed as axiomatic in the definitions of the encapsulated models, as in MESM. A more pragmatic scientific approach is to make the factors that promote categoriality a proper object of study in their own right, without abandoning the insight that lexical contrasts and morphological alternations are more granular than phonetics alone requires. One way to do this is to view the discrete (or quasi-discrete) aspects of phonology as embedded in a continuous description, arising from cognitive processes that establish preferred regions in the continuous space and that maximize the sharpness and distinctness of these regions. That is, instead of viewing the discreteness of phonology as simply *sui generis*, we view it as a mathematical limit under the varied forces that drive discretization. The complexity of phonological categories can then be appreciated as fully as we appreciate the complexity of colour perception.

Some specific factors contributing to discretization are already under active exploration. First, there is the idea that phonology prefers to exploit non-linearities in the physical system; the nature of the preference is, however, controversial. Stevens (1989) proposes that languages prefer vowels whose acoustics remain stable under small changes in articulation; Lindblom and his colleagues (Liljencrants and Lindblom 1972; Lindblom *et al.* 1983) hold, in contrast, that language prefer vowel systems for which minimal articulatory effort produces maximal contrasts. Similarly, Pisoni (1977) argues that the preference for voiceless stops effectively exploits psychoacoustic non-linearities that render the stop bursts both objectively distinctive and psychologically salient; Summerfield (1981) and others, by contrast, point to boundary shifts with place of articulation, as well as to the attested integration of the Voice Onset Timing (VOT) cue and the F1 cutback cue, as evidence for language-specific articulatory habits as the source of the discretization of the VOT continuum. (See Benkí 1998 for a recent review of these two opposing views, and Damper 1998 for new evidence on the role of psychoacoustic non-linearities.)

Second, the use of speech sounds to contrast meanings requires that the sounds be robustly discriminable. This factor does not define any single region of the phonetic space as preferred, but it tends to push apart preferred regions in relation to each other. Results related to this factor include the finding by Johnson, Flemming, and Wright (1993) that the 'best' vowels are more extreme than the most typical vowels, and a substantial body of work by Lindblom and colleagues on deriving vowel inventories from considerations of contrastiveness (see Lindblom (1992), for a summary review of successive refinements to the original 'dispersion' model over the last two decades).

Third, connectionist modelling demonstrates the generic tendency of neural networks to warp the parameter space that is being encoded. Guenther and Gjaja (1996) show that when a neural network is trained on steady state vowel tokens selected from Gaussian distributions centred on the average F1/F2 values for a language's distinct vowel categories, a language-specific warping of the F1/F2 space occurs in the perceptual map even with unsupervised learning—that is, even when the vowel categories are not provided as the output nodes in training and testing. Makashay and Johnson (1998) show that, when this sort of network is trained on a more natural distribution of tokens (that is, steady state vowels that reflect normal inter-gender variability), there is less clear convergence to vowel 'prototypes'; however, distinct vowel categories re-emerge if F0 is included in the parameters of the space, to allow the model (in effect) to correlate inter-token variability with speaker identity. Damper and Harnad (forthcoming) show related results for neural network modelling of VOT categories. They demonstrate that the sharp S-shaped boundary that is a hallmark of classical 'categorical perception' is exhibited by a broad class of connectionist models, when the model is trained on tokens that cluster around the endpoints of the continuum. However, as Damper 1998 shows, the input to the model must be spectra that have been passed through an auditory front-end in order for the boundary to shift with place instead of falling at the centre of the continuum (as predicted for perceptual learning in general by Macmillan *et al.* 1987).

Last, we may consider issues of cognitive complexity. Lexical contrasts and morphological alternations involve knowledge not of sounds alone, but of the relationship between sounds and meanings in the lexicon. As discussed in Werker and Stager (2000), children begin to master the association between word form and lemma at about 14 months by manipulating extremely coarse-grained phonetic contrasts. This is so despite their exquisite sensitivity to speech sounds as such, and despite a pattern of response to fine phonetic detail that is already language specific at 11 months, as demonstrated by Werker and Tees (1994), among others. Given the amount of neural circuitry that must be established to encode the relationships between word forms and word meanings, there may be limits on the ultimate extent of phonological differentiation possible. (See Beckman and Pierrehumbert, forthcoming, for further development of these ideas.)

7. COMPETENCE AND PERFORMANCE

In the previous section, we developed a picture of implicit knowledge of sound structure that marks a significant departure from the most phonetically sophisticated generative model—namely, MESM. This picture has important consequences for the understanding of linguistic competence and the competence/ performance distinction. The following quote from Chomsky (1995: 14) may serve to introduce our discussion of this issue:

We distinguish between Jones's competence (knowledge and understanding) and his performance (what he does with the knowledge and understanding). The steady state constitutes Jones's mature linguistic competence.

A salient property of the steady state is that it permits infinite use of finite means, to borrow Wilhelm von Humboldt's aphorism. A particular choice of finite means is a particular language, taking a language to be a way to speak and understand, in a traditional formulation. Jones's competence is constituted by the particular system of finite means he has acquired.

We find much to agree with in this quotation. Language does put finite means to infinite use. To explain the diverse and productive linguistic behaviour that people exhibit, we impute abstract, implicit, and synoptic knowledge of language to individuals. The ability to acquire and apply such knowledge is a hallmark of the human species. However, the concept of linguistic competence carries with it in the generative literature a number of further axiomatic assumptions to which we take strong exception.

One assumption concerns the relationship of the various types of data gathered by linguists to theories of linguistic competence. Much of the generative literature assumes that well-formedness judgements provide the most direct and revealing data about competence, with other types of data presenting difficulties of interpretation that compromise their relevance. This assumption is articulated particularly clearly in an essay by Soames (1984), who undertakes to define linguistics proper in an a priori fashion on the basis of the data it deals with. However, studies in the sociolinguistics and psycholinguistics literature (e.g. Labov 1973; Bard *et al.* 1996) cast serious doubt on the reliability and predictiveness of well-formedness judgements. Well-formedness judgements are opinions. They are high-level meta linguistic performances that are highly malleable. They do not represent any kind of direct tap into competence, but are rather prone to many types of artefacts, such as social expectations, experimenter bias, response bias, and undersampling. Hence, well-formedness judgements are just one type of evidence among many, and not a particularly good type of evidence as currently used (see the constructive criticisms of Bard *et al.* 1996).

All data about language come from performance, and all present difficulties of interpretation relating to the nature and context of the performance. Like scientists in other fields, we must assess the weight to assign to various types of data; statistics provide one tool for making such an assessment. But no matter how we weight the data, we must acknowledge that all data ultimately originate in performance. The notion that some data represent 'mere performance' does not in itself constitute sufficient grounds for discarding data.

A second assumption involves universals. Discussion in Chomsky (1995) articulates his conception of linguistic competence in terms of a UG: UG provides an overarching description of what all mature human languages have in common; simultaneously, it is claimed to describe the initial state of the child who embarks on language acquisition. This dual characterization of UG forces the view that language acquisition is a process of logical instantiation. UG provides logical schemata that describe all languages, and the child, armed with the schemata, instantiates the variables they contain so as to achieve a grammar of a particular language.

This understanding of UG is not logically necessary, nor is it supported by the available results on acquisition of phonology. At its root is the assumption that, to achieve a formal model of language, the model must be formalized using the resources of logic. However, it is clear that phonetics must be formalized using continuous mathematics, and the experimental literature on phonological development makes it clear also that phonological knowledge depends in an inextricable fashion on phonetic skills, including the gradual acquisition of spatial and temporal resolution and coordination (see e.g. Elbers and Wijnen 1992; Locke and Pearson 1992; Edwards *et al.* 1999). As speakers acquire more practice with a category, the variance in their productions of the category gradually reduces, and this process continues well into late childhood (Lee *et al.* 1999). When children are first acquiring a phonological contrast, they often fail to reproduce an adult-like phonetic expression of the contrast. For example, Finnish children often produce disproportionately long geminate consonants. When children are acquiring the American English or Taiwanese Chinese contrast between aspirated and unaspirated initial stops, the VOT values for the aspirated stops contrast may be exaggerated, or they may be so small as to appear to fall into the unaspirated category (Macken and Barton 1980; Pan 1994). Similarly, an adult-like control of the spectrum of /s/ that differentiates it robustly from both /θ/ and /ʃ/ in English may not be achieved until 5 years of age, or even later in children with phonological disorder (Baum and McNutt 1990; Nittrouer 1995). As discussed in Scobbie *et al.* (2000), the trajectory from insufficient (or 'covert') phonetic contrasts to robust mature contrasts is a gradual one. Hence it cannot be modelled as a process of logical instantiation, but only using statistics over a continuous space.

Additional patterns in acquisition that demand a statistical treatment are provided by investigations of babbling and early word productions, as well as by patterns of perceived substitution in children with and without phonological disorder. For example, vowel qualities in the earliest stages of variegated babbling show the impact of the frequencies of different vowels in the vowel space of the ambient adult language (de Boysson-Bardies *et al.* 1989). Consonants in later stages of variegated babbling that are concurrent with the acquisition of the first twenty-five words in production reflect cross-language differences in the relative frequencies of different places and manners of articulation (de Boysson-Bardies and Vihman 1991). Also, coronals are more frequent than either labials or dorsals in both English and Swedish, and children acquiring these languages already show language-specific differences in the fine acoustic details of coronal stops by the age of 30 months (Stoel-Gammon *et al.* 1994). This is so even though they may not yet have learned robustly to differentiate the spectra for dorsal place from coronal place of contact, making /t/ for /k/ one of the most commonly perceived substitutions in English-acquiring children (Edwards *et al.* 1997). Finally, although infants at the reduplicated babbling stages universally produce multisyllabic productions with simple CV alternations, children acquiring English (but not those acquiring French) show a marked increase in monosyllabic babbles, and in babbling productions ending with consonants, beginning at the first word stages (Vihman 1993). This difference reflects the predominant shapes of the most frequent words in the two languages.

In connection with these observations, we would reiterate our opposition to dualism. A mature language is instantiated in individual brains. The physical state of these brains represents an equilibrium state that is reached from an initial condition—the human genetic endowment—through interactions with the physical environment. For physical systems in general, it is a conceptual error to equate the initial conditions with generalizations over the equilibrium states that may evolve from these conditions. For example, the current state of our solar system (with nine planets moving nearly on the same plane on elliptical orbits around the sun) is an equilibrium state. In so far as this solar system is typical—with its sun, its small number of discrete planets, and its orbital plane—one might imagine a kind of 'meta-grammar' of equilibrium states of the form:

(1) Solar system → Sun, planet+

With a binding condition for orbital planes:

(2) For all i, Plane(planet[i] = Plane(planet[i+1])

However, the initial condition for our solar system was an unformed cloud of debris containing a mixture of heavy elements from a previous supernova explosion. Neither (1) and (2) nor any discrete abstraction of them sensibly describes an unformed cloud of debris; nor is the current state sensibly viewed as the logical instantiation of the parameters of such a cloud. Describing how the planets arose from the debris requires gravitational field theory. That is, the discreteness of our own solar system does not arise from logical instantiation of the discrete elements of a metagrammar. Instead, it arises as the discrete limit of continuous processes, much as we have shown for the case of phonological acquisition.

A third objection to Chomsky's conception of competence is its continued reliance on the assumption of an idealized uniform speaker-hearer community. According to Chomsky, this idealization is justified by the obvious absurdity of imagining that language acquisition would proceed better in a varied speech community than in a uniform community. However, there is much evidence that uniformity impedes the process of language acquisition, and that variability facilitates it, yielding exactly the result that Chomsky believes to be absurd. This evidence comes from several areas of research. Experiments on second-language learning show that learners who are exposed to varied examples of a phonemic category learn the category better than those who are exposed repeatedly to the same example (Logan *et al.* 1991). The variation in examples permits the learners to generalize to new cases and to transfer perceptual learning to production (Bradlow *et al.* 1997). Research on first-language acquisition of affixal categories similarly points to the role of variability in the morphological context—for example, of exposure to a sufficient number of different roots before the affix can be abstracted away as a productive independent morpheme. Thus, for the English past tense affix, Marchman and Bates (1994) show that (contra the model and claims of Pinker and Prince 1988), the single best predictor of when over-regularized past tense forms begin to appear is the number of different verbs that the child has acquired. That is, acquiring a large variety of regular past tense verb forms permits the child to project the principles of regular past tense formation, overpowering the high token frequency of some irregular verbs. Derwing and Baker (1980) similarly show that the syllabic plural allomorph is acquired later than the two consonantal allomorphs, in keeping with its lower type frequency.

Such results gain an intuitive interpretation when one reflects that *variability causes the need for abstraction*. The entire point of an abstraction such as the morpheme *-ed* or the phoneme /i/ is that it represents the same thing across differences in the root to which it is affixed or in the speaker's larynx size and vocal tract length, the speech style and effort of articulation, the segmental and prosodic context, and other kinds of systematic token-to-token variability. If these sources of variability did not exist, then lexical items could be encoded directly in terms of invariant phonetic templates. Abstractions are cognitively expensive. They are learned because variability makes them necessary. There is no reason why they should be learned in the absence of variability.

Laboratory phonologists share with other phonologists the aim of developing an explanatory theory of language. Overall, the issue is where the deep structural regularities of language come from. Work in the Chomskian tradition has emphasized the possibility that humans have a genetically innate predisposition to language, which is manifested through logical instantiation of the universal schemata of UG. However, there are also a number of other potential sources of deep, abstract, and universal characteristics of language. These include necessary or optimal properties of communication systems as such (as explored by Wiener (1948), in his work on cybernetics; also much subsequent work in information theory); objective consequences of the characteristics of the human vocal and auditory apparatus; and general cognitive factors (such as general facts about categorization, memory, and temporal processing). For the laboratory phonology community as a whole the interplay amongst these various possible factors is treated as an open question.

APPENDIX

The fundamental similarity between the PF representation of current Minimalist theory and the surface phonological representation of Chomsky and Halle (1968) can be deduced from a quotation such as the following:

> Let us recall again the minimalist assumptions that I am conjecturing can be upheld: all conditions are interface conditions; and a linguistic expression is the optimal realization of such interface conditions. Let us consider these notions more closely.
>
> Consider a representation π at PF. PF [*sic*] is a representation in universal phonetics, with no indication of syntactic elements or relations among them ... To be interpreted by the performance systems A[rticulatory]-P[erceptual], π must be constituted entirely of *legitimate PF objects*, that is elements that have a uniform language-independent interpretation at the interface [to the articulatory-perceptual system] ...
>
> To make ideas concrete, we must spell out explicitly what are the legitimate objects at PF and LF. At PF, this is the standard problem of universal phonetics ...   (Chomsky 1993: 26–7; emphasis in original)

This characterization of PF involves objects that are categorical and that support a universal phonetic interpretation. These assumptions are critical to some work in the Minimalist framework, such as Halle and Marantz's (1993) theory of Distributed Morphology (DM). DM claims that the PF level is the result of instantiating the lexical items in the morphological representation with phonological segments and features that can be manipulated by categorical rules and constraints. Thus, it presupposes the modular division between a language-specific categorical component and a universal quantitative phonetics that is clearly non-viable.

It is possible, however, to read much of the Minimalist literature in a different light—as an abdication of Chomsky and Halle's original claim that sound structure as such has a 'grammar', in the sense of an abstract computational system that is capable of generating novel forms. As Jackendoff (1997: 15) points out, in the Minimalist Program 'the fundamental generative component of the computational system is the syntactic component; the phonological and semantic components are "interpretive" ' (see also the discussion in Burton-Roberts, this volume). One almost might interpret this research programme as acknowledgement in advance by its proponents of some of the problems we raise regarding efforts to explain implicit knowledge of sound structure in terms of a categorical phonological module. At the same time, the Minimalist Program appears to make no pretence that its key concepts (such as grammaticality, UG, or linguistic competence) in any way pertain to language sound structure, and we are possibly being unfair in attacking these concepts as if they were claimed to pertain. However, this interpretation strikes us as regrettable, for many reasons.

First, it leads one to disregard the ways in which phonology and phonetics are grammar-like, enabling the speaker to create morphological neologisms, to make additions to the lexicon, and to produce regular allophonic patterns when saying novel phrases and sentences. To the extent that there are abstract parallels in sound structure across languages, these suggest the kind of deep universals that are the traditional target of linguistic theory. Even if these quasi-grammatical properties of phonology are embedded in an understanding of the physical world and of general cognitive capabilities, they are still scientifically important and tell us something about the human capacity for language.

Second, it leads one to disregard the ways in which morphological and syntactic relationships are echoed in quantitative effects in the phonetics (e.g. Sereno and Jongman 1995; Fougeron and Steriade 1997; Hay *et al.*, forthcoming), which surely are the reflexes of the fact that phonetic knowledge is intertwined with the linguistic system rather than being decoupled from it.

Third, the interpretation undermines the effort to find parallels between phonology and syntax in the way that they relate to physical events in the world and to the language user's conceptualization of these events. It may turn out that, thanks to its restricted physical domain and advanced instrumentation, phonology is simply in the lead in an enterprise in which syntax will eventually catch up. If the relationship of syntax to this 'world understanding' is eventually proven to resemble that of phonology (as we have described it here), then the Minimalist Program will have been carried through to its logical—truly 'minimalist'—conclusion.

REFERENCES

Atal, B. S., Chang, J. J., Mathews, M. V., and Tukey, J. W. (1978), 'Inversion of Articulatory-to-Acoustic Transformations in the Vocal Tract by a Computer-Sorting Technique', *Journal of the Acoustical Society of America*, 64: 1535–55.
Badin, P., Beautemps, D., Laboissière, R., and Schwartz, J.-L. (1995), 'Recovery of Vocal

Tract Geometry from Formants for Vowels and Fricative Consonants Using a Midsagittal-to-Area Function Conversion Model', *Journal of Phonetics*, 23: 221–9.

Bailly, G., Laboissière, R., and Schwartz, J.-L. (1991), 'Formant Trajectories as Audible Gestures: An Alternative for Speech Synthesis', *Journal of Phonetics*, 19: 9–23.

Bard, E., Robertson, D., and Sorace, A. (1996), 'Magnitude Estimation of Linguistic Acceptability', *Language*, 72: 32–68.

Baum, S. R. and McNutt, J. C. (1990), 'An Acoustic Analysis of Frontal Misarticulation of /s/ in Children', *Journal of Phonetics*, 18: 51–63.

Beckman, M. E. and Edwards, J. (2000), 'Lexical Frequency Effects on Young Children's Imitative Productions', in M. Broe and J. Pierrehumbert (eds.), *Papers in Laboratory Phonology V* (Cambridge: Cambridge University Press), 208–17.

—— and Pierrehumbert, J. B. (forthcoming), 'Interpreting "Phonetic Interpretation" over the Lexicon', in J. Local, R. Ogden, and R. Temple (eds.), *Papers in Laboratory Phonology VI* (Cambridge: Cambridge University Press).

—— Edwards, J., and Fletcher, J. (1992), 'Prosodic Structure and Tempo in a Sonority Model of Articulatory Dynamics', in G. Docherty and D. R. Ladd (eds.), *Papers in Laboratory Phonology II* (Cambridge: Cambridge University Press), 68–86.

Bell, A. and Hooper, J. (1978), (eds.) *Syllables and Segments* (Amsterdam: North-Holland).

Benkí, J. (1998), 'Evidence For Phonological Categories from Speech Perception', Ph.D. dissertation (University of Massachusetts, Amherst).

Berlin, B. and Kay, P. (1991), 'Basic Color Terms: Their Universality and Evolution' (Berkeley and Los Angeles: University of California Press).

Bird, S. (1995), 'Computational Phonology: a Constraint-Based Approach' (Cambridge: Cambridge University Press).

—— and Klein, E. (1990), 'Phonological Events', *Journal of Linguistics*, 26: 33–56.

Boysson-Bardies, B. de and Vihman, M. M. (1991), 'Adaptation to Language: Evidence from Babbling and First Words in Four Languages', *Language*, 67: 297–319.

—— Hallé, P., Sagart, L., and Durand, C. (1989), 'A Cross-linguistic Investigation of Vowel Formants in Babbling', *Journal of Child Language*, 16: 1–17.

Bradlow, A. (1995), 'A Comparative Acoustic Study of English and Spanish Vowels', *Journal of the Acoustical Society of America*, 97: 1916–24.

—— Pisoni, D., Akahane-Yamada, R., and Tohkura, Y. (1997), 'Training Japanese Listeners To Identify English /r/ and /l/: IV. Some Effects of Perceptual Learning on Speech Production', *Journal of the Acoustical Society of America*, 101: 2299–310.

Bromberger, S. and Halle, M. (1992), 'Types and Tokens in Linguistics', in S. Bromberger (ed.), 'On What We Know We Don't Know' (Chicago: University of Chicago Press, CSLI Publications), 170–208.

—— —— (this volume), 'The Ontology of Phonology (Revised)'.

Browman, C. P. and Goldstein, L. (1990a), 'Tiers in Articulatory Phonology, with Some Implications for Casual Speech', in J. Kingston and M. Beckman (eds.), *Papers in Laboratory Phonology I* (Cambridge: Cambridge University Press), 341–76.

—— —— (1990b), 'Representation and Reality: Physical Systems and Phonological Structure', *Journal of Phonetics*, 18: 411–24.

Bruce, G. (1977), *Swedish Word Accents in Sentence Perspective* (Lund: Gleerup).

—— (1990), 'Alignment and Composition of Tonal Accents', in J. Kingston and M. Beckman (eds.), *Papers in Laboratory Phonology I* (Cambridge: Cambridge University Press), 107–15.

Bullock, D. and Grossberg, S. (1988), 'Neural Dynamics of Planned Arm Movements: Emergent Invariants and Speed-Accuracy Properties During Trajectory Formation', *Psychological Review*, 95: 49–90.

Burton-Roberts, N. (this volume), 'Where and What is Phonology? A Representational Perspective'.

Bybee, J. (2000), 'The Phonology of the Lexicon: Evidence from Lexical Diffusion', in M. Barlow and S. Kemmer (eds.), *Proceedings of the Rice Symposium on Usage-Based Models of Language* (Stanford, Calif.: CSLI Publications).

Caramazza, A. and Yeni-Komshian, G. H. (1974), 'Voice Onset Time in Two French Dialects', *Journal of Phonetics*, 2: 239–45.

Chiba, T. and Kajiyama, M. (1941), *The Vowel, its Nature and Structure* (Tokyo: Kaisekian).

Cho, Y. Y. (1990), 'Syntax and Phrasing in Korean', in S. Inkelas and D. Zec (eds.), *The Phonology-Syntax Connection* (Chicago: University of Chicago Press), 47–62.

Choi, J. D. (1995), 'An Acoustic-Phonetic Underspecification Account of Marshallese Vowel Allophony', *Journal of Phonetics*, 23: 323–47.

Chomsky, N. (1964), *The Logical Structure of Linguistic Theory* (The Hague: Mouton).

—— (1977), 'On Wh-Movement', in A. Akmajian, T. Wasow, and P. Culicover (eds.), *Formal Syntax* (Cambridge, Mass.: MIT Press), 71–133.

—— (1993), 'A Minimalist Program for Linguistic Theory', in K. Hale and S. J. Keyser (eds.), *The View from Building 20: Essays in Linguistics in Honor of Sylvain Bromberger* (Cambridge, Mass.: MIT Press), 1–52.

—— (1995), *The Minimalist Program* (Cambridge, Mass.: MIT Press).

—— (1998), 'Minimalist Inquiries: The Framework', MS, Massachusetts Institute of Technology.

—— and Halle, M. (1968), *The Sound Pattern of English* (New York: Harper & Row).

—— and Lasnik, H. (1995), 'The Theory of Principles and Parameters', in N. Chomsky (ed.), *The Minimalist Program* (Cambridge, Mass.: MIT Press), 13–128.

Clements, G. N. (1985). 'The Geometry of Phonological Features', *Phonology Yearbook*, 2: 225–52.

Coleman, J. S. (1992), 'YorkTalk: "Synthesis-by-Rule" without Segments or Rewrite Rules', in G. Bailly, C. Benoit, and T. R. Sawallis (eds.), *Talking Machines: Theories, Models, and Designs* (Amsterdam: Elsevier), 211–24.

—— (1994), 'Polysyllabic Words in the YorkTalk Synthesis System', in P. A. Keating (ed.), *Papers in Laboratory Phonology III* (Cambridge: Cambridge University Press), 293–324.

—— (1998), *Phonological Representations—their Names, Forms, and Powers* (Cambridge: Cambridge University Press).

—— and Local, J. K. (1992), 'Monostratal Phonology and Speech Synthesis', in P. Tench (ed.), *Studies in Systemic Phonology* (London: Pinter Publishers), 183–93.

Cooper, W. E. and Eady, S. J. (1986), 'Metrical Phonology in Speech Production', *Journal of Memory and Language*, 25: 369–84.

Damper, R. I. (1998). 'The Role of the Auditory Periphery in the Categorization of Stop Consonants', in *Proceedings of the Joint Meeting of the International Conference Acoustics and the Acoustical Society of America*, 1973–4.

—— and Harnad, S. R. (forthcoming), 'Neural Network Models of Categorical Perception', *Perception and Psychophysics*.

Dell, G. (2000), 'Counting, Connectionism and Lexical Representation', in M. Broe and J. Pierrehumbert (eds.), *Papers in Laboratory Phonology V* (Cambridge: Cambridge University Press), 334–47.

Derwing, B. L. (1992), 'A "Pause-Break" Task for Eliciting Syllable Boundary Judgments from Literate and Illiterate Speakers: Preliminary Results from Five Diverse Languages', *Language and Speech*, 35: 219–35.

—— Baker, W. J. (1980), 'Rule Learning and the English Inflections (with Special Emphasis on the Plural)', in G. D. Prideaux, B. L. Derwing, and W. J. Baker (eds.), *Experimental Linguistics: Integration of Theories and Applications* (Ghent: E. Story-Scientia), 248–72.

Durand, J. and Laks, B. (1996) (eds.), *Current Trends in Phonology: Models and Methods* (Salford: University of Salford Publications).

Edwards, J. (1992), 'Compensatory Speech Motor Abilities in Normal and Phonologically Disordered Children', *Journal of Phonetics*, 20: 189–207.

—— Gibbon, F., and Fourakis, M. (1997), 'On Discrete Changes in the Acquisition of the Alveolar/Velar Stop Consonant Contrast', *Language and Speech*, 40: 203–10.

—— Fourakis, M., Beckman, M. E., and Fox, R. A. (1999), 'Characterizing Knowledge Deficits in Phonological Disorders', *Journal of Speech, Language, and Hearing Research*, 42: 169–86.

Elbers, L. and Wijnen, F. (1992), 'Effort, Production Skill, and Language Learning', in C. A. Ferguson, L. Menn, and C. Stoel-Gammon (eds.), *Phonological Development: Models, Research, Implications* (Timonium, Md.: York Press), 337–68.

Fant, G. (1959), 'Acoustic Analysis and Synthesis of Speech with Applications to Swedish', Ericsson Technics Report, No. 1.

—— (1960), *The Acoustic Theory of Speech Production* (The Hague: Mouton).

Feyerabend, P. (1975), *Against Method* (Medawah, NJ: Humanities Press).

Flemming, E. S. (1995), 'Auditory Representation in Phonetics', Ph.D. dissertation (University of California, Los Angeles).

Fougeron, C. and Steriade, D. (1997), 'Does Deletion of French Schwa Lead to Neutralization of Lexical Distinctions?', *Proceedings of the 5th European Conference on Speech Communication and Technology* (University of Patras), vi. 943–6.

Frisch, S. (1996), *Similarity and Frequency in Phonology*, Ph.D. dissertation (Northwestern University).

—— (2000), 'Temporally Organized Lexical Representations as Phonological Units', in M. Broe and J. Pierrehumbert (eds.), *Papers in Laboratory Phonology V* (Cambridge: Cambridge University Press), 283–9.

Fujimura, O. and Lovins, J. (1977), 'Syllables as Concatenative Phonetic Units' (Bloomington, Ind.: Indiana University Linguistics Club).

Goldsmith, J. A. (1976), 'Autosegmental Phonology', doctoral dissertation, MIT, Cambridge, Mass. (Published, New York, Garland Publishing, 1979).

Grabe, E. and Warren, P. (1995), 'Stress Shift: Do Speakers Do It or Do Listeners Hear It?', in B. Connell and A. Arvaniti (eds.), *Papers in Laboratory Phonology IV* (Cambridge: Cambridge University Press), 95–110.

Guenther, F. H. and Gjaja, M. N. (1996), 'The Perceptual Magnet Effect as an Emergent Property of Neural Map Formation', *Journal of the Acoustical Society of America*, 100: 1111–21.

Halle, M. and Marantz, A. (1993), 'Distributed Morphology and the Pieces of Inflection', in K. Hale and S. J. Keyser (eds.), *The View from Building 20: Essays in Linguistics in Honor of Sylvain Bromberger* (Cambridge, Mass.: MIT Press), 111–76.

—— and Vergnaud, J. R. (1987), *An Essay on Stress* (Cambridge, Mass.: MIT Press).

Harrington, J., Beckman, M. E., Fletcher, J., and Palethorpe, S. (1998), 'An Electropalatographic, Kinematic, and Acoustic Analysis of Supralaryngeal Correlates of Word and Utterance-Level Prominence Contrasts in English', in *Proceedings of the 5th International Conference on Spoken Language Processing Sydney, Australia, December 1998* (Australian Speech Science and Technology Association Inc.), 1851–4.

Harris, J. and Lindsey, G. (this volume), 'Vowel Patterns in Mind and Sound'.

Harris, K. (1978), 'Vowel Duration Change and its Underlying Physiological Mechanisms', *Language and Speech*, 21: 354–61.

Hay, J., Pierrehumbert, J., and Beckman, M. (forthcoming), 'Speech Perception, Well-Formedness and Lexical Frequency', in J. Local, R. Ogden, and R. Temple, (eds.), *Papers in Laboratory Phonology VI* (Cambridge: Cambridge University Press).

Hayes, B. (1984), 'The Phonology of Rhythm in English', *Linguistic Inquiry*, 17: 467–99.

—— (1995), *Metrical Stress Theory* Chicago: University of Chicago Press).

Hertz, S. (1990), 'The Delta Programming Language: An Integrated Approach To Nonlinear Phonology, Phonetics, and Speech Synthesis', in J. Kingston and M. Beckman (eds.), *Papers in Laboratory Phonology I* (Cambridge: Cambridge University Press), 215–57.

—— (1991), 'Streams, Phones and Transitions: Toward a New Phonological and Phonetic Model of Formant Timing', *Journal of Phonetics*, 19: 91–109.

Hockett, C. F. (1953), review of *The Mathematical Theory of Communication*, Claude L. Shannon and Warren Weaver, *Language*, 29: 69–93.

—— (1954), 'Two Models of Grammatical Description', *Word*, 10: 210–34.

Hoeksema, J. (1985), 'Formal Properties of Stress Representations', in H. van der Hulst and N. Smith (eds.), *Advances in Nonlinear Phonology* (Dordrecht: Foris), 83–99.

Huffman, M. (1991), 'Time-Varying Properties of Contextually Nasalized Vowels: Acoustics and Perception', in Congress Committee and Organizing Committee (eds.), *Proceedings of the XIIth International Congress of Phonetic Sciences* (Aix-en-Provence: Université de Provence Aix-Marseille), 130–3.

Hull, D. L. (1988) (ed.), *Science as a Process* (Chicago: University of Chicago Press).

—— (1989), *The Metaphysics of Evolution* (Albany, NY: State University of New York Press).

Hyman, L. M. (forthcoming), 'The Limits of Phonetic Determinism in Phonology: *NC Revisited', in E. Hume and K. Johnson (eds.), *The Role of Speech Perception in Phonology* (New York: Academic Press).

Jackendoff, R. (1997), *The Architecture of the Language Faculty* (Cambridge, Mass.: MIT Press).

Jakobson, R., Fant, G., and Halle, M. (1952), *Preliminaries to Speech Analysis. The Distinctive Features and their Correlates* (Acoustics Laboratory of the MIT, Technology Report 13; Cambridge, Mass.: MIT Press).

Johnson, K. (1990), 'The Role of Perceived Speaker Identity in F0 Normalization of Vowels', *Journal of the Acoustical Society of America*, 88: 642–54.

—— Flemming, E., and Wright, R. (1993), 'The Hyperspace Effect: Phonetic Targets are Hyperarticulated', *Language*, 69: 505–28.

Jun, S.-A. (1994), 'The Domains of Laryngeal Feature Lenition Effects in Chonnam Korean', *Ohio State University Working Papers in Linguistics*, 43: 15–20.

Keating, P. A. (1984), 'Phonetic and Phonological Representation of Stop Consonant Voicing', *Language*, 60: 286–319.

—— (1990a), 'The Window Model of Coarticulation: Articulatory Evidence', in J. Kingston and M. Beckman (eds.), *Papers in Laboratory Phonology I* (Cambridge: Cambridge University Press), 451–70.

—— (1990b), 'Phonetic Representation in a Generative Grammar', *Journal of Phonetics*, 18: 321–34.

Kingston, J. (1990), 'Articulatory Binding', in J. Kingston and M. Beckman (eds.), *Papers in Laboratory Phonology I* (Cambridge: Cambridge University Press), 406–34.

—— and Diehl, R. (1994), 'Phonetic Knowledge', *Language*, 70: 419–54.

Klatt, D. H. (1976), 'Linguistics Uses of Segmental Duration in English: Acoustic and Perceptual Evidence', *Journal of the Acoustical Society of America*, 59: 1208–21.

Kornai, A. (1991), 'Formal Phonology', Ph.D. dissertation (Stanford University).

Kripke, S. (1972), 'Naming and Necessity', in D. Davidson and G. Harman (eds.), *Semantics and Natural Language* (Dordrecht: Reidel), 253–355.

Kubozono, H. (1992), 'Modeling Syntactic Effects on Downstep in Japanese', in G. J. Docherty and D. R. Ladd (eds.), *Papers in Laboratory Phonology II* (Cambridge: Cambridge University Press), 368–88.

Kuhl, P. K., Williams, K. A., Lacerda, F., Stevens, K., and Lindblom, B. (1992), 'Linguistic Experience Alters Phonetic Perception in Infants by 6 Months of Age', *Science*, 225: 606–8.

Kuhn, T. (1962), *The Structure of Scientific Revolutions* (Chicago: University of Chicago Press).

Labov, W. (1973), 'Where do Grammars Stop?', in R. W. Shuy (ed.), *Sociolinguistics: Current Trends and Prospects.* 23rd Annual Round Table (Monograph Series on Languages and Linguistics, 25), 43–88.

Lacerda, F. (forthcoming), 'Distributed Memory Representations Generate the Perceptual-Magnet Effect', *Journal of the Acoustical Society of America*.

Ladd, D. R., Verhoeven, J., and Jacobs, K. (1994), 'Influence of Adjacent Pitch Accents on Each Other's Perceived Prominence: Two Contradictory Effects', *Journal of Phonetics*, 22: 87–99.

Laeufer, C. (1992), 'Patterns of Voicing Conditioned Vowel Duration in French and English', *Journal of Phonetics*, 20: 411–40.

Laudan, L. (1983), *Science and Values* (Berkeley and Los Angeles: University of California Press).

—— (1996), *Beyond Positivism and Relativism: Theory, Method, and Evidence* (Boulder, Colo.: Westview Press).

Lee, S., Potamianos, A., and Narayanan, S. (1999), 'Acoustics of Children's Speech: Developmental Changes of Temporal and Spectral Parameters', *Journal of the Acoustical Society of America*, 105: 1455–68.

Liberman, M. Y. and Prince, A. (1977), 'On Stress and Linguistic Rhythm', *Linguistic Inquiry*, 8: 249–336.

Liljencrants, J. and Lindblom, B. (1972), 'Numerical Simulation of Vowel Quality Systems: The Role of Perceptual Contrast', *Language*, 48: 839–62.

Lindblom, B. (1963), 'Spectrographic Study of Vowel Reduction', *Journal of the Acoustical Society of America*, 35: 1773–81.

—— (1992), 'Phonological Units as Adaptive Emergents of Lexical Development', in C. A.

Ferguson, L. Menn, and C. Stoel-Gammon (eds.), *Phonological Development: Models, Research, Implications* (Timonium, Md.: York Press), 131–63.

Lindblom, B., Lubker, J., and Gay, T. (1979), 'Formant Frequencies of Some Fixed-Mandible Vowels and a Model of Speech-Motor Programming by Predictive Simulation', *Journal of Phonetics*, 7: 147–62.

—— MacNeilage, P., and Studdert-Kennedy, M. (1983), 'Self-Organizing Processes and the Explanation of Phonological Universals', in B. Butterworth, B. Comrie, and Ö. Dahl, *Explanations of Language Universals* (The Hague: Mouton), 181–204.

Locke, J. L. and Pearson, D. M. (1992), 'Vocal Learning and the Emergence of Phonological Capacity', in C. A. Ferguson, L. Menn, and C. Stoel-Gammon (eds.) *Phonological Development: Models, Research, Implications* (Timonium, Md.: York Press), 91–129.

Loevenbruck, M., Collins, M. J., Beckman, M. E., Krishnamurthy, A. K., and Ahalt, S. C. (1999), 'Temporal Coordination of Articulatory Gestures in Consonant Clusters and Sequences of Consonants', in O. Fujimura, B. D. Joseph, and B. Palek (ds.), *Proceedings of the 1998 Linguistics and Phonetics Conference* (Prague: Karolinum Press).

Logan, J. S., Lively, S. E., and Pisoni, D. B. (1991), 'Training Japanese Listeners to Identify English /r/ and /l/', *Journal of the Acoustical Society of America*, 89: 874–86.

Lotto, A. J., Kluender, K. K., and Holt, L. H. (2000). 'Effects of Language Experience on Organization of Vowel Sounds', in M. Broe and J. Pierrehumbert (eds.), *Papers in Laboratory Phonology V* (Cambridge: Cambridge University Press), 218–26.

Lucy, J. (1996), 'The Linguistics of "Color"', in C. Hardin and L. Maffi (eds.), *Color categories in Thought and Language* (Cambridge: Cambridge University Press).

McCarthy, J. J. (1985), *Formal Problems in Semitic Phonology and Morphology* (New York: Garland Press).

—— (1988), 'Feature Geometry and Dependency: A Review', *Phonetica*, 43: 84–108.

Macken, M. and Barton, D. (1980), 'A Longitudinal Study of the Acquisition of the Voicing Contrast in American-English Word-Initial Stops, as Measured by Voice Onset Time', *Journal of Child Language*, 7: 41–72.

Macmillan, N. A., Braida, L. D., and Goldberg, R. F. (1987), 'Central and Peripheral Effects in the Perception of Speech and Non-Speech Sounds', in M. E. H. Schouten (ed.), *The Psychophysics of Speech Perception* (Dordrecht: Martinus Nijhoff), 28–45.

Maddieson, I. and Ladefoged, P. (1993), 'Phonetics of Partially Nasal Consonants', in M. Huffman and R. Krakow (eds.), *Nasals, Nasalization, and the Velum (Phonetics and Phonology 5)* (San Diego: Academic Press), 251–301.

Maeda, S. (1991), 'On Articulatory and Acoustic Variabilities', *Journal of Phonetics*, 19: 321–31.

Makashay, M. J. and Johnson, K. (1998), 'Surveying Auditory Space using Vowel Formant Data', in *Proceedings of the Joint Meeting of the International Conference on Acoustics and the Acoustical Society of America* (Acoustical Society of America), 2037–8.

Marchman, V. and Bates, E. (1994), 'Continuity in Lexical and Morphological Development: A Test of the Critical Mass Hypothesis', *Journal of Child Language*, 21: 339–66.

Miller, J. L. and Dexter, E. R. (1988), 'Effects of Speaking Rate and Lexical Status on Phonetic Perception', *Journal of Experimental Psychology: Human Perception and Performance*, 14: 369–78.

Myers, S. (this volume), 'Boundary Disputes: The Distinction between Phonetic and Phonological Sound Patterns'.

Nittrouer, S. (1995), 'Children Learn Separate Aspects of Speech Production at Different Rates: Evidence from Spectral Moments', *Journal of the Acoustical Society of America*, 97, 520–30.

Odden, D. (1992), 'Simplicity of Underlying Representation as Motivation for Underspecification', *Ohio State University Working Papers in Linguistics*, 41: 83–100.

Pan, H. (1994), 'The Acquisition of Taiwanese (Amoy) Initial Stops', Ph.D. dissertation (Ohio State University).

Pierrehumbert, J. B. (1990), 'Phonological and Phonetic Representation', *Journal of Phonetics* 18, 375–94.

—— (1994*a*), 'Syllable Structure and Word Structure: A Study of Triconsonantal Clusters in English', in P. A. Keating (ed.), *Papers in Laboratory Phonology III* (Cambridge: Cambridge University Press), 168–88.

—— (1994*b*), 'Knowledge of Variation', in K. Beals, J. Denton, R. Knippen, L. Mielmar, H. Suzuki, and E. Zeinfeld (eds.), *Papers from the 30th Meeting of the Chicago Linguistic Society*, ii. *Papers from the Parasession on Variation* (Chicago: Chicago Linguistic Society), 232–56.

—— and Beckman, M. (1988), *Japanese Tone Structure (Linguistic Inquiry Monograph, 15)* (Cambridge, Mass.: MIT Press).

—— and Talkin, D. (1992), 'Lenition of /h/ and Glottal Stop', in G. Docherty and D. R. Ladd (eds.), *Papers in Laboratory Phonology II* (Cambridge: Cambridge University Press), 90–117.

Pinker, S. and Prince, A. (1988), 'On Language and Connectionism: Analysis of a Parallel Distributed Processing Model of Language Acquisition', *Cognition*, 28: 73–193.

Pisoni, D. B. (1977), 'Identification and Discrimination of the Relative Onset Time of Two-Component Tones: Implications For Voicing Perception in Stops', *Journal of the Acoustical Society of America*, 61: 1352–61.

Pullum, G. (1991), *The Great Eskimo Vocabulary Hoax* (Chicago: University of Chicago Press).

Putnam, H. (1973), 'Meaning and Reference', *Journal of Philosophy*, 7: 699–711.

—— (1978), *Meaning and the Moral Sciences* (London: Routledge & Kegan Paul).

Quine, W. V. O. (1954/1966), 'The Scope and Language of Science', repr. in *The Ways of Paradox and Other Essays* (New York: Random House), 215–32.

—— (1960), *Word and Object* (Cambridge, Mass.: MIT Press).

—— (1961), *From a Logical Point of View* (2nd edn., Cambridge, Mass.: Harvard University Press).

Rialland, A. (1994), 'The Phonology and Phonetics of Extrasyllabicity in French', in P. A. Keating (ed.), *Papers in Laboratory Phonology III* (Cambridge: Cambridge University Press), 136–59.

Saltzman, E. L. and Munhall, K. G. (1989), 'A Dynamical Approach to Gestural Patterning in Speech Production', *Ecological Psychology*, 1: 333–82.

Scobbie, J. M. (1999), *Attribute-Value Phonology* (New York: Garland Press).

—— Gibbon, F., Hardcastle, W. J., and Fletcher, P. (2000), 'Covert Contrast as a Stage in Acquisition of Phonetics and Phonology', in M. Broe and J. Pierrehumbert (eds.), *Papers in Laboratory Phonology V* (Cambridge: Cambridge University Press), 194–207.

Selkirk, E. O. (1984), *Phonology and Syntax: The Relation between Sound and Structure* (Cambridge, Mass.: MIT Press).

Sereno, J. A. and Jongman, A. (1995), 'Acoustic Correlates of Grammatical Class', *Language and Speech*, 38: 57–76.

Shattuck-Hufnagel, S., Ostendorf, M., and Ross, K. (1994), 'Stress Shift and Early Pitch Accent Placement in Lexical Items in American English', *Journal of Phonetics*, 22: 357–88.

Silva, D. (1992), 'The Phonetics and Phonology of Stop Lenition in Korean', Ph.D. dissertation (Cornell University).

Silverman, K. and Pierrehumbert, J. (1990), 'The Timing of Prenuclear High Accents in English', in J. Kingston and M. Beckman (eds.), *Papers in Laboratory Phonology I* (Cambridge: Cambridge University Press), 72–106.

Smith, C. (1995), 'Prosodic Patterns in the Coordination of Vowel and Consonant Gestures', in B. Connell and A. Arvaniti (eds.), *Papers in Laboratory Phonology IV* (Cambridge: Cambridge University Press), 205–22.

Soames, S. (1984), 'Linguistics and Psychology', *Linguistics and Philosophy*, 7: 155–80.

Steriade, D. (1993), 'Closure, Release, and Nasal Contours', in M. Huffman and R. Krakow (eds.), *Nasals, nasalization, and the velum* (Phonetics and Phonology 5; San Diego, Calif.: Academic Press), 401–70.

Stevens, K. N. (1972), 'The Quantal Nature of Speech: Evidence from Articulatory-Acoustic Data', in E. E. David and P. B. Denes (eds.), *Human Communication: A Unified View* (New York: McGraw-Hill), 51–66.

—— (1989), 'On the Quantal Nature of Speech', *Journal of Phonetics*, 17: 3–45.

Stoel-Gammon, C., Williams, K., and Buder, E. (1994), 'Cross-Language Differences in Phonological Acquisition: Swedish and American /t/', *Phonetica*, 51: 146–58.

Summerfield, Q. (1981), 'Differences between Spectral Dependencies in Auditory and Phonetic Temporal Processing: Relevance to the Perception of Voicing in Initial Stops', *Journal of the Acoustical Society of America*, 72: 51–61.

Swadesh, M. (1971), *Origin and Diversification of Language* (Chicago: Aldine Atherton).

't Hart, J. and Cohen, A. (1973), 'Intonation by Rule: A Perceptual Quest', *Journal of Phonetics*, 1: 309–27.

Thompson, E., Palacios, A., and Varela, F. (1992), 'Ways of Coloring: Comparative Color Vision as a Case Study in Cognitive Science', *Behavioral and Brain Studies*, 15: 1–74.

Treiman, R., Kessler, B., Knewasser, S., Tincoff, R., and Bowman, M. (2000), 'English Speaker's Sensitivity to Phonotactic Patterns', in M. Broe and J. B. Pierrehumbert (eds.), *Papers in Laboratory Phonology V* (Cambridge: Cambridge University Press), 259–73.

Vihman, M. M. (1993), 'Variable Paths to Early Word Production', *Journal of Phonetics*, 21: 61–82.

Werker, J. F. and Stager, C. L. (2000), 'Developmental Changes in Infant Speech Perception and Early Word Learning: Is There a Link?', in M. Broe and J. Pierrehumbert (eds.), *Papers in Laboratory Phonology V* (Cambridge: Cambridge University Press), 181–93.

—— and Tees, R. C. (1994), 'Cross-Language Speech Perception: Evidence for Perceptual Reorganization during the First Year of Life', *Infant Behavior and Development*, 7: 49–63.

Wiener, N. (1948), *Cybernetics* (New York: John Wiley & Sons).

Willerman, R. (1994), 'The Phonetics of Pronouns: Articulatory Bases of Markedness', Ph.D. dissertation (University of Texas, Austin).

Zsiga, E. (1995), 'An Acoustic and Electropalatographic Study of Lexical and Postlexical Palatalization in American English', in B. Connell and A. Arvaniti (eds.), *Papers in Laboratory Phonology IV* (Cambridge: Cambridge University Press), 282–302.

—— (forthcoming), 'Phonetic Alignment Constraints: Consonant Overlap and Palatalization in English and Russian', *Journal of Phonetics*.

12

Phonetics and the Origins of Phonology

MARILYN VIHMAN AND SHELLEY VELLEMAN

1. INTRODUCTION

The chief difficulty for a constructivist account of language development is explaining the origin of specifically linguistic structure—meaning phonology and syntax, the domains of formal linguistic theory and description. The position taken in this chapter will be that the phonetic grounding of phonology, like the semantic grounding of syntax, provides an entry point into linguistic structure. Our main goal here will be to establish that an incipient phonological system can be identified within the single word period, and that it can be seen to emerge out of phonetic structure. At the same time, we will locate the origins of phonology not only in an automatic, passive process of 'self-organization' (Lindblom 1992) but also in the individual child's implicit work of systematization. We ultimately trace the individual differences in both phonetic patterning and the first phonological organization to the children's personal filtering of the adult input in relation to their own vocal production. And we affirm that emergent phonological structure serves a critical function for the child, helping to support representational memory for a growing lexical repertoire and limiting the learning space—in different ways for different children, but always leading to the same multifaceted adult system.

We take it to be uncontroversial that phonetics, like semantics, is embedded in experiences external to language proper, and is universal in that sense. Despite this fact, both phonetic and semantic structure can be taken to be language particular to a degree, and therefore learned, not biologically 'given'. The specifics of phonetic and semantic structure can be seen to result from the imposition of particular ambient language filters on the 'natural world' of possible vocal output and of perceptible differences between different such possible vocal patterns, as

We would like to thank Sari Kunnari for generously sharing her dissertation data with us, and for willingly answering all of our questions. We also thank Satsuki Nakai for her very helpful critical reading of an earlier version of this chapter as well as help and advice on the acoustic and statistical analyses and graphics. This study was supported in part by a grant to M. M. Vihman from the Economic and Social Research Council (R000 23 708), to which we are also grateful.

regards phonetics (Best 1994), and on the way humans experience the physical and social world around them, as regards semantics (Wierzbicka 1992). From the developmental perspective, the shaping of the raw vocal output of the infant's production mechanism as a reflection of exposure to input patterns from a particular language is what can be taken to yield the 'phonetic starting point', just as the changes in cognition that reflect both maturation and experience, including exposure to the semantic categories of a particular language, provide the starting point for the transition into syntax (see Vihman 1999a and the various papers collected in that volume).

There are differences of opinion about the degree of ambient language influence on the production of infants in the prelinguistic and first word period. In particular, adult perceptual judgements of infant vocalizations have yielded conflicting results (see e.g. Thevenin, *et al.* 1985; Boysson-Bardies *et al.* 1989; and Vihman 1991 for a review). However, it is generally accepted that some degree of phonetic 'drift' toward the values of the adult language can be identified in babbling and early word vocalizations if one analyses frequencies of occurrence of categories that are within the babbling repertoire (proportion of labials or stops, extent of final syllable lengthening or rising pitch in disyllabic vocalizations— roughly, end of the first year of life: see Boysson-Bardies and Vihman 1991; Whalen *et al.* 1991). That consensus is in harmony with experimental findings regarding the earliest adult language influence on the discrimination of segmental contrasts (again, toward the end of the first year: Werker and Tees 1984; Best 1994).

Some have proposed that accommodation to the adult language is the primary criterion for the origin of phonology (e.g. Locke 1983). In contrast, Laver (1994) distinguishes the 'organic' from the 'phonetic' level and includes any 'voluntary . . . learnable aspects of the use of the vocal apparatus' under the latter (p. 28). Similarly, Kingston and Diehl (1994) have argued persuasively that much phonetic knowledge is independently controlled, or *voluntary*. For example, they show that different coarticulatory effects are selected by different languages; they are not the completely automatic results of motoric imprecision, as has often been assumed. The consequences are that much phonetic variation, while motivated by physiological constraints, is language specific and therefore *learned* rather than universal.

Under these views, the evidence of learning that we detect in early vocal production or perception does *not* serve to demarcate the starting point for phonology but merely marks the entry into speech-related vocal production, a path that merges rather seamlessly from a purely 'organic' level of vocal production (involving no supraglottal segmental production—the 'precanonical' stage (Oller 1980); see also Vihman (1996: ch. 5) for a review of the early period of infant vocal production) into phonetics.

If these accommodations to the ambient language are taken to be phonetics, when—if ever—does phonology begin?

1.1. *Phonology all the way down?*

Some argue that phonology is present from birth. Many scholars who have applied the concepts of current phonological theories to development have assumed (often without considering the results of decades of research into developmental phonology) that knowledge of all the potential types of phonological organization and patterns is present at birth. Within Optimality Theory (OT), for example, phonology is taken to consist primarily of universal sets of 'markedness constraints', which specify which features, patterns, or structures are typically avoided by languages, and 'faithfulness constraints', which specify which features, patterns, or structures of the 'input' (roughly, the underlying representation) are preferentially preserved. Markedness is casually referred to as corresponding to the speaker's ease of production, while faithfulness corresponds approximately to the listener's ease of perception. Lindblom (1998) warns that this definition of markedness is circular (languages avoid difficult things because they are marked; we classify them as marked because they are avoided). Archangeli and Pulleyblank (1994) avoid this circularity by defining markedness constraints as 'cross-linguistic statistical skewings of ... behavior' (pp. 164–5), which will typically but not obligatorily be 'grounded in their phonetic substance' (pp. 176–7).

Within OT, each language has an established 'ranking' for this universal set of faithfulness and markedness constraints, which determines which characteristics of a given input are actually preserved and which are sacrificed in a given output. The common assumption is that these constraints are present in all humans at birth: 'The ranking, but not the constraints, differs from language to language. The constraints are therefore universal. If phonological constraints are universal, they should be innate' (Gnanadesikan 1995: 1).

The issue for these linguists is the order of the initial ranking: is the child's 'initial state' one in which all markedness constraints are given higher priority (e.g. Gnanadesikan 1995; Smolensky 1996), one in which all faithfulness constraints are given higher priority (e.g. Hale and Reiss 1996, 1997), or a random ranking that differs from child to child (Pulleyblank and Turkel 1997)? Whatever the answer, the phonology is provided in the genes, and needs only to be adjusted to the ambient language, according to these views. However, these adjustments are not typically seen to be phonetic (as described above), but phonological. What then is the role of phonetics in phonological development?

Autonomous roles for phonetics versus phonology are proposed by Hale and Reiss (1996, 1997), Stemberger and Bernhardt (1999), and Pulleyblank and Turkel (1997). Hale and Reiss (1996, 1997) suggest that phonetic learning is essentially a red herring to those who would study phonological acquisition. In their view, 'deviations from target forms—in children's as well as adults' grammars—are to be attributed to performance effects, including non-linguistic cognitive and motor processing' (1997: 2). They propose a parallel between learning to walk and learning to talk; babies know how to do both from birth, but physiological factors interfere with their demonstration of this knowledge. Eventually, 'the child's performance system catches up with the innate knowledge of how to walk [and talk]' (1997: 25). Smolensky (1996), in contrast, opposes the idea that all errors can be attributed to performance difficulties, citing developmental research documentation of phonological regression, which suggests that children sometimes seem to lose the ability to produce forms that they had previously produced correctly. Such regressions appear unlikely to result from motor performance difficulties.

Bernhardt and Stemberger (1998) express doubts about the possibility of a universal order of constraint acquisition. Stemberger and Bernhardt (1999) suggest that phonology (specifically, the phonological constraint hierarchy) is not a form of innate linguistic knowledge, but the result of 'the universality of other characteristics of human beings: vocal tract design, perceptual systems, cognitive systems, and aerodynamics' (p. 429). They propose that phonology, unlike other aspects of language, does not pose a learning problem because 'most words have been produced before, and the sounds of a given morpheme are simply memorized by the speaker' (p. 432). Despite this view and its child data sources, they, like Hale and Reiss (1996, 1997), deny the phonetic basis or 'groundedness' (Archangeli and Pulleyblank 1994) of phonology. They state that markedness constraints could not be motivated by ease of articulation, because a child could not learn that certain units or structures are difficult without first producing them. In order for this to be the mechanism for learning markedness constraints, 'the child must attempt to produce a very wide range of sounds, and we know that they do not (Locke 1983; Vihman 1996). In our opinion, few constraints, if any, exist for articulatory reasons ...' (Stemberger and Bernhardt 1999: 434). They also reject perceptual phonetic bases for markedness constraints. They do not see 'ease of perception' as a possible source of child voicing errors, for example, because 'a child with normal hearing *can* hear voicing in codas. It does not make sense to argue that a child would eliminate some feature from his or her production of words that he or she can hear, when its elimination causes communication problems with adults' (p. 434).

Pulleyblank and Turkel (1997), too, see phonetic factors as irrelevant to phonology: 'we assume that there are no rankings that are ruled out a priori by Universal Grammar, and that maturational factors do not prevent certain hypotheses from being entertained' (p. 157). Goad (1997), based upon a study of child consonant harmony (CH), concludes that phonetic factors must be relevant to child speech patterns. However, in her view, these findings imply that child phonetics is distinct from phonology: 'The absence of CH from adult languages suggests that the explanation for its presence in child language must lie outside the formal devices provided by the theory. ... the motivation for the process must be functional i.e. independent of the grammar' (p. 138).

Macken (1995) concurs, on the premiss that all children exposed to the same language quickly arrive at the same adult phonology. This could not be true, in her opinion, unless miracles occur or language acquisition is 'a formal problem space' (p. 695). Individual differences can neither reflect nor affect the phonological system, she says, because 'stochastic learning is cumulative and where paths differ, outcomes differ' (p. 695).

Others see functionality as one foundation for phonology, and have claimed that markedness constraints do typically arise from phonetic factors. Archangeli and Pulleyblank (1994), from a theoretical position based upon adult phonologies, arrive at a conclusion similar to our own: that phonetics provides the foundation for a child's phonology, which then takes on an organization and character of its own that may relate far less directly to articulatory or acoustic factors. They propose an interaction between physiology and the formal elements of an innate linguistic system:

phonological phenomena cannot be understood solely in terms of formal patterns, in isolation from the physical properties of the system. At the same time, the physical properties alone [are] inadequate in defining the systematic behavior of sounds in particular languages. . . . it is through the interaction of the formal and substantive theories that an explanation of feature patterns is found.   (p. 428)

On the basis of this proposal, they suggest that children's initial phonologies 'reflect physically motivated conditions quite closely, but that more marked configurations . . . are developed in the face of positive evidence' (p. 183). Simply put, physical (organic) aspects of phonetics ground phonology, but the complex structure of the ambient language requires the child to develop more abstract patterning.

Myers (1997) attempts to create a conceptual bridge from the functionality of phonetics to the abstractions of phonology. He claims that this is made possible, in part, by the markedness component of OT. This theory, in his view, is 'better able . . . to express the correspondence between phonetically natural phonological patterns and their phonetic counterparts . . . [and] better suited . . . to distinguish natural phonological patterns from unnatural ones' (p. 125). In this endeavour, Myers has provided a useful characterization of the difference between phonetics and phonology. Phonetics is optional, gradient, rate-dependent, insensitive to morphological categories. Phonology is obligatory, categorical, independent of speech rate, and may be restricted to certain morphological categories, among other things. Phonetics is the foundation of and the explanation for phonological patterns. Phonology moulds gradient, functional phonetic variation into abstract, categorical patterns.

1.2. Phonetics all the way up?

Lindblom (1983, 1992, 1998, 1999), MacNeilage (1994, 1997), MacNeilage and Davis (1990), and Studdert-Kennedy (1987) approach the problem from the opposite end. They focus on phonetic development, paying little or no attention to the ultimate phonological system that emerges. In MacNeilage's terms, which ironically parallel those of Stemberger and Bernhardt (1999), despite his underlying assumptions being diametrically opposed to theirs, 'Learning to speak the ambient language basically involves developing a set of input–output relationships, direct and indirect. The direct relationship is evident in our ability to imitate ... Indirect input–output relationships are evidenced when we spontaneously utter a word, the auditory representation of which we originally learned from the input' (1997: 319).

Studdert-Kennedy (1987), similarly, lists the following steps in the development of phonology: 'diversifying articulatory routines ... narrowing the domain within a word to which an articulatory routine applies ... the systematic grouping of phonetic variants into phoneme classes, and the discovery of language-specific regularities in their sequencing' (p. 79).

Sound patterns, in this view, evolve in response to biological constraints on speech production, speech perception, and learning. Segments and, eventually, contrastive phonemes are seen to 'emerge' and 'self-organize' from these bases. 'For the child, phonology is not abstract. It represents an emergent patterning of phonetic substance' (Lindblom 1999: 13). But what is this emergent patterning? What is the process and, more importantly, what is the outcome of this 'self-organization'? According to MacNeilage (1997), 'the main form of development might be rather gradual changes in the ability to produce sounds independent of context' (p. 326). While he, like Smolensky (1996), acknowledges that children exhibit changing patterns that appear to reflect phonetic regression, he states that such changes are phonetically based. He poses the question, 'What is to be gained by regarding such events as evidence of an autonomous phonological component?' (p. 330) and answers it: 'It is likely as we come to understand more about ... the phonetics of early speech—we will have less and less need for postulation of independent phonological causal factors' (p. 331).

If we accept that phonological structure arises gradually out of the phenomena of phonetics, we should expect a continuous incremental improvement in the child's ability to approximate adult word targets. The types of phenomena that could be taken to characterize phonological structure as it emerges out of phonetic learning would include:

- *Categorization*: physically different sounds (variable individual tokens or 'segments') 'count' as belonging to the same category.
- *Paradigmatic network of relations*: repeated use of the same articulatory gestures in different segments implies componentiality (which may or may not accord with adult language categories).
- *Prosodies*:
  (a) A range of different phonotactic structures occur, falling into an implicit hierarchical organization.
  (b) Gradient prosodic phenomena such as segmental duration are differentiated into categorical oppositions ('short' versus 'long' vowels or consonants).

  (c) Adult-like accentual patterns function to bind groups of syllables into
        words or short phrases.

At what point in the developmental trajectory can we say that 'phonology' can
be identified then? When the child has outgrown the CV associations typical of the
first period of babbling (Davis and MacNeilage 1990), implying componentiality?
When the repertoire comes to include some of the less common segments peculiar
to the ambient language, breaking free of a physiologically based universal
repertoire (Pye *et al.* 1987)? When prosody begins to be controlled more by the
parameters that characterize the adult language than by speech production factors
(Hallé *et al.* 1991; Vihman *et al.* 1998)? Or should we set the criterion higher,
requiring evidence of specific contrastive features at the level either of segmental
patterning or of prosody, or of both? If the emergence of phonological structure
out of phonetics is only gradual, it is difficult to see how a particular onset point for
phonology can be selected. The problem is magnified by the fact that children may
initially mark phonological contrasts articulatorily in ways that are not detectable
without careful acoustic analysis. For this reason, according to Scobbie (1998),
only developmental phonetic changes can be directly observed.

1.3. The paradox

We take a different position here. However paradoxical this may seem, we suggest
that discontinuity as well as continuity is evident in speech development, and
therefore it is possible to identify the onset of a child's phonological system.
Different children arrive at different solutions to the conflict between their
phonetic skills and the demands of the ambient language. In many children, these
solutions consist of recognizable word templates (Menn 1978), which are initially
expressed as lexical selectivity (Ferguson and Farwell 1975). Over time, these
templates—nascent phonological systems—break free of phonetics and impose
themselves upon lexical items that do not fit the same structural descriptions.
These 'distortions' or 'adaptations' of adult word shapes defy direct phonetic
explanation. Thus, the emergence of phonological organization can be detected in
a child-based distributional analysis, in which the extent of parallel patterning
across different word forms is established and tracked longitudinally. By following
that approach it is possible to observe the idiosyncratic development of word
templates in some children and a more cautious step-by-step constraint-loosening
approach in others (Macken 1978, 1979; Vihman and Velleman 1989; Vihman
1996).

1.4. Phonetic patterns and phonological organization in development

In order to achieve a satisfactory, empirically based understanding of the
emergence of phonology we must begin by distinguishing between the phonetic

patterns of the prelinguistic and first word period and the incipient phonological structure that can be identified by the end of the single word period, when a child has a vocabulary of fifty words or more.

Exploration of his or her own vocal capacities in babbling serves to provide the child with a range of segmental and prosodic patterns that can be produced voluntarily. Command of a sufficient number of such patterns or 'vocal motor schemes' has been shown to be a prerequisite for the transition to referential word use (McCune and Vihman 1987, forthcoming). Deployment of vocal motor schemes reflects (1) the exercise of emergent neuromuscular control within the framework of a changing vocal tract, (2) implicit learning of the distributional patterns in the input, such as the vowel space characteristic of the particular ambient language (Boysson-Bardies *et al.* 1989), and (3) the 'reinforcing' effect of the auditory match of the child's own vocalizations to input patterns—yielding proprioceptive knowledge of how specific sound patterns may be produced. We term the process of matching own vocal patterns to the input the ARTICULATORY FILTER (Vihman 1993; Vihman *et al.* 1994).

It is important to note that from the beginning adult-like vocal production is influenced by both speech production constraints, the physiological parameters of the vocal apparatus (markedness constraints, in OT terms), and the ambient language as filtered through the child's perceptual system (roughly, faithfulness constraints). Furthermore, the means of production, even of roughly the same sound patterns, are variable across individual children and even within the same child—resulting generally in the domination or 'highest ranking' of neither markedness nor faithfulness constraints but in 'pairwise ranking' instead, reflecting the child's selectivity—owing to the ongoing operation of the articulatory filter (Velleman and Vihman, 1999; Velleman *et al.* 1999). Finally, variability in the extent and timing of ambient language influence relates both to the individual child and to the difficulty of the sound pattern in question.

When, at a later stage, the child begins to exhibit consistent patterning in the production of different adult words, including the distortion of some words to fit them into the child's individual production template, we identify this as the first evidence of phonological organization. We see this first phonological structuring as having two functions. First, it supports representational memory for the production of a growing repertoire of distinct lexical patterns. Thus, it begins to play a role only as the cumulative lexicon grows to something like fifty words. It is not seen in the form of the first words, which tend to be relatively accurate and not formally interrelated—much like the earliest syntactic combinations, according to some current analyses (Tomasello 1992; Lieven *et al.* 1997). Secondly, it limits the learning space, creating self-paced sequences of emergent phonological categories, relations, and prosodies. Even within a group of children learning the same language there are wide differences in the aspects that are mastered first, so that some but not all children focus on final consonants in English (Vihman *et al.* 1986), rising pitch in French, glottal closure in Japanese (Hallé *et al.* 1991), and geminates in Finnish (to be elaborated below).

Whereas the first words, which typically lack systematicity in production and which closely resemble the repertoire of babbling patterns typical of the individual child (Vihman *et al.* 1985), are seen as the product of implicit learning and the articulatory filter, the incipient phonological organization of the later stage of single word production reflects the child's attention-guided response to selected aspects of the input. What is salient itself depends on at least four distinct factors, two of them properties of the input, two of them internal to the individual child: (1) recurrent input patterns (input frequency), (2) prosodic heightening in the input, (3) the child's personal interests ('situational filter'), and (4) the child's perceived match between his or her particular vocal motor schemes and patterns in the input, mediated by the articulatory filter, arguably a prelinguistic precursor of phonological memory (see Baddeley *et al.* 1998). In addition, however, word production at this later stage reflects the child's *generalization* from selected patterns in the input, leading to 'distortions' or 'adaptations' of words that do not fit the child's word template. The template itself can be seen as a 'routine' that automatizes the process of word production, facilitating expansion of the lexicon. The process of generalization, which depends on implicit comparison across differing word targets and/or child word forms, represents an advance towards a linguistic system, although it is commonly manifested in regressions in accuracy in the production of particular word forms.

Thus, the emergence of phonological organization itself, which we view as the first step towards specifically linguistic structure, is the product of (1) the development of phonetic resources through babbling, (2) lexical expansion (receptive and expressive), and (3) representational advance, which is undoubtedly neurologically based although little is known about this in any detail (see Mills *et al.* 1994). At the outset phonological structure lacks any evident connection with morphology and is in fact only loosely connected with the phonology of the targeted lexical patterns in the ambient language. Instead, the first phonological structure is characterized by general linguistic principles of organization at a primitive level, primarily systematicity, expressed in idiosyncratic ways by individual children. It appears to reflect the child's implicit comparison of different production plans and their 'rationalization' into some kind of a primitive system. These initial systems vary from fairly specific templates with a constant frame and variable slots (much like the pivot-open structure of some children's first word combinations) to broader templates with restricted phonotactic options but more variable segmental elements (Vihman 1996: chs. 6, 9).

Many aspects of early phonological development are reminiscent of learning in other domains (for example, motor learning) and in other aspects of language:

1. High variability often closely precedes the stabilization of patterns (as predicted by dynamic systems models: see e.g. Thelen 1989).

2.   Regressions in accuracy (U-shaped curves) reflect cycles of organization and reorganization (Macken and Ferguson 1983; Karmiloff-Smith 1992).
3.   Structure develops piecemeal—at different rates and in different sequences even for children learning the same language (see e.g. Carey 1978, and Gathercole 1983, for the piecemeal acquisition of semantics, Gathercole *et al.* (1999), for piecemeal advances in Spanish morphology, and Tomasello (1992), for the piecemeal learning of syntactic structure in early verbs; Macken (1979), provides a rare case-study account of development from whole word template to segment-based phonology).

All of these empirically well-established phenomena cast doubt on formal theories of a smooth 'unfolding' or 'maturation' of pre-existing knowledge or innate principles as well as on the gradualist idea of a wholly automatic emergence of phonological structure out of phonetic patterning.

2. A DEVELOPMENTAL STUDY OF THE SHIFT FROM PHONETICS TO PHONOLOGY

The natural variation across languages in the use of segmental quantity as an element in phonological structure provides a good testing ground for the emergence of phonology. One advantage of the study of the acquisition of quantitative contrast is that it combines both segmental and suprasegmental or prosodic aspects, and affects phonotactic structure as well. Another advantage is that the issue readily lends itself to both phonetic and phonological analysis. Here we focus on the acquisition of gemination in Finnish, with data from English and French as points of comparison.

The basic question for an empirical phonetic study of the development of geminates is what kind of evidence we can accept as indicating emergent phonological opposition. In principle, we might expect to find that an initially undifferentiated 'durational space' for child medial consonants will divide into a bipolar short:long pattern, and also that a tie-in with the adult lexicon will become evident, such that all tokens of words with medial singletons in the target will fall into the short range while words with target medial geminates will fall into the long range.

Our phonetic analyses will concentrate on tracking the length of medial consonants in both the word and non-word vocalizations of five children in each of the three language groups at two points in time, one at the outset of lexical development, the other toward the end of the single word period. On the basis of earlier work in both segmental and prosodic aspects of phonological development (e.g. Vihman *et al.* 1986; Boysson-Bardies and Vihman 1991; Vihman *et al.* 1994) we expect to see the children in each language group display greater within-group variability at the earlier lexical point and less at the later one, and we expect the children across the different language groups to show greater similarity at the earlier lexical point and less at the later one. Arguably, this reflects the influence of physiological (or 'markedness') constraints on early production and the increasingly felt guiding role of the ambient language ('faithfulness constraints') once lexical learning is more advanced.

Finally, we will look at the specific lexical patterns of individual children acquiring Finnish. We ask whether there is evidence that geminates play a particular role in the initial organization of phonology for one or more of the children, and if so, how that is manifested. Additionally, we ask whether there is any apparent connection, for individual children, between such a structure-oriented (categorical or 'digital') analysis and the findings of our acoustic (gradient or 'analogue') analysis.

2.1. Method

Data at two word points from five children each acquiring English, French, and Finnish were analysed acoustically (see Table 12.1 for child age and numbers of word types at each session). Data for English were collected in California, USA, for French in Paris, France. The word points are defined on the basis of the number of words produced spontaneously in a thirty-minute audio-and video-recorded session of unstructured play between mother and child; a small microphone was hidden inside a soft vest worn by the child. Words were identified according to the procedures described in Vihman and McCune (1994). The earlier developmental point is the first one of two sessions in which the child produces at least four different word types spontaneously; the later point is based on approximately twenty-five spontaneous words produced in a session. Each of these lexically based developmental points corresponds to a cumulative lexicon of approximately twice as many words by parental record (Vihman and Miller 1988; Kunnari 1998)—so 8–10 and 50+ words, respectively.

The Finnish data were collected by Sari Kunnari as part of her Ph.D. thesis for the Department of Finnish, Saami, and Logopedics, University of Oulu, Finland. Ten first-born children acquiring Finnish in Oulu, five girls and five boys, were video-recorded monthly from age 5 months until they had a cumulative vocabulary of about fifty words according to parental diary records. A high-quality microphone was placed near parent and child as they interacted in unstructured play sessions. In addition to the transcription of infant vocalizations, five mothers' speech to their child was transcribed and analysed for words used and for the distribution of consonants, all based on 4-word-point sessions. The word identification procedures carried out for English and French were also employed for Finnish (Kunnari 1998).

We restrict our acoustic analyses to disyllables, both identifiable words and non-words (whether babble or unidentifiable words); these form the overwhelming majority of multisyllabic productions in all three languages. Utterances selected for inclusion minimally contained two open (vocalic) phases separated by

Table 12.1. Subjects and sessions used in acoustic analyses

Child	Session					
	4-word point I		4-word point II		25-word point	
	Age	Word types	Age	Word types	Age	Word types
AMERICAN						
Deborah	0;11.4	4	0;11.11	4	1;3.24	20
Emily	1;1.0	5	1;1.7	5	1;3.29	25
Molly	0;10.15	4	0;10.23	3	1;2.20	19
Sean	1;0.19	6	1;0.24	6	1;3.23	31
Timmy	0;11.7	4	0;11.27	6	1;4.22	23
FRENCH						
Carole	0;10.26	4	0;11.10	7	1;2.5	28
Charles	0;11.13	5	1;0.10	5	1;3.19	20
Laurent	0;10.10	4	0;11.7	2	1;5.15	27
Marie	1;1.2	3	1;1.23	5	1;7.24	21
Noël	1;0.29	4	1;1.10	3	1;5.23	27
FINNISH						
Atte	1;5.0	6	1;6.3	9	1;8.0	26
Eelis	1;7.0	4	1;7.30	5	1;10.4	30
Eliisa	1;1.4	5			1;3.5	25
Mira	1;1.0	5	1;2.0	7	1;5.4	29
Venla	0;11.0	5	1;0.3	9	1;1.2	20

Note: Only spontaneous word types are used to establish word points; accordingly, the numbers given here are for spontaneous word types only.

a closed (consonantal) phase; we included every disyllable that lent itself to objective analysis by the methods available. Syllabic consonants were included as syllable nuclei. Disyllables with interfering talking or other noise were not used. We also included no more than three successive repetitions of a single word type, on the grounds that a single 'prosodic set' could be inferred and such mechanical repetition would unduly bias the results.

Phonetic transcriptions of the sessions were consulted for information as to word identity and segmental shape; the tokens were retranscribed as necessary on the basis of the additional acoustic information, especially as regards voicing, which is not reliably transcribable by ear alone.

The children's disyllabic vocalizations, whether words or babble, were extracted from the original recordings and digitally recorded using a 16-bit Audiomedia board at a sampling rate of 22.2 Hz. They were acoustically analysed using the SoundScope Speech Analysis Package implemented on a Power PC. The disyllables were segmented following rules devised as part of an earlier study (DePaolis *et al.* 1996), drawing on previous research (Peterson and Lehiste 1960;

Delattre 1966; Klatt 1976). Medial consonant duration measurements were made using concurrent information from the amplitude trace, narrow and wide band spectrograms, and intensity curve. Additionally, time scales were expanded on separate screens, to allow closer examination of transition points from C to V or V to C around manually placed markers (see Vihman *et al.* 1998: fig. 2).

2.2. Finnish geminates

To obtain some preliminary idea of the role of geminates in the acquisition of Finnish we consider first the distribution of words with geminates in the mothers' speech (Table 12.2) as well as in the words attempted and produced by the children (Table 12.3). As in other studies of the phonetics of the mothers' speech within different language groups (Vihman *et al.* 1994), the mothers are quite similar (s.d. 0.05), with a mean of 38 per cent content words with geminates, while the children are far more diverse, both in the percentage of geminate words that they attempt and in their production of geminates. The mean proportion of geminate words attempted at the 25-word point (target words) was 43 per cent, s.d. .0.14; the mean proportion of words produced with a geminate in at least one token (based on transcription) was 47 per cent, s.d. .0.14. More than half the words attempted included geminates for five of the ten children participating in the study. The five children whose data were analysed acoustically include three of those who attempted many words with geminates (Atte, 58%, Eelis, 55%, and Eliisa, 50%) and two who attempted relatively fewer such words (Venla, 43%, and Mira, 30%).

Table 12.2. Proportion of geminate words in Finnish mothers' speech to their children

Mother of	Content words with geminates	Total content words	%
Atte	274	678	40
Eliisa	151	368	41
Matti	161	411	39
Mira	114	402	28
Saini	293	730	40
MEAN	198.6	517.8	38 (s.d. 0.05)

2.3. Results

2.3.1. Acoustic analyses

The group results are given in Table 12.4. The children produce a wide range of medial consonant durations at the 4-word point, with somewhat higher variability (mean s.d.) within the French and Finnish children's vocalizations than the American but greater within-group homogeneity (group s.d.) in Finnish and

Table 12.3. *Proportion of geminate words attempted and produced at the 25-word point*

Child	Age	Words attempted with geminates		Words produced with geminates	
		Words with geminates/ all words	Proportion	Words with geminates/ all words	Proportion
Atte	1;8.0	15/26	0.58	18/26	0.69
Eelis	1;10.4	18/33	0.55	22/33	0.67
Eliisa	1;3.5	16/30	0.50	15/30	0.50
Emma	1;7.2	7/24	0.32	9/24	0.39
Ilari	1;11.0	10/26	0.38	10/26	0.38
Matti	1;6.5	19/38	0.50	21/38	0.55
Mira	1;5.4	10/29	0.30	12/29	0.41
Saini	1;3.15	12/22	0.55	9/22	0.41
Venla	1;1.2	10/24	0.43	11/24	0.46
Verneri	1;5.28	4/24	0.16	5/24	0.21
TOTAL		121/276	0.43 (s.d. 0.14)	112/276	0.47 (s.d. 0.14)

French than in English. No clear pattern is evident across children in any language group. At the 25-word point the groups diverge, in clear relationship to the structure of the adult languages. Here, the children acquiring English and French, adult languages that make no contrastive use of consonantal length, show a decrease in mean length and an even more striking decrease in group heterogeneity with lexical advance. Furthermore, the individual children's mean variability also drops (from an s.d. of 72 to 50 for English and 111 to 54 for French).

Table 12.4. *Medial consonant length in three languages*

Language	4-word point			25-word point		
	Mean in ms	Mean child s.d.	Group s.d.	Mean in ms	Mean child s.d.	Group s.d.
English	207.97	71.8	82.51	121.87	50.10	28.81
French	149.56	111.34	43.68	139.98	54.00	8.18
Finnish	205.74	132.96	46.99	297.82	150.67	96.07

The Finnish data show the opposite trend in every respect: The mean consonantal duration increases, from 206 ms to nearly 300 ms; individual child variability increases somewhat, from s.d. 133 to 150; and the group of children becomes more rather than less diverse, with the standard deviation for the group increasing from 47 to 96. Comparing Finnish with English and French, we can see that at the 25-word point English and French show a fall in every index while Finnish shows a rise.[1]

These same results can be seen graphically in Figures 12.1–12.6. The American and French infants display a good deal of variability at the 4-word point but 'pull together' at the short end of the duration range by the 25-word point to display similar profiles, both as individual children and as groups. On the other hand, over this same developmental period the Finnish children noticeably increase their variability as well as their mean medial consonant length. Some of the Finnish children develop sufficient sensitivity to the duration-based contrast in the adult language to begin to have what could be seen as a 'bipolar' profile by the 25-word point, as discussed below, prefiguring a full-blown phonological contrast, while others continue to explore a full range of possible consonantal durations.

We will now consider the individual developmental profiles of two of the Finnish children, then the relationship of those profiles to the words attempted. Lastly we will turn to their incipient phonological organization. Figures 12.7–12.8 show two different starting points (4-word points) for the two Finnish children, comparable to the varied starting points seen in Figures 12.1 and 12.3 for the English and French children. Eliisa shows two peaks, both at relatively short durations; she

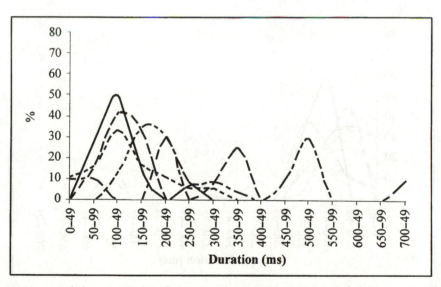

Fig. 12.1. Medial consonant lengths at 4-word point: Five American infants

[1] This pattern holds true of every child in every language group, with the exception of one French-learning child. This particular child had the shortest mean medial consonant duration of any child at the 4-word point (79.5 ms). At the 25-word point his medial consonant durations increase to durations similar to those of other French children (132.2 ms), almost 100 ms lower than any Finnish child at the 25-word point.

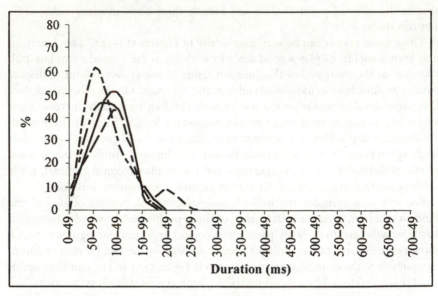

Fig. 12.2. Medial consonant lengths at 25-word point: Five American infants

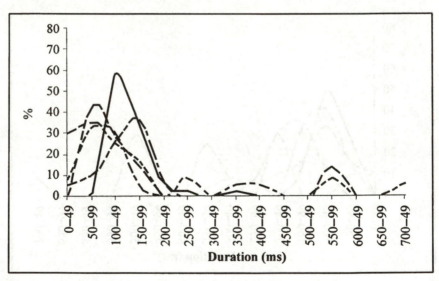

Fig. 12.3. Medial consonant lengths at 4-word point: Five French infants

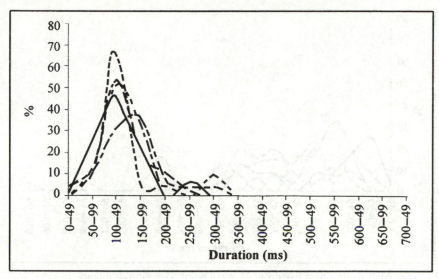

Fig. 12.4. Medial consonant lengths at 25-word point: Five French infants

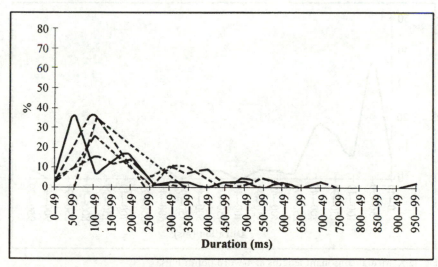

Fig. 12.5. Medial consonant lengths at 4-word point: Five Finnish infants

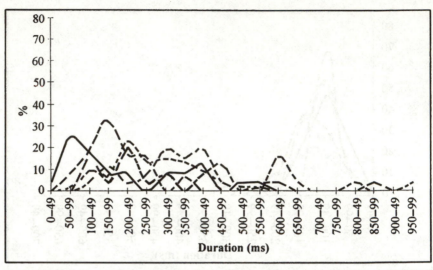

Fig. 12.6. Medial consonant lengths at 25-word point: Five Finnish infants

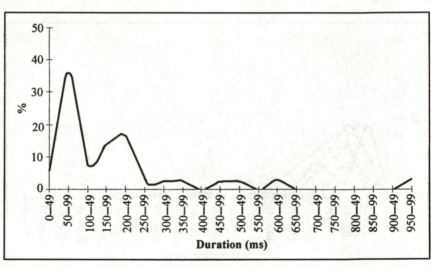

Fig. 12.7. Medial consonant lengths at 4-word point: Eliisa

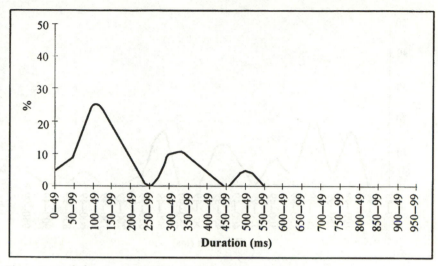

Fig. 12.8. Medial consonant lengths at 4-word point: Atte

also has a few vocalizations whose medial consonants are quite long. Atte also shows two separate peaks, at about 100–49 ms and then at about 300–400 ms.

At the 25-word point both children have begun to produce long medial consonants (Figs. 12.9–12.10). Although Eliisa has something resembling a bipolar distribution, Atte's profile now appears far less bipolar and also far less organized than it had been at the 4-word point.

To supplement these profiles, which are based on proportions of vocalizations

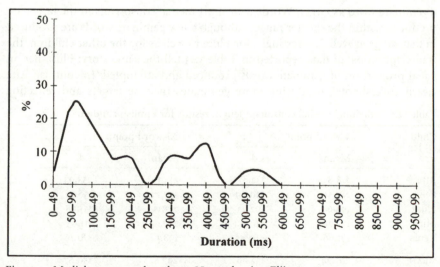

Fig. 12.9. Medial consonant lengths at 25-word point: Eliisa

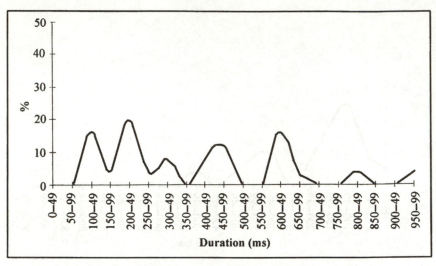

Fig. 12.10. Medial consonant lengths at 25-word point: Atte

at each medial consonant duration range, we plot the distribution of consonantal length in relation to the length-status (singleton versus geminate) of the medial consonant in the target. (Notice that this analysis can be undertaken at the 25-word point, when the majority of the children's productions have an identifiable target, but not at the 4-word point, when few vocalizations are identifiable as words.) As can be seen in Figs. 12.11–12.12, Eliisa appears to have fairly successfully sorted out her singletons from her geminates by the 25-word point. All of her longer productions, those over her mean of 213 ms. (see Table 12.5), are vocalizations with a geminate word as target. Words with short medial consonants in the target are produced within the shorter range, although a few geminate words are produced in that range as well. Interestingly, for Eliisa as well as for the other children, the transcription based data reported in Table 12.3 tell the same story: Eliisa has an equal proportion of geminate words produced and attempted. In contrast, Atte clearly 'overshoots', producing more geminates than he targets and reflecting

Table 12.5. Individual medial consonant length results for Finnish children

Child	4-word point		25-word point	
	Mean	s.d.	Mean	s.d.
Atte	218.8	132.87	413.16	253.03
Eelis	282.56	210.09	377.72	156.19
Eliisa	198.6	192.73	213.13	151.98
Mira	137.06	65.64	287.03	111.03
Venla	191.66	63.45	198.1	81.16
MEAN	205.74	132.96	297.82	150.67

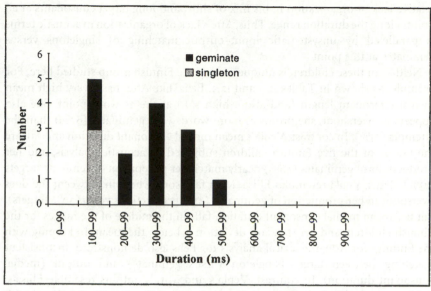

Fig. 12.11. Distribution of medial consonant length in relation to the length status of the medial consonant in the target: Eliisa, 25-word point

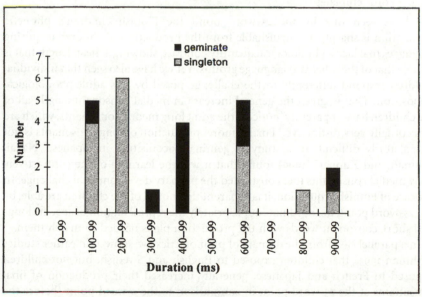

Fig. 12.12. Distribution of medial consonant length in relation to the length status of the medial consonant in the target: Atte, 25-word point

relative lack of organization in his mix of short and long target consonants at all points along the duration range. Thus, Atte's lack of organization in acoustic terms is paralleled by unsystematic input–output matching of singletons versus geminates at this point.

Neither of these children is unique among the Finnish group studied here. For example, as shown in Tables 12.3 and 12.5, Eelis, like Atte, has a very high mean medial consonant length (and also a high s.d.) at the 25-word point. She also appears to overshoot; she produces more words with geminates (67%) than she attempts (55%). In contrast, Venla's mean medial consonant duration and s.d. are the lowest of the five Finnish children subjected to acoustic analysis, and her productions of geminates (46%) nearly match her proportion of geminate targets (43%). Thus, Venla resembles Eliisa. Mira falls somewhere in between; she does overshoot in her production of geminates (41% productions versus 30% targets), but her mean medial consonant duration falls in the middle of the ranges for the Finnish children, and her standard deviation is below the mean. In keeping with the findings for Atte, the lexical analysis for Eelis also demonstrates inconsistent matching between target (singleton versus geminate) and output (medial consonant duration). In contrast, Venla's and Mira's outputs resemble Eliisa's: they approach the adult pattern more closely (target geminates produced with longer durations).

2.3.2. Word templates

We have seen that by the 25-word point the Finnish children's phonetic production is sharply distinguishable from the production of children acquiring languages that lack a phonological quantity contrast, showing a mean length that is double that of the other two language groups. Yet we have also seen that individual children respond differently to the challenge posed by this adult phonological opposition. That is, given the general increase in medial consonant length, all of the children have apparently 'noticed' the adult long medial consonants, which are perceptually very distinctive.[2] Furthermore, production of long consonants is not articulatorily difficult. In a study of geminate acquisition in Japanese, Nakai, Vihman, and Kunnari (1999) found that it was the learning of the contrastively *short* medial consonants that constituted the primary developmental challenge. In the case of Finnish acquisition, it is apparent that not all of the children are able, by the 25-word point, to coordinate appropriately the representation of specific long- and short-consonant words with the production plans needed to match them.

In a parallel case from the domain of phonotactics, we showed in earlier studies (Vihman 1993) that children exposed to English and Swedish, but not children exposed to French and Japanese, generally increased their production of final consonants at the 25-word point in comparison to the 0 word point (before the onset of word use). Indeed, one French child, Carole, produced 41 per cent final

---

[2] Richardson (1998) has demonstrated that (Finnish) 6-month olds discriminate the synthetically designed nonsense forms [ata] from [atta] at a category boundary similar to that of Finnish adults.

consonants in babble, but essentially ceased to produce any at the 25-word point (only 1 per cent final consonants). By the 25- but not the 4-word point, two out of five American children frequently produced final consonants, while the remaining three continued to produce primarily the more universally distributed open syllables. In a longitudinal microanalysis of Molly, one of the two children who focused on final consonant production from early on, we found that the phonological treatment of final consonants did not emerge directly out of her earlier production of such consonants in babbling and first words. She ranked only third among the American children in final consonant use in babbling (7 per cent use), but moved up to a strong second place (23 per cent use) by the 25-word point. In between these two points was a period of focused exploration of a variety of word shapes, highly variable productions, and phonological reorganization (Vihman and Velleman 1989). The result was a CVNV/CVC^h pattern in which the final consonant of a target CVC word was preserved (faithfulness), but either as the onset of a second syllable (for nasal targets, as in [panːə] for *Brian*, [wanːə] for *around*) or as a highly aspirated or affricated coda (for obstruent targets, as in [hit^h], [ʔɪtʃ] for *eat*). These patterns were applied to inappropriate target words as well (producing, for example, *Nicky*, in which the target nasal is not word final, as [ɪnːi] and *cheese* as [itʃ]). Such child-based patterning is typical of a word template.

Achieving the ability to produce differing consonants in a sequence of syllables is one of the key developmental challenges for phonological learning. Whereas implicit phonetic learning in the period of babbling and first words results in the subtle shaping of child vocalizations in the direction of the adult language (shifting frequencies of production of segmental and prosodic categories towards ambient language values (Boysson-Bardies and Vihman, 1991; Vihman *et al.* 1998)), representation-based patterning at the 25-word point can be seen to lead, in some cases, to radical restructuring of adult target forms to fit the child's preferred word template or templates (see Vihman 1996: ch. 9, for references to a number of earlier case studies that illustrate this point, such as Priestly 1977; longitudinal data from individual children acquiring English and French are also included in Vihman 1996: app. C). Typically, the majority of tokens of all word types conform to a single template, with a small residue of forms that may be more or less accurate but that fall outside the systematized production pattern(s) (McCune and Vihman forthcoming).

We will begin our consideration of incipient phonological organization in Finnish by summarizing the results of an analysis of the word tokens transcribed at the 25-word point for all ten children. The column headings in Table 12.6 indicate the five phonological patterns found in the children's identifiable word productions at the 25-word point, based on transcription. In each case the child's word types and tokens could be exhaustively categorized as falling into one or more of these patterns only—namely, monosyllables, disyllables lacking a medial consonant, disyllables lacking an initial consonant ('null onset'), disyllables with

Table 12.6. Early word templates in Finnish

Child	Single consonant				VCV		Consonant sequence			
	(C)VV(C)		(C)V.V				C1VC1V		C1VC2V	
	Instances/total	Proportion	Instances/total	Proportion	Instances/total	Proportion	Instances/total	Proportion	Instances/total	Proportion
Atte	11/33	**0.33**			16/26	**0.61**	10/26	**0.38**		
Eelis	3/31	0.10			14/33	**0.39**	8/33	0.27		
Eliisa	9/26	**0.35**	4/31	0.13	7/31	0.23	17/31	**0.55**		
Emma	4/25	0.16			6/26	0.23	6/26	0.23	5/26	0.19
Ilari	4/42	0.10			7/25	0.28	8/25	0.32	6/25	0.24
Matti	4/32	0.13			19/42	**0.45**	10/42	0.24	9/42	0.21
Mira	8/26	0.31			1/32	0.03	22/32	**0.69**	5/32	0.16
Saini					6/26	0.23	10/26	**0.38**	2/26	0.08
Venla	2/24	0.08			7/24	0.29	15/24	**0.63**		
Verneri	10/28	**0.36**	1/28	0.04	10/28	**0.36**	6/28	0.21	1/28	0.04
MEAN		0.19		0.02		0.31		0.39		0.09

Notes: C1 . . . C1 indicates a consonant harmony constraint (CH).
Italics indicate that the template applies to words with geminates only.
Bold face is used for all patterns that account for more than 33% of the child's tokens, and also for the names of the five children whose data were analysed acoustically for this study.

harmonizing consonantal onsets, and disyllables with differing consonantal onsets.

These patterns are based on the child's forms. It is also informative to consider them in relation to the adult target. Here we distinguish two subtypes: (*a*) 'selected' forms are those that derive directly from the target (allowing for changes in vowel or consonant that do not affect the basic structure) while (*b*) 'adapted' forms are those that involve more radical changes to the adult target. Specifically, 'adaptation' includes consonant assimilation to achieve consonant harmony, consonant omission to achieve V.V or VCV patterns, and syllable omission to achieve the monosyllable pattern. The proportion of each child's distinguishable tokens that are accounted for by each pattern is indicated on Table 12.6, with bold face highlighting the cases where a single pattern accounts for over one-third of a child's differing tokens.[3] Examples of each of the patterns follows, drawing for illustration on the child who makes the greatest use of the pattern:[4]

1. *Monosyllables (C)VV(C): Verneri*
   (*a*) /ei/ 'no' [ei]; /puu/ 'tree' [puu]; /pois/ 'off, away' [poi];
   (*b*) /paini(nalle)/ 'wrestling (teddy)' [pai]; /kiinni/ 'closed' [ki(i)].
2. *No medial consonant (C)V.V: Eliisa*
   (*a*) [no instances];
   (*b*) /kirja/ 'book' [ki:a]; /piiloon/ 'into hiding' [i.o]; /haloo/ 'hello (telephone)' /a.o/.
3. *Null onset VCV: Atte*
   (*a*) /auto/ 'car' [autto]; /äiti/ 'mother' [äitti]; /isi/ 'father' [içi]; /aŋkka/ 'duck' [akka];
   (*b*) /kala/ 'fish' [ala]; /pallo/ 'ball' [allo]; /loppu/ 'end, finished, all done' [oppu]; /nalle/ 'teddybear' [alle].
4. *Harmonizing consonant sequences C1VC1V: Mira*
   (*a*) /paapaa/ 'is sleeping' [paapaa]; /nenä/ 'nose' [nenä]; /tüttö/ 'girl' [titto]; /kukka/ 'flower' [kakkʰa];
   (*b*) /loppu/ 'end, finished, all done' [poppu]; /nalle/ 'teddybear' [ʎaʎʎe].
5. *Non-harmonizing consonant sequences C1VC2V: Ilari*
   (*a*) /piiloon/ 'into hiding' [piilo]; /pikku/ 'little' [pikku]; /pois/ 'away' [poiʃ];
   (*b*) [no instances].

The V.V pattern plays only a minor role for a single child (and there is no

---

[3] Where the tokens of a single word type fit more than one pattern, they are assigned to each, but all tokens conforming to a single pattern are counted once only. Thus the number of instances of patterns indicated on the table for each child are occasionally greater than the total number of different word types targeted but are always less than the total number of tokens produced.

[4] In citing Finnish adult and child forms we will follow Finnish orthographic convention in using double letters to indicate long vowels and geminate consonants and the letter <ä> for the low front vowel.

'selection' of corresponding adult patterns to ground it). The C1VC2V pattern also fails to play a major role for any of the children, though it is of somewhat higher mean occurrence (9 per cent), and when it does occur, it represents something close to the 'end state' for the words in question. In this case there are no 'adapted' instances. Neither of these patterns can be seen as serving as a word template for any of the children. The three remaining patterns dominate the children's early word forms, yielding monosyllables and disyllables only; there were few longer forms produced (5 per cent, if onomatopoeia and interjections are included (Kunnari 1998)), and only slightly more attempted (9 per cent; in maternal input at the 25-word point Kunnari (1998), finds 10 per cent, including onomatopoeia and interjections).

1. *Monosyllables* (mean 23%) played a dominant role for three children, with adaptation in the form of second syllable omission in several cases. This is most striking in the case of Saini, who omits final syllables from geminate words as well as words with singletons: /pallo/ 'ball' > [ba], /tuossa/ 'there' > [tu]. Some children showed first instead of second syllable omission: see Verneri /tonttu/ 'brownie' and /istu/ 'sit' both > [tu], Matti: /kiikkaa/ 'swing (V)' > [ka]. Two of the children (Eelis and Verneri) omit the geminate nasal along with the following vowel in /kiinni/ 'closed', yielding [kii]. Four of the children sometimes omit initial consonants from adult monosyllabic targets, yielding onsetless monosyllables, but all are onomatopoeic words: Matti: /mää/ > [ää] 'sheep sound', Emma and Saini: /nam(nam)/ > [am] 'yum' as well as Saini /ammu/ > [am] 'moo'.

2. *Disyllables with no initial consonant* (mean 31%) were often arrived at through 'adaptation' (initial consonant omission). The pattern played a dominant role for four children. The Finnish accent pattern is trochaic, yet the initial consonant—so rarely omitted in English child production in general that a tendency to do so is viewed as a sign of disordered phonology (Howell & Dean, 1994; Velleman 1998)—is frequently omitted (see also Savinainen-Makkonen, 1996).

3. *Disyllables with harmonizing consonants* (mean 39%) characterized more than half of the forms for three children, and constituted a dominant form for two more children. Venla presents a special case: Of her 15 harmonizing patterns, 10 include labials. Since Finnish has only three labial consonants—/p/, /m/ and /v/, which patterns like a glide, the child shows a good deal of homophony. For example, her forms [pappa] and [bappa] derive from /pallo/ 'ball', /palikka/ 'block', /varpaat/ 'toes' and /plektra/ 'plectrum, or guitar pick' (compare the bilingual child Raivo, whose early Estonian and English word forms displayed a high level of homophony, identified as an organizational strategy in Vihman, 1981). Eelis shows harmony forms only for targets with geminates (stops and nasals); Eliisa harmonizes only to stops. Saini assimilates only to alveolars, whether in initial or medial position: /tini/ (proper name) > [titi / titti]; /nalle/ 'teddybear' > [nanne]; /lintu/ 'bird' >

[ninnu]. Atte shows regressive harmony only, as does Mira, with a single exception (/kaataa/ 'overturns' > [kaakaa]).

Table 12.7 indicates the extent to which the two most common patterns are either 'selected' or 'adapted' to yield the child forms for each child. We see that adaptation accounts for just under half of the children's forms in both cases. The main point of interest here is the role of geminates. Of the 115 child forms that harmonize, 64 (56 per cent) derive from adult targets with geminates, as against 33 from singletons and 18 from clusters. Similarly, 41 (48 per cent) of the 85 onsetless child disyllables derive from geminate targets. Of the null onset child forms with geminate targets, over half are adapted. It is important to note that geminate words are overrepresented in these patterns compared to their incidence overall (53 per cent combined mean, 43 per cent geminate words over all words attempted, but 38 per cent geminate words in the input: Tables 12.2 and 12.3). The double 'augmentation' of the geminate pattern in adult words—by child selection of geminate targets, first of all, and then by child construction of templates around geminates—provides strong evidence of the children's role in 'constructing' phonology.

Table 12.7. The role of geminates in Finnish early word templates

Medial	Select/adapt	CH	Null onset	Total
C	select	22	27	49
	adapt	11	8	19
CC	select	40	18	58
	adapt	24	23	47
C₁C₂	select	[not applicable]	2	2
	adapt	18	7	25
TOTAL		115	85	200
		(46% adapted)	(45% adapted)	

The combined effect of 'selection' and 'adaptation' is what we take to be the child's initial phonological organization: The preferred word production plans conform to dominant characteristics of the adult language (such as the incorporation of geminates for Finnish, final consonants for English), but also differ from one child to the next, allowing for the well-documented individual paths from phonetics into phonology (Vihman 1993). Returning now to the findings of our acoustic analyses for just five of the children (Table 12.5), we can ask whether there is anything about the phonological patterns we have identified that separates Eliisa, Venla, and perhaps Mira, with their relatively greater progress towards organizing an opposition based on consonantal length, from Atte and Eelis. And indeed when we turn back, with this question in mind, to Table 12.6, which charts the extent to which the children's productions conform to any one pattern, we observe that the three children with the strongest harmonizing patterns are (in order of most to least) Mira, Venla, and Eliisa; the only other child with a single equally strong pattern is Atte, who omits initial consonants more often than he harmonizes the onset consonants.

It may be that early development of a harmony production pattern is one way for a child to begin to master the prosodic opposition between long and short consonants—both syntagmatically (first versus second syllable onset) and paradigmatically (comparing across words with medial singletons versus geminates). That is, the C1VC1V frame may serve to focus the child's attention on the length contrast. To test this hypothesis we examined the shapes of the word tokens produced by these five children at the 4-word point. They are listed in Table 12.8 in order of most to least consonant harmony forms at the later 25-word point. Here we see that the children who have begun to master the length opposition by the 25-word point are in fact the children whose earliest word forms were most exclusively centred on harmony patterns. These children did not target or produce more such patterns, but they failed to produce many other patterns—suggesting that for some time prior to the 25-word point most of their productions of word tokens fit the harmony pattern. Among the alternative paths followed by the Finnish children are omission of initial or medial consonants or final syllables of

Table 12.8. Production of consonant harmony forms at the 4-word point (five children only)

Child	Harmony forms (%)	Harmony forms	Non-harmony forms
Mira	100	*mammaa* 'milk' *mamma* 'Muumi mama' tätä 'this' *pallo* 'ball' > **papu**	
Eliisa	75	*kiikkuu* 'swing' *lamppu* 'lamp' > **papu** *pallo* 'ball' > **papu**	**hau** 'woof'
Venla	67	*kakka* 'caca' leipää 'bread' > ***päppää*** *pallo* 'ball' > ***bappo*** vauva 'baby'	**hauva** 'bowwow, dog' *pallo* 'ball' > **pa**
Eelis	50	heppa 'horse' > **beppa** *kiikkaa* 'swing' *kukka* 'flower'	äiti 'mother' anna 'give' kaatui 'fell' > **kaa**
Atte	40	*kukka* 'flower' *mummu* 'grandmom' *pappa* 'grandpa' **tutututu** 'toottoot'	äiti 'mother' anna 'give' > **na** heppa 'horse' *mummu* > **ummo, mu** *pappa* > **pa** 'grandpa' *tonttu* 'brownie' > **to**

Note: Child forms are in bold; words with geminate consonants are in italics.

disyllabic words, but none of these strategies would plausibly lead to the sharpening of focus on the short/long opposition that the harmonic frame affords.

3. DISCUSSION

We have focused on two lexically defined developmental points in our data analyses, but it should be pointed out that there is nothing definitive about these 'word points'. They provide a convenient marker for comparing across children learning the same or different languages; they certainly constitute a more meaningful basis for comparison than age-based markers would (notice that the Finnish children range in age from 13 to 22 months at the 25-word point, and that some of the children reach the 25-word point at a younger age than other children reach the 4-word point). But our acoustic analysis of the production of medial consonants shows clearly that the 25-word point defines no single phonetic 'stage' in the development of the short/long opposition.

We would also like to emphasize that a finding of increase or decrease in group coherence with lexical advance depends on the particular parameter being considered. With respect to labial production, for example, all four groups included in Vihman (1993)—English, French, Japanese, and Swedish—showed a drop in standard deviation from the prelexical level (0-word point) to the end of the single-word period (25-word point). The percentage of labials in words was higher than in babble for all four languages, reaching ambient adult levels by the 25-word point. For final consonants, which are relatively rarely produced in the early period, English shows the increase in standard deviation that reflects the beginnings of use for two out of five of the children while French shows a drop, as all the French children agree on producing very few final consonants at the 25-word point. Similarly here, although we found a drop in group variability for both English and French with respect to medial consonant duration, Finnish showed the increase in group variability that corresponds to the emergent opposition between short and long consonants for two or three of the five children.

Let us review the developmental path from phonetics to incipient phonology as we understand it. In the prelexical period infants develop favoured production patterns through babbling, which results in both perceptual and proprioceptive familiarity or 'knowledge' of those patterns. Children whose lexical development is relatively precocious are those who show an early sensitivity to the presence of speech patterns in the input that provide a rough match to their own developing vocal patterns (McCune and Vihman forthcoming). In fact, we see the child's (unintentional, implicit) matching of vocal motor schemes developed through exploratory babbling as the solution to the paradox of experimentally validated 'selection on phonological grounds' (Schwartz and Leonard, 1982): How does the child know what to avoid, without having first tried out what he or she cannot produce (a question raised by Stemberger and Bernhardt 1999, as discussed above)? The answer, we believe, is that the child does not 'know what to avoid' but instead is drawn to reproduce patterns familiar from own vocal production as well as from adult input. Thus the vocally precocious child 'knows what he or she knows', not what he or she does not know.

In our view, then, 'selection on phonological grounds' reflects the child's unconscious matching of own patterns to input, and consequent tendency to produce as identifiable words, in context, just those patterns that are relatively close to pre-existing babbling patterns from his or her repertoire. Once the child's representational abilities have also made an advance, based on the neurological changes that occur at the end of the first year and are apparently consolidated in the first months of the second year (Scheibel 1993; Mills *et al.* 1994), production of those 'selected' word patterns leads to a more abstract representation of 'pronounceable word forms': this is the word template. Achievement of such a more structured or abstract representation permits the child to 'overgeneralize', disregarding details that stand in the way of a match. As a result, he or she now begins to produce some old words less accurately than before and a good many more new words, some of them radically adapting adult forms to fit the template.

The word templates are not generally equivalent to adult phonology; the child will have to outgrow the need for them as his or her representations of adult words continue to improve and stabilize and as he or she gradually masters the phonetic challenges of the particular adult language. But they do constitute a (discontinuous) step beyond gradual phonetic accommodation: they show that the child is implicitly comparing across the representations of different word types, selecting one or more production plans from among those that are familiar and therefore efficiently executed, and adding new word types to those relatively abstract—so 'phonological'—patterns.

It seems appropriate here to mention one more cross-domain parallel in the early learning of structure. According to Ninio (1999*a,b*), children typically embark on adult-like verb use with one or two 'generic' verbs of high frequency in the input. Recurrent use of just one or two such verbs over an extended period of time appears to lead the child to induce an abstract notion of predication, eventually resulting in a sharp increase in the use of new verb types. (Ninio's data are from children acquiring English and Hebrew; see Vihman (1999*b*) for confirmatory data from a child acquiring Estonian and English.) The children could be described as 'learning by doing', or 'picking up' an abstract structural notion from active use of a 'model exemplar'. In the Finnish data we seem to see the same process: active production of consonant harmony frames over an extended period of time appears to be a way of inducing the short/long opposition in medial consonants.

The model we are proposing does assume the continuity of phonetics throughout development. However, a discontinuity is present as well: the onset of phonological systematization is superimposed upon ongoing phonetic learning, and in time this system begins to take a primary role in shaping output. The development of such a system is, in our view, mandated by 'faithfulness'—the complexity of patterning of the ambient language. The child takes advantage of phonetic grounding but focuses at any one time on only a subset of the word forms made available by prior phonetic experience, in order to establish a phonological system. Templates are typically based upon features of the ambient language, but also upon the patterns that represent the child's prior phonetic learning, resulting in adaptations of the target forms that, as a result, are no longer 'faithful' or accurate. These nascent phonologies arise as the child's individual solution to the tension between production ease (markedness) and ambient language require-ments (faithfulness) and signal the onset of truly phonological organization.

REFERENCES

Archangeli, D. and Pulleyblank, D. (1994), *Grounded Phonology* (Cambridge, Mass.: MIT Press).

Baddeley, A., Gathercole, S., and Papagno, C. (1998), 'The Phonological Loop as a Learning Device', *Psychological Review*, 105: 158–73.

Bernhardt, B. and Stemberger, J. P. (1998), *Handbook of Phonological Development: From the Perspective of Constraint-Based Nonlinear Phonology* (San Diego, Calif.: Academic Press).

Best, C. T. (1994), 'The Emergence of Language-Specific Phonemic Influences in Infant Speech Perception', in J. C. Goodman and H. C. Nusbaum (eds.), *The Development of Speech Perception: The Transition from Speech Sounds to Spoken Words* (Cambridge, Mass.: MIT Press), 167–224.

Boysson-Bardies, B. de and Vihman, M. M. (1991), 'Adaptation to Language: Evidence from Babbling and First Words in Four Languages', *Language*, 67: 297–319.

—— Hallé, P., Sagart, L., and Durand, C. (1989), 'A Cross-Linguistic Investigation of Vowel Formants in Babbling', *Journal of Child Language*, 16: 1–17.

Carey, S. (1978), 'The Child as Word Learner', in M. Halle, J. Bresnan, and G. A. Miller (eds.), *Linguistic Theory and Psychological Reality* (Cambridge, Mass.: MIT Press), 264–93.

Davis, B. L. and MacNeilage, P. F. (1990), 'Acquisition of Correct Vowel Production: A Quantitative Case Study', *Journal of Speech and Hearing Research*, 33: 16–27.

Delattre, P. C. (1966), 'A Comparison of Syllable Length Conditioning among Languages', *International Journal of Applied Linguistics*, 4: 182–98.

DePaolis, R., Vihman, M. M., and Davis, B. L. (1996), 'Acoustic and Perceptual Evaluation of Stress', paper presented at the 10th International Conference on Infant Studies, Providence, RI, April.

Ferguson, C. A. and Farwell, C. B. (1975), 'Words and Sounds in Early Language Acquisition', *Language*, 51: 419–39.

Gathercole, V. C. (1983), 'Haphazard Examples, Prototype Theory, and the Acquisition of Comparatives', *First Language*, 4: 169–96.

—— Sebastian, E., and Soto, P. (1999), 'The Early Acquisition of Spanish Verbal Morphology: Across-the-Board or Piecemeal Knowledge?', *International Journal of Bilingualism*, 3: 133–82.

Gnanadesikan, A. E. (1995), 'Markedness and Faithfulness Constraints in Child Phonology', MS, University of Massachusetts, Amherst and Rutgers University; Rutgers Optimality Archive ROA-67.

Goad, H. (1997), 'Consonant Harmony in Child Language: An Optimality-Theoretic Account', in S. J. Hannahs, and M. Young-Scholten (eds.), *Focus on Phonological Acquisition* (Amsterdam: John Benjamins), 113–42.

Hale, M. and Reiss, C. (1996), 'Competence and Performance in Child Phonology', MS, Concordia University, Montreal.

—— —— (1997), 'Formal and Empirical Arguments Concerning Phonological Acquisition', MS, Concordia University, Montreal.

Hallé, P., Boysson-Bardies, B. de, and Vihman, M. M. (1991), 'Beginnings of Prosodic Organization: Intonation and Duration Patterns of Disyllables Produced by French and Japanese Infants', *Language and Speech*, 34: 299–318.

Howell, J. and Dean, E. (1994), *Treating Phonological Disorders in Children: Metaphon—Theory to Practise* (2nd edn., London: Whurr Publishers Ltd.).

Karmiloff-Smith, A. (1992), *Beyond Modularity: A Developmental Perspective on Cognitive Science* (Cambridge, Mass.: MIT Press).

Kingston, J. and Diehl, R. L. (1994), 'Phonetic Knowledge', *Language*, 70: 419–54.

Klatt, D. H. (1976), 'Linguistic Uses of Segmental Duration in English: Acoustic and Perceptual Evidence', *Journal of the Acoustical Society of America*, 59: 1208–21.

Kunnari, S. (1998), 'Syllable Number in Early Words', in K. Heinänen, and M. Lehtihalmes (eds.), *Proceedings of the Seventh Nordic Child Language Symposium, Oulu, 27–28 November* (Oulu: Publications of the Department of Finnish, Saami and Logopedics), 85–8.

Laver, J. (1994), *Principles of Phonetics* (Cambridge: Cambridge University Press).

Lieven, E. V. M., Pine, J. M., and Baldwin, G. (1997), 'Lexically-Based Learning and Early Grammatical Development', *Journal of Child Language*, 24: 187–219.

Lindblom, B. (1983), 'Economy of Speech Gestures', in P. F. MacNeilage (ed.), *Speech Production* (New York: Springer), 217–45.

—— (1992), 'Phonological Units as Adaptive Emergents of Lexical Development', in C. A. Ferguson, L. Menn, and C. Stoel-Gammon (eds.), *Phonological Development: Models, Research, Implications* (Timonium, Md: York Press) 131–63.

—— (1998), 'Systemic Constraints and Adaptive Change in the Formation of Sound Structure', in J. R. Hurford, M. Studdert-Kennedy, and C. Knight (eds.), *Approaches to the Evolution of Language: Social and Cognitive Bases* (Cambridge: Cambridge University Press), 242–64.

—— (forthcoming), 'Emergent Phonology', *Berkeley Linguistics Society 25* (University of California, Berkeley).

Locke, J. L. (1983), *Phonological Acquisition and Change* (New York: Academic Press).

McCune, L. and Vihman, M. M. (1987), 'Vocal Motor Schemes', *Papers and Reports on Child Language Development*, 26: 72–9.

—— —— (forthcoming), 'Phonetics and Semantics of Single Words: Integration and Redirection', *Journal of Speech, Language and Hearing Research*.

Macken, M. A. (1978), 'Permitted Complexity in Phonological Development: One Child's Acquisition of Spanish Consonants', *Lingua*, 44/2–3: 219–53.

—— (1979), 'Developmental Reorganization of Phonology: A Hierarchy of Basic Units of Acquisition', *Lingua*, 49: 11–49.

—— (1995), 'Phonological Acquisition', in J. A. Goldsmith (ed.), *The Handbook of Phonological Theory* (Oxford: Blackwell), 671–98.

—— and Ferguson, C. A. (1983), 'Cognitive Aspects of Phonological Development: Model, Evidence and Issues', in K. E. Nelson (ed.), *Children's Language*, iv (Hillsdale, NJ: Lawrence Erlbaum), 256–82.

MacNeilage, P. F. (1994), 'Prolegomena to a Theory of the Sound Pattern of the First Spoken Language', *Phonetica*, 51: 184–94.

—— (1997), 'Acquisition of Speech', in W. J. Hardcastle and J. Laver (eds.), *The Handbook of Phonetic Sciences (Oxford: Blackwell)*, 301–32.

—— and Davis, B. L. (1990), 'Acquisition of Speech Production: Frames, then Content', in M. Jeannerod (ed.), *Attention and Performance XIII: Motor Representation and Control* (Hillsdale, NJ: Lawrence Erlbaum), 453–75.

Menn, L. (1978), *Pattern, Control, and Contrast in Beginning Speech: A Case Study in the Development of Word Form and Word Function* (Bloomington, Ind.: Indiana University Linguistics Club).

Mills, D. L., Coffey-Corina, S. A., and Neville, H. J. (1994), 'Variability in Cerebral Organization during Primary Language Acquisition', in C. Dawson and K. W. Fischer (eds.), *Human Behavior and the Developing Brain* (New York: Guilford Press), 427–55.

Myers, S. (1997), 'Expressing Phonetic Naturalness in Phonology', in I. Roca (ed.), *Derivations and Constraints in Phonology* (Oxford: Oxford University Press), 125–52.

Nakai, S., Vihman, M. M., and Kunnari, S. (1999), 'The Acquisition of Geminates by Japanese Children', paper presented at the first annual meeting of the Chester Language Development Group, 30 April – 2 May.

Ninio, A. (1999*a*), 'Model Learning in Syntactic Development: Intransitive Verbs', *International Journal of Bilingualism*, 3: 619–53.

—— (1999*b*), 'Pathbreaking Verbs in Syntactic Development and the Question of Prototypical Transitivity', *Journal of Child Language*, 26: 111–31.

Oller, D. K. (1980), 'The Emergence of the Sounds of Speech in Infancy', in G. Yeni-Komshian, J. F. Kavanagh, and C. A. Ferguson (eds.), *Child Phonology*, I. *Production* (New York: Academic Press), 93–112.

Peterson, G. E. and Lehiste, I. (1960), 'Duration of Syllable Nuclei in English', *Journal of the Acoustical Society of America*, 32: 693–703.

Priestly, T. M. S. (1977), 'One Idiosyncratic Strategy in the Acquisition of Phonology', *Journal of Child Language*, 4: 45–66.

Pulleyblank, D. and Turkel, W. J. (1997), 'Gradient Retreat', in I. Roca (ed.), *Derivations and Constraints in Phonology* (New York: Oxford University Press), 153–85.

Pye, C., Ingram, D., and List, H. (1987), 'A Comparison of Initial Consonant Acquisition in English and Quiche', in K. E. Nelson, and A. Van Kleek (eds.), *Children's Language*, VI (Hillsdale, NJ: Lawrence Erlbaum), 175–90.

Richardson, U. (1998), 'Familial Dyslexia and Sound Duration in the Quantity Distinctions of Finnish Infants and Adults', *Studia Philologica Jyväskyläensia*, 44: 9–211.

Savinainen-Makkonen, T. (1996), 'Lapsenkielen fonologia systemaattisen kehityksen kaudella' [The phonology of child language during the period of systematic development]; licentiate thesis (University of Helsinki).

Scheibel, A. B. (1993), 'Dendritic Structure and Language Development', in B. de

Boysson-Bardies, S. de Schonen, P. Jusczyk, P. MacNeilage, and J. Morton (eds.), *Developmental Neurocognition: Speech and Face Processing in the First Year of Life* (Dordrecht: Kluwer), 51–62.

Schwartz, R. G. and Leonard, L. B. (1982), 'Do Children Pick and Choose? An Examination of Phonological Selection and Avoidance in Early Lexical Acquisition', *Journal of Child Language*, 9: 319–36.

Scobbie, J. M. (1998), 'Interactions Between the Acquisition of Phonetics and Phonology', paper presented at CLS 34, Chicago. (Published in M. C. Gruber, D. Higgins, K. Olson, and T. Wysocki (eds.), *CLS 34* (Chicago: Chicago Linguistic Society, 1998), 343–58.)

Smolensky, P. (1996), 'On the Comprehension/Production Dilemma in Child Language', *Linguistic Inquiry*, 27: 720–31

Stemberger, J. P. and Bernhardt, B. H. (1999), 'The Emergence of Faithfulness', in B. MacWhinney (ed.), *The Emergence of Language* (Mahwah, NJ: Lawrence Erlbaum), 417–46.

Studdert-Kennedy, M. (1987), 'The Phoneme as a Perceptuomotor Structure', in A. Allport, D. MacKay, W. Prinz, and E. Scheerer (eds.), *Language Perception and Production* (New York: Academic Press), 67–84.

Thelen, E. (1989), 'Self-Organization in Developmental Processes: Can Systems Approaches Work?', in M. Gunnar, and E. Thelen (eds.), *Systems in Development: The Minnesota Symposia in Child Psychology* (Hillsdale, NJ: Lawrence Erlbaum), 77–117.

Thevenin, D. M., Eilers, R. E., Oller, D. K., and Lavoie, L. (1985), 'Where's the Drift in Babbling Drift? A Cross-Linguistic Study', *Applied Psycholinguistics*, 6: 3–15.

Tomasello, M. (1992), *First Verbs* (Cambridge: Cambridge University Press).

Velleman, S. (1998), *Making Phonology Functional: What Do I Do First?* (Boston: Butterworth-Heinemann).

—— and Vihman, M. M. (1999), 'The Optimal "initial state"', MS, University of Massachusetts, Amherst, and University of Wales, Bangor.

—— —— and Lleó, C. (1999), 'Resources, Constraints, and Patterning in the Acquisition of Phonology', MS, University of Massachusetts, Amherst, University of Wales, Bangor, and University of Hamburg.

Vihman, M. M. (1976), 'From Prespeech to Speech: On Early Phonology', *Stanford Papers and Reports on Child Language Development*, 12: 230–44.

—— (1981), 'Phonology and the Development of the Lexicon: Evidence from Children's Errors', *Journal of Child Language*, 8: 239–64.

—— (1991), 'Ontogeny of Phonetic Gestures: Speech Production', in I. G. Mattingly and M. Studdert-Kennedy (eds.), *Modularity and the Motor Theory of Speech Perception: Proceedings of a Conference to Honor Alvin M. Liberman* (Hillsdale, NJ: Lawrence Erlbaum), 69–84.

—— (1993), 'Variable Paths to Early Word Production', *Journal of Phonetics*, 21: 61–82.

—— (1996), *Phonological Development: The Origins of Language in the Child* (Oxford: Blackwell).

—— (1999*a*), 'Cross-Linguistic Studies of Early Grammar', *International Journal of Bilingualism*, 3: 105–10.

—— (1999*b*), 'The Transition to Grammar in a Bilingual Child: Positional Patterns, Model Learning, and Relational Words', *International Journal of Bilingualism*, 3: 267–301.

—— and McCune, L. (1994), 'When is a Word a Word?', *Journal of Child Language*, 21: 517–42.

—— and Miller, R. (1988), 'Words and Babble at the Threshold of Lexical Acquisition', in M. D. Smith, and J. L. Locke (eds.), *The Emergent Lexicon: The Child's Development of a Linguistic Vocabulary* (New York: Academic Press), 151–83.

—— and Velleman, S. L. (1989), 'Phonological Reorganization: A Case Study', *Language and Speech*, 32: 149–70.

—— Macken, M. A., Miller, R., Simmons, H., and Miller, J. (1985), 'From Babbling to Speech: A Reassessment of the Continuity Issue', *Language*, 61: 397–445.

—— Ferguson, C. A., and Elbert, M. (1986), 'Phonological Development from Babbling to Speech: Common Tendencies and Individual Differences', *Applied Psycholinguistics*, 7: 3–40.

—— Kay, E., Boysson-Bardies, B. de, Durand, C., and Sundberg, U. (1994), 'External Sources of Individual Differences? A Cross-Linguistic Analysis of the Phonetics of Mothers' Speech to One-Year-Old Children', *Developmental Psychology*, 30: 651–62.

—— Velleman, S. L., and McCune, L. (1994), 'How Abstract is Child Phonology? Towards an Integration of Linguistic and Psychological Approaches', in M. Yavas (ed.), *First and Second Language Phonology*, (San Diego, Calif.: Singular Press), 9–44.

—— DePaolis, R. A., and Davis, B. L. (1998), 'Is there a "Trochaic Bias" in Early Word Learning? Evidence from Infant Production in English and French', *Child Development*, 69: 935–49.

Werker, J. F. and Tees, R.C. (1984), 'Cross-Language Speech Perception: Evidence for Perceptual Reorganization During the First Year of Life', *Infant Behavior and Development*, 7: 49–63.

Whalen, D. H., Levitt, A. G., and Wang, Q. (1991), 'Intonational Differences Between the Reduplicative Babbling of French- and English-Learning Infants', *Journal of Child Language*, 18: 501–16.

Wierzbicka, A. (1992), *Semantics, Culture and Cognition: Universal Human Concepts in Culture-Specific Configurations* (Oxford: Oxford University Press).

Name Index

Note: Multiple authored references are indexed under the leading author's name.

Language Index

Subject Index